MW00352807

Pricing Carbon

The European Union's Emissions Trading Scheme (EU ETS) is the world's largest market for carbon and the most significant multinational initiative ever taken to mobilize markets to protect the environment. It will be an important influence on the development and implementation of trading schemes in the United States, Japan and elsewhere. As is true of any pioneering public policy experiment, however, this scheme has generated much controversy. *Pricing Carbon* provides the first detailed description and analysis of the EU ETS, focusing on the first, 'trial', period of the scheme (2005 to 2007). Written by an international team of experts, it allows readers to get behind the headlines and come to a better understanding of what was done and what happened based on a dispassionate, empirically based review of the evidence. This book should be read by anyone who wants to know what happens when emissions are capped, traded and priced.

A. DENNY ELLERMAN is Senior Lecturer at the Sloan School of Management, Massachusetts Institute of Technology.

FRANK J. CONVERY is Heritage Trust Professor of Environmental Policy at University College Dublin.

CHRISTIAN DE PERTHUIS is Associate Professor of Economics at the University Paris-Dauphine and Head of the Mission Climat of the Caisse des Dépôts, France.

Pricing Carbon

The European Union Emissions Trading Scheme

Principal authors

A. DENNY ELLERMAN
Massachusetts Institute of Technology

FRANK J. CONVERY
University College Dublin

CHRISTIAN DE PERTHUIS
Mission Climat of the Caisse des Dépôts and University Paris-Dauphine

Contributing authors

EMILIE ALBEROLA
Mission Climat of the Caisse des Dépôts

BARBARA K. BUCHNER
International Energy Agency

ANAÏS DELBOSC
Mission Climat of the Caisse des Dépôts

CATE HIGHT
Mission Climat of the Caisse des Dépôts

JAN HORST KEPPLER
University Paris-Dauphine and Institut Français des Relations Internationales

FELIX C. MATTHES
Öko-Institut

 CAMBRIDGE
UNIVERSITY PRESS

CAMBRIDGE UNIVERSITY PRESS
Cambridge, New York, Melbourne, Madrid, Cape Town, Singapore,
São Paulo, Delhi, Dubai, Tokyo

Cambridge University Press
The Edinburgh Building, Cambridge CB2 8RU, UK

Published in the United States of America by Cambridge University Press, New York

www.cambridge.org
Information on this title: www.cambridge.org/9780521196475

First published 2010

Printed in the United Kingdom at the University Press, Cambridge

A catalogue record for this publication is available from the British Library

Library of Congress Cataloging-in-Publication Data

Ellerman, A. Denny.
   Pricing carbon : the European Union Emissions Trading Scheme / principal authors,
A. Denny Ellerman, Frank J. Convery, Christian de Perthuis; contributing authors,
Emilie Alberola, Barbara K. Buchner.
      p.   cm.
   ISBN 978-0-521-19647-5 (Hardback)
   1. Emissions trading–European Union countries. 2. Carbon offsetting–European
Union countries. I. Convery, Frank J. II. Title.
   HC79.P55E514 2010
   363.738′746–dc22

                                                                        2009038173

ISBN 978-0-521-19647-5 Hardback

Contents

Figures

Tables

Boxes

Appendices

Frequently used abbreviations

AA	aviation allowance
AAU	assigned amount unit
ATS	Aviation Trading Scheme
BAT	best available technology
BAU	business-as-usual
BOF	basic oxygen furnace
BSA	burden-sharing agreement
CCGT	combined-cycle gas turbine
CCS	carbon capture and storage
CCX	Chicago Climate Exchange
CDM	Clean Development Mechanism
CER	certified emission reduction
CITL	Community Independent Transaction Log
CO_2	carbon dioxide
CO_2e	carbon dioxide equivalent
COP	Conference of Parties
CRF	common reporting format
EAF	electric arc furnace
ECX	European Climate Exchange
EEA	European Environment Agency
EEX	European Energy Exchange
ERU	emission reduction unit
EU ETS	European Union Emissions Trading Scheme
EUA	European Union allowance
GHG	greenhouse gas
IEA	International Energy Agency
IMF	International Monetary Fund
IPCC	Intergovernmental Panel on Climate Change
ITL	international transaction log
JI	Joint Implementation
LPG	liquefied petroleum gas

MIT	Massachusetts Institute of Technology
MRV	monitoring, reporting and verification
NAP	national allocation plan
NER	new entrant reserve
OTC	over-the-counter
UCD	University College Dublin
UNFCCC	United Nations Framework Convention on Climate Change
VER	verified emission reduction

Preface

Pricing Carbon is the result of a multinational research collaboration primarily between researchers (leader in brackets) at the Mission Climat of the Caisse des Dépôts and the University Paris-Dauphine in Paris (Christian de Perthuis), University College Dublin (UCD) (Frank Convery) and the Massachusetts Institute of Technology (MIT) (Denny Ellerman) but also involving researchers from the International Energy Agency (IEA) (Richard Baron and Barbara Buchner), the Öko-Institut in Berlin (Felix Matthes) and the University Paris-Dauphine (Jan Horst Keppler).

The project has been motivated by the belief that the European Union's Emissions Trading Scheme is a significant public policy experiment that should be subjected to a comprehensive and rigorous *ex post* evaluation. It is the world's first cap-and-trade programme for greenhouse gases, by far the largest environmental market in the world and the possible prototype for a global climate policy regime that would be based on emissions trading.

As an *ex post* exercise, the research reported in this book is resolutely backward-looking and focused mostly on the first three years that constituted the trial period of the EU ETS. The tone of the book is more descriptive or positive than normative. The objective is to describe, analyse, and understand what has transpired and not to prescribe what should be, or should have been. The normative preferences of the authors may intrude here and there, but the intent has been to keep these judgements to a minimum and to let every reader draw his or her own conclusions about the European experience during the trial period. Our aim is that readers come away at least well informed, and perhaps persuaded that the problems and solutions are a little more complex than how they are often presented.

Each chapter has a leader (name in brackets) with overall responsibility for delivery, delegated as follows: chapter 2, 'Origins and development of the EU ETS' (Frank Convery); chapter 3, 'Allowance allocation' (Denny Ellerman); chapter 4, 'Effects of free allocation' (Barbara Buchner); chapter 5, 'Market development' (Christian de Perthuis); chapter 6, 'Emissions abatement' (Denny Ellerman); chapter 7, 'Industrial competitiveness' (Richard Baron); chapter 8, 'Costs' (Frank Convery); and chapter 9, 'Linkage and global implications' (Christian de Perthuis). Felix Matthes of the Öko-Institut contributed the first drafts of the introductory and concluding chapters, and Jan Horst Keppler of the University Paris-Dauphine contributed the annex on electricity.

There have been substantive contributions to most of these chapters by other scholars, however. Chapter 4 benefited from the work of Sara de Pablos (IEA) and Mar Reguant-Ridó (MIT). In chapter 5, Anaïs Delbosc and Emilie Alberola, in charge of European carbon market monitoring at the Mission Climat, made major contributions. Raphaël Trotignon (Mission Climat) was the recognized master of the data in the central registry of the EU ETS, the Community Independent Transaction Log (CITL). As such, he was primarily responsible for developing the programme that allowed the surrender data to be exploited, and he did the work of separating the electric utility power plants from other combustion sources.

Chapter 6 could not have been written without the contributions of Erik Delarue from the University of Leuven, Belgium, and his thesis supervisor, Professor William D'haeseleer, who graciously agreed to the use of the model they developed to support the project. Meghan McGuinness and Stephan Feilhauer at MIT also contributed significantly to the case studies of the United Kingdom and Germany. A final noteworthy, albeit more indirect, contributor to this chapter was Anke Herold of the Öko-Institut in Berlin. Without her earlier work in comparing the two main data sources for greenhouse gas data in Europe, the CITL and the United Nations' common reporting format data, it would not have been possible to develop the longer data series for the ETS sectors that allowed projections of counterfactual emissions to be made.

Chapter 7 was a team effort to which many contributed. Neil Walker (UCD) provided the section on the cement sector, Romain Lacombe (MIT) that on refineries and Julia Reinaud (IEA) the sections on the iron and steel sector and aluminium. Philippe Quirion of the Centre International de Recherche sur l'Environnement et le Développement (CIRED) also contributed to the sections on cement and iron and steel. In chapter 8, Jurate Jaraite (UCD) provided the unique analysis of transaction costs and a very useful survey of modelling and other analyses concerning the expected cost of the EU ETS. Chapter 9 benefited from the contributions of Cate Hight (Mission Climat), who wrote the section on expanding the scope of the EU ETS, Benoît Leguet (Mission Climat), an expert on the Kyoto project mechanisms, and Morgan Hervé-Mignucci (Mission Climat and University Paris-Dauphine), who studied the links between European allowance prices and Kyoto credit prices on the world carbon market.

In addition to those who contributed directly, we have benefited from the support and insights of the following: from University College Dublin, Corrado Di Maria provided quality control and encouragement in equal measure, while Barry Anderson and Luke Redmond also provided suggestions. At MIT, Paul Joskow, Henry Jacoby, John Parsons and Mort Webster were invaluable colleagues in their unflagging interest and support. The project also benefited from the insights of Jean-Marie Chevalier, Patrice Geoffron and Jan Horst Keppler, the energy economics team at the University Paris-Dauphine. Another virtual participant was Dora Fazekas of Corvinus University of Budapest and Columbia University, whose work on auctions and how Hungarian firms responded to the EU ETS provided valuable insights. Workshop and administrative logistics would have been impossible without the able assistance of Malika Boumaza at the Mission Climat, Frances Goldstein and Joni Bubluski at MIT and Sarka Sebkova at the University of Prague.

We would be very remiss if we did not acknowledge the contributions of the European Environment Agency in Copenhagen, in particular the interest and help from Hans Vos and Andreas Barkman. Peter Zapfel at the European Commission has also been extremely supportive of our efforts and helpful in making sure that we understood many of the decisions that were made. They are not implicated in any of the conclusions that we have drawn.

A project of this scale and import cannot happen without resources. We were fortunate indeed to garner what was necessary from generous donors on both sides of the Atlantic. The head of the Caisse des Dépôts, Augustin de Romanet, understood at an early stage the importance of this research project, and was instrumental in bringing together the coalition of French companies that provided the funds for the European participants in the project and in supplying much of the administrative and logistical support that this effort required. The European funds were managed by the Association pour la Promotion de la Recherche sur l'Economie du Carbone (APREC), a non-profit association launched by the Caisse des Dépôts and University Paris-Dauphine under the direction of Pierre Ducret. BlueNext, Electricité de France, Euronext, Orbeo, Suez, Total and Veolia were the main contributors to this association. To all these companies, and to their employees, who were tireless in sharing their insights with us, particular thanks are due. The American side of the collaboration could not have occurred without the generous financial support of the Doris Duke Charitable Foundation. Andrew Bowman, the foundation's director of climate change programmes, deserves special credit for providing just the right combination of encouragement and guidance. Finally, we readily acknowledge the many unsung ways in which the institutions with which the authors are associated provided encouragement, not least in providing salary support and tolerating the demands of this project on our time. In this group, particular gratitude is due the International Energy Agency, and especially to Claude Mandil for his early support to this project.

Good writing requires freedom from the daily pressure of meetings, e-mails, phone calls and sundry intrusions that most are heir to at their home base. Some of us were fortunate to escape for a writing interlude to the welcoming embrace of the offices of Mission Climat of the Caisse des Dépôts in Paris and the Center for Energy and Environmental Policy Research at MIT, and this helped move the project forward.

Many of the research results in this volume were initially presented at a series of four workshops held in April 2007 in Paris, January 2008 in Washington, June 2008 in Prague and September 2008 in Paris. The questions and comments by participants have had more impact in shaping our thinking than those who made them might imagine. We are very grateful to all of them, as well as to the organizations that hosted these meetings: the Caisse des Dépôts for the two meetings in Paris, MIT's Center for Energy and Environmental Policy Research for the meeting in Washington and Jirina Jilcova and her team at the Institute for Economic and Environmental Policy, University of Economics, Prague. A highlight of the social side was the dinner graciously hosted in his residence by the French ambassador to the United States, Pierre Vimont, which provided an opportunity for

American and European carbon market experts to engage in a very productive dialogue.

To all we extend our thanks, both for their direct contributions and their sharing of our belief in the need for objective, dispassionate analysis and better understanding of public policy experiments, which by their nature are always controversial.

1 | *Introduction*

This book focuses on the first period (2005–7) of the European Union Emissions Trading Scheme (EU ETS), known also as the 'pilot' or 'trial' period. The EU ETS is one of the most exciting and important initiatives ever taken to limit the greenhouse gas emissions that cause climate change. It will be an important influence on the development and implementation of trading schemes in the United States, Japan and elsewhere. As such, it can provide the cornerstone for an eventual global trading regime, which will be an important component of the set of policies that will be needed to address climate change.

The audience for this book are those in all walks of life who want to understand how the EU ETS came about, and (especially) how it functioned in its early life. It is written by economists, but for a general audience, defined as those who take more than a passing interest in how to address our planet's climate change challenge and who are neither technically nor temperamentally attuned to the economics literature. It will also be of value to those with an interest in understanding how the European Union can function effectively in developing and executing a climate policy that has global implications.

Ever since the profession of environmental economics came into being, the integration of the environment and the economy via markets has been a core objective, and the reason why many entered the field in the first place. Carbon emissions trading in Europe has finally lifted the environment from the boiler room to the boardroom, from ministries of environment to ministries of finance, from local councils to Cabinet tables. For chief executives of many major corporations, the environment and the carbon market has become an omnipresent, if not always welcome, guest at their strategic tables. Carbon now has a price in Europe, and the impact of the EU ETS on policy and business continues to progress and intensify. The EU ETS is orders of magnitude more significant in terms of its scope, ambition and likely impact than any other application of environmental economics. Several billion euros cross frontiers on a monthly basis, and abatement – the technical term for emission reduction – happens in all kinds of interesting and surprising ways. Its effects spill over to influence other markets, notably the volume and value of projects undertaken in developing countries under the aegis of the Clean Development Mechanism (CDM). There are thousands of people involved, including prime ministers and bureaucrats, entrepreneurs and inventors seeking to create lower-cost ways of reducing carbon; carbon market analysts, brokers and bankers mediating and funding markets; CEOs (chief executive officers) developing their carbon strategies; engineers in the control room changing the order in which electricity generation plants come on-stream; and academics analysing and discussing evidence so as to give some intellectual shape to what is happening. For all of these, it should be of interest to know how the scheme came about, and how it performed it its first trading period.

The EU ETS draws its inspiration from Dales' (1968) observation that '[i]f it is feasible to establish a market to implement a policy, no policy maker can afford to do without one'. A key underlying reason for the problem of climate change is the failure of the market to recognize the scarcity value of the atmosphere as a sink for anthropogenic greenhouse gas (GHG) emissions. There is no price that signals this increasing scarcity, and therefore no incentive to reduce emissions. Economists recognize two broad policy instruments to repair this failure, aimed at introducing price incentives that will encourage the parsimonious use of diminishing environmental endowments and stimulate innovation to find new and better ways of reducing such pressure. The first is to introduce environmental taxes, whereby a tax is levied on every unit of emissions produced. This was the instrument first proposed by the European Commission, in the form of a carbon energy tax. The story of its introduction and failure to be accepted is told in chapter 2, but in essence it failed because of the human reluctance noted by Edmund Burke over two centuries ago: 'To tax and to please, no more than to love and be wise, is not given to men.'[1]

The second market-based policy instrument is emissions trading, which draws on humanity's singular impulse to trade. In its simplest

---

[1] Edmund Burke, 'On American taxation', British House of Commons, 1774.

expression, this involves setting an overall cap per unit of time on the emissions to be permitted and allocating allowances or permits to emitters such that the sum of the allocations does not exceed the cap. These emitters can then pollute as much as they wish, but only on the condition that they hold sufficient allowances at the end of the period to 'cover' their emissions. If they wish to emit more than the allowances they have received, they must buy allowances from those who emissions are lower than the quantity of allowances they hold. These transactions produce a price per unit of pollution that provides the incentive to polluters to reduce emissions and sell the surplus to those who need to buy to cover their emissions. Emissions trading also provides a signal to innovators to come up with new and better ways to reduce emissions. Because those who can do so at least cost will reduce most, the overall burden on the economy of meeting the cap is likely to be achieved at close to minimum cost. The European Union Emissions Trading Scheme is the creation of a Europe-wide market for carbon dioxide (CO_2). The inspiration for, and some of the design of, the European scheme came from the United States, where, for over a decade, trading has evolved on a 'learning by doing' basis, culminating in a trading scheme for sulphur dioxide (SO_2) in the power sector.

In telling the story of this market in its early stages, the concern has been to be as factual as the available evidence allowed, sharing the view of Pablo Neruda that 'the reality of the world should not be under-prized'. Accordingly, the emphasis is on the positive – what has happened – rather than the normative – what should have happened.

In proposing the three-year pilot period that is the focus of this book, the European Commission was anxious to have a window of experience from which to learn and which would inform later stages of the trading scheme. What is described and analysed here is 'out of date', therefore, in the sense that lessons have been learnt, and the second and subsequent stages differ from what comprised the first period. All the same, this volume will contribute to a sound understanding of this evolution and inform the development of other trading systems that are evolving around the world.

One of the most interesting aspects of the EU ETS is its multinational character. The twenty-seven member states of the European Union are engaged in achieving greater economic and political integration, but they are still sovereign nations, with a wide range of political structures and traditions, and sometimes widely differing commitments in the framework of multilateral policies (e.g. under the United Nations Framework Convention on Climate Change or the Kyoto Protocol). The coordination that has been required, as well as the implications for national policy-making, is an important and often underestimated aspect of the EU ETS.

Outline of the book

The EU ETS had its origins in the necessity for the European Union to convert the commitments, targets and visions expressed via the Kyoto Protocol and elsewhere into action, in the knowledge, as expressed in the Japanese proverb, that 'vision without action is a dream; action without vision is a nightmare'. Creating a carbon market at the heart of Europe was a means of providing not only a price signal, but also a practical fulcrum that could enhance the effectiveness and coherence of other, parallel EU policies, demonstrate global leadership by the European Union and provide encouragement to, and a framework for, the rest of the world to join in the effort. This vision took the practical form of the Emissions Trading Directive. The development of this centre for European climate policy is described in chapter 2, and the key features of the EU ETS are summarised in box 1.1.

A key step in the creation of a trading scheme is deciding on the scope of coverage – the gases and sectors to be included – and the level – upstream or downstream – to which coverage applies. These decisions were made in the enabling legislation, the ETS Directive, and the choices were to go downstream to the level of installations and to limit the coverage in the pilot period to carbon dioxide and to the power sector and heavy industry (the latter including oil-refining, cement and lime, steel, ceramics and glass, pulp and paper). The next step – deciding the cap and allocating allowances to affected installations – was left to the member states and the European Commission. How they dealt with the problem and the outcomes decided upon are the subject of chapter 3.

The free allocation of allowances triggered some controversy about consequences. Chapter 4 addresses these issues, with particular atten-tion to the effects of the extent of trading and the effects of free

---

Box 1.1 Key features of the EU ETS in the pilot period

A cap-and-trade scheme with a pilot, or 'learning', period

A cap on emissions from the covered sectors is fixed (see coverage and allocation below). The scheme operates over discrete periods, with the first or pilot period (2005–7) being the subject of this book, with a review and appropriate amendment to follow for subsequent periods, of which two have been specifically defined. The second period, corresponding to the first commitment period of the Kyoto Protocol, will extend from 2008 to 2012, and it will be followed by a third period, from 2013 to 2020.

Relationship to the Kyoto Protocol

Those countries that ratified the Kyoto Protocol agreed to meet emission targets in the 2008–12 period. The European Union target for the then fifteen member states was a reduction of 8 per cent below 1990 emissions levels. This overall objective was subsequently redistributed in the form of fifteen separate national targets to the member states under the European burden-sharing agreement (BSA). The twelve new member states are also signatories of the Kyoto Protocol, and ten accepted individual country targets. There is no direct link between Kyoto and the EU ETS, in that the latter was agreed before Kyoto entered into force, and will continue post-Kyoto. Nevertheless, the EU ETS is the anchor around which EU-level climate change policy is structured, and it contributes towards meeting the Kyoto targets.

Coverage was partial

The pilot period was confined to carbon dioxide emissions from combustion installations (electric power and other) with a rated thermal input in excess of 20 MW (megawatts) (except municipal or hazardous waste incinerators), oil refineries, the production and processing of ferrous metals, the manufacture of cement (capacity > 500 tonnes per day), the manufacture of lime (capacity > 50 tonnes/day), ceramics including bricks, glass, and pulp, paper and board (>20 tonnes/day). This coverage accounted for about a half of CO_2 emissions and 40 per cent of total greenhouse gas emissions. About 11,500 installations in all twenty-seven member states were covered, embracing emissions of about 2 billion tonnes of CO_2 annually. Reductions achieved by the use of sinks – e.g. planting trees – were not allowed.

Allocation was free and decentralized

Member states had the option to auction up to 5 per cent of their allowances, but most chose not to do so. Allocations – called European Union

Box 1.1 *(cont.)*

allowances (EUAs) – were denominated as tonnes of CO_2. The allocation process was decentralized to the member states, each of which prepared a national allocation plan (NAP), but had to follow the procedures and criteria specified in the directive; each NAP had to be approved by the Commission. Most used emissions in a past period as a basis for allocation.

Full banking and borrowing within the period

This was allowed within the pilot period, but not between the first and second periods. Allowances were issued by the end of February, two months before allowances had to be surrendered for the previous year. This overlap provided installations with the ability to meet last year's emissions targets using allowances from next year's allocation.

Monitoring, reporting and verification (MRV) and enforcement

Once the allocations had been approved by the Commission, each member state had to establish a registry to record the creation, transfer and surrender of allowances. There is also a central registry in Brussels – the Community Independent Transaction Log (CITL) – which records all transactions, including among installations located in different member states; this requirement allowed the Commission to block any transfers that were out of compliance. Annual emissions for each installation had to be verified, typically by a certified independent verifier. Emitters whose emissions exceed their allowances are liable both to make up the deficit and to pay an automatic penalty, of €40 per EUA in the first period and €100 in the second period. This is the only EU law that prescribes financial penalties that must be applied automatically for non-compliance. A degree of uniformity was maintained by the issuance of regulations and guidelines concerning monitoring, reporting and verification and enforcement.

There was a provision to include project-based emissions reductions

The amendment to the directive to provide for linkage allowed qualifying project-based reductions in the pilot period to be used to comply with obligations under the EU ETS, up to certain ceilings specified by member states with the approval of the Commission. These are known as certified emission reductions (CERs), achieved via the Clean Development Mechanism in developing countries and certified by the United Nations Framework Convention on Climate Change (UNFCCC) Clean Development Mechanism Executive Board.

Box 1.1 *(cont.)*

There were provisions for a new entrant's reserve and for the closure of installations

Most member states exercised the option of setting aside a quota of emissions to give free to new entrants, including in some cases for expansions of existing facilities. Most member states exercised the option to require installations that closed to surrender post-closure allowances – i.e. such allowances could not be sold.

---

allocation on profitability and operations, in both the short run and the long run.

Once the framework had been established and allocations had been made, trading commenced. Trading strategies were conditioned by the extent to which firms were left short or long, the extent to which they understood trading, including the provisions relating to banking and borrowing, and perceptions with regard to overall supply and demand. The market developed in three stages, related to the evolution of allowance prices over the pilot period. The volume of trades likewise evolved over time, and a variety of intermediaries and products entered to facilitate the working of the market. These issues of conditioning factors, pricing and institutional development are the subject of chapter 5.

The extent to which abatement occurred is a key consideration. Although the pilot period was established primarily to get the system up and running, as opposed to achieving substantial progress as regards abatement, whether such occurred remains nevertheless of great interest and is the topic of chapter 6.

Competitiveness can be described variously (OECD [Organisation for Economic Co-operation and Development] 1996a), but it is a dominant consideration for the industrial sectors involved and policy-makers alike. In chapter 7, this issue is addressed with regard both to industries inside the EU ETS – cement, steel and refineries – and to those outside the scheme (notably aluminium) that could be affected by the need to incorporate carbon prices into inputs, such as electricity.

An important consideration in designing and implementing any trading scheme is the extent to which costs are incurred to set up and operate the scheme, including the buying and selling of allowances. These transaction costs can affect the efficiency or even the feasibility of trading. It is interesting to compare what the analytical community expected to happen *ex ante* as regards overall costs – impacts on gross domestic product (GDP), marginal costs of abatement, etc. – and the *ex post* reality. Chapter 8 addresses the issues of transactions costs and *ex ante* and *ex post* comparisons.

The reach of the EU ETS has been global. Emission reductions outside the European Union, made through the project-based mechanisms of the Clean Development Mechanism and Joint Implementation (JI), have been given status and reality in the marketplace by the fact that they can be used, up to a point, to meet EU ETS obligations. The EU ETS has also stimulated the development of pilot projects at the member state level, and created a template that may be linked to trading schemes elsewhere. These themes are addressed in chapter 9. The final chapter, 10, provides our conclusions and the lessons that we draw from the pioneering experience of the EU ETS.

The electricity sector is the most important of those included in EU ETS, whether judged in terms of emissions, share of allowances or its role in the carbon market. This important issue is addressed in a separate annex authored by Professor Jan Keppler of the University Paris-Dauphine. The treatment includes addressing the link between CO_2 prices and electricity prices, the effects on electricity demand, the interface with international competitiveness and security of supply, and the windfall profits issue.

The book also contains some textual and data appendices. Appendix A is a timeline describing the sequence of events in the development of the EU ETS and the Linking Directive. Appendix B provides data tables concerning allowance allocation and emissions, carbon and energy prices, and allowance trading volumes.

The authors have tried to be faithful to their objective of being as true as possible to the evidence before us, but we are always conscious of Einstein's admonition 'Whoever undertakes to set himself up as judge of Truth and Knowledge is shipwrecked by the laughter of the gods'. We hope our readers will find that our best has been good enough to make the reading worthwhile.

2 | *Origins and development of the EU ETS*

Introduction

In a context of which Nietzsche would have approved, the European Union Emissions Trading Scheme grew out of failure. He admonishes us:

> Examine the lives of the best and most fruitful people and peoples and ask yourselves whether a tree that is supposed to grow to a proud height can dispense with bad weather and storms; whether misfortune and external resistance, some kinds of hatred, jealousy, stubbornness, mistrust, hardness, avarice, and violence do not belong among the favourable conditions without which any great growth even of virtue is scarcely possible. (Nietzsche, *Beyond Good and Evil*, 1886)

The sapling that became EU ETS was a product of two failures. First, the European Commission failed in its initiative to introduce an effective EU-wide carbon energy tax in the 1990s. Second, the Commission fought unsuccessfully against the inclusion of trading as a flexible instrument in the Kyoto Protocol in 1997. This chapter explores how these apparent setbacks were followed by the successful creation of an EU-wide market in carbon dioxide.

Before delving into the political foundations of the EU ETS, some background knowledge will be useful. The first section of this chapter describes the political decision-making process within the European Union, in which power is shared between the Commission, the European Parliament and the Council of Ministers. The second section explores the academic and experiential platform that made the EU ETS possible, from the work of economists Coase, Dales, Crocker and Montgomery, to the American SO_2 trading programme to intellectual development within Europe.

The material in this chapter draws heavily from Convery (2009).

With this background in hand, sections three and four explore the political foundations that supported the creation of the EU ETS: the carbon tax failure, the Kyoto Protocol, the EU burden-sharing agreement, the Commission's Green Paper on climate policy, and the EU ETS and Linking Directives. Section five of the chapter focuses on some of the people who played key roles in moving market-based environmental policy forward in Europe. Section six concludes.

The European Union and the environment: legislative and institutional context

The Single European Act of 1986 is a fundamental building block of the European Union and its environmental policy efforts. It made the idea of a single European market – which hitherto had been largely theoretical – a reality by guaranteeing the free movement of goods, people and capital and by providing the legislative and institutional support to ensure that these provisions were implemented. The act also added a separate section on the environment to the treaty establishing the European Community, which created the legal foundation for Community action in this area based on qualified majority voting.

The Treaty on European Union, signed in Maastricht in 1993, created new forms of co-operation between the member state governments, including the introduction of the euro. It and the Treaty of Amsterdam (1997) substantially enhanced the role of the European Parliament in the legislative process.

Three institutions are key to policy formulation, development and implementation within the European Union. The first is the European Commission, which is organised into a number of Directorates General, of which one is Environment. It is often, incompletely, described as the bureaucracy of the European Union. It is that – but much more as well. It has the singular right to initiate legislation, it is the fulcrum that levers the various other actors towards decision, it provides the evidence and analytical ballast to drive an agenda forward, and it has the responsibility of ensuring implementation, including, when necessary, taking delinquent member states to court.

The second key actor is the Council of Ministers, consisting of representatives of the member states, who, in the case of emissions trading, are typically ministers for the environment. They are a key decision-making hub; nothing can be enacted without their approval.

This does not mean that each member state has a veto, however. The qualified majority mechanism[1] means that decisions can be taken without unanimity. Although the Council of Ministers cannot initiate legislation, it can request the Commission to examine an issue and come forward with proposals.

The third key player is the European Parliament, which is directly elected every five years. The Parliament transacts its business through committees, the most relevant for emissions trading being the Committee on the Environment, Public Health and Food Safety, which has sixty members. Its role is central, but rather baroque. Under the co-decision procedure (see figure 2.1), the Parliament has the right to propose amendments to a Commission proposal over a period of two readings. The Parliament can veto the adoption of the whole proposal if it thinks that its amendments have not been taken into account sufficiently in the final text. It can adopt amendments not accepted by the Commission only on the second reading, with the support of an absolute majority of its constituent members.

The Commission is arguably the first amongst equals in this triumvirate, for the following reasons. It is permanent: Members of Parliament and government ministers come and go, but the Commission endures. It commands the agenda and information. It is required to conduct impact assessments of policy choices, which involves examining the choices available, and tracing their impact on the economy, the environment and society as an aid to decision-making; steering this process involves not just learning but, associated with this, an accretion of influence. It is the hub in a wheel of spokes, in which the Parliament and the Council must perforce at times represent the rim.

Three-legged races are awkward affairs at the best of times, however. Getting over the line in reasonable time and good order requires all three parties to have mutual respect and to collaborate. There are other actors that provide input that can be influential. These include the European Environment Agency, with a brief to provide high-quality

---

[1] In the Council of Ministers, each member state is allocated a number of votes according to its population, with extra weight given to the smaller member states. Since 1 January 2007 the threshold for a qualified majority has been set at 255 votes out of 345 (73.91 per cent). A qualified majority decision also requires a favourable vote from the majority of member states (i.e. at least fourteen member states). In addition, a member state may request verification that the qualified majority includes at least 62 per cent of the European Union's total population.

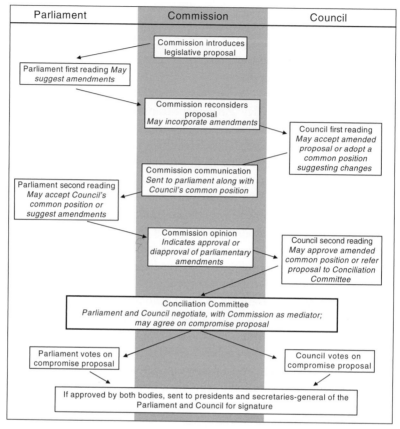

Figure 2.1 How a European legislative proposal becomes law: the co-decision process

Source: European Commission's co-decision website: http://ec.europa.eu/codecision/index_en.htm

information in a timely fashion to support the policy process. A report on whether progress is adequate or not in the climate change arena can be influential in driving policy. Within the European Parliament, the Committee of the Regions and the Economic and Social Committee have the right of input and commentary. In Brussels, there is a constellation of economic interest groups and lobbies of a scale and sophistication that matches those of Washington, DC. It is their job to influence, and at times they can be very effective. In regard to climate change policy, key actors are the Union of Industrial and Employers' Confederations of Europe (UNICE, now BusinessEurope), which represents business and industry, and more specialised sectoral lobbies, including the European Chemical Industry Council and Cembureau, which represents the cement industry. Environmental NGOs (non-governmental organizations) that are engaged and influential include the Foundation for International Law and Development (FIELD), Climate Action Network and the World Wide Fund for Nature (WWF). These bodies all, of course, have their analogues in the member states.

The intellectual and experiential platform

Theoretical foundations

An important precursor condition for the adoption of emissions trading within Europe was the development of the intellectual platform that gave it status as a policy instrument. Coase, in his famous article 'The problem of social cost' (Coase 1960), provides a trenchant argument that the assignment of suitably defined property rights would allow for the use of environmental endowments to negotiate and trade their way to the economically efficient outcome. The correction for market failure could be achieved without recourse to the use of external cost-internalizing taxes, as advocated by Pigou (1920). Coase was awarded the Nobel Prize for economics in 1991, and this – the ultimate intellectual accolade in the field – provided further validation for the general approach.

Coase's theoretical frame was given more explicit expression as a way of creating an emissions market by Crocker (1966), Dales (1968) and Montgomery (1972), but still using hypothetical cases to illustrate the potential. They all make the case that fixing the quantity of emissions, allocating quotas to the emitters such that the sum of these did not exceed the overall ceiling then allowing a price to emerge as the product of trades would allocate abatement automatically to those market participants who could abate at least cost. In addition, the price signal would create a continuing incentive to innovate, thereby yielding dynamic efficiency, and the approach adhered to the 'polluter pays principle' by automatically rewarding those who reduced emissions, and penalizing those who did the contrary.

The US experience with emissions trading

It was the application of these ideas in the United States, and the careful documentation of this experience, that provided the meat in the analytical sandwich, and nourished the development of the instrument in Europe. Tietenberg (2006) provides an excellent summary of the US experience, which, in essence, amounted to learning by doing, often emerging as a pragmatic response to situations in which flexibility was required, all other options were inoperable and desperation became the mother of invention. The initial efforts were broadly unsuccessful, as markets were thin, limiting liquidity, restrictions on trading were routine, participation was restricted and banking and borrowing was either not allowed or highly restricted. What it took to make such markets work soon emerged, however, lessons were learnt – albeit somewhat fitfully at times – and successes were recorded. The core criteria defining success were political and administrative feasibility and the achievement of the environmental target at lower costs than the alternatives. Dynamic efficiency – the innovation dividend – received less attention.

The flagship of the US emissions trading family has been the Acid Rain Program, whereby substantial reductions in sulphur dioxide emissions by power stations were achieved at costs that were substantially below the likely alternative policies. The evolution of this programme, its design characteristics and economic and environmental performance was meticulously documented by Ellerman *et al.* (2000). The Acid Rain Program experience and the associated analyses provided European economists with insights to apply to the European situation, and provided officials in both the member states and in the Commission with a body of literature and people to interrogate and to learn from.

The European intellectual platform

Klaassen (1997) is credited with providing the first comprehensive review of the potential for using emissions trading to deal with the problem of climate change in the European Union. The European intellectual platform evolved quickly, and much of it crystallized or found expression via the initiatives of the Concerted Action on Market-Based Instruments programme, which operated from 1996 to 1998, and then the Concerted Action on Tradable Emission Permits. These brought together leading scholars from around the world in a series of workshops. Each workshop typically combined invited speakers and a choice of submitted papers, which were all available on the Web. Policy practitioners and other stakeholders were often involved as well. From these workshops, a series of policy briefs focused on conveying key insights from research to the policy process were produced and disseminated widely,[2] and a series of books were published.

A book in this series edited by Sorrell and Skea (1999) brought together the key emerging insights about emissions trading, including theory, design and application related to the European context. Inevitably, there was – and still is – nothing like unanimity about the merits of emissions trading amongst the academic community; to have such would be very alarming. Many economists regard an appropriate carbon tax with recycling as the first best option for addressing climate change, and therefore regard emissions trading with misgivings. Some are so committed to a tax that in its absence they act like a jilted lover, preferring chastity to the embrace of an inferior. Others recognize the power of emissions trading, but only if allowances are auctioned and the revenues recycled. Still others accept the fact that emissions trading with free allocation is perhaps only the third best option, but that having a price that signals scarcity in terms of the capacity of the planet to absorb more greenhouse gasses is a fundamental achievement.

Keynes, as always, has the *mot juste* to capture the idea:

The ideas of economists, both when they are right and when they are wrong, are more powerful than is commonly understood. Indeed, the world is ruled by little else. Practical men, who believe themselves to be quite exempt from any intellectual influences, are usually the slaves of some defunct economist. Madmen in authority, who hear voices in the air, are distilling their frenzy from some academic scribbler of a few years back. I am sure that the power of vested interests is vastly exaggerated, compared with the gradual encroachment of ideas. (Keynes, quoted in Skidelsky 2003)

The concept of emissions trading is a product in part of talented academic scribblers. Europe has had its share of madmen in authority, but, this time, it was the quiet achievers who embraced the idea. These intellectual rivulets fed intermittently but persistently into the stream of ideas that eventually shaped policy choices and, in effect, gave

[2] These policy briefs can be accessed at www.ucd.ie/gpep/gpepinfo/workingpapers/index.html.

emissions trading parity of esteem with taxes and charges in the environmental policy canon.

The political foundations of the EU ETS

The European Union Emissions Trading Scheme was the product of two failures: the Commission's failure to win pan-European support for the introduction of a carbon tax, and the failure of European negotiators to insert their desired policy initiatives in the Kyoto Protocol.

The failure of the carbon energy tax proposal

The European Commission proposed an EU-wide carbon energy tax in 1992 (European Commission 1992). Opposition to the proposal came from two powerful sources. First, some nations regard member state autonomy in taxation as a core value, not to be relinquished even if the environment would benefit. The view is that the power of taxation is so central to management of an economy that, if it is forgone, national autonomy will be compromised. While the carbon energy tax was presented, correctly, as a special case, it was regarded by some as the thin edge of the wedge, to be followed inevitably by other taxing initiatives that would incrementally leak fiscal autonomy from member states to the Commission. Because fiscal measures require unanimity, this strong ideological opposition proved impossible to overcome. Second, the main industry lobbies, represented most clearly by UNICE, also opposed the tax, with consistent and persistent case-making at the member state and EU levels.

In the end, there was some harmonization with regard to the minimum rate of taxes and excise duties applicable to energy products. These moves mostly codified what was already in place at the member state level, without any features specific to carbon or greenhouse gases. The opposition to the carbon energy tax proved too strong; the proposal was formally withdrawn in 1997.

The Kyoto negotiations

The third Conference of Parties (COP) to the United Nations Framework Convention on Climate Change convened in Kyoto, Japan, in December 1997. Three features characterized the European Union's negotiating position at Kyoto: (1) a commitment to mandatory caps on emissions by developed countries; (2) an undifferentiated target of 15 per cent below 1990 emissions levels; and (3) an antipathy towards emissions trading as a mechanism for achieving these targets, on the basis that some participants whose caps included surplus emissions allowances, or 'hot air', would benefit without making an effort and would compromise the overall objective. Participating nations agreed to caps in the resulting Kyoto Protocol, but the European negotiators achieved neither the 15 per cent reduction nor the undifferentiated target. In addition, at the insistence of the US delegation, led by then Vice-president Al Gore, emissions trading between countries was included as a flexible measure, together with the Clean Development Mechanism and Joint Implementation. Six months after opposing emissions trading, the Commission embraced it. As the Psalmist puts it: 'The stone which the builders rejected has become the cornerstone.'

It is noteworthy that proponents of the European single market, as well as some representatives from industry, supported the inclusion of emissions trading in the Kyoto Protocol. This position was predicated on the assumption that the United States would be a participant, and was informed by the fact that British energy company BP, the former British Petroleum, had introduced an internal company trading scheme, with some success.

The emergence of emissions trading in the European Union[3]

The burden-sharing agreement and the Kyoto–EU-ETS link

Following the Kyoto negotiations, during subsequent COP meetings in Buenos Aires and Marrakech, Japan opposed any enforcement mechanisms that would give the UN the power to take legal sanctions against a party to the protocol for not complying with its targets. This convinced the Commission that, if trading was to be successful in the first instance, it would have to be 'domestic', in the sense of being internal to the Union, and that the Commission and ultimately the

---

[3] This section is based largely on the analysis in Skjaerseth and Wettestad's excellent 2008 book *EU Emissions Trading: Initiation, Decision-making and Implementation*.

European Court of Justice would have to guarantee the integrity of what was proposed.

A key decision that enabled the emergence of trading within Europe was the BSA of June 1998 (European Council 1998), whereby the then fifteen member states agreed to varied national targets – the sum of which amounted to the overall Kyoto target of 8 per cent below 1990 emissions levels by the 2008–12 period – which were subsequently made legally binding. It was also in June that the Commission issued *Climate Change: Towards an EU Post-Kyoto Strategy* (European Commission 1998), in which it stated that the Community *could* set up its own internal trading scheme by 2005, which would give practical familiarity and even a leading edge to the European Union in using the instrument. The Commission also acknowledged that the United States was likely to embrace emissions trading as a key policy instrument, if and when it addressed climate change seriously, and that compatibility of approach could be a useful stimulus to US action and facilitate international trading.

While the European Commission from the outset made it clear that the EU ETS was a 'domestic scheme' that would proceed independently of what happened with the Kyoto Protocol, the Kyoto–EU-ETS link moved to centre stage after the rejection of the protocol in March 2001 by US president George W. Bush. The steps required to achieve ratification of the protocol in light of the US withdrawal were daunting. To come into effect, the agreement required ratification by fifty-five parties accounting for at least 55 per cent of developed countries' emissions (1990 being the reference year). Since the United States contributed 34 per cent of 1990 emissions, it meant that, in addition to the European Union, all the major players – Japan, Canada, Russia – had to ratify the protocol if it was to succeed. The US decision animated a 'Save Kyoto' campaign by the Union and the member states, which was in a sense a coming of age. It required the Union to take leadership at the various Conferences of the Parties to the Kyoto Protocol so as to facilitate continuing engagement and support from others, notably Japan and Canada.

Russia was the final domino that needed to fall for the Kyoto Protocol to come into effect. On October 2004 it was approved by the Russian parliament, with European Union support for Russian membership in the World Trade Organization (WTO) as the quid pro quo. Russia's ratification was a demonstration that the Union could be effective at mobilising 'soft power' to lead the world in shaping climate change policy, and showed the Bush administration that progress was possible without US leadership or participation. Throughout this process, the EU ETS moved to centre stage as the core evidence that the European Union could be innovative, courageous and effective inensuring that its own performance matched its rhetoric. Progress was further animated by the publication in 2002 of the European Environment Agency's greenhouse gas inventory, showing unsatisfactory progress over the period from 1990 to 2000 (EEA 2002).

In other words, Kyoto placed the EU ETS rocket on the launch pad, but it was President Bush and his administration that lit the fuse that finally put it into orbit.

Early action by member states

Member states were the first to act on the potential that emissions trading seemed to offer. The United Kingdom had emerged during the 1990s as the leader in Europe in the mobilization of markets to address a range of environmental challenges, focused initially on the use of taxes. In 1993 the Conservative government introduced the fuel price escalator as a way of both raising revenue and discouraging car use on environmental grounds. The escalator, which annually raised petrol prices above the rate of inflation, was set at 3 per cent in 1993 and later increased to 5 per cent. When the Conservatives left office in 1997 the United Kingdom had the highest transport fuel costs in the Union, with tax as a proportion of total cost standing at 76.3 per cent.

The negotiation of the Kyoto Protocol occurred not long after the new Labour government had taken office, and attention turned naturally to implementation. A first measure was the imposition of a climate change levy, beginning in April 2001, on energy use by business, with the proviso that 80 per cent of the tax would be excused if businesses achieved energy efficiency targets established in climate change agreements negotiated with the government. In late 1998 a commission chaired by Lord Marshall recommended the introduction of trading among firms subject to climate change agreements and the establishment of a pilot emissions trading scheme (Marshall 1998). Industry in the United Kingdom, which opposed the energy tax, advocated forcefully for emissions trading and established a group to work with the government in developing ways to implement the Marshall recommendations. The result was the rather complex UK

Emissions Trading Scheme, which started in April 2002 and which consisted of two components: a voluntary cap-and-trade system and sector-based intensity targets. Installations were encouraged to participate in the voluntary cap-and-trade programme through incentive payments totalling £30 million (about €48 million), which were distributed to participants through a subsidy auction for emission reductions and participation in the UK Emissions Trading Scheme.

Denmark had a long tradition of using environmental taxes, and so it was also politically and temperamentally disposed to use markets to support environmental objectives. In 1999 the Danish parliament adopted a measure that imposed a descending absolute cap on emissions from the Danish electricity sector beginning in 2001. The cap was initially set at a level that roughly approximated the demand for electricity from within Denmark and with a non-compliance penalty of 40 Danish kroner (about €5.4) per tonne. Since Danish electricity generation is highly variable, depending on hydroelectric reservoir levels in the Scandinavian electricity market and coal-fired power generation on the margin, this system effectively levied a tax on electricity exports.

Other member states were also contemplating emissions trading schemes. The Netherlands had long been an advocate of purchasing Joint Implementation credits through auction mechanisms, and in August 2000 it set up a commission to consider the possibility of a national emissions trading system. Sweden convened a commission, which recommended the introduction and use of emissions trading to help the country meet its Kyoto obligations. Similar commissions or study groups were established and proposals were discussed for introducing emissions trading systems in France and Germany (Ellerman 2000).

In all these cases, it was the enthusiasm of industry to avoid or to mitigate proposals for carbon taxes that drove the support for emissions trading; and it was this early action at the member state level that encouraged the Commission and others to move quickly at the Union level. Otherwise, Europe would end up with a patchwork of schemes combining lack of scope and scale and probable incompatibilities, making the whole much less than the sum of the parts. In particular, the baroque nature of the UK scheme reinforced the predisposition to keep the EU design simple. Attlee observed: 'Democracy is government by discussion, but it is only effective if you can stop people talking.' The ability and institutional positioning of the Commission as the agenda setter was crucial in giving coherence and focus to the emerging fissiparous tendencies of policy, and to move from talk to effective action at the EU level.

The Green Paper

In 1999 the Commission initiated a process to move the Union from thinking about setting up a scheme to actually doing so. In May the Commission adopted a communication to the Council and the Parliament on climate change that emphasized the need for a 'sustained policy response' (European Commission 1999). This was followed less than a year later – in March 2000 – by a Green Paper on emissions trading by the Commission (European Commission 2000). The Green Paper was intended to launch a discussion on the key policy options that needed to be decided upon in order to establish a framework for the implementation of a Community-wide trading scheme.

The shape and style of the Green Paper was influenced by three papers commissioned by the European Commission. Some of the economic case for trading was supported by a study by Capros and Mantzos (2000), which analysed the cost savings associated with implementing a Europe-wide emissions trading programme rather than a number of national schemes. Lessons from other trading experiences, notably those of the United States, were compiled in a paper by the Center for Clean Air Policy (1999), an organization with its headquarters in Washington, DC, that was a key player in the evolution of trading in the United States. Lastly, the development of the Green Paper was also supported by studies by FIELD, which established some of the legal parameters.[4]

Although the Green Paper did ask 'Should there be a common emissions trading scheme within the European Community for certain sectors in the interest of fair competition, maximum transparency and legal certainty for companies?', the tone and tenor of the paper assumed that the decision to establish a Community-wide emissions trading scheme had already been taken. The focus was on the 'How?' options for design and implementation. It made the case for a pilot period beginning in 2005 'to gain experience in its implementation

---

[4] Cited in Delbeke (2006: 292).

before the international emissions trading scheme starts in 2008', and suggested that those sectors already covered by command-and-control regulation via the Large Combustion Plant[5] and Integrated Pollution Prevention and Control Directives[6] could comprise the sectors in the trading scheme. The Green Paper noted that 'the key to limiting the risks of distortion between large point sources and small, and between trading and non-trading sectors, is the application of strict policies and measures to non-trading sources, with the possibility for these firms to voluntarily opt-in to the trading system' (European Commission 2000).

Implicit in the Green Paper's focus on the power sector and heavy industry was the decision to regulate emissions downstream. Going upstream would involve including the importers and producers of fossil fuels, and capping emissions at this level.[7] Resistance to upstream regulation came from two sources. First, the predominant view was that the additional fuel price rise that would be engendered by an allowance price in the order of €15–30 would have modest effects on consumption and therefore emissions. Second, finance ministers from individual member states – each of which charged high excise duties on petrol and diesel, amounting to up to €200 per tonne of CO_2 equivalent (CO_2e) – believed that upstream regulation could create the basis for removing excise duties in order to avoid 'double taxation'. Environmental NGOs supported the finance ministers' position, on the grounds that upstream trading could undermine the level and therefore the environmental effectiveness of excise duties on fuel.

The Green Paper emphasized that the cost to energy producers and energy intensive industry of meeting Kyoto obligations through an

[5] Directive 88/609/EEC of 24 November 1988, as modified by Directive 94/66/EEC of 15 December 1994. The Large Combustion Plant Directive applies to combustion plants with a thermal output of greater than 50 MW.

[6] Council Directive 96/61/European Commission of 24 September 1996 concerning integrated pollution prevention and control, and in particular annex I. The Integrated Pollution Prevention and Control Directive concerns highly polluting new or existing industrial and agricultural activities, as defined in annex I to the Directive (energy industries, production and processing of metals, mineral industry, chemical industry, waste management, livestock farming, etc.).

[7] Downstream programmes regulate emissions at their source (such as an industrial installation), whereas upstream programmes regulate the entities that produce materials that will emit pollutants when they are used (such as oil refineries that produce gasoline for use in automobiles).

EU-wide emissions trading scheme would be nearly one-fifth lower (about €1.7 billion annually) than a range of national schemes. The paper also stressed the benefits of using a centralized system to set national emissions caps, the importance of the internal market and the benefits-of-scale effects from operating at the EU rather than the national level, which would 'allow for significant cost savings'.[8]

The paper devoted considerable time to the issue of allowance allocation, comparing free allocation and auctioning. It noted that 'how the permits are allocated does not affect the environmental outcome', but that auction is 'technically preferable' because it generates revenues that can be used to reduce other taxes or fund new environmental programmes, avoids the difficult and politically delicate decision of how much to give to each company and reduces state aid and competition complications as well as those regarding new entrants. Respondents were invited to react to these and other issues by September 2000.

In very broad terms, there was support for the Green Paper, but industry was preoccupied with competitiveness while environmental NGOs were concerned that ambitious targets be set and met. The position of UNICE was of particular interest. In its response to the carbon energy tax proposals, it had posited emissions trading as an alternative. It had also supported the inclusion of emissions trading in the Kyoto Protocol, but this was on the presupposition that the United States would ratify the protocol. When it became clear that the US administration would not seek to ratify, the conditions for support changed fundamentally. Nevertheless, after some internal debate, UNICE decided to support the trading scheme, and this was key to subsequent progress. At the member state level, the main scepticism was expressed by Germany. German industry had obtained numerous forms of tax relief in the government's eco-tax package introduced in 1998, in exchange for taking on a voluntary agreement, whereby reduction targets were set as intensity targets and no strong compliance mechanism was implemented. This arrangement was very comfortable for industry, and there was considerable antagonism towards the proposed mandatory emissions trading scheme that would supersede it.

---

[8] Böhringer *et al.* (2006) have demonstrated, however, that the efficiency losses of splitting the abatement effort between the non-trading and trading sectors could be high, because of the likely differences in marginal abatement costs.

The EU ETS Directive

Following the formal feedback period, and the more informal but perhaps more important interactions between Commission officials and key stakeholders, the draft proposal was submitted in 2001 for formal consideration by the Council of Ministers and the European Parliament. The key interactions with the European Council (the member states) took place prior to drafting the proposal, but continued thereafter. The interface with the European Parliament crystallized only when the directive was in draft form. A key issue within the Parliament was the need to secure the support of the Christian Democrat bloc of German MEPs, who reflected the opposition of German industry to the scheme. With some difficulty, this support was secured, and, together with the support of the Socialists, this ensured that the directive would become law.

The Parliament finished its first reading of the draft directive in October 2002 and the Council presented its common position on 18 March 2003 (European Council 2003). The Parliament's first reading and the Council's position differed on several points. First, the Parliament supported a more directive 'top-down' allocation process administered by the Commission. It also favoured the use of mandatory auctioning for a share of the allocation. The Council, on the other hand, strongly favoured free allocation and wished to defer to member states on how allowances would be allocated. Second, Parliament wanted to implement a temporary opt-out option for installations only, whereas the Council wanted to allow member states to exclude installations, activities and sectors. Last, the Parliament wanted member states to have the option to include other sectors (in particular aluminium and chemicals) and other greenhouse gases from 2005, while the Council wanted to include this option from 2008 onward.

The Parliament presented its amendments based on the Council's position in spring 2003 (European Parliament 2003). The amended draft directive was adopted by the European Parliament at its second reading on 2 July 2003 and was accepted by the Council of Ministers at its meeting on 22 July 2003. The outcome kept allocation as a first and primary responsibility of the member states, but guided by criteria specified in the directive, and – most crucially – subject to the review of the Commission. Auctioning by member states was an option to a maximum of 5 per cent in the first trading period (2005–7) and

10 per cent in the second period (2008–12). Member states were permitted to 'opt out' installations only during the first period. Last, member states could include additional installations and sectors from 2005, while they could include additional gases starting in 2008.

On 13 October 2003 the Emissions Trading Directive was formally issued, with trading to commence on 1 January 2005 (European Parliament and Council 2003).

The Linking Directive

As the entry into force of the Kyoto Protocol remained uncertain during the negotiation of the EU ETS Directive, the Commission decided to consider as a separate issue the prospect of linking the EU ETS to emissions reduction projects in other nations through the project-based mechanisms established by the Kyoto Protocol. Linking the EU ETS to CDM and JI projects would enable installations to use Kyoto project credits to meet a portion of their EU ETS obligations. Proponents argued that the Linking Directive would provide fungibility between the EU ETS and the CDM/JI markets, thus stimulating these markets and expanding the transfers to developing and transition countries. Margot Wallström, the then European commissioner for the environment, made the case: 'The Commission will propose to open the new market to emission credits gained by companies internationally under the Joint Implementation and Clean Development Mechanism. This will mean that other countries, for example Russia, will benefit from our EU emissions trading market' (Environment News Service 2003).

The draft Linking Directive was proposed in July 2003 – immediately following the agreement on the EU ETS Directive – and discussions were highly contentious. Industry favoured maximum access to project credits, arguing that an expanded credit supply would reduce allowance prices. NGOs and a few member states – notably Germany – opposed linking or argued for highly restrictive conditions and limits, on the basis that to do otherwise would dilute the effectiveness of the EU ETS and could lead to a price collapse. In the final agreement, the question of capping access to CDM and JI credits was left to the member states, which were allowed to use CDM credits from 2005 and JI credits from 2008. The European Council and Parliament reached agreement on the Linking Directive in April 2004 (European Parliament and Council 2004).

Leadership and people matter

The implementation of the European Union Emissions Trading Scheme was the result of hard work by a variety of stakeholders and institutions. Among these groups, a few individuals were key to both promoting the idea and its execution.

Jos Delbeke and his team at the European Commission[9] were central to the effort. They brought the scars of history from the failed European carbon tax proposal, an interdisciplinary focus combining economics, law and political science, and great skill in meeting the pragmatic need to adapt to pressure but doing so in a fashion that did not weaken the essentials, and with a fierce determination that this time they would not fail.

---

[9] The Commission team that drove the development, enactment and implementation of EU ETS included the following. Jos Delbeke, economist, then head of unit; Delbeke steered the study of the single market and the environment in 1990, led the attempt to introduce the carbon energy tax and served as a staff member at the International Monetary Fund (IMF) before joining the Commission in 1986; he was awarded the Outstanding Achievement Award by the European Association of Environmental and Resource Economists in 2005 for his work in leading the EU ETS to realization. Olivia Hartridge, political scientist, co-wrote the rules for the UK Emissions Trading Scheme before joining the Commission team in 2003. Jürgen Lefevere worked with FIELD on climate change and energy, including the Commission's Green Paper on emissions trading, before joining the Commission in 2003, where he focused on the development of the Linking Directive. Damien Meadows worked as a legal adviser to the UK Department of Environment, Transport and the Regions and the UN Climate Change Secretariat before joining the Commission; he was responsible for EU ETS implementation and review. Arthur Runge-Metzger, resource economist, has been head of 'market-based instruments including greenhouse gas emissions trading' in the Commission since 2003, with an earlier focus in the Commission on developing countries. Yvon Slingenberg served as a member of the Cabinet of the then environment commissioner, Wallström, and in the Commission's Climate Change Policy Unit. Matti Vainio, economist, was head of the Energy and Environment Unit of the European Commission; he carried out the economic analysis of the EU ETS in 2000/1 and led the Clean Air for Europe programme. Peter Vis, economist, was the main author of the Green Paper on emissions trading and led the day-to-day discussions of the Commission proposal tabled in 2001. Finally, Peter Zapfel, economist, coordinated the EU ETS team, having focused earlier in particular on the allocation of allowances.

The director generals of the Commission's Environment Directorate were key advocates and leaders when it was most needed. Jim Curry was the director general after the Kyoto Protocol period. He was an economist who understood the logic and salience of the emissions trading idea, and led and facilitated the change of direction. His successor, Catherine Day, was also an economist, who in her early career had worked for an industry lobby group in Ireland, and she understood the motivations and modalities of interest groups. She also served in the Cabinet of Peter Sutherland's Directorate General for Competition when the European Union was making a reality out of the rhetoric of the single market, and led the accession process of many new member states. Thus, she was intellectually favourably disposed to market approaches and had the practical experience and skills to move the agenda forward.

Margot Wallström was commissioner for the environment during the crucial 1999–2004 period. As a national of a country with a long history of concern for the environment, she understood the importance of market signals as animators of environmentally responsible behaviour. To an unusual degree at this level, she brought qualities of charm and persuasiveness that proved very important in securing the support of her fellow commissioners and then steering the directive from concept to reality.

In addition, after some initial hesitation and antagonism, the commissioners for competition and the internal market – Mario Monti and Frits Bolkestein, respectively – supported the EU ETS, because it was a logical way to proceed in order to avoid the competition-inhibiting Balkanization of trading into twenty-seven different national jurisdictions with differing coverage and rules. In this case, environment trumped industry because of the long shadow of the single market. The Commission also had a number of advisers and supporters on its fringes who helped move the idea forward.

The Danish presidency was timely, in that its six months steering the Union occurred at a crucial moment in which substantive opposition, notably from Germany, had to be reconciled with the view of the Commission, Parliament and some other member states. The Danes proved to have the experience, skill and ambition to find a way forward successfully. Subsequently, the Irish presidency prioritized securing agreement on the Linking Directive.

The United Kingdom was a steady and consistent supporter of trading, even though what the Commission proposed and what was eventually enacted differed substantially from the country's own voluntary scheme. At the level of the European Parliament, Jorge Moreira da Silva as rapporteur proved to be the right man in the right place at the right time. In a less high-profile way, parliamentary rapporteur Alexander de Roo fulfilled the same role for the Linking Directive.

Key stakeholder groups in industry were also crucial, none more so than BP, and their chief lobbyist in Brussels at the time, Mike Wrigglesworth. BP legitimated emissions trading by creating its own internal scheme, and acted as a behind-the-scenes supporter, which had the effect of diluting industry opposition.

There is an American baseball expression that says: 'Good pitching will cancel out good hitting and vice versa.' The protagonists in the main resisted the temptation to devote their energies to simply cancelling each other out, and instead sought and found ways forward. Moreover, all were helped by the sense that emissions trading was an idea whose time had come.

Some conclusions and implications

On 1 January 2005 the European Union Emissions Trading Scheme went into effect. With approximately 11,500 participating installations spread across the twenty-seven member states of the Union, the European Union is the initiator and operator of the world's first and largest international emissions trading scheme. The trading scheme is now the cornerstone of EU environmental policy, and provides a platform for subsequent action at the global level. It is estimated that the sources to which the trading scheme applies will account for 45 per cent of CO_2 emissions in 2010, and a little less than 40 per cent of total greenhouse gas emissions in that year.

As a result of the adoption of the EU Emissions Trading Directive, a somewhat paradoxical situation has emerged in the international climate change arena. In a very short period of time, emissions trading has evolved from being a non-option for the European Union to the cornerstone of European climate policy. Meanwhile, the United States, so long the proponent of emissions trading, turned largely to voluntary measures as part of its climate strategy and refusal to ratify the Kyoto Protocol.[10] Considering that it was only in 1997 that trading began moving from being a mainly academic interest to taking centre stage in Europe, progress with adopting this instrument has been remarkable. The European Environment Agency describes this situation as one in which Europe has gone 'from follower to leader' in terms of both understanding and applying this economic instrument to environmental policy (EEA 2005).

The Union has a population of almost 500 million people, living in twenty-seven countries, embracing twenty-three languages, with per capita GDP in 2005 on a purchasing power parity basis ranging from €32,197 (Ireland) to €7,913 (Bulgaria) (Eurostat 2008a). It is not always a harmonious club. Sometimes it seems that Edward Mortimer's view captures the Union's essence: 'A nation ... is a group of people united by a common dislike of their neighbours, and a shared misconception about their ethnic origins.'

Why was agreement reached? Several factors contributed to the successful establishment of the EU ETS.

First, the idea of the European common market and the Single European Act of 1986 that made it a reality were fundamental to the creation of the emissions trading scheme. By enabling the free movement of goods, people and capital across borders, the act linked the economies of member states and made the idea of a common emissions reduction objective – as expressed in the burden-sharing agreement of 1998 – a real possibility. It also helped member states overcome industry's objections to the implementation of a pan-European trading system.

Second, both the content and the political fallout of the Kyoto Protocol were key to the introduction of emissions trading within the European Union. European negotiators failed to prevent the inclusion of emissions trading in the Kyoto Protocol. It was precisely this failure, however, that led the Union to reconsider its GHG management strategy and to turn from a tax-centred approach to the creation of a carbon market. Then the US refusal to ratify the Kyoto Protocol prompted Europe to take the lead in moving the treaty forward.

---

[10] It is important to note that, as only voluntary measures have been implemented at the federal level in the United States so far, a number of American states are taking steps to establish mandatory emissions trading schemes. The so-called Waxman–Markey bill could set up a mandatory cap-and-trade scheme at the federal level by 2013, however.

The Union's ability to make trade-offs on the world stage – and in particular to secure Russian agreement to ratify the Kyoto Protocol in exchange for EU support for WTO membership – allowed the protocol to come into effect, which in turn re-emphasized the role of the EU ETS.

Third, early actions by individual European member states gave further impetus to the swift creation of a pan-European trading scheme following the Kyoto negotiations. States such as the United Kingdom, Denmark and the Netherlands were choosing to pursue their own environmental taxation and trading schemes in the absence of European action. Fears about the further expansion of this regulatory patchwork – and the implications it could have for the proper functioning of the common market – enabled the tripartite EU government to come to agreement on the EU ETS in a relatively short period of time. This agreement was facilitated by supportive information on trading from the United States, which, based on its experience with the Acid Rain Program, relayed the message that business can co-exist and prosper with emissions trading.

Finally, the design features of the EU ETS itself facilitated consensus between the EU government, industry and NGOs. A firm limit on emissions and the prospective availability of transparent data from installations assuaged environmental advocates; free allowances and allocation at the member state level helped diminish industry opposition; and the inclusion of an obligatory three-year pilot period temporarily indulged some member state preoccupations, including opt-out and pooling,[11] and served as a way of identifying weaknesses to be corrected after 2007. These provisions, combined with a willingness on all sides to compromise and a high degree of skill and commitment at the levels of the European Commission, European Parliament, member states and some businesses and NGOs, enabled the EU ETS to go forward.

So, while European negotiators may have lost their initial battles to introduce a carbon tax and to exclude emissions trading from the Kyoto Protocol, they appear to have won the war. The EU ETS has

---

[11] Pooling provisions authorize a company or any other legal entity to centralize the allowance management of several installations located in the same country, using a single account in the corresponding national registry.

resulted in the establishment of an effective price signal for CO_2 emissions, and the pilot period has provided Europe with a number of important lessons for the future operation of the trading scheme. As noted by Egenhofer *et al.* (2006), 'Emissions trading is one of the crucial pillars upon which both the EU's climate change policy and the (yet to emerge) global regime is expected to rest.'

3 | *Allowance allocation*

Introduction

A *unique feature of cap-and-trade systems*

Cap-and-trade systems operate through the creation and distribution of tradable rights to emit, usually called allowances, to installations. Since a constraining cap creates a scarcity rent, these allowances have value, and there are many claimants for them, not least the owners of installations required to surrender allowances equal to their emissions. The distribution of these rights, usually for free, is what is called allocation, and it is the unique feature of cap-and-trade systems.

Allocation is often portrayed as contentious and sordid, but it should be remembered that similar rights, rents and value are created by any system that effectively constrains emissions. An emissions tax is relatively straightforward. It creates a fixed price on emissions, instead of a fixed quantity limit, and the right to emit is acquired by paying the tax. The government is typically the recipient of the tax revenues, although cases exist in which the revenues are returned to emitters, such as the NOx (nitrogen oxides) tax in Sweden (Millock and Sterner 2004). 'Command-and-control' approaches are more common and less transparent, but they create the same rights and rents. Firms acquire implicit rights to emit by meeting the prescribed regulatory standard, or whatever derogations may be granted. The value created by the constraint is conveyed to facilities meeting the new standard through the increase in the price of output due to the new regulatory requirement, which often places more demanding standards on new entrants.

At bottom, allowance allocation involves a tough political decision concerning who is to be the recipient of the value created by the constraint. Setting aside whether the price is fixed or variable, a cap-and-trade system differs from a tax only to the extent that the allowances created by the cap are distributed for free to entities other than the government. If allowances are auctioned, as often advocated, the government is the initial recipient of the value created by the cap. As is the case with a tax, a decision still has to be be made about distributing the auction revenues, but the starting point is different. Conventional command-and-control regulation is distinctive in removing any possibility that the government would be the recipient of the value created by the emissions constraint. In this respect, it is like a fully grandfathered cap-and-trade system. The main difference is that the magnitude of the rents – as well as the identity of the recipients – is almost totally obscured. In contrast, allowance allocation has the dubious distinction of making both the magnitude and the recipients readily evident.

Allocation in the EU ETS

Allocation in the EU ETS has taken on a broader significance to include setting the cap in addition to the distribution of allowances to affected facilities. The structure for accomplishing allocation in the first and second periods was specified in article 9 of the ETS Directive (European Parliament and Council 2003):

> For each period . . . each Member State shall develop a national plan stating the total quantity of allowances that it intends to allocate for that period and how it proposes to allocate them.

These national allocation plans are to be developed using objective and transparent criteria that are given in annex III of the directive. The ETS Directive also requires member states to take public comment into account in developing their NAPs, and it specifies timelines for the submission or notification of NAPs to the Commission.

The role of the European Commission is also clearly laid out in article 9:

> Within three months of notification of a national allocation plan . . ., the Commission may reject that plan, or any aspect thereof, on the basis that it is incompatible with the [specified] criteria.

The Commission must state the reason for rejection; member states cannot distribute allowances to installations until the grounds for the Commission's rejection have been removed, however. Notably, the directive does not give the Commission authority to 'approve' national allocation plans. It has the authority only to review and to reject, in part or in whole; if the NAP is not rejected, it is accepted. This may be a distinction without a difference, but it is an important one in a multinational setting in which the constituent members are sovereign states and the powers exercised by the central authority are delegated, and in this case limited to ensuring that the implementing actions of member states are consistent with the previously agreed common interest.

Certain consequences flow from this decentralized structure of allocation. The most obvious is that the cap for the EU ETS is the sum of twenty-seven separate decisions concerning the total number of allowances that each member state can distribute. Consequently, the EU-wide cap is not known until all the member state totals have been decided.[1] These totals are sometimes called 'caps' or 'targets', although in reality they are neither, since a member state's total does not limit its emissions, and there is no expectation that each member state's emissions will be equal to its total. Nevertheless, this part of the allocation process is usefully termed 'cap-setting', as the EU-wide cap is the sum of these totals.

Another consequence of decentralized allocation is that the distribution of the totals to installations in various member states may be done differently, so that installations competing in the same markets may receive different free allocations of allowances. The resulting perception of unfairness and possible competitive advantage has led to the calls for harmonization that have been prominent in the EU ETS.

The degree of decentralization in the EU ETS reflects the political reality of the European Union, in which member states are sovereign nations that have ceded limited authority to central institutions.

---

[1] The European Union consisted of twenty-five member states when the EU ETS was launched in 2005. In 2007 Bulgaria and Romania joined the European Union, and they became part of the EU ETS the same year. This change in regional scope as well as the total cap of the EU ETS created separate time frames for the development, the notification and the approval of the NAPs for the EU25 and the two new member states. Although, technically, the cap for the entire period was not known until these last two NAPs were accepted, for all practical purposes the first-period NAP process was concluded when the NAPs for the EU25 were accepted. For this reason, most of the subsequent discussion of the first period in this chapter will focus on the allocation process for the EU25.

The NAP structure represents the particular balance of central and member state authority that was possible when the ETS Directive was negotiated. This decentralized structure also accommodates the often very different legal requirements among member states. In France, for example, the development of the NAP was a purely administrative procedure, whereas in Germany legislative approval was required.

The EU ETS is a significantly more decentralized system than any earlier cap-and-trade programme. For instance, in the US Acid Rain Program for trading SO_2 permits, allocation is completely a federal matter: both the cap and the allocations to installations are decided at the federal level. Installations are located in different states, but the role of the states is negligible. The US NOx Budget Program operates in a more decentralized manner that is closer to the EU ETS. The federal Environmental Protection Agency (EPA) decides the overall cap and its apportionment to individual states (the 'budget'), but each state is free to allocate allowances to installations without further review by the EPA. At the extreme of decentralization, one can imagine a trading system of constituent cap-and-trade programmes linked through mutual recognition and in which both the cap and the allocations to installations are determined independently by each constituent member with little or no central review. The EU ETS, which can be seen as twenty-seven linked cap-and-trade systems, approaches this limiting case, but the role of the European Commission is considerably more important than in this fictional, heuristic example.

Allocation is one aspect of the EU ETS about which an *ex post* perspective can be taken with respect to more than the trial period. The allocation process for the second trading period was completed in 2007, and the amendments to the ETS Directive adopted in 2008 have changed the allocation process after 2012 fundamentally. The next two sections of this chapter discuss cap-setting in the first and second periods, for which the conditions and results differed substantially. The following section focuses on the allocation to installations within member states, which was not significantly different in the first and second periods. The next section of the chapter explains the post-2012 amendments, which fundamentally change both cap-setting and the manner by which installations obtain allowances for compliance. The final section concludes.

Cap-setting in the first compliance period

Conditions of implementation

Cap-setting in the first period has been much criticized because of the end-of-period surplus. This *ex post* result cannot be properly judged, however, without taking into account the difficult conditions under which cap-setting in the first period was conducted and the self-contained nature of the first period, notably poor data availability and impossible deadlines. These factors compounded what would have been a difficult problem anyway, because of the modest ambition of the first period and the inherent uncertainty of future emission levels.

Modest ambition and emissions uncertainty

The objective for the trial period was not to achieve significant emission reductions in 2005–7 but to establish the infrastructure and institutions and to gain the experience to make the subsequent, 'real', period a success. Moreover, the trial period was not part of the Kyoto Protocol. The cap that was to be decided for the trial period was a voluntary one assumed by the European Union to prepare for the subsequent trading period when a legally binding obligation would exist. As a result, the criteria for cap-setting in the trial period were closely tied to expected business-as-usual (BAU) emissions. The specific criterion for member state totals was the lesser of BAU emissions or a level of emissions that would not jeopardize the member state's achievement of its Kyoto/BSA target in the second period. This latter 'path to Kyoto' criterion applied only to member states for which recent emissions were above a straight line drawn from the 1990 emission level to the Kyoto/BSA target. As of 2004, when the first-period NAPs were being prepared, nine of the EU15 were judged to be not on track and thus subject to this criterion (EEA 2004). For the other member states, including the new member states with the exception of Slovenia, the allowed national total for the ETS sectors was estimated BAU emissions. Thus, the criteria for cap-setting implied that ten member states would have totals below expected BAU emissions and the totals for the remaining fifteen would be at BAU emissions. As noted by Ellerman, Buchner and Carraro (2007: 354), however, the final first-period totals were close to expected BAU emissions, even for member states that were deemed off the path to Kyoto.

When combined with the inherent uncertainty of future emissions, the modest ambition of the first period made an end-of-period surplus more likely than if the reduction objective had been more demanding. An EU-wide cap that was expected to be at or a little below BAU emissions would run a significant chance of being slack, which could lead to an allowance price of zero at the end of the period. For example, if the final cap were 2 per cent below expected BAU emissions, and emissions fluctuated by as much as 5 per cent from year to year, there would be a non-negligible chance that emissions would be below the cap on an *ex post* basis even without any abatement. BAU uncertainty is present in any cap-setting exercise, but a slack constraint and a zero price will not result when the prospective cap imposes a much greater reduction of emissions. For instance, if the ambition of the cap is a 50 per cent reduction, as it was in the US SO_2 trading programme, a variation of even as much as 10 per cent in BAU emissions would still produce a price and be binding. The allowance price might be lower than expected but it would be positive and significant. In addition, the self-contained nature of the trial period, created by the short time period and the inability to bank first-period allowances for use in the second period, made a zero price at the end of the period inevitable if the constraint was slack, as it turned out to be.

Poor data

The task of setting a cap that was at or close to BAU emissions was made enormously more difficult by poor data. The problem was that no member state government had a good idea of the exact emissions within the ETS sectors. While good inventory data had been developed at the national and sector levels and reported through the UNFCCC processes, these data were calculated on an upstream basis – that is, based on fuel consumption at the sectoral and economy-wide levels. Moreover, the definition of sectors differed, as did the criteria by which installations and emissions were included in the ETS.[2] As a

---

[2] The data collection and verification procedures under the EU ETS led to significant revisions and improvements of the national greenhouse gas inventories, however, because the installation-based data collection provided a wide range of new insights into emission sources and emission factors. For instance, in both Hungary and the Czech Republic, the public consultations with industry revealed that actual ETS emissions were higher than originally estimated, by 14 per cent and 17 per cent, respectively (Bart 2007).

result, there were no data and no models that could predict ETS sector emissions. The data problem was even worse in the new member states of eastern Europe, where the problem of forecasting was made more difficult by the ongoing structural transformations of the economy. The result was a set of approximations of what EU ETS sector emissions were thought to have been in the recent past and what they were expected to be in the first trading period.

The problems created by poor data were not limited to cap-setting; they extended into the allocation of allowances to installations, which required installation-level emissions data. Where such data were thought to exist, differences in definitions or inadequacies in quality made the data unusable. In Germany, for instance, the data were simply not available (Matthes and Schafhausen 2007), and in Sweden the previously collected data turned out to be unreliable (Zetterberg 2007).

The only remedy for this problem was a crash effort to collect installation-level data that could be used for the allocation to installations and to determine the scope of the ETS sectors when summed. Because there was no legal and regulatory framework for collecting these data – and such a framework would have taken too long to set up – the practical expedient was dependence on the voluntary submission of data by the owners of included installations. Not surprisingly, since allocations to these installations depended on the data submitted, industrial firms were forthcoming, although there has always been a suspicion that the intended use of the data imparted an upward bias to these data. As reported by nearly every contributor to Ellerman, Buchner and Carraro (2007), those in charge of allocation checked these data submissions for consistency with related data, but the deadlines were such that there was no time for careful verification of these data submissions.

Impossible deadlines

The final condition shaping the NAP1 process was the demanding time schedule specified in the ETS Directive. This agreement among the EU15 member states, which was substantively concluded in July 2003 and formally issued in October 2003, required first-period national allocation plans to be submitted by the end of March 2004. Moreover, the ten new member states, mostly eastern European, that were to join the European Union on 1 May 2004 were to submit their NAPs by that date. Then the Commission was to complete its review within three months of having been notified of each member state's NAP. In theory, the entire process would be concluded and the cap determined by August 2004, five months before the scheduled start of the system on 1 January 2005.

Given the novelty of the exercise and what would be required both practically and legally in developing and assessing NAPs, however, this schedule proved to be impossible. In fact, only four of the EU15 member states, and none of the new member states, met the deadline for notifying NAPs to the Commission, although four member states missed it by ten days or fewer. By the end of July 2004 all the EU15 member states except Greece had notified their NAPs to the Commission, and in early November the last of the new member state plans was formally received. The final NAP, from Greece (against which the Commission had to initiate enforcement proceedings), was notified in January 2005.

The Commission's assessment of notified NAPs was completed in batches, with the first eight announced in early July 2004, another eight in October and another five in late December. By the start of 2005 twenty-one of the twenty-five plans had been approved. The remaining four were relatively large emitters (Poland, the Czech Republic, Italy and Greece), with almost 30 per cent of the emissions covered by the ETS. The last NAP, that for Greece, was accepted on 20 June 2005, six months into the first period. From start to finish, the review process had taken fifteen months. Table 3.1 shows the stages by which NAPs were accepted and the percentage of the eventual EU-wide cap that was determined as of each date.

The delays incurred resulted not only from late submissions but from the Commission's review. The time between the initial notification and the conclusion of the Commission's assessment was often much greater than three months. Only eight of the twenty-five NAPs were reviewed within three months of notification, and the average time required was 4.3 months, with the longest assessment being that for Italy, which required a little more than ten months. Often the initial notifications were found to be incomplete, and the Commission developed the expedient of not starting the three-month clock until adequate data for assessment had been provided.

The delayed submissions and staged reviews did have some advantages. Member states that were late in preparing their NAPs frequently adopted provisions from earlier submissions, particularly those of the

Table 3.1 *NAP1 review results*

Review concluded	Number of NAPs	Member states	Three-year totals (million EUAs)[1]	Cumulative percentage
7 July 2004	8	Germany, United Kingdom, Netherlands, Denmark, Austria, Sweden, Ireland, Slovenia	2,880	44
20 October 2004	8	France, Belgium, Finland, Portugal, Luxembourg, Slovakia, Estonia, Latvia	1,081	60
27 December 2004	5	Spain, Hungary, Lithuania, Cyprus, Malta	680	71
8 March 2005	1	Poland	717	82
12 April 2005	1	Czech Republic	293	86
25 May 2005	1	Italy	698	97
20 June 2005	1	Greece	223	100

Note: [1]As initially approved and therefore not including opt-ins, opt-outs and later refinements of the list of installations.
Source: Zapfel (2007).

United Kingdom and Germany. The announcement of the first batch of concluded reviews on 7 July 2004 also provided the Commission with an opportunity to explain its reasoning, particularly in regard to *ex post* adjustments. It also provided more specific guidance so that member states that had yet to submit their NAPs could make appropriate changes.

Co-ordination and guidance

Given the impossible deadlines and the lack of familiarity with emissions trading, it is doubtful that the EU ETS would have emerged at all had it not been for the facilitating and educational role that the Commission assumed in the preparation of the first-period NAPs. Without this guiding hand, the start of the EU ETS would have been even more difficult than it was. This assistance was aimed at 'overcoming know-how gaps' among regulatory authorities and stakeholders, and it took the form of studies on certain technical aspects, non-official papers suggesting practical steps for developing NAPs, and the elaboration of official guidance on how the Commission interpreted the assessment criteria contained in the ETS Directive (Zapfel 2007). The Commission was also active in organizing various working groups and other mechanisms to facilitate the exchange of information among member state authorities. The result was, as remarked by Zapfel (2007), 'a remarkably high degree of harmonization'.

The Commission's success in guiding the first NAP process to a successful conclusion was also due to its prioritization of the potentially conflicting criteria laid out in the ETS Directive. Attention was focused on the features that were necessary to create an EU-wide allowance market that would enable a least-cost achievement of the needed emission reductions. The proposed total number of EUAs to be issued by each member state and the absence of *ex post* adjustments were the two features that received the most attention. The first was aimed at ensuring that the EU-wide cap would be constraining so that an EUA price would appear, while the latter was targeted against provisions that would have impeded the development of an allowance market. Many member states proposed readjusting allocations at the end of the period to correspond more closely to an installation's actual emissions. The Commission feared that this 'quota management' would encourage firms to seek this form of administrative relief instead of trading allowances and would discourage the incorporation of a carbon price into production decisions.

In the interests of expediting matters, the Commission also developed the expedient of accepting a member state's NAP conditional on certain technical changes being made, at which time the NAP would automatically become fully accepted. This avoided a second review and diplomatically spared member states from having their NAP rejected. In most cases, these technical changes had already been agreed through more informal and back-channel communications between the member state authorities and the Commission. Throughout the process there was a high degree of informal communication and information exchange through working groups and bilateral communications.

Results

In exercising its delegated powers to review and reject member state NAPs, the Commission required reductions in the proposed member state totals, as shown in table 3.2.

The Commission required reductions totalling 4.3 per cent of what would otherwise have been the EU-wide cap, or about 100 million tonnes on an annual average, from fourteen member states. Two-thirds of this reduction in proposed totals was in six eastern European new member states and almost a half of the EU-wide total was in Poland alone. Among the EU15 member states, and with the exception of Italy, the required reductions were small in both absolute and percentage terms.

In view of the surplus that appeared at the end of the first period, it needs to be emphasized that, until the release of the 2005 verified emissions data in April 2006, the EU-wide cap was not viewed as being too lax. If anything, the higher than expected EUA prices and analyst forecasts suggested the opposite.[3] Documenting earlier expectations quantitatively is always difficult, but the case studies in Ellerman, Buchner and Carraro (2007) provide relevant data for a

---

[3] An example of the latter is an ill-timed first-page guest viewpoint in Point Carbon's *Carbon Market Europe*, published a week before the price collapse in April 2006, when prices were skirting their highs of €30, which bore the headline 'CO$_2$ price still too low' (Lekander 2006).

Table 3.2 Proposed and allowed EU25 member state totals, first-period NAPs

Member state	Proposed annual amount (million EUAs)	Allowed annual amount (million EUAs)	Required reduction (million EUAs)	Percentage reduction from proposed amount
Austria	33.2	33	-0.2	-0.60
Belgium	62.6	62.1	-0.5	-0.80
Denmark	33.5	33.5	0	
Finland	45.5	45.5	0	
France	157.8	156.5	-1.3	-1.00
Germany	499	499	0	
Greece	74.4	74.4	0	
Ireland	22.5	22.32	-0.18	-0.80
Italy	246.1	223.1	-23	-8.80
Luxembourg	3.51	3.36	-0.15	-4.50
Netherlands	98.3	95.3	-3	-3.10
Portugal	39.6	38.9	-0.7	-1.80
Spain	174.4	174.4	0	
Sweden	22.9	22.9	0	
United Kingdom	245.3	245.3	0	
EU15 subtotal	*1,758.6*	*1,729.6*	*-29*	*-1.6*
Cyprus	5.7	5.7	0	
Czech Republic	107.66	97.6	-10.06	-9.30
Estonia	21.6	18.95	-2.65	-12.30
Hungary	31.3	31.3	0	

Table 3.2 (*cont.*)

Member state	Proposed annual amount (million EUAs)	Allowed annual amount (million EUAs)	Required reduction (million EUAs)	Percentage reduction from proposed amount
Latvia	6.43	4.57	−1.87	−29.00
Lithuania	14.17	12.27	−1.9	−13.40
Malta	2.9	2.9	0	
Poland	286.2	239.1	−47.1	−16.50
Slovakia	35.47	30.5	−4.97	−14.00
Slovenia	8.8	8.8	0	
EU10 subtotal	*520.2*	*451.7*	*−68.5*	*−13.20*
EU25 total	*2278.8*	*2181.3*	*−97.6*	*−4.30*

Notes: The proposed and allowed final amounts for Belgium, France, Italy and Portugal differ from the totals given in the initial NAP proposals, news reports and the acceptance decision from the Commission as a result of subsequent amendments to the list of installations that were required to bring the list into conformity with the Commission's interpretation of the applicability of the ETS Directive. The allowed amounts in this table are those given in European Commission (2007), which takes these changes into account. The required reductions are those announced initially and they are added to the final allowed amounts to yield an adjusted proposed annual amount.

Sources: Authors' compilation, based on news reports, Commission decisions on NAP assessments and European Commission (2007).

subset of member states that constitute approximately a half of EU ETS emissions. Table 3.3 presents these data.

The main point is that what would have been indicated as an expected shortfall of 4 per cent became an actual surplus of 4 per cent. Even if the Polish forecast of expected emissions is discounted, as the Commission obviously did in requiring a reduction of the cap to a level that still allowed a more than 3 per cent annual growth of emissions, an expected aggregate deficit remains.[4] Table 3.3 also shows that the entire actual surplus for the subset as a whole is located in the eastern European countries. The notable feature here is not so much that their verified emissions were lower than their respective caps but that they were lower than pre-2005 emissions. The explanation is not a decline in economic growth, which remained robust during these years, but the continuing significant improvements in energy and carbon efficiency per unit of GDP in eastern Europe. This trend, which had been pronounced since the early 1990s as part of the restructuring of the eastern European economies, was uniformly viewed as having been largely exhausted by 2005, and this expectation was embedded in the NAP predictions of BAU emissions (Chmelik 2007; Jankowski 2007). This faulty assumption only compounded the problem of poor data.

Four further features of the EU-wide cap in the first period are needed for a technically correct accounting of the cap and the resulting surplus: the accession of Romania and Bulgaria in 2007; the European Court of First Instance's ruling on Germany's challenge to the Commission's disallowance of *ex post* adjustments; the treatment of opt-outs and opt-ins; and the incomplete distribution of allowances in the new entrant reserves (NERs). None of these had a substantive impact on the EUA market, but they are necessary for a complete description of the trial-period cap and a final accounting of the surplus.

Although Romania and Bulgaria were technically a part of the EU ETS in 2007, they were, in the spirit of the trial period, effectively self-contained experiments in setting up a cap-and-trade system.

---

[4] The inclusion of other member state data on expected emissions might change these percentages somewhat, but the general directions would remain the same. For instance, Spain and Italy received caps that were clearly less than expected BAU emissions, and that turned out to be less than verified emissions, while other countries received caps that were close to or even above expected emissions (see Godard 2005 for a revealing analysis of the French NAP).

Table 3.3 *Expected and actual EUA surpluses, seven member states, 2005–7*

Country	Recent emissions (Mt CO$_2$, annual average) (year)	Predicted 2005–7 emissions (Mt CO$_2$, annual average)	ETS cap (Mt CO$_2$, annual average)[1]	Verified emissions (Mt CO$_2$, annual average)	Expected surplus (% of cap)	Actual surplus (% of cap)
Czech Republic	91 (2004)	97.6	97.6	84.6	0	+13 (13%)
Hungary	31.0 (2002)	31.3	31.3	26.3	0	+5 (16%)
Poland	217 (2003)	260	239	207	−21.0 (−9%)	+32 (13%)
Germany	507 (2002)	495	499	480	+4.0 (+0.8%)	+19 (3.8%)
Ireland	22.5 (2003)	23	22.3	21.6	−0.7 (−3.1%)	+0.7 (3.1%)
Denmark	30.7 (2002)	39.3	33.5	30	−5.8 (−17%)	+3.5 (10%)
United Kingdom[2]	251 (2003)	246	224	248	−22 (−10%)	−24 (−11%)
Total	NA	1,192	1,147	1,098	−45 (−3.9%)	+49 (4.3%)

Notes: [1]As given in Ellerman, Buchner and Carraro (2007) to maintain comparability with predicted BAU emissions, which are taken from the same source.

[2]Verified emissions do not include installations for which the opt-out was exercised during the first period. To maintain comparability, the EUAs included in the UK NAP for these installations are deducted from the totals that are given in Ellerman, Buchner and Carraro (2007) for recent and predicted emissions and the ETS cap: 267.1 million tonnes (Mt) and 245.4 million EUAs, respectively. The quantity of EUAs not issued to opt-outs was 24 Mt in both 2005 and 2006 and 14 Mt in 2007. BAU emissions for opted-out units are assumed equal to allowances not issued.

Sources: Compiled from CITL data and Ellerman, Buchner and Carraro (2007).

Installations in those countries were liable for their emissions and submitted verified emission reports, but the registries in both countries were not operating in time to permit any significant trading with other member states. The two countries added 117 million EUAs to the EU-wide cap for the first period, 109 million tonnes of additional emissions and a surplus of 8 million EUAs – equal to about 7 per cent of their combined totals.

A more substantial change was effected by the court ruling on Germany's legal challenge to the Commission's position on *ex post* adjustments. The German NAP contained a provision that gave existing installations the option of choosing an allocation based on plant-specific projected production instead of the historical baseline, with the proviso that allowances would be taken back if production was less than planned (Matthes and Schafhausen 2007). The Commission rejected this provision, on the reasoning that extra allowances issued as a result of this option were subtracted from other allocations, since the overall total for Germany remained unchanged, and that the takeback associated with this option constituted an *ex post* adjustment. The court ruled in favour of Germany on 7 November 2007 (European Court of First Instance 2007), and 70 million EUAs were subsequently withdrawn from the registry accounts of installations that had received an allowance surplus through this option[5] (DEHst [Deutsche Emissionshandelsstelle – the German emissions trading authority] 2009). This withdrawal converted Germany's apparent surplus of 58 million EUAs into a deficit of 8 million EUAs.

The final two features were the net effect of installations that were subject either to an opt-out or an opt-in subsequent to the NAP acceptances and the EUAs set aside for new entrants but not distributed. The Commission's conditional acceptances of NAPs did not take account of installations that were subsequently opted out or opted in. The CITL data, as presented in the data appendix, provide the definitive numbers, which indicate that the net effect was a reduction of 77 million EUAs. The largest adjustments were opt-outs of 61.5 million in the United Kingdom and 19.1 million in the Netherlands, and an extra 15.9 million EUAs in Spain for a group of

---

[5] Some *ex post* adjustments also resulted from bonus allocations for co-generation, hardship clauses and transfer provisions with incomplete transfer of production.

Table 3.4 *Final first-period cap and emissions*

(data in millions)	EUAs	Verified emissions	Surplus
Initial EU25 NAP result	6,544	6,091	453
Plus: Bulgaria and Romania	117	109	8
Less: German *ex post* adjustment	−70	NA	−70
Less: net of opt-outs and opt-ins	−77	NA	−77
Less: undistributed new entrant reserves	−47	NA	−47
Final first-period results	6,467	6,200	267

Source: Compiled by the authors.

installations that were not initially included in the Spanish NAP. Additionally, 47 million EUAs remained in the reserves that were set aside for new entrants, which will be explained presently. The final accounting of the first-period cap and its surplus after these adjustments is given in table 3.4.

The final result is still a surplus for the European Union as a whole, but the magnitude is about half as large because of the German *ex post* adjustment, the net effect of opt-outs and opt-ins, and the undistributed NERs.

Cap-setting in the second compliance period, 2008–12

Conditions of implementation

Most of the problems that had plagued the first-period NAP process had disappeared by the time the second-period NAPs were developed and reviewed. The problem of poor data was solved at one fell swoop by the release of verified emissions data for 2005 just before the date for submission of second-period NAPs. A rigorous and consistent measure of the emissions from the installations included in the EU ETS then became available. In addition, the deadline for the submission of NAPs (June 2006) was no longer an impossible one, since it had been known since the passage of the ETS Directive in 2003. Finally, the ambition with respect to emission reductions was greater for the second compliance period, so the interaction with BAU uncertainty posed less of a problem and the ability to bank second-period allowances for use in the post-2012 period eliminated any prospect of a zero price at the end of the period. Nonetheless, the first-period problems were replaced by new ones created by the EU ETS' status in the second period as a cap within a cap and the need to make sure that the second-period allocation did not jeopardize the European Union's achievement of its obligations under the Kyoto Protocol.

Second-period NAP submissions were due on 30 June 2006, and, had the Commission's review been completed within three months, the second-period cap would have been known by the end of September 2006, fifteen months before the start of the second period. Only two member states, however, Germany and Poland, notified their NAPs by the June deadline, but another four were received by mid-July, and by the end of September 2006 the total had risen to fifteen. The last twelve trickled in at the rate of one or two a month until the last one, from Denmark, was notified in March 2007. The Commission issued its first set of approvals in November 2006, but it was not until 26 October 2007, barely two months from the start of the second period, that the last NAP, from Romania, was approved. In all, the process took sixteen months, one month longer than had been required for the first period. All the same, the earlier start ensured that the final EU-wide cap was known before the start of the second trading period – something that was not true for the first period. The delay can be largely credited to the reaction to the release of verified emissions data for 2005 on the eve of when submissions were due and the change in expectations and in guidance that that event occasioned.

Furthermore, the EU ETS' role as the primary European instrument for ensuring compliance with the Kyoto Protocol presented problems of co-ordination that had not been present beforehand. These problems concerned the trade-off required by the fact that the ETS was now a cap within a broader cap and that limits on the use of credits from Joint Implementation and the Clean Development Mechanism had to be determined.

The 'cap within a cap' problem arose from the consequences of issuing EUAs to ETS installations. Since ETS emissions were included within the Kyoto/BSA targets, each EUA issued by a member state carried with it an allowance issued to that member state under the

Kyoto Protocol, known as assigned amount units (AAUs). Tying EUAs to AAUs ensured that every member state's ETS emissions would be in compliance with the Kyoto Protocol whatever the degree of trading, but it also meant that the quantity of AAUs remaining to each government to cover non-ETS emissions depended on the member state's allocation to the ETS installations. Moreover, any shortfall in AAUs to cover a member state's non-ETS emissions implied government expenditures to buy JI/CDM credits or AAUs from other signatories to the Kyoto Protocol. Thus, for any member state anticipating a potential problem in meeting its Kyoto/BSA obligation, the greater the NAP2 total the lower the number of remaining AAUs, and the higher the level of potential government expenditure for Kyoto credits – and vice versa. Since JI or CDM credits (but not AAUs) could be used for compliance within the ETS, lowering the NAP2 total effectively shifted the burden of purchasing the needed credits away from the Treasury and onto the ETS participants.

A lower NAP2 total also increased the member state's chances of meeting its Kyoto obligations and, by extension, the binding character and accountability of the international regime. Since the compliance regime for the EU ETS is considerably stronger than that for the Kyoto Protocol, member state governments could be assured that the share of the total reduction assigned to the ETS sectors would be accomplished either within the member state or elsewhere through trading. In effect, this part of the member state's Kyoto burden was privatized. Governments gave up some control over reductions in the ETS sectors, but this allowed them to focus more on the policies and measures for the non-ETS sectors and called for a somewhat different policy mix.

The other Kyoto-related problem in the second NAP round was establishing a limit on the use of JI and CDM credits, as required by the Linking Directive, which amended the ETS Directive to allow the use of these credits for compliance (European Parliament and Council 2004). This limit responds to the 'supplementarity' criterion in the Kyoto Protocol, whereby the use of foreign allowances and JI/CDM credits is to be supplementary to domestic reduction efforts. Supplementarity was never defined precisely, but the position of the European Union, which was the chief advocate of this provision in the Kyoto Protocol, was that no more than a half of a signatory's reduction effort could be performed outside of country. Since the reduction necessary to comply with a country's limit can only be estimated, however, making this criterion operational required some expedient.[6] The first step in making supplementarity operational was a provision of the Linking Directive that made the allocation to installations the point of reference for the JI/CDM limit and required member states to include this limit in the second-period NAP if the member state chose to allow the use of these credits for compliance:

Member States may allow operators to use [JI or CDM credits] up to a percentage of the allocation of allowances to each installation, to be specified by each Member State in its national allocation plan. (Article 11a [1])

Co-ordination and guidance

As it had done for the first period, the Commission provided guidance for the preparation of second-period NAPs. Two guidance documents were issued, one in December 2005 (European Commission 2005c) and the other in November 2006. The latter included changes in guidance occasioned by the release of 2005 verified emissions and it accompanied the announcement of the results of the Commission's review of the first ten NAPs for the second period.

The December 2005 guidance (European Commission 2005c) used the only firm reference point that was available at the time: the NAP1 totals. As in the first NAP round, the criterion for the member state total was the lower of (1) BAU emissions for those on track to comply with their Kyoto commitments or (2) a level of ETS emissions that would ensure achievement of the Kyoto/BSA limits taking other measures into account. An estimated EU-wide gap of about 300 million tonnes was to be closed by a combined use of the ETS, other policies and measures affecting non-ETS emissions, and government purchases of AAUs or JI and CDM credits. A balanced use of all three was expected, and the Commission explicitly warned against proposing an ETS total that would place the entire burden of compliance

---

[6] The emission reduction required of any signatory would be the difference between the country's Kyoto 'cap' and what its emissions would have been in the absence of the measures taken to comply with the Kyoto Protocol. Since the latter is not observed, emission reductions can only be estimated. A more complete discussion of this point is contained in chapter 6, where estimates of the emission reductions achieved as a result of the EU ETS are presented.

with the Kyoto Protocol on other policies and measures and on government purchases of AAUs and Kyoto credits. In this context, the Commission announced its expectation that the second-period EU-wide cap would be 6 per cent lower than the comparable first-period cap on an annual basis.

Moreover, in part responding to criticism that the first NAP assessment had lacked consistency and transparency, the Commission announced that it would apply uniform assumptions concerning the growth of CO_2 emissions – an annual rate of growth of 0.3 per cent for the EU15 and 0.2 per cent for the new member states – instead of relying primarily on member state projections, as it had done in the first NAP process. In addition, this early guidance provided a uniform definition of combustion installations that was to be applied by all member states and stated the Commission's opposition to the use of first-period emissions data for installations in determining second-period allocations to those installations.

The November 2006 guidance was necessitated by the intervening release of the 2005 verified emissions data, which the Commission characterized, with some understatement, as being 'of particular importance' (European Commission 2006b). Since these data revealed ETS emissions to be about 7 per cent lower than the first-period cap, the previously intended 6 per cent reduction in the EU-wide cap would have implied very little further emission reduction. In addition, the Commission announced that the economic growth and intensity improvement factors to be used in projecting BAU emissions would be member-state-specific and based on 'a single and coherent methodology and set of assumptions', as contained in a model (PRIMES) that had been widely used to inform EU environmental policy-making. Two other measures were also adopted that would have the effect of ensuring a binding cap. The carbon intensity improvement factor was increased by 0.5 per cent a year and the growth in transport emissions was introduced as another factor in determining whether proposed totals should be reduced.[7]

The November 2006 guidance also clarified a number of other points. Most importantly, an explicit formula was provided for

[7] Specifically, if the projected growth in transport emissions in the NAP was less than that from projections that the Commission was using (implying less of a problem in meeting the member state's Kyoto/BSA target), the trading sector's share of the difference would be deducted from the allowed cap.

calculating the JI/CDM credit limit. The Commission announced its intent to disallow any guarantees of allocation beyond the current trading period, as well as any implied guarantees from the prior trading period. This restriction was aimed explicitly at a provision in Germany's first-period NAP, which had promised a fourteen-year allocation to new entrants. Finally, the Commission dealt with the potential for the banked allowances that the first-period NAPs from France and Poland would have allowed. Any first-period allowances banked for use in the second period would be deducted from the approved member state total and substantiated as resulting from real reductions (instead of being merely surplus allowances).[8] At the same time, the guidance made it clear that banking from the second trading period into subsequent trading periods would be allowed.

Another distinguishing feature of the second round of national allocation plans was the change of style on the part of the Commission in exercising its responsibilities for review. Gone was the velvet glove of allowing member states to take the initiative in proposing totals and then negotiating with the Commission during the review process. The formal procedure was the same as it had been in the first period, but the reality was different. What had been a some-what ad hoc set of negotiations between the Commission and member states now became a determination of whether the proposed member state totals conformed to clearly specified formulae. In effect, the EU-wide cap for the second period and its apportionment among the member states were largely determined and imposed by the Commission. While being more assertive with respect to its role in cap-setting, the Commission for the most part stayed away from passing judgement on the internal distribution of allowances by member states, as it had in the first round. The main exceptions were the continuing opposition to *ex post* adjustments and the new warnings against the use of 2005 verified emissions data as the basis for installation allocations and against allocation guarantees beyond the current period.

---

[8] Banking allowances from the first to the second period were left to member state discretion in the first NAP round. All member states apart from France and Poland stated that they would not allow any banking for fear of complicating compliance with the Kyoto Protocol, which did not recognize banked EUAs for compliance.

Results

Comparison of the second-period EU cap with the first-period cap is complicated by an increase in the number of installations covered, which increased covered emissions by about 2.5 per cent. As shown in table 3.5, when emissions from these new installations are excluded, the NAP2 total for the EU27 is 11.8 per cent below the first-period total and 5.2 per cent below average first-period emissions.

The relationship of each member state's second-period total to its first-period total and its average 2005–7 emissions is displayed graphically in figure 3.1.

When first- and second-period NAPs are compared (after eliminating the emissions from additional installations included in period 2), nearly every member state's total was lower than its first-period total, as shown by the vertical axis. The story is different with respect to verified emissions, for which the relationship is given on the horizontal axis. Twelve of the twenty-seven member states, mostly new member states, were allowed second-period totals that were greater than first-period emissions. In the three cases of significant increases – Slovakia, Latvia and Lithuania – special circumstances, usually shutting down an old Russian-style nuclear reactor, justified the increase.

As was the case in the first period, the totals proposed by member states were generally greater than what the Commission was willing to accept. Only four member states (Denmark, France, the United Kingdom and Slovenia) had their initially-proposed totals accepted. The reductions required by the Commission ranged from the trivial (0.3 per cent for Spain) to more than a half (55 per cent for Latvia). In all, the required reductions totalled 243 million tonnes on an annual basis, slightly more than 10 per cent of the initial proposals and, proportionately, about two and a half times greater than in the first NAP round. Most of this required reduction affected, again, the new member states. As shown in table 3.6, the totals proposed by new member states were significantly higher than their first-period totals, not to mention their average annual emissions during the first period.

The significant reductions required of the new member states consisted mostly of reducing proposed totals that were seen as non-constraining. The aggregate 27 per cent reduction in the totals that had been proposed by the new member states still allowed emissions growth of 2.6 per cent, considerably more than was the

Table 3.5 *Second-period NAP totals*

Member state (annual amounts [Mt/EUAs])	NAP1 totals	Average 2005–7 emissions	Proposed NAP2 totals	Allowed NAP2 totals	Emissions from additional installations	Comparable NAP2 totals
Austria	33	32.5	32.8	30.7	0.35	30.35
Belgium	62.1	54.3	63.3	58.5	5	53.5
Denmark	33.5	30	24.5	24.5	0	24.5
Finland	45.5	40	39.6	37.6	0.4	37.2
France	156.5	128.3	132.8	132.8	5.1	127.7
Germany	499	480	482	453.1	11	442.1
Greece	74.4	71.3	75.5	69.1	NA	69.1
Ireland	22.3	21.6	22.6	22.3	NA	22.3
Italy	223.1	226.6	209	195.8	NA	195.8
Luxembourg	3.4	2.6	3.95	2.5	NA	2.5
Netherlands	95.3	79	90.4	85.8	4	81.8
Portugal	38.9	33.6	35.9	34.8	0.77	34
Spain	174.4	182.4	152.7	152.3	6.7	145.6
Sweden	22.9	18.2	25.2	22.8	2	20.8
United Kingdom	245.3	248.1	246.2	246.2	9.5	236.7
EU15 subtotal	*1,729.6*	*1,648.4*	*1,636.5*	*1,568.8*	*44.8*	*1,524*
Cyprus	5.7	5.2	7.12	5.5	NA	5.5
Czech Republic	97.6	84.6	101.9	86.8	NA	86.8
Estonia	19	13.4	24.4	12.7	0.31	12.4

Table 3.5 (*cont.*)

Member state (annual amounts [Mt/EUAs])	NAP1 totals	Average 2005–7 emissions	Proposed NAP2 totals	Allowed NAP2 totals	Emissions from additional installations	Comparable NAP2 totals
Hungary	31.3	26.3	30.7	26.9	1.43	25.5
Latvia	4.6	2.9	7.7	3.4	NA	3.4
Lithuania	12.3	6.4	16.6	8.8	0.05	8.75
Malta	2.9	2	3	2.1	NA	2.1
Poland	239.1	207.3	284.6	208.5	6.3	202.2
Slovakia	30.5	25.1	41.3	32.6	1.78	30.8
Slovenia	8.8	8.9	8.3	8.3	NA	8.3
EU10 subtotal	*451.8*	*381.9*	*525.6*	*395.6*	*9.87*	*385.8*
EU25 total	*2,181.4*	*2,030.3*	*2,162*	*1,964.4*	*54.7*	*1,909.7*
Bulgaria[1]	42.3	39.2	67.6	42.3	NA	42.3
Romania[1]	74.8	69.6	95.7	75.9	NA	75.9
EU27 total[2]	*2,298.5*	*2,139.12*	*2,325.3*	*2,082.7*	*54.7*	*2,027.9*

Notes: [1]NAP1 total and verified emissions data are for 2007 only.
[2]EU27 total is average 2005–7 emissions for EU25 plus 2007 emissions for Romania and Bulgaria.
Source: European Commission (2007), except for average 2005–7 emissions, which are from appendix B.

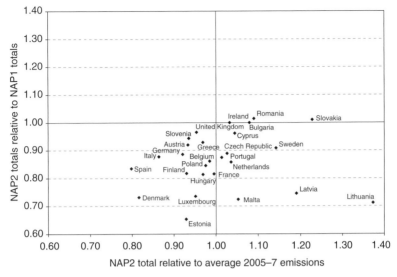

Figure 3.1 The relationship of member states' NAP2 totals to NAP1 totals and first-period emissions
Source: Compiled by the authors

case for the EU15 or the EU27 as a whole. While the contrast between east and west in the relationship of the allowed totals to 2005–7 emissions can be seen as a form of differentiation in favour of lower-income member states, this contrast is also in keeping with the criteria for cap-setting in the first period and implicit in the second period: compliance with the Kyoto Protocol. Those in no danger of exceeding their Kyoto limits were allowed totals that approximated BAU emissions while those that would have more trouble received totals that were much below first-period emissions. The three countries in figure 3.1 with the lowest ratios relative to 2005–7 emissions – Spain, Denmark and Italy – are the three with the greatest challenge in meeting the Kyoto/BSA limits.

The reductions required of nine of the eastern European new member states (all but Slovenia) led these member states to challenge the Commission's actions before the European Court of First Instance. Slovakia subsequently withdrew its complaint, but the other eight remain. These challenges seek annulment of the Commission's rejection of the member states' NAPs for the second period. The arguments brought forward in these cases are based on both procedural and sub.stantive points, but

Table 3.6 *NAP2 cap relationships by region*

(million EUAs)	EU15	New member states	EU27
NAP1 'caps'	1,730	569	2,299
Average annual emissions, 2005–7	1,648	491	2,139
Proposed NAP2 'caps'	1,598	679	2,277
Allowed NAP2 'caps'	1,524	504	2,028
	Ratios		
NAP2 proposed to NAP1 cap	0.924	1.193	0.99
NAP2 proposed to 2005–07 emissions	0.97	1.383	1.065
NAP2 allowed to proposed	0.954	0.731	0.891
NAP2 allowed to 2005–7 emissions	0.925	1.026	0.948

Source: Compiled from table 3.5.

the central argument is that the Commission applied inappropriate assumptions in rejecting the NAPs and thereby exceeded its authority by intruding into the member state's prerogatives concerning energy policy (Poland 2007; Estonia 2007). These challenges raise the possibility that the cap decided in the NAP process for the second period may not be final, as was the case in the first period, with the difference that the EU-wide cap would be increased instead of being reduced.

The Commission's guidance of November 2006 also laid out an explicit formula for calculating the limit on JI/CDM use. It is one-half of the maximum gap between the member state's Kyoto/BSA target and (1) its base-year emissions (generally 1990), (2) its 2004 greenhouse gas emissions or (3) its projected 2010 greenhouse gas emissions, less any planned government purchases of Kyoto units. This quantity would then be expressed as a percentage of the member state's allowed annual ETS total for the second period, with the further proviso that, if this percentage were less than 10 per cent, a minimum 10 per cent threshold would be allowed. This formula effectively permitted all installations to use JI/CDM credits for compliance and ensured that the EU-wide limit would be at least 10 per cent of the EU-wide cap. Table 3.7 provides the limits included in the final approved NAPs and the corresponding quantity of project credits allowed, assuming that all installations took advantage of this provision.

Table 3.7 *Second-period member state totals and JI/CDM limits*

Member state	Allowed NAP2 totals (million EUAs)	JI/CDM limit (percentage of NAP2 total)	JI/CDM amount (million credits)
Austria	30.7	10.00	3.07
Belgium	58.5	8.40	4.91
Denmark	24.5	17.00	4.17
Finland	37.6	10.00	3.76
France	132.8	13.50	17.93
Germany	453.1	20.00	90.62
Greece	69.1	9.00	6.22
Ireland	22.3	10.00	2.23
Italy	195.8	15.00	29.35
Luxembourg	2.5	10.00	0.25
Netherlands	85.8	10.00	8.58
Portugal	34.8	10.00	3.48
Spain	152.3	20.60	31.37
Sweden	22.8	10.00	2.28
United Kingdom	246.2	8.00	19.70
EU15	*1,568.8*	*14.50*	*227.9*
Cyprus	5.5	10.00	0.55
Czech Republic	86.8	10.00	8.68
Estonia	12.7	0	0
Hungary	26.9	10.00	2.69
Latvia	3.4	10.00	0.34
Lithuania	8.8	20.00	1.76
Malta	2.1	TBD	0
Poland	208.5	10.00	20.85
Slovakia	32.6	7.00	2.28
Slovenia	8.3	15.80	1.31
EU10	*395.6*	*9.70*	*38.5*
EU25 total	*1,964.4*	*13.60*	*266.4*
Bulgaria	42.3	12.60	5.31
Romania	75.9	10.00	7.59
EU27 total	*2,082.7*	*13.40*	*279.3*

Note: TBD = to be decided.
Sources: European Commission (2007) and authors' calculations.

Access to JI/CDM credits will have two effects on the cost of compliance with the ETS Directive. The first operates through the increased possibilities for abatement in meeting the EU-wide cap. Since these credits are fully substitutable for EUAs, their price should be equal to the EUA price, and the EUA price would be lower, to the extent that cheaper abatement is available through these project credits. So long as the prices of these credits and EUAs are equal, this would be the only cost-reducing effect of the Linking Directive. The second effect arises if the price of JI or CDM credits is lower than that of EUAs. This separation could occur either because there is some risk associated with the use of JI/CDM credits that is reflected in the discount or because the aggregate JI/CDM limit is fully subscribed. As is discussed in chapter 9, whenever this separation occurs, another cost-reducing possibility is created. Firms could lower the cost of compliance by selling EUAs that they would otherwise use for compliance and buying JI or CDM credits up to the limit applicable to the firm's affected installations. Such a separation appeared in the first year of the second period and was the basis of what came to be known as CER swaps. In this circumstance, the installation-level JI/CDM limit determined the extent to which firms participating in this arbitrage were able to take advantage of this further cost-reducing opportunity.

The allocation of member state totals to installations

The allocation of EUAs to installations within member states did not differ significantly between the two periods. There were fewer EUAs to be distributed in the second period, so installations generally did not receive as many allowances as in the first period, but the main features of the internal distributions were similar. For that reason, both periods are discussed together in this section.

For what was a highly decentralized process, member states made remarkably similar choices in distributing allowances to installations. The considerable co-ordination and exchange of information among member states and the sequential nature of NAP submissions, which allowed later submissions to adopt provisions from earlier ones, explain much of this similarity. It would be a mistake to ignore the broader considerations that were at play and that were common to all member states, however. Examples are the political demands of initiating such a system and the concern over trade impacts. These broader considerations explain the notable similarity of allocation in the EU ETS to that in earlier cap-and-trade programmes in the United States for conventional pollutants, but they also motivated new allocation features, such as new entrant reserves and the assignment of the expected shortage, which seem likely to characterize allocation in future CO_2 cap-and-trade programmes.

Auctioning and grandfathering

In cap-and-trade programmes, allowances can be distributed to installations either by grandfathering,[9] which grants some quantity of free allowances, or by government auctioning, which requires a payment and generates revenue for the government. In this choice, the EU ETS conformed to all previous cap-and-trade systems in adopting a high degree of grandfathering.

This outcome was the topic of some discussion in the legislative process leading up to the adoption of the ETS Directive, however, and the controversy became greater as the programme was implemented. The Commission's early consultations with stakeholders in 2002 convinced it that grandfathering would be necessary to gain the support of the industry upon which the new obligation was being imposed. During the subsequent co-decision process, the European Parliament attempted to make some degree of auctioning mandatory in the first and second periods, but ultimately it had to yield to gain the agreement of the two largest member states, Germany and the United Kingdom, to abandon their position in favour of voluntary participation in the trial period (Skjaerseth and Wettestad 2008). The final ETS Directive did recognize the Parliament's position by including an option that would allow member states to auction up to 5 per cent of their totals in the first period and up to 10 per cent in the second. This formulation implicitly mandates free allocation for up to 95 and

---

[9] The use of the term 'grandfathering' grew out of the 'Jim Crow' laws in the post-civil-war southern United States, whereby persons whose grandfathers had the right to vote were exempted from various tests determining voter qualifications aimed at disenfranchising former slaves and their descendants. As applied to allocation in cap-and-trade systems, it does not imply exemption from having to surrender allowances equal to emissions, only from having to pay for those allowances that are 'grandfathered' to the installation.

Table 3.8 *Member state auction reserves for the first and second periods*

Member state	Annual quantity (million tonnes)		Percentage of member state total	
	2005–7	2008–12	2005–7	2008–12
Denmark	1.675	0.08	5.00	0.3
Hungary	0.78	0.54[1]	2.5	2.0
Lithuania	0.18	0.26[1]	1.5	2.9
Ireland	0.17	0.11	0.75	0.5
Germany	0	40	0	8.8
United Kingdom	0	17.23	0	7.0
Netherlands	0	3.2	0	3.7
Austria	0	0.4	0	1.3
EU ETS total	2.81	61.82	0.13	3.00

Note: France also announced its intention to auction some allowances to supplement the new entrants reserve (France, 2008).

[1] The quantities for Hungary and Lithuania reflect announced intentions pending final notifications of the second-period amounts in the CITL.

Sources: National allocation plans and CITL data.

90 per cent, respectively, of a member state's total in the two periods, and it does not exclude 100 per cent free allocation.

For both periods most member states chose not to auction any EUAs, but some did, and there is a clear tendency to greater auctioning in the second period both in the number of member states choosing to do so and in the total quantity of EUAs to be auctioned. Table 3.8 presents the member states auction reserves in one or both periods, the annual amounts and the percentages of the respective member state totals.

Only four member states auctioned any amounts in the first period, but that number grew to eight in the second period. The volume increased more than twentyfold, albeit from a very small number. Only one member state chose to auction the full allowed amount – Denmark, in the first period – but it auctioned almost none in the second period. Italy, Poland, Belgium and Luxembourg proposed auctions in their initial NAP2 notifications, but eliminated auctioning when the Commission reduced the allowed member state total. The Netherlands reduced its auction reserve in response to the same requirement.

Establishing an auction reserve does not mean that an auction will occur or that the EUAs placed in the reserve will be the only EUAs auctioned. In the first period, Denmark did not conduct an auction, but sold the set-aside into the market through market intermediaries. Germany is doing the same thing for the first two years of the second period while it prepares for conducting auctions in the remaining three years. In addition, some member states have chosen to auction EUAs placed in NERs that were not issued by the end of the period. For instance, in the first period, Ireland and Denmark auctioned or sold an additional 700,000 and 500,000 EUAs, respectively, from NERs (Fazekas 2008a).

From a technical standpoint, the three member states that did organize formal auctions conducted sealed-bid, uniform-price auctions. The clearing price ranged from €26.32 for Ireland's first auction in January 2006 to 6 eurocents for Lithuania's single auction in September 2007. According to Fazekas (2008a), of the approximately 9.7 million allowances that were either sold or auctioned by member state governments (including unclaimed NERs), slightly more than half were placed on the market in 2006. No allowances were auctioned or sold directly in 2005, and only Ireland managed to organize an auction before the price collapse in April 2006. With the exception of Ireland and Lithuania, auction proceeds went to the Treasuries of the respective member state governments. Ireland's auction revenues were specifically earmarked to pay for the government's expense for administering the ETS, and the amount set aside for auctioning was determined by this budget requirement. Lithuania had intended its auction revenues to be a part of general revenues, but the proceeds were approximately equal to the cost of conducting the auction.

The very limited auctioning during the first and second periods raises an obvious question of why governments made so little use of the option that they were given in the ETS Directive. Free allocation for 95 or 90 per cent of the member state totals was mandated, but nothing required member states to allocate all allowances for free, as most did. The answer seems to be political acceptance of the new system, and perhaps a sense that some compensation was due to those that had made prior investments when no CO_2 price existed and that might be disadvantaged by the new system. Free allocation in the first period did lay the foundation for the controversy over 'windfall profits', however, which would lead to the subsequent increased resort to auctioning by the United Kingdom, Germany and the Netherlands in the second period and to the post-2012 amendments that radically changed the rules of allocation in favour of more auctioning starting in 2013.

Benchmarking and recent historical emissions

A benchmarked allocation was much advocated in the EU ETS but little practised. Benchmarking refers to an emission rate that characterizes efficient production and that, it is argued, should be the basis for allocation with appropriate adjustment for the level of past or expected production.[10] It is argued that such an allocation would penalize energy-inefficient producers and reward energy-efficient ones. In nearly all cases, allocation to installations is based on recent historical emissions – that is, the installation's historical emission rate times its historical production. Consequently, installations with a higher emission rate received proportionately more allowances than installations producing the same quantity and good with a lower emission rate.

There are three reasons for the general failure to adopt benchmarking in the EU ETS. The first is the circumstances surrounding the initial allocation of allowances: impossible deadlines and poor data. A benchmarked allocation requires two data points: an agreed-upon standard and past or expected production. An allocation based on recent historical emissions requires only one data point: emissions. When time is short and data poor, the simplest solution succeeds.

The second reason is more fundamental: the heterogeneity of goods produced and of the processes and conditions under which similar goods are made. No one would maintain that the same benchmark should be set for cement and steel, but within each of these sectors the goods and the processes used can be highly variable. Flat sheets are

---

[10] A careful distinction must be made between a once-and-for-all benchmarked allocation and one that is 'updated' or adjusted according to actual production. The latter, often called a dynamic benchmark, is expressly ruled out by the Commission's effective prohibition of *ex post* adjustments. Thus, in the EU ETS, the advocacy of a benchmarked allocation implies one that may be based on past expected production but, once granted, is fixed and not subject to further change.

different products from rolled products and the latter require more processing, which implies more expenditure of energy and higher emissions. Moreover, the same steel mill may produce different products in varying quantities depending on demand. The processes used to produce the same good may be different in one location from another because of past investment, differing access to resources and, potentially, other government policies. Even electricity, which would seem to be highly homogeneous, can be viewed as a differentiated product. Electricity generated to meet peak demand during the day has a different price from that produced during the night, and the efficient processes to produce each are typically different. The ultimate implication of a benchmarked allocation could be dozens if not hundreds of benchmarks, each crafted to meet some particular subproduct and varying circumstances of production.

The failure of benchmarking suggests that the premise underlying the arguments for benchmarking – rewarding the energy-efficient and penalizing the energy-inefficient – is invalid. The fact may be that, if all installations are energy-efficient – as might be expected in a reasonably competitive economy – and the heterogeneity of products and processes is such that no two installations are alike, then each installation would have its own benchmark, which would be identical to recent historical emissions. As is suggested by research reported in chapter 4, recent emissions may reflect better than anything else the carbon implications of efficient production and thereby provide the best standard for allocation.

The third reason for the failure of benchmarking was the absence of any pre-existing standard with sufficient legal and institutional force to impose itself as a benchmark. The best counter-example to the EU ETS in this regard is the US SO_2 trading programme. Allocation in this programme is benchmarked on an emission rate standard of 1.2 pounds of sulphur dioxide emissions per million BTU (British thermal units) of heat input, which was the first New Source Performance Standard (NSPS) for SO_2 emissions, adopted in the early 1970s. This standard had been applicable to all new power plants until it was subsequently superseded by a later technology mandate, so that by 1990, when the US SO_2 programme was enacted, it applied to about 60 per cent of total coal-fired generation. In this US case, a pre-existing standard of considerable legal, institutional and practical force was available to provide an obvious common reference point.

No comparable standard for CO_2 exists in Europe, the United States or elsewhere. Reference is commonly made to best available technology (BAT), but exactly what this is remains undefined and subject to some debate. Although conceptually clear, in practice it tends to degenerate into what is expressed wonderfully by the British acronym BATNEEC (best available technology not entailing excessive cost) – a standard that is effectively tailored to each case.

While benchmarking was not generally adopted, there are some notable exceptions. The most obvious is the allocation to new entrants. This allocation is always explicitly benchmarked on BAT because new installations have no historical emissions and BAT, however defined in specific instances, is the obvious reference point. Since all new facilities could be expected to be using best available technology, the typical new entrant allocation was expected allowance need, although there were exceptions. For instance, Denmark's new entrant benchmark was based on capacity instead of expected production. Some member states, notably the United Kingdom and Spain, chose a non-fuel-differentiated benchmark for new capacity in the electricity sector based on gas-fired combined-cycle technology, although usually no new coal plants were expected to be built. Sweden specifically excluded new fossil fuel power plants from the new entrant provisions, although, again, no new power plants were planned.

When benchmarking was used for allocations to existing facilities, as it was for some sectors in Denmark, Italy, Spain and Poland, the benchmark had no technological basis. It tended to be simply an average of the allowances available to some subset of installations differentiated according to capacity or past production. This was the case for the Danish electricity sector, as it was for most installations in Spain, with the interesting variant that, for coal-fired power plants, the benchmark was further adjusted inversely according to whether the plant had a higher or lower emission rate than the average (Del Rio, 2007: 192). In Italy, the electricity benchmark was determined by expected generation during the trial period, not historical production. In Poland, as in Italy, some sectors were allowed to have a benchmarked allocation if they could agree on what it should be.

In the second NAP exercise, benchmarking made some progress, but mostly in the electricity sector and then only when differentiated by fuel type or other process parameters. For instance, in the United Kingdom, there were five benchmarks for power production that depended on the fuel type and whether heat was also produced, and, for coal plants, the status with respect to the requirements of the Large Plant Combustion Directive. Germany similarly adopted different benchmarks for power production from different fuels and three different benchmarks for cement production. In Spain, the first period benchmark, which had favoured lower emitting coal units, was discarded in favour of one that favoured plants required to use domestically produced coal and plants installing SO_2 and NOx control equipment. This example shows that a benchmarked allocation provides no guarantee against allocation being used to promote other policy goals.

New entrant and closure provisions

A notable new feature that the EU ETS has introduced into allocation in cap-and-trade systems is the awarding of free allowances to new entrants and the forfeiture of allowances granted to existing facilities that have closed. In some member states, the transfer of allowances from closed facilities to new facilities is also allowed. Together, these measures constitute the new entrant and closure provisions. These allocations are fundamentally different from those to existing sources, in that the receipt or loss of allowances depends on the actions of the recipient. As such, they create incentives to expand capacity or to keep facilities open, although only those that are CO_2-emitting. For example, new nuclear or renewable energy facilities do not receive any allowances from the new entrant reserves even though they produce the same product as a new gas- or coal-fired electricity generating plant. Chapter 4 discusses the effect of these provisions; here the purpose is only to describe this new feature of allowance allocation.

The new entrant component of these provisions required that a reserve of EUAs be set aside from within the member state total for new facilities and expansions of existing facilities. The latter usually presented the greater demand on the NERs. In Germany, for example, eighteen new facilities received 9.67 million EUAs during the three-year trial period, and 131 existing facilities received 13.51 million additional EUAs for expansions of capacity (DEHst 2009). In most member states, post-closure forfeitures were typically added to the NER, and the forfeiture started following the year in which the facility closed. Closure was usually defined as some minimum level of production or emissions, but the level varied from country to country.

The closure provisions led to a third hybrid component, known as a transfer provision. This provision allowed the owner of a closed facility to transfer allowances from that facility to a new replacement facility if the replacement took place within a certain window of time. The transfer would be proportionate to the capacity of the smaller of the two facilities with the difference for the larger being either forfeited or provided from the NER. Germany was the first member state to develop a transfer provision, and several of the later NAP submissions, notably those of Poland and Hungary, adopted similar provisions.

The motivation for new entrant and closure provisions was always fear of the employment effects of not having them. No government wanted to be seen to be creating a disincentive to new investment. Similarly, the absence of a closure provision was seen as an incentive to move production elsewhere. In the allocation debate in Germany, failing to require the forfeiture of post-closure allowances came to be equated with creating a 'shutdown premium' (Matthes and Schafhausen 2007). The concern here was not so much leakage outside the European Union as transfer of production facilities to eastern Europe. A revealing feature of transfer provisions is that they are applicable only for new facilities built within the same member state.

The incentives to over-build and to keep old facilities online that were created by these provisions were widely recognized at the technical level, but to little avail. Recommendations not to include such provisions were made in many member states, but were invariably overruled at the political level (Ellerman, Buchner and Carraro 2007). Sweden and the Netherlands were two notable exceptions in deciding not to include closure provisions.

The decentralized implementation of these provisions also led to some potential contraventions of EU policy with respect to market integration, state aid and, more generally, equal treatment in a single EU market. As pointed out by Matthes, Graichen and Repenning (2005), the differences in new entrant endowments for similar facilities could be considerable. For instance, the difference in the new entrant endowment to a similar coal-fired plant in Germany and the United Kingdom is 384 EUAs per gigawatt-hour, which at €20/EUA would translate into a cost advantage of €7.68 per megawatt-hour, or about 10 per cent of the wholesale electricity price.

These perverse incentive effects are inherent in the interaction between free allocation and the multi-period compliance structure of the EU ETS, however. The allocation for each period is based on a list of installations that exist at the beginning of each period. By definition, those that closed or opened in the preceding period would be deleted or added to the list. Accordingly, the new entrant and closure provisions can be seen as an intra-period accommodation to what would happen at the beginning of each successive compliance period.

The creation of new entrant reserves also required a decision as to what to do about the difference between what was set aside and what would be needed. The usual provision for dealing with an NER that turned out to be inadequate was simply not to provide any more, although Germany stated that it would replenish the NER as needed through market purchases, which it did in fact in an amount of 19 million EUAs (DEHst 2009). Germany's decision to supply all demand was in part a response to the difficulty created by the transfer provision in estimating new entrant needs. When a transfer provision is present, sizing the reserve is no longer just a matter of expected new facilities but also of how many will take advantage of the transfer rule, thereby reducing demand on the reserve.

In the case of an end-of-period reserve surplus, six member states indicated that they would cancel unused allowances (France, Spain, Germany, Denmark, Latvia and Lithuania), three made no provision (Malta, Cyprus and Slovakia) and the rest indicated that they would either auction or sell unclaimed reserve allowances in the final year of the period (Dufour and Leseur 2006). Nearly all member states had surpluses remaining, but only Belgium, Ireland, Austria and the United Kingdom reported selling or auctioning any (EEA 2008). Most countries appear not to have sold the EUAs remaining in the reserve, perhaps because of the near-zero prices prevailing in the last year of the trial period.

In the first period the size of the NERs varied from less than 1 per cent of the member state total (Germany, Cyprus, Poland, Slovakia and Slovenia) to as much as 26 per cent (Malta) (see table 3.9). The average percentage set-aside for the EU25 was 2.7 per cent. Four member states exhausted all or virtually all their reserve (2 per cent or less remaining: Germany, Italy, Lithuania and Slovenia), while one member state, Malta, distributed none of its reserve. On average, 74 per cent of the EUAs set aside for new entrants plus forfeitures were distributed.

The second-period NERs are notably larger as a percentage of the EU-wide cap and on an annual basis. For the EU25, the percentage set-aside is doubled, from 2.7 to 5.4 per cent, and, after adding

Table 3.9 *New entrant reserves, first- and second-period NAPs*

Member state	First period (2005–7)			Second period (2008–12)	
	Annual average (million EUAs)	Percentage of total	Remaining at end of period (million EUAs, percentage of three-year total)	Annual average (million EUAs)	Percentage of total
Austria	0.33	1.00	0.88 (89%)	0.31	1.00
Belgium	2.55	4.00	8.37 (106%)	5.55	9.50
Denmark	1	3.00	2.22 (74%)	0.46	1.90
Finland	0.83	1.80	0.16 (6%)	1.4	3.70
France	5	3.20	11.36 (67%)	2.74	2.10
Germany	4	0.80	0 (0%)[1]	22.7	5.00
Greece	3.16	4.20	3.90 (41%)	3.35	4.80
Ireland	0.33	1.50	0.23 (23%)	1.93	8.70
Italy	15.33	6.90	0.04 (~%)	16.89	8.60
Luxembourg	0.13	3.80	0.36 (30%)	~	<0.1
Netherlands	2.5	2.60	3.00 (40%)	6.37	7.40
Portugal	1.25	3.30	0.95 (10%)	4.3	12.40
Spain	3.36	1.90	0.86 (9%)	6.28	4.10
Sweden	0.73	3.20	1.83 (84%)	2.68	11.80
United Kingdom	15.6	6.40	5.93 (13%)	16.32	6.60
EU15 subtotal	*56.11*	*3.20*	*40.09 (24%)*	*91.28*	*5.80*
Cyprus	0.04	0.70	0.06 (50%)	0.74[2]	13.40
Czech Republic	0.35	0.40	0.19 (18%)	1.29	1.50
Estonia	0.19	3.40	0.20 (10%)	0.96[2]	7.60
Hungary	0.63	1.90	0.33 (18%)	3.23[2]	12.00

Latvia	0.52	11.30	0.95 (61%)	0.8	23.30
Lithuania	0.61	5.40	0 (0%)	0	0
Malta	0.76	26.30	2.29 (100%)	0	0
Poland	0.82	0.40	2.45 (87%)	6.71[2]	3.20
Slovakia	0	0	0 (0%)	1.30[2]	4.00
Slovenia	0.07	0.80	~ (2%)	0.17	2.00
EU10 subtotal	*3.99*	*0.90*	*6.47 (54%)*	*15.2*	*3.80*
EU25 total	*60.1*	*2.70*	*46.56 (26%)*	*106.48*	*5.40*
Bulgaria	NA			9.95[2]	23.50
Romania	NA			4.35	5.70
EU27 total				*120.78*	*5.80*

Notes: [1]EEA (2008) reports a remaining reserve of 61.9 million EUAs, but this figure includes the 69.8 million EUAs taken back in *ex post* adjustments. Germany's NER provisions stated that, if the NER were exhausted, the government would purchase the required allowances to meet new entrant claims. The NER was also to be the source of any additional allowances that would have to be issued as a result of legal claims. Germany set aside 11.8 million EUAs as a new entrant reserve for the three years, but ended up issuing 23.5 million EUAs for new entrants and capacity expansions and 16.5 million EUAs for legal claims. The difference was made up by 5.1 million allowances from post-closure forfeitures and the purchase of 19 million EUAs, and the balance was provided by *ex post* adjustments (DEHst 2009).
[2]The NER amounts for these countries have not been entered into the CITL. The numbers shown are the initially proposed NERs scaled down in proportion to reductions required in the review process.

Sources: First-period data from EEA (2008); second-period data compiled by Öko-Institut; percentages calculated from first- and second-period totals as given in European Commission (2007).

Bulgaria and Romania, the total per cent reserve is 5.8 per cent. All member states increased their NERs except for six: Austria, Denmark, France, Luxembourg, Lithuania and Malta. Two explanations are given for the increase in these reserves. First, when the second-period NAPs were prepared, more investment was expected in the second period than in the first, especially in the power sector. Second, a greater margin of error appears to have been built in, since most member states had the same experience as Germany in having more demand from capacity expansions, which have shorter lead times and are less easy to anticipate than completely new facilities. Nevertheless, given the experience of the first period in not distributing a quarter of the NERs plus forfeitures, not to mention the economic slowdown that arrived in the course of 2008, the likelihood that the second-period reserves will be less than fully distributed seems large.

Among the implications of larger new entrant reserves, as well as larger auction reserves, is that the reduction in free allocation to incumbent installations is greater than the reduction in the overall cap. In the first period the new entrant and auction reserves were 2.8 per cent of the total, so approximately 97.2 per cent was freely allocated to incumbents. The comparable second-period EU-wide cap (excluding added installations) is 11.8 per cent lower than the first-period cap, and another 8.0 per cent has been set aside for auctioning and new entrant purposes. The resulting reduction in free allocation to incumbent installations varies between member states, from 2 per cent in Malta to 43 per cent in Latvia, and the average for the EU27 as a whole is 18 per cent.

Assignment of shortage to power sector and emergence of trade exposure as a basis for allocation

Any regulatory authority establishing a cap-and-trade system that will limit emissions to less than they would otherwise be must decide how to allocate the expected shortage. When allowances are allocated for free, this assignment is done through the number of allowances issued to individual facilities or sectors. For instance, if the shortage were to be assigned proportionately, all would receive X per cent fewer allowances than some reference level.

The EU ETS is not only the first CO_2 cap-and-trade system of any consequence, but more importantly, the first to incorporate facilities from a number of different sectors of the economy.[11] This presented the possibility of splitting the member state total into sectoral allocations, as most member states did, and then allocating to installations within each sector or subsector. The multisectoral nature of the system also involved deciding whether all sectors should be treated alike in sharing the expected shortage.

The answer in the EU ETS was remarkably consistent. Nearly every member state expecting a shortage assigned it entirely to the electric power sector. In distinct contrast, facilities in other sectors were allocated allowances approximately equal to their expected emissions or 'need'. The reason for doing so was twofold. First, abatement was believed to be easier and cheaper for installations in the electric utility sector. Second, the electric power sector did not face any non-EU competition that would occasion leakage. Installations in the industrial sectors were seen to be competing in a world market, in which the prices were set outside the European Union, and the grant of free allowances was believed to be a means of allowing them to avoid raising prices and thereby losing market share. In contrast, power stations competed in strictly European markets and would thereby be able to pass on their added CO_2 costs. That many of the customers that would be paying the additional costs would be the very industrial firms that were assumed unable to pass on the additional CO_2 cost seems not to have figured in the debate at the time of allocation. Nonetheless, this effect became a major part of the windfall profits controversy and would affect second-period allocations and the amendments to the directive that were adopted for the post-2012 period.

The validity of the argument concerning the trade impact can be questioned, and some evidence on this point is presented in chapter 7. For instance, many facilities in the industrial sectors are protected by high transport costs or other factors that shield them from international competition. An example is inland cement manufacture. Nevertheless, in the allocation for the trial period, when time was short and data poor, the simple electricity/non-electricity divide was an easy distinction to make. The important new allocation criterion

---

[11] For instance, the SO_2 and NOx programmes in the United States are largely limited to the electric utility sector. The RECLAIM programme in the Los Angeles Basin is a multi-sector programme, but it is relatively small in terms of its geographic scope and the number of affected installations.

that emerged from this process is competitive effects, understood as exposure to competitors that do not have any CO_2 costs. The arguments for this new criterion were politically powerful, and they prevailed despite questions that could be raised concerning market structure and behavioural assumptions.

In the first period international trade effects became a criterion for allocation only in those member states, such as the United Kingdom and Spain, in which a shortage was expected and had to be assigned. Elsewhere, among the new member states and in several of the EU15, the member state total was set at the level of expected emissions and there was no shortage to assign. Moreover, combined heat and power plants typically received some type of bonus allocation to reward their greater efficiency, with the result that the assignment of the expected shortage to the electricity sector was largely restricted to single-purpose generating plants owned by electric utilities. Nevertheless, the principle of more favourable treatment for facilities facing international competition that could occasion leakage became firmly established in the first-period allocation, and it would become the basis for distinctly different treatment in the post-2012 amendments.

The post-2012 changes in allocation

No discussion of allocation in the EU ETS would be complete without a discussion of the significant changes introduced by the amendments to the ETS Directive proposed on 23 January 2008, and approved in December 2008. The changes were more than technical corrections; they wrought a fundamental restructuring of the cap-setting procedures and in the distribution of the cap to affected installations. These amendments were the end result of a long process of assessment and stakeholder consultation that consisted of the following steps.

- Article 30 of the ETS Directive, which directed the Commission to draw up a report on the application of the directive by mid-2006, addressing a number of enumerated concerns in light of the experience to date (European Parliament and Council 2003).
- This ETS review report, submitted in November 2006, in which the Commission explicitly announced its intent to propose amendments for the post-2012 period by the end of 2007 after further consultation with stakeholders. This document also laid out four areas of

consultation: the scope of the directive; compliance and enforcement; harmonization and predictability; and linkage to other systems (European Commission 2006a).

- The Council of Ministers meeting on 20 February 2007, at which the irrevocable EU target of a 20 per cent reduction of GHG emissions relative to 1990 to be achieved by 2020 was announced, the importance of the EU ETS in meeting this target was re-emphasized and the Commission was called upon 'to review the ETS Directive' and 'bring forward proposals' to 'create the right incentives for forward-looking, low-carbon investments' (European Council 2007).
- The stakeholder consultation through the European Climate Change Programme Working Group on Emissions Trading, which consisted of four two-day meetings on each of the four areas of consultation extending from March to June 2007, and for which a report of conclusions was published.[12]
- The proposed amendments released on 23 January 2008, which were part of a much broader energy-climate package addressing a number of interrelated issues (European Commission 2008c).
- The European Parliament's draft report on the proposal (Doyle Report) on 11 June 2008, which contained the amendments from the European Parliament (European Parliament 2008a).
- Agreement on the final compromise in the Council of Ministers meeting on 12 December 2008 (European Council 2008) and acceptance by the European Parliament on 17 December 2008 (European Parliament 2008b).

There were many parts in the proposed and approved amendments, but the principal changes for allocation concerned auctioning, harmonization and cap-setting.

Auctioning

The most radical and most contested issue in the debate over the proposed amendments was auctioning. The Commission's proposal consisted of a principle and a proposal for implementation. The principle was that free allocation would be ended and allowances

---

[12] This report and other material from these meetings can be accessed at http://ec.europa.eu/environment/climat/emission/review_en.htm.

distributed entirely through auctioning. The proposed implementation consisted of three elements.

- The power sector would receive no free allowances from 2013 on, except for heat delivered to district heating or for industrial uses.
- Installations in non-power sectors would receive a free allocation of 80 per cent of their share of the cap in 2013, which would be reduced by ten percentage points each year so that free allocation would be phased out in 2020.
- Energy-intensive sectors or subsectors that face a significant risk of carbon leakage from competitors in countries without equivalent CO_2 measures could receive free allowances of up to 100 per cent of their need. Alternatively, these industries could benefit from the imposition of a 'carbon equalization system' or border tax adjustment that would place competing imported products from countries without equivalent measures on the same footing as industry within the European Union.

In the debate, between January and December 2008, the principle of eventual auctioning was never called into serious question. The main debate was over the pace of the phase-out and how to deal with the exception for sectors subject to trade impacts and leakage. The final compromise made the following principal changes to the Commission's proposal for implementing full auctioning.

- A temporary derogation from full auctioning in the electricity sector for member states meeting certain criteria. In qualifying countries, no more than 70 per cent of average 2005–7 verified emissions in the electricity sector could be allocated freely in 2013, and that percentage would be phased down to zero by 2020, with a possibility of extension. The criteria for this exemption, which involves connection to the European grid, per capita GDP and dependence on a single fuel, limit its applicability mostly if not entirely to new member states.[13]
- A slower phase-out of free allocation in the non-power sector, which would delay the complete phase-out until 2027 and allow up to 30 per cent free allocation in 2020.

[13] An early analysis by Deutsche Bank judged that all the new member states, with the exceptions of Latvia, Slovakia and Slovenia, would qualify (Deutsche Bank 2008).

- Installations in sectors or subsectors deemed to be exposed to a significant risk of carbon leakage could be allocated up to 100 per cent free allocation, based on benchmarks that would reflect the average emission rate of the top 10 per cent of qualifying facilities. These sectors or subsectors will be determined by the Commission after discussion with the Council, based on criteria specified in the amendments and subject to periodic review.[14]

A further change in the Commission proposal on auctioning concerned the use of auction revenues. The Commission's proposed amendments would have required member states to use at least 20 per cent of the auction revenue for specified climate purposes and to report on the use of these funds. The final compromise reflects EU member states' sensitivity to any direction from Brussels or common European institutions concerning how to spend national revenue. The final compromise 'recalls' that member states will determine the use of auction revenues 'in accordance with their respective constitutional and budgetary requirements' and 'takes note of their willingness' to use at least a half of these revenues for climate-related purposes. Furthermore, a specific declaration is made that member states 'may' use auction revenues generated between 2013 and 2016 to support up to 15 per cent of the total costs of investment for new highly efficient power plants that are 'ready' for carbon capture and sequestration.

Public headlines and the rhetoric of the debate tend to identify 'windfall profits' as the motivating force for the adoption of auctioning, but two other factors also contributed: the demand for harmonized allocation and a nagging sense that free allocation does not provide the proper incentives. Whatever the merits of these arguments – and grounds to question them exist, as are presented in subsequent

---

[14] These criteria are that (1) direct CO_2 costs and indirect CO_2 costs from the pass-through of CO_2 costs in power prices are more than 30 per cent of gross value added (GVA); or (2) that the non-EU trade intensity (exports plus imports as a share of production plus imports) is greater than 30 per cent; or (3) the cost to GVA criteria is 10 per cent or larger *and* the non-EU trade intensity is greater than 10 per cent and other qualitative criteria (investments, market structures, profit margins) indicate exposure to a significant risk of carbon leakage. The Commission is also to take into account the extent to which world production in sectors deemed at risk occurs in countries that have taken comparable measures to reduce greenhouse gas emissions.

chapters – these arguments were politically effective. Auctioning provided a single answer to both problems. It harmonizes everyone at zero free allocation and renders moot any question of whether agents take the cost of carbon into account in their production decisions.

Large scale auctioning will transform the mechanics and psychology of compliance. There is something comforting about having most of the allowances needed for compliance in hand and resorting to the market only for the differences between allocations and emissions, which have been relatively small to date. Starting in 2013, the demand will increase enormously. In theory, the supply will be there, but the supply will need to be front-loaded if price disturbances due to delays or breakdowns of auction mechanisms are to be avoided. An even more invidious problem will be the tendency to adjust the quantity of allowances auctioned in order to moderate price fluctuations. In theory, this should not occur, because the schedule and quantities to be auctioned would be pre-specified and immutable, but the pressures to change schedules or quantities when prices fall or rise to what some see as unacceptable levels will be strong. All these problems can be solved. Whether the solution offered by auctioning will be any easier, or more equitable or efficient, than those found during the first two periods of the EU ETS remains to be seen.

Harmonization

While full auctioning solves the problem of harmonization by abolishing free allocation, a problem remains during the transitional phase-out. The Commission's proposed amendments anticipate 'Community-wide and fully harmonized implementing measures' for the transitional free allocation in the industrial sectors, as well as for those industrial sectors or subsectors deemed to be at significant risk of carbon leakage. Also, 5 per cent of the annual EU-wide free allocation is to be set aside for new entrants in the industrial sectors only and the closure rule is to be applied uniformly without provision for transfer. Thus, from 2013 onwards not only will the transitional free allocation to industrial facilities be harmonized within sectors and subsectors but the NER will be administered at the European Union level, presumably without regard to national origin. The feasibility of EU-wide harmonization can be questioned, but the problem is to be solved through an already existing committee of member state representatives established by the original ETS Directive. In any case, it will be a transitional problem of progressively less concern.

While the transitional industrial sector free allocations will be harmonized, the derogations granted for the electricity sector mean that power sector allocations will not be completely harmonized until 2020. These derogations are the basis for the only remaining vestiges of the previous national allocation plans. Member states desiring this derogation will be required to submit applications to the Commission that will include the grounds for the qualification, a proposed methodology for allocation and the list of qualifying installations. As was the case with NAPs during the pre-2012 compliance periods, the Commission will have the power to reject these applications (but within six months of their submission) if specified criteria are not met. These criteria are largely those that pertained during the NAP process, albeit with one addition. The submission must include a national plan for 'investments in retrofitting and upgrading of [member state] infrastructure and clean technology and for diversification of their energy mix and sources of supply' with monitoring and enforcement mechanisms to ensure the plan's fulfilment.

Cap-setting

Given the earlier agreement in the European Council that the Union would reduce its greenhouse gas emissions to at least 20 per cent below the 1990 level, the Commission's proposal concerning the EU-wide cap for the ETS was accepted without amendment. The essential elements are that the first post-2012 compliance period will be lengthened from five to eight years and the 2020 level of the ETS cap is to be 21 per cent below 2005 verified emissions. Since EU27 greenhouse gas emissions in 2005 were already 7.9 per cent below the 1990 baseline (EEA 2007), the ETS target implies a more than proportionate reduction by these sectors.[15] Both the eight-year

---

[15] The projection contained in EEA (2007) predicts EU27 GHG emissions increasing slowly from 8 per cent below 1990 levels in the 2008–12 period to 6 per cent below 1990 by 2020. Thus, the expected reduction in GHG emissions in 2020 would be approximately 14 per cent. Other elements of the post-2012 amendments establish an emissions reduction target of 10 per cent below 1990 levels for the non-ETS sectors of the economy.

compliance period and the predetermined cap are seen as providing the long-term perspective and increased predictability that will promote long-term investments in efficient abatement (European Commission 2008c).

The cumulative EU cap for the 2013–20 period will be calculated by an annual reduction factor of 1.74 per cent, applied from 2010. This annual reduction factor is the linear decrement required to get from the midpoint of the second-period EU-wide cap to a level 21 per cent below 2005 verified emissions. Bearing in mind that the annual decrement does not have any effect until 2013 and that the second-period EU cap is 5.9 per cent below 2005 verified emissions (after adjustment for added installations), the third-period cap will be 11.3 per cent below the second-period cap and 16.5 per cent below 2005 verified emissions, without considering increases in the scope of the system in the third period. Moreover, the 1.74 per cent annual decrement in the total number of allowances does not stop in 2020. It continues indefinitely, subject to review in 2025.

A centrally determined cap does not address the issue of how the cost burden is to be shared among the participating member states. In addition, since member states are no longer free to determine the distribution of allowances internally, differentiation can be achieved only by the assignment of auction rights and the resulting revenue. The Commission's proposal in this respect consisted of two elements: a basic entitlement determined by the member state's share of 2005 verified emissions and an additional amount to some member states 'for the purpose of Community solidarity and growth'. Ninety per cent of the allowances to be auctioned would be distributed as the basic entitlement and the remaining 10 per cent would be awarded to nineteen member states according to percentages that were specified in the proposed amendments. Since the Commission's initial proposal envisaged full auctioning by 2020 and that the EU-wide cap would be 21 per cent below 2005 verified emissions, all member states would be moving towards a basic entitlement of auction rights equal to 71 per cent $[0.9 \times (1 - 0.21)]$ of their 2005 verified emissions. Those benefiting from the extra supplement would receive from 2 per cent (Italy) to 56 per cent (Latvia) more.

The final compromise accepted this redistribution, but added a new component that increased the differentiation in favour of member states with lower per capita income. The basic entitlement to 90 per cent of auction revenues is reduced to 88 per cent and the extra two percentage points are redistributed as an early-action bonus to nine eastern European member states that 'had achieved in 2005 a reduction of at least 20 per cent in greenhouse gas emissions compared with the reference year set by the Kyoto Protocol'. Thus, the final post-2012 distribution of auction rights will be the result of the basic entitlement plus the solidarity adder and an early-action bonus. Table 3.10 presents the resulting redistribution expressed as a percentage of each member state's share of 2005 verified emissions.

These percentages express the adjustment of the member state's share of 2005 verified emissions to be used in apportioning auction rights among member states. A percentage of 100 would mean that the member state would receive auction rights equal to its share of 2005 verified emissions. In effect, a group of eight relatively high-income EU15 member states agreed to reduce their claims by 12 per cent in order to redistribute auction rights to generally lower-income southern or eastern European member states. Although the redistribution is not entirely from west to east, the EU15 as a whole reduced their auction rights by 9.1 per cent in order to provide 32 per cent more to new member states.

The actual amounts to be auctioned will depend upon the level of the EU-wide cap relative to 2005 verified emissions and the extent of free allocation to the industrial and trade-impacted sectors. Free allocations in accordance with derogations in the electricity sector will not reduce the EU-wide amount of auction rights but be taken from the member state's share of auction rights, thereby reducing the quantity auctioned by it. In 2027, when, in principle, free allocation will be completely phased out, the EU-wide cap will be approximately 70 per cent of 2005 verified emissions, assuming continuation of the 1.74 per cent annual decrement to that year. The actual amounts auctioned by each member state will be the final percentages in table 3.10 multiplied by 2005 emissions times 0.7. Only those with a final share greater than 1.43 (= 1.00/0.70) will be auctioning more EUAs than their 2005 verified emissions, and the eight member states with the 88 per cent claims will be auctioning allowances equal to about 62 per cent of their 2005 emissions.

Pricing Carbon

Table 3.10 *Post-2012 distribution of auction rights (percentages)*

Member state	Basic entitlement	Solidarity adder	Early-action bonus	Final entitlement
Austria	88.00			88.00
Denmark	88.00			88.00
Finland	88.00			88.00
France	88.00			88.00
Germany	88.00			88.00
Ireland	88.00			88.00
Netherlands	88.00			88.00
United Kingdom	88.00			88.00
Italy	88.00	1.80		89.80
Luxembourg	88.00	7.00		95.00
Sweden	88.00	8.80		96.80
Belgium	88.00	8.80		96.80
Spain	88.00	11.40		99.40
Portugal	88.00	14.10		102.10
Greece	88.00	15.00		103.00
EU15 subtotal				*90.90*
Cyprus	88.00	17.60		105.60
Slovenia	88.00	17.60		105.60
Malta	88.00	20.20		108.20
Czech Republic	88.00	27.30	2.10	117.40
Hungary	88.00	24.60	8.10	120.70
Poland	88.00	34.30	5.70	128.00
Slovakia	88.00	36.10	5.10	129.20
Estonia	88.00	37.00	20.20	145.20
Bulgaria	88.00	46.60	15.70	150.30
Romania	88.00	46.60	17.40	152.00
Lithuania	88.00	40.50	45.10	173.60
Latvia	88.00	49.30	59.60	196.90
EU12 total				*132.00*

Source: Compiled by the authors.

Concluding observations

The European Union's experience with allocation is notable both for what it has achieved in the face of formidable difficulties and for the alacrity and completeness with which the structure and rules for allocation were changed. The relatively decentralized NAP process adopted for the first two periods presents a model of how allocation can be handled in a multinational setting. For all the criticism the process has received, its achievements cannot be gainsaid. A cap thought to be constraining was adopted, the requisite rights to emit were distributed, and a market and price for carbon emerged. If there is any fundamental lesson arising from this experience, it is the importance of good emissions data for the facilities to be included in the scheme, both as a basis for cap-setting and for allocating free allowances to those installations.

The stronger and more assertive role of the Commission in the second period reflected the logic of the initial 'trial' period. Rehearsals are never as demanding as real performances, and the second period was opening night. Given the seriousness with which the European Union viewed its obligations under the Kyoto Protocol and the central role that the ETS had come to assume in the fulfilment of these obligations, the relatively accommodating stance taken in the first period was bound to change. The change was also a response to the first-period allocation, however, for which the Commission was criticized first for being inconsistent in its review of NAPs and then, when an end-of-period surplus became evident, for not being tough enough. Both criticisms implied a need for greater uniformity and centralization in cap-setting. This more assertive role has, however, also spawned serious legal challenges to the Commission's exercise of its review authority.

While the decentralized structure of national allocation plans has worked reasonably well, the post-2012 amendments constitute a nearly complete rejection of this decentralized approach to allocation. The EU-wide cap, its apportionment among participating member states and the distribution of allowances to installations are now completely centralized, not in any authority given the Commission but in commonly agreed formulae negotiated through the multinational institutions of the European Union. In less time than it took to complete either NAP process, member states gave up the initiative and room for debate with the Commission that they possessed under the NAP structure in favour of a hard-wired EU-wide cap and sharing of the cost burden. They also gave up any direct means of influencing the distribution of allowances to installations within their jurisdictions.

This surprising and radical change in cap-setting may be a distinctly European phenomenon, made possible by the pre-existing institutions and practices of the European Union, but it raises the intriguing issue of whether such top-down, treaty-like approaches are more conducive to agreement than decentralized, bottom-up structures. While many factors contributed to this outcome, there is also a sense of fatigue on the part of the member states with the unrewarding process of getting national totals accepted by the Commission and then allocating the allowed total among affected facilities. The post-2012 amendments effectively free member states of all these worries, except for those seeking a temporary derogation for the electricity sector, and Brussels is saddled with the task of allocating the remaining free allowances to the appropriate installations.

The allocation choices made during the NAP phase of the EU ETS were similar to those made in earlier cap-and-trade systems and in other contexts, such as fisheries, where limited but tradable rights are created to constrain access to a previously free resource. As in all these earlier examples, allocation in the EU ETS showed great deference to prior-use claims – that is, to those that were previously using the newly created right that is now limited. What is new in the European experience is how quickly a consensus was formed to move from free allocation to auctioning. Indeed, the more general lesson from the European experience would seem to be that, while free allocation may be necessary for the introduction of a limit on carbon, the resulting emission rights and associated value are not granted in perpetuity, as has been done in other contexts. Instead, free allocation is a transitional feature, both expedient and equitable, that will yield to more socially valuable uses of the scarcity rents created by the cap. How this radical change in allocation will work out is the new public policy experiment on which the EU ETS will embark as it prepares for the third compliance period.

4 | *Effects of free allocation*

Introduction

The preceding chapter discussed the issues of how and on what basis allowances were allocated. This chapter addresses a second question: what is the effect of allocation when the affected installations receive a free allocation of allowances? The debate surrounding auctioning and free allocation suggests that it matters a great deal. The purpose of this chapter is to explain how, and in what ways, allocation does (and does not) matter.

Price effects and allocation effects

Two key distinctions must be made. The first concerns the effects of free allocation itself, distinct from what would be attributed to the price created by the cap-and-trade system. If full auctioning is the means chosen for distributing allowances to installations, there will be no allocation effects because there would be no free allocation. The only effects would be those associated with the price for CO_2 emissions. Free allocation raises the question of whether the allocation itself has effects beyond or additional to those associated with the carbon price.

In the classic economic explanation advanced by Coase (1960), an up-front, fixed assignment of rights to emit will have no effect on the supply and demand for the good in question – in this case emissions. Under certain idealized conditions, such as complete information or the absence of significant transactions costs, trade would occur until marginal valuations and marginal costs are equalized.[1]

The distinction between allocation and price effects, and the assumed independence of these effects, also raise questions about behaviour. Are the producers that receive free allowances as rational,

[1] Transaction costs in the EU ETS are addressed in chapter 8.

or as rigorously profit-maximizing, as assumed in standard neoclassical economics? If they are not, it is possible that a greater or smaller allocation would cause them to produce more or less (or to abate less or more). It certainly is the case that recipients will argue that an excessively small allocation will restrict their production, while an overgenerous allocation given to a competitor will create a competitive advantage for that firm.

Financial and operational effects

The second distinction that must be drawn in discussing allocation effects is that between financial and operational consequences. In the classical Coasian formulation, the grant of allowances has financial consequences but no operational consequences. While the operator will be better off – and will enjoy higher profits – if allowances are received for free instead of being purchased, operational decisions will be determined by the allowance price alone. This is so because each allowance surrendered incurs an opportunity cost equal to the revenue that could have been earned had the allowance been sold. Regardless of whether allowances are distributed for free or purchased through auction, the operator incurs a cost with each allowance it surrenders, and it is this cost that informs operational decisions concerning levels of production.

The financial effect is what is intended by the charge of 'windfall profits' – the idea that operators that receive allowances for free pass along the opportunity cost of allowances to the consumers of their products. This concept logically implies rational, profit-maximizing behaviour on the part of the operators. If operators fail to capture these rents for various regulatory, behavioural or strategic reasons, the financial effects are less pronounced.

An example would be 'cost-of-service' regulation. This common form of electric utility regulation allows only actually incurred costs to be incorporated into the electricity rates charged to customers. Under this form of regulation, the opportunity cost of using an allowance could not be recovered so that the value of the free allocation would be passed on to consumers in the form of a lower electricity rate. A distortion in overall economic efficiency would be incurred, however. All else being equal, these privileged consumers will not pay the full price of the CO_2 emissions they use and will thus consume more electricity (with associated CO_2 emissions). With a fixed cap, this extra demand will drive up the price of CO_2 emissions – and of all the goods whose production results in CO_2 emissions – to the disadvantage of consumers who do not benefit from this type of regulation.

The remaining sections of this chapter discuss three ways in which allocation has mattered. The effect of allocation on the extent of trading as implied by the 'trade part' of the cap-and-trade couplet is looked at first. The next section focuses on the effects of free allocation on short-term profitability and competitiveness. The following section addresses the longer-term effects on investment. The final section concludes.

Effects on the extent of trading

Introduction

With free allocation, the extent of trading depends upon the discrepancies that arise between the allocation of allowances to installations and those installations' actual emissions. A remote theoretical possibility exists that there would be no trading: if the regulator allocated allowances such that every facility had exactly the number of allowances it needed to surrender each year, there would be no surpluses or deficits to be traded.[2] In reality, there will always be discrepancies, for three reasons: equity, abatement and randomness. When free allocation is the prevailing mode of distributing allowances, these three causes will interact to create discrepancies at all levels, from the installation to the system as a whole. Although it could as easily be said that these discrepancies are created by emissions, they are typically attributed to allocation, which is a matter of programme design.[3]

In the context of the EU ETS, several examples of equity considerations in the allocation process come readily to mind. The ETS

---

[2] It is a little hard to imagine how, in this situation, a price to co-ordinate abatement and production decisions would emerge. In keeping with the heuristic value of this case, one must assume a 'virtual price' that all affected facilities respond to, and subsequently find that, after taking that price into account, facilities' emissions are exactly equal to the allowances received from the omniscient regulator.

[3] In similar manner, the economist Marshall once famously remarked that it was no more possible to determine whether supply or demand determined price than it was to say whether the upper or lower blade of a pair of scissors cuts a piece of paper.

Directive itself specified criteria for deciding member state totals that implied more allowances for some states than for others – namely those that were on track to meet their Kyoto/BSA targets. Equity considerations also motivated the redistribution of auction rights in the post-2012 amendments to the ETS Directive. In both these instances, some states (and the installations located in those states) will receive more than others according to some standard of comparison. Another example is the explicit decision in many national allocation plans to allocate all the expected shortage to the electricity sector, on the grounds that power plants could abate more easily and that they face no foreign competition. Other examples can be observed in extra allocations for combined heat and power facilities or for early action. With a fixed cap, any such preferential treatment creates surpluses (or smaller deficits) for some and has the opposite effect on all others. All these examples involve some concept of fairness and all create discrepancies between allocations and emissions that can be expected to create opportunities for trading.

A second cause of discrepancies is abatement. A fixed, lump-sum endowment that is not adjusted *ex post* according to actual emissions encourages firms for which abatement is cheaper than the market price to abate, and thus to benefit from the sale of unneeded allowances. Although it can be imagined that allocation would take expected abatement into account, no authority knows exactly the amounts of abatement that would be undertaken by installations in response to a given CO_2 price. Often operators themselves do not have a full appreciation of all the abatement possibilities available to them until they have an incentive to reduce emissions. Furthermore, even if the extent of abatement were known at the time of allocation, innovation in response to the CO_2 price could be expected to create new abatement possibilities, and these would create surpluses that could and should be traded to ensure least-cost abatement at all times.

The last and inescapable cause of the discrepancies that determine the extent of trading is the unexpected and largely random variation in the conditions that determine production and emissions. For example, some facilities may experience a temporary breakdown, which implies that competing facilities produce more to meet demand for their common output. Such unpredictable events increase the demand for allowances at some facilities and decrease it at others. Similar variations in emissions can occur as a result of the differential effects of the weather, energy prices or the level of economic activity on affected firms. All these normal vagaries in the factors that determine emissions will create discrepancies that will need to be eliminated through trading if the aggregate limit is to be met efficiently.

The extent of trading in the EU ETS

The degree to which these discrepancies determined the need for trading in the EU ETS is revealed by the data in the Community Independent Transaction Log, which records annually both emissions and freely allocated allowances at the installation level. As is characteristic of cap-and-trade systems, very few installations in the EU ETS had emissions exactly equal to the allowances allocated to them. Out of more than 30,000 observations (three years for more than 10,000 installations), there were only twenty-seven instances in which emissions and the annual allocation were the same (Trotignon and Ellerman 2008). For all practical purposes, all installations were either 'long' (an annual allocation greater than emissions) or 'short' (an allocation less than emissions), and therefore all installations were potential participants in trading. The distribution of these long and short positions is summarized in tables 4.1 and 4.2 and illustrated in figure 4.1.

The truncation of the centre in figure 4.1 illustrates a fundamental feature of cap-and-trade systems: most of the potential demand and supply is in the tails. Moreover, in the EU ETS, and as shown in the figure, the deficits are more concentrated than the surpluses. Only 7 per cent of the installations have differences of more than 250,000 tonnes, and, when compared with the surplus side, those on the deficit side are smaller in number (280 versus 498) and hold a larger percentage of all deficit positions (84 versus 65 per cent).

The CITL data indicate an aggregate deficit at short installations of about 650 Mt CO_2 for the period as a whole and an aggregate surplus of slightly over 800 Mt. Thus, a transfer of at least 650 million EUAs is indicated for all installations to be in compliance. The number of transfers that were actually required for compliance is probably fewer, however, because distributions from new entrant and other reserves are not shown in the CITL data on allocations that are publicly available. Installations recorded in the CITL with a zero allocation almost surely received EUAs from NERs and may not have been short at all. Similarly, some installations recorded in the CITL with initial positive allocations received additional allowances for expansions of capacity

Table 4.1 *Installation EUA surpluses and deficits, 2005–7*

	Short installations			Long installations		
	Number of installations	Emissions (000 tonnes)	Deficit (000 tonnes)	Number of installations	Emissions (000 tonnes)	Surplus (000 tonnes)
2005	2,954	944.2	181.3	8,251	1,068.7	264.7
2006	3,148	997.6	227.7	8,093	1,037.5	264.2
2007	3,091	1,037.4	241.6	7,784	1,003.5	279.3
Period 1	3,064[1]	2,979.1	650.5	8,043[1]	3,109.8	808.2

Note: [1] Average for the three years.
Source: CITL.

Table 4.2 *Size distribution of installations by EUA deficits and surpluses, 2005–7*

Installation category	Number of installations	Sum of all differences (Mt)	Percentage of total surplus/deficit
Surplus greater than 250,000 tonnes	498	526.3	65
Surplus less than 250,000 tonnes	7,545	281.9	35
Surplus total	*8,043*	*808.2*	*100*
Deficit less than 250,000 tonnes	2,784	–103.9	16
Deficit greater than 250,000 tonnes	280	–546.6	84
Deficit total	*3,064*	*–650.5*	*100*

Source: CITL.

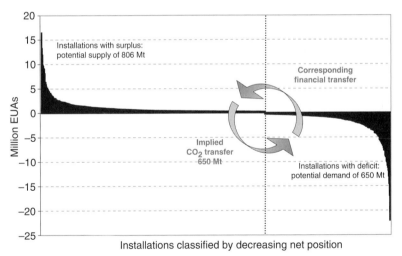

Figure 4.1 Installations' net positions and implied trading flows, 2005–7
Note: For the sake of illustration, only the installations that had deficits or surpluses greater than 250,000 tonnes are shown. If not, there would be a very long line in the centre, indistinguishable from the zero axis
Source: Adapted from Trotignon and Delbosc (2008)

or for other reasons, and therefore may have held positions that were longer (or less short) than those indicated by the CITL data. Most of these unrecorded allowances were probably distributed to short installations, so the actual extent of trading was less, perhaps between 500 million and 550 million EUAs. All the same, EUAs distributed from reserves account for about 2 per cent of the total EU-wide cap. While their distribution can have important consequences in individual cases, the overall picture is not greatly changed. The bulk of the potential buying and selling sides of the market are revealed by the CITL data.[4]

With these qualifications in mind, the distribution of short and long positions at the installation level by member state and by sector indicates the sources of potential demand and supply for EUAs. Figure 4.2 presents the sum of all the EUA deficits and surpluses at installations in each member state for the period as a whole.

The top panel includes the EU15 countries and the bottom panel the ten new member states. The gross short and long positions, which are shown by the striped bars, indicate, respectively, the sum of all the deficits at installations that are short and the sum of the surpluses at installations that are long. The solid portion of the bar indicates the difference, or the net position of installations in the member state.

As is immediately evident, virtually all the short installations were located in the EU15, while the long installations were more evenly distributed between the EU15 and the new member states. Five of the six countries that are indicated as short on balance – the United Kingdom, Spain, Italy, Greece and Ireland – are among the EU15, and only one new member state, Slovenia, was net short (although by a very small amount). Germany is the only member state whose position was significantly affected by the adjustments discussed previously. The *ex post* withdrawal of 70 million EUAs from accounts in surplus at the end of the period reduced Germany's gross surplus from 137 million EUAs to 67 million EUAs and converted it from what would otherwise have been a net long position of 46 million tonnes to a net short position of 24 million tonnes.[5]

---

[4] In general, installations that were long or short in one year were long or short in all years. The correlation coefficients for the net positions of installations are +0.915 for 2005 with both 2006 and 2007 and +0.959 for 2006 with 2007 positions.

[5] The distribution of new entrant reserves in Ireland and Greece converted both these member states from being slightly short to being slightly long in the aggregate and reduced the net short positions of Spain, Italy and the United Kingdom (Trotignon and Ellerman 2008).

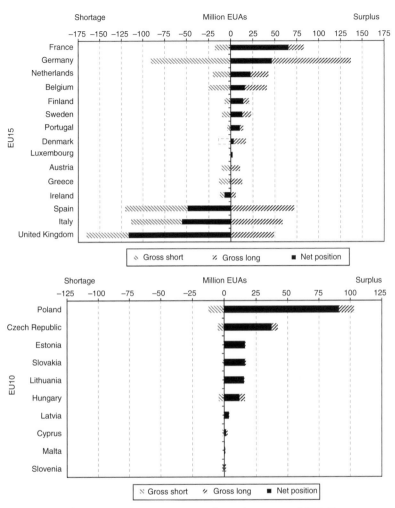

Figure 4.2 The gross and net positions of member states, 2005–7
Source: Trotignon and Delbosc (2008)

The indicated directions of allowance transfers among member states were mostly to the United Kingdom, Spain and Italy. The supply from long installations was more equally distributed, although those in France, Poland and the Czech Republic probably figured prominently given the size of the net surpluses in these three countries. Germany would appear to have also been a large supplier, but at least a half of its surplus at the installation level was in all probability retained pending resolution of the litigation concerning *ex post* adjustments.

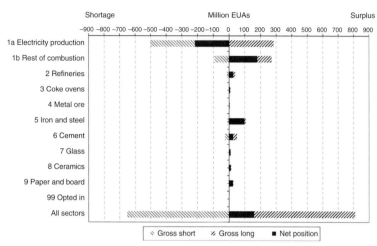

Figure 4.3 Short and long positions by economic sector, 2005–7
Source: Trotignon and Delbosc (2008)

Member states are not the only group into which the installation data can be aggregated. Another breakdown is by economic sector, as shown in figure 4.3. By this grouping, the short installations are mostly located in the power sector (77 per cent), which, together with the rest of combustion, covers more than 90 per cent of the short installations. The same two sectors account for almost 70 per cent of the long installations and, when combined with the main industrial sectors – iron and steel, cement and refineries – contribute 748 million of the 808 million EUAs in surplus, or about 92 per cent of the total. When viewed from this perspective, the power sector and the rest of combustion dominate the potential market. Virtually all the compliance demand for EUAs in the first period came from these categories, as well as more than two-thirds of the likely supply.

In light of the important role the electricity sector plays in the market, Figure 4.4 provides more detail on this sector. The countries have been split into two groups: the largely western European EU15 and the largely eastern European new member states. Figure 4.4 highlights that most of the net demand from the electricity sector originated from the United Kingdom, Spain and Italy. These countries, together with Germany and Belgium, account for more than 80 per cent of the short positions in the electricity sector. While a few short positions existed in eastern European countries, virtually all the

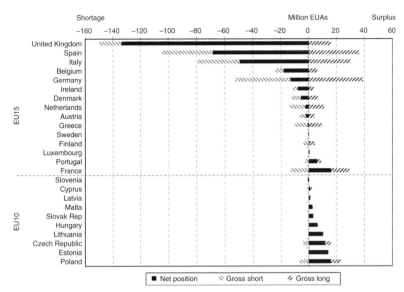

Figure 4.4 Short and long positions in the electricity sector, 2005–7
Source: Trotignon and Delbosc (2008)

demand came from the EU15. In contrast, most of the net long positions among electric utilities are located in eastern Europe, mainly Poland, Estonia and the Czech Republic, although a sizeable net long position also characterized the French electric utility sector. When looking at all long positions for electric utilities, significant supply comes from the EU15, where more than 70 per cent of the long positions at the power plant level are found.[6]

The CITL data presented thus far show implied transfers and not necessarily actual transfers. As already noted, the allocation data is not complete, so these observed discrepancies can be viewed only as indicative. Another part of the CITL database allows the analyst to observe actual transfers among member states for the purpose of compliance. These data indicate the registry of origin of every allowance surrendered for compliance, but they do not reveal the installation to which the EUA was issued or the sector to which that installation belongs. Table 4.3 shows the net flows among member

---

[6] Although owners of multiple facilities can be expected to transfer EUAs internally before resorting to the market, it does not follow that sectors or member states were netted out before making sales or purchases involving other sectors or member states.

Table 4.3 *Net EUA export and import flows by country and year, 2005–7*

(million EUAs)	Net exporters					Net importers			
	2005–7	2005	2006	2007		2005–7	2005	2006	2007
EU15	89.61	12.37	26.81	55.37	EU15	−216.52	−21.10	−59.97	−140.38
France	41.89	5.38	9.50	27.01	United Kingdom	−106.98	−8.57	−28.71	−69.70
Netherlands	13.36		6.66	6.99	Spain	−41.17	−9.72	−8.34	−23.11
Finland	9.13	3.26	1.00	4.87	Italy	−35.32	−0.35	−16.63	−18.34
Portugal	6.81		2.47	5.09	Germany	−29.72		−4.01	−28.26
Belgium	6.48	0.91	3.00	2.57	Austria	−2.29	−0.76	−2.28	
Denmark	6.26		1.32	5.20	Ireland	−1.04	−0.41		−0.86
Sweden	3.50	0.27	1.07	2.16	Portugal		−0.75		
Greece	1.12	0.00	1.23		Netherlands		−0.28		
Luxembourg	1.06	0.00	0.33	0.72	Denmark		−0.26		
Germany		2.55			Greece				−0.11
Austria				0.76					
Ireland			0.23						
EU10	128.07	8.73	33.36	85.98	EU10	−1.16	0.00	−0.20	−0.97
Poland	52.65	0.08	8.92	43.65	Slovenia	−1.16		−0.20	−0.97
Czech Republic	27.66	5.66	8.86	13.15					

					EU25			
Slovakia	12.03	1.32	3.99	6.72				
Estonia	11.69	1.00	5.71	4.98				
Lithuania	10.93	0.42	2.36	8.15				
Hungary	9.50	0.07	2.80	6.62				
Latvia	3.09	0.17	0.70	2.22				
Cyprus	0.52	0.00	0.02	0.49				
Slovenia		0.01						
EU25	217.68	21.10	60.17	141.35	EU25	−217.68	−21.10	−60.17	−141.35

Source: Trotignon and Ellerman (2008).

states indicated by these data. Net flows represent the balance between EUAs originating in the indicated member state that were surrendered for compliance in other member states and the EUAs originating in other member states that were surrendered for compliance in the indicated member state.[7] The fact that a 'foreign' allowance was surrendered in a member state indicates that a cross-border transfer occurred, although not necessarily in the year indicated. For instance, EUAs surrendered in 2007 may have been transferred out of a particular country in 2006 and held in one or several accounts before being surrendered. In any event, these net balances can be interpreted as net exports or imports of EUAs by each member state.

These data are arranged with net exporters on the left and net importers on the right, with a division between the EU15 and the ten new member states. The order of listing is determined by the total net volume for the period as a whole. These flows confirm what would be expected based on the net positions of member states as shown in figure 4.2. The net importers are, with the exception of Slovenia, EU15 member states, with the United Kingdom accounting for half the importing side and Spain, Italy and Germany accounting for most of the rest. On the export side, the supply is about evenly split between the surplus countries of the EU15 and the new member states, with France, Poland and the Czech Republic accounting for 56 per cent of this total.

Summary: what explains these flows?

All the factors mentioned earlier – equity, abatement and randomness – contributed to the flow of allowances between installations and member states. The basic trading patterns in the first period of the EU ETS were shaped strongly by the allocation process. In particular, the criterion for cap-setting largely determined the trading outcome. Member states that were predicted to have problems meeting their Kyoto/BSA obligations were held to a more constraining cap (on an expected basis) than countries that were on track to meet these targets. In the latest status report when NAPs were being decided, the European Environment Agency listed nine member states as not being

---

[7] For instance, the net inflow to the United Kingdom of 107 million EUAs is the difference between 751 million non-UK EUAs surrendered by UK installations and 644 million UK-originated EUAs that were surrendered by non-UK installations elsewhere in the EU ETS. Nearly every net flow shown reflects a similar difference.

on track to meet these targets: Austria, Belgium, Denmark, Finland, Greece, Ireland, Italy, Portugal and Spain (EEA 2004). None of the member states with large surpluses that are shown in figure 4.2 or table 4.3 are on this list, and those that are on the list were either in deficit or closely balanced.

The exceptions are Germany and the United Kingdom. Germany would have had a large surplus at the installation level if it had lost its court challenge to the Commission's ruling on *ex post* adjustment. As indicated in table 4.3, Germany's position as a net importer of EUAs for the period as a whole was determined by net imports of about 28 million EUAs in 2007. The surrender data do not indicate whether this surge in imports was a response to the court ruling, which would have required any installations that had already sold surpluses to purchase first-period allowances to give back to the regulator. As can also be observed on table 4.3, other countries that were net importers also surrendered larger quantities of non-domestic EUAs for compliance. As is discussed in chapter 5, this pattern of net imports is also consistent with borrowing allowances from the year-ahead allocations for compliance in 2005 and 2006.

The United Kingdom was the largest net importer because it proposed a more constraining NAP1 total, in part to meet its tougher domestically set target of cutting emissions to 20 per cent below the 1990 level rather than the Kyoto/BSA target of 12 per cent below, which the country has never been in danger of not achieving. As the first member state to publish its national allocation plan (in January 2004, as part of a public consultation exercise) and as a self-styled leader in emissions trading, the United Kingdom adopted what was claimed, and what was largely recognized, as a constraining total. The United Kingdom's large deficit is also explained by the unexpected, however. When the country developed its NAP, natural gas prices were expected to be much lower than they turned out to be. As a member state with liberalized electricity markets and significant shares of electricity generated by coal and natural gas, higher than expected gas prices during the first period meant more coal and less natural gas generation than had been projected in setting the NAP1 total. This unexpected change in the relationship between coal and natural gas prices also probably created a larger deficit for Spain, another member state with relatively liberalized wholesale electricity markets and significant reliance on both coal- and natural-gas-fired generation.

Random factors were also important in explaining other member state net positions and net flows. The drought in southern Europe in 2005 contributed to the short position of Spain, and the relatively high rainfall during the same period made the balances in Denmark, Sweden and Finland larger than they would otherwise have been.[8] In Finland, a prolonged strike in the pulp and paper industry had a noticeable effect on the balance in 2005. Other examples of random factors are not hard to find as one examines the detail regarding different countries.

A final factor in affecting flows is abatement, but its influence is not easy to identify. Abatement would increase the surplus of installations that are long, and as such it may explain some of the end-of-period surplus in the EU ETS. When abatement occurs at installations that are short, however, the effect is that of avoided purchases or transfers. As is discussed in more detail in chapter 6, much of the abatement in the first period occurred in the electric utility sector from fuel-switching. Therefore, the main effect of abatement was probably to reduce import demand, especially in the United Kingdom, Spain and Italy, where the short positions of the electricity sector were large. Without abatement, the demand for EUAs from those countries and the import flows would have been even greater.

Even after taking random variations and abatement into account, the main explanation of the observed differences between allocation and emissions in the first period remains allocation. Two relatively non-controversial choices largely determined the extent and direction of trading: the decision to expect more of some countries than others, and the decision to grant fewer allowances to electric utilities than to industrial facilities. Poor data and faulty assumptions in emissions projections compound the effects of allocation in eastern Europe, but this could also be seen as a form of randomness, since projections always turn out to be wrong to some extent.

Effects on short-term profitability and competitiveness

Free allocation obviously affects profitability, although these financial effects can easily be overstated. The more interesting and less easily answered question is whether free allocation has effects beyond the

---

[8] For an excellent examination of the effects of differing rainfall on emissions in the first year of the EU ETS, see Houpert and de Dominicis (2006).

obvious financial ones. Notwithstanding the theoretical argument to the contrary, the argument is often made that allocation does have operational effects. In addition, a new issue related to free allocation has emerged in the EU ETS: harmonization. The call for harmonization has arisen out of the readily observed differences in allocation to apparently similar installations that have resulted from decentralized free allocation to installations. At the very least, these differences are seen as unfair and as potentially creating a competitive advantage for those that receive more generous allocations.

In this section, examples are drawn from the refining sector to place the financial effects of free allocation in perspective and to consider the feasibility of reducing the disparities in free allocation that can be observed. Evidence on the effect of free allocation on output and emissions in refining and in electricity generation is also presented.

The refining sector as a case study of financial effects[9]

The refinery sector provides an attractive case study because of its size, the small number of facilities, the sophistication of its operators, the careful planning and close monitoring of refinery runs and the availability of information on plant characteristics and emissions at the plant level. One hundred and thirty-nine refineries are included in the EU ETS, and data on crude input, refinery type, and emissions can be assembled for ninety of these. Once the dominant share of the power sector is excluded, the refining sector ranks third in terms of allowances distributed over the first period, with 8 per cent or 473 million EUAs, close behind the iron and steel and cement sectors (8.1 and 9.1 per cent of the EU cap, respectively).

Over the three years of the first period the combined allowance allocation to the refining sector was 7 per cent greater than its emissions, suggesting that, in general, the sector did not face a shortage of allowances. The picture changes if we look at the sector in more detail, however, as is made possible by figure 4.5.

The sum of the annual net positions of individual refineries, grouped by country, is given for all three years of the first period. When the horizontal bar is all on one side or the other, the refinery was either

---

[9] Lacombe (2008) provides an excellent analysis of the economic impact that the EU ETS had on the refinery sector.

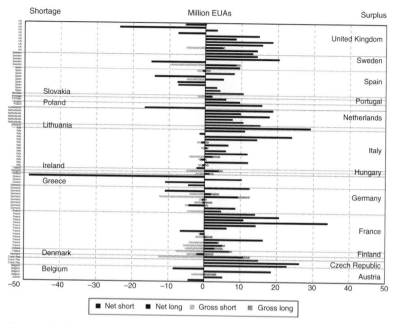

Figure 4.5 Short and long positions of refinery installations, 2005–7
Source: CITL

long or short for all three years. When a line appears on both sides, the refinery was short in one or two years and long in the others, and the net balance for the period is indicated by the difference between the two. Of the ninety refineries that are depicted, twenty-six fall into the category of being both short and long in different years.

This large sample of the entire universe of refineries included in the EU ETS shows that there were significant differences in the balance between allowances and emissions at various installations and that differences existed within member states as well as between them. When considered *ex post*, only the Netherlands and the Czech Republic managed to allocate allowances to individual installations in a manner that was roughly equal.

Table 4.4 presents a quasi-realistic example of the effects of allocation on the two refineries that represent the two extremes in this sample: the Berre refinery in France, which had a 34 per cent allowance surplus, and the Corinth refinery in Greece, which faced a deficit equal to 49 per cent of its allocation.

Table 4.4 *Illustration of the financial effects of allocation:*
two refineries

		Berre	Corinth
1	Name of refinery	Berre	Corinth
2	Member state	France	Greece
3	Type	Complex	Ultracomplex
4	Daily crude input (barrels)	82,000 (78,000 in 2007)	100,000
5	Annual EUA allocation	1,368,000	1,207,000
6	Average annual verified emissions	903 000	1,793,000
7	Average annual net position	465	−586
8	Percentage of allocation	34	−49
9	CO_2 emissions (kg/1,000 bls.)	30.6	49.1
A	Illustrative annual refinery profit ($6/bl. of crude input)[1]	€145 million	€177 million
B	Value of allowance endowment, annual (@€15/EUA)	€20.6 million	€18.2 million
C	Percentage of annual profit	14	10
D	Value of over-/under-allocation, annual	+€7.1 million	−€8.7 million
E	Percentage of illustrative margin	5	−5
F	Cost of annual crude input ($50/bl.)[1]	€1,207 million	€1,472 million
G	Full cost of emissions	€13.55 million	€26.90 million
H	Percentage of crude input cost	1.12	1.83
I	Equivalent cost per barrel crude input	$0.56/bl.[1]	$0.91/bl.[1]

Note: [1]Exchange rate of $1.24/€1.
Sources: Derived from CITL data, Lacombe (2008) and *Oil & Gas Journal*
(2005, 2006, 2007).

Rows 1 to 9 provide the basic data concerning these two refineries.
When measured in terms of daily crude input, Berre is a smaller
refinery than Corinth and is also less complex: Berre lacks the hydrocracking capability that not only allows Corinth to process heavier
crudes and to produce a lighter slate of petroleum products, but also
causes Corinth to consume more energy and produce more CO_2
emissions per unit of crude input. Despite the Corinth plant's complexity, it received about 12 per cent fewer EUAs than Berre as an
annual allocation. As a result, it ran a significant deficit in all years,
while Berre enjoyed a sizeable surplus in all years.

Rows A to I attempt to place these different allocations in perspective by comparing various CO_2-related items to what might be

imagined to be the annual profits of these refineries. These estimates are based on an assumed refinery margin of $6 per barrel of crude input (row A; converted to euros at $1.24/€1) and the cost of the major expense item for any refinery: the cost of crude oil (row F). Row B gives the value of the annual allowance allocation when valued at €15 per EUA and row C expresses this as a percentage of the illustrative profit of each refinery.

The effect of free allocation on profitability for firms in general and for these two refineries in particular depends on the ability to pass CO_2 costs on to customers. Although many variations exist, and all costs must be recovered eventually for a firm to remain viable, two limiting cases can be used to illustrate these effects. One limiting case is that all costs are passed through (but no more), reflecting the standard economic assumptions of a competitive market. In this case, the effect of free allocation is indicated by rows B and C in table 4.4. Firms would charge the marginal cost, whether that be an incurred cost as at Corinth, which must buy additional allowances, or an opportunity cost as at Berre, which will sell the allowances it was allocated but does not need to cover emissions. Profits will increase by 14 per cent at Berre, and by 10 per cent at Corinth, because of the free allocation of allowances.

The other limiting case is that none of the additional CO_2 costs can be passed on to customers. In this case, the value of the free allocation is the cost avoided, which would be the same as just presented, although it would not show up on most accounting statements. What would show up are the differential effects: the additional allowances that Corinth, representing short installations, would have to buy and the surplus that Berre, representing long installations, would be able to sell. In this particular example, Berre's profits would be boosted by 5 per cent and Corinth's reduced by 5 per cent. Although the value of the free allocation does not show up here, it would if all allowances had to be purchased at auction. Again, assuming that these costs could not be passed through to customers, profits would be reduced by about 9 per cent at Berre and by 15 per cent at Corinth.

These simple examples illustrate three points. First, the more important financial effects are those associated with the endowment of free allowances, not with the differences in these endowments between installations. The example used here purposefully took the two extreme cases. By design, the differential effects for other refinery comparisons would be even smaller, as can be readily seen by referring to figure 4.5 and comparing these two extremes to the *ex post* outcomes at the other refineries. Second, the differential effects of free allocation are greater the less the ability of recipients to pass CO_2 costs through in product prices. If there is full pass-through, the *ex post* comparison of these two refineries is 114 versus 110, or a 3.6 per cent difference, whereas if no pass-through is possible the *ex post* comparison is 105 versus 95, a 10 per cent difference.[10] The third point is that, if costs cannot be fully passed through, auctioning does not eliminate differential effects. The only combination that has no direct effect on profitability of the firm is auctioning with full cost pass-through.

Finally, rows F to I in table 4.4 place the cost of CO_2 emissions (always at €15/EUA) in the context of the major cost item in any refinery, that of crude input, here valued at $50/barrel and converted to euros at $1.24/€1. With these assumptions, the new cost of CO_2 emissions is equal to 1 to 2 per cent of the cost of crude input: an increase in the cost of crude input of between $0.50 and $1.00 a barrel. Different crude oil, EUA or exchange rate assumptions could change these figures somewhat, but they would all show that the cost of CO_2 is small relative to crude input costs, which are typically assumed to be passed on to customers absent some regulatory constraint.

Can inter-refinery allocation differences be reduced?

While small in relation to other input costs and less important in financial effect than the free allocation itself, the elimination of these inter-installation differences in allocation is the object of the calls for harmonized allocation in the EU ETS. The premise behind this demand is that an appropriate benchmark based on technical conside-rations and independent of lobbying would reduce these disparities. Equivalently, a harmonized allocation would reduce the disparities observed between installation-level emissions and allocations in the first period, which are illustrated graphically in figure 4.6.

Since the annual allocation was the same in all three years, individ-ual refineries can be identified by the three symbols that line up vertically. The 45° line in figure 4.6 represents the ideal, of an

[10] By assumption, the *ex ante* comparison is 100 versus 100.

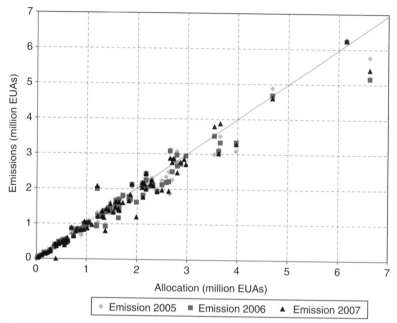

Figure 4.6 The relation between allocations and actual emissions in period 1
Source: Compiled by authors based on CITL data

allocation with no disparities between allocations and *ex post* emissions. This ideal could never be achieved, if for no other reason than the random factors that affect emissions from year to year, but the premise is that a harmonized allocation would result in a closer clustering around the 45° degree line that what is observed in this figure. Statistically, the degree of clustering is measured by the R^2. Perfect alignment is indicated by a value of 1.00, and the lower the R^2 value the greater the differences. Thus, the test in attempting to construct a harmonized technical benchmark would be whether the R^2 has a higher value than what is obtained when observed emissions are regressed on the annual allocation. Alternatively, a harmonized benchmark would predict actual emissions with less scatter than is observed in figure 4.6.

The refinery industry is one for which there is considerable public information concerning the technical characteristics that determine emissions, and this could be used as the basis for a technically based benchmark that would reflect efficient production, incorporating data such as the crude input, the refinery characteristics that determine complexity, and the amount of processing and emissions involved in transforming crude oil into marketable petroleum products. These data can be used to construct a benchmark that would reduce the inter-installation differences between emissions and free allocations. A simple econometric approach was applied in which observed emissions were regressed on installation-specific independent variables for:

- the crude input, as a proxy for capacity and output under full utilization;
- the total charge capacity of the processes that the installation uses;
- a complexity factor developed by a refinery industry consultant;[11] and
- refining technologies (hydro-crackers etc.).

As might be expected, when more technical detail is added as independent variables to a simple linear regression on emissions, the fit improves. The crude input is clearly correlated with emissions, and its inclusion in the regression equation greatly improves the fit. Charge capacity, a slightly more sophisticated indicator of refinery size, reduces the variations when it is added to the equation. Including the different technologies found at refineries and the complexity factor also helps reduce variance. When all these factors are included, the R^2, or 'fit', with observed annual emissions is 0.954. While close, the fit is not as good as that obtained when emissions are regressed on allocations ($R^2 = 0.989$). Surprisingly, these same factors do an even better job of predicting the first-period allocations ($R^2 = 0.988$), although it is worth noting that these differences in R^2 are all small.

This exercise suggests that a benchmark based on purely technical factors would do no better than the existing allocations based on recent historical emissions. The deeper insight may be that recent historical emissions provide the best information concerning the carbon implications of efficient production at installations. If so, recent historical emissions, averaged over several years in order to reduce the effect of random annual variations, provide the best benchmark for harmonizing allocation, and the first-period allocations in

[11] The complexity factor is proposed by Purvin & Gertz in their *Global Petroleum Market Outlook* (Purvin & Gertz 2008), and is calculated using factors for each process unit at individual refineries.

the EU ETS are both benchmarked and harmonized. The differences that remain are not the result of some inappropriate bias introduced by a 'messy' or corrupted allocation process but the result of random influences and other factors that determine allocations.

One such factor that would appear to be applicable here is differentiation, or the considerations of equity that lead to different member state totals in the EU ETS. Such a consideration may explain the differences that can be observed in the examples of the Berre refinery in France and Corinth refinery in Greece. When the first-period cap was being decided, Greece was one of the countries viewed as not on a trajectory to meet its Kyoto/BSA target, unlike France. A strict application of the cap-setting criterion – progress towards the Kyoto/BSA target – implied that Greece would choose or be held to a lower cap relative to expected business-as-usual emissions than would France; and, indeed, this appears to have been the case, based on the differences between member state totals and their emissions in the first period, as shown in figure 4.2. Greece's emissions were virtually equal to its 'cap' while France enjoyed the largest surplus among the EU15 and the second largest in the EU25, after Poland.

The difference in the member state totals for Greece and France would have repercussions on the *ex post* positions of installations in these countries, and that appears to be the case in this comparison between Greece and France. Of the thirteen refineries in France included in figure 4.5, seven were long in all three years of the trial period, four fluctuated from year to year but were net long for the three years as a whole, and two were short in all three years. Among the four refineries in Greece, one was long in all three years and three were short in all three years. On average, French refineries were 9 per cent long while Greek refineries were 20 per cent short. Although other factors may also be relevant, such as how different sectors were treated within any single country, the differentiation expressed in the totals for Greece and France explain at least part of the observed differences in the free allowance endowments and in the *ex post* outcomes.

This comparison points out a fundamental problem with harmonization, namely: how to reconcile it with differentiation. One standard implies that similar installations in different countries be treated alike; the other implies that they be treated differently because of other characteristics, whether they be per capita income, Kyoto commitments or some other equity consideration. The post-2012 amendments to the EU ETS reconcile this conflict by achieving differentiation through auction rights while seeking to achieve harmonization in the remaining free allocation through the use of a best-practice benchmark, the average emission rate for the 10 per cent of installations in a sector or subsector with the lowest emission rates. The question that will have to be addressed is: what defines the sector or subsector to which the benchmark applies and from which the 10 per cent best installations are selected? To return to the examples of the Berre and Corinth refineries, the issue will be whether they belong in the same subset. As shown in row 9 of table 4.4, Corinth has a significantly higher emission rate per unit of crude input than Berre, but it is also a more complex refinery. Taking this complexity or other factors influencing efficient best-practice emission rates into account implies more benchmarks and smaller subsets, while failing to take these factors into account will perpetuate differences in allocation and the financial effects that flow from them.

Could allocation determine production?

One remaining question concerning short-term effects is whether allocation influences emissions. If it does, then the high degree of correspondence between allocations and emissions observed in figure 4.6 is not surprising. One casual means of addressing this issue for refineries is to examine crude input both before and after the start of the EU ETS, as is presented by the two panels of figure 4.7, which show crude input at the refineries that had the largest allowance deficits and surpluses during the first period of the ETS.

The overall picture is one of little change. None of the nine refineries with the shortest positions show any decline in crude input in the last three years corresponding to the EU ETS. A refinery in Poland experienced considerable growth in input despite being short. The picture for the refineries with the longest positions is also one of little change. A refinery in Belgium experienced an increase in crude input of about 50,000 barrels per day, but one in Lithuania experienced an even greater decline in crude input. Other long refineries show minor increases or decreases.

Although crude input is a reasonable proxy for output levels, emissions can vary from year to year according to the quality of the crude

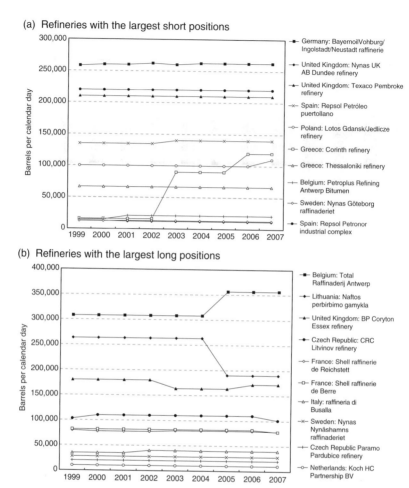

Figure 4.7 Developments in crude input at the shortest and longest installations, 1999–2007

Source: Oil & Gas Journal (1999, 2000, 2001, 2002, 2003, 2004, 2005, 2006, 2007)

input and of the product slates. Thus, there is still a possibility that emissions might be influenced by allocation even if there appears to be little effect on input or output. Data on pre-2005 emissions at ETS installations are often not publicly available or easy to obtain. One notable exception, however, is the United Kingdom, which has published the pre-2005 CO_2 emissions data that were used for determining the allocation to the facilities included in the ETS. Figure 4.8 presents verified emissions for 2005 to 2007 as a ratio to

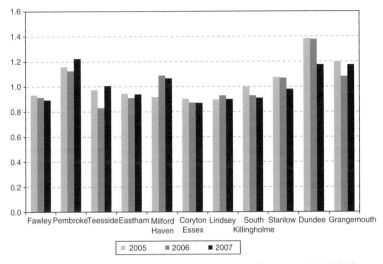

Figure 4.8 UK refinery CO_2 emissions, 2005–7, relative to 1999–2003 average
Source: Derived from UK Department of Environment, Food and Rural Affairs spreadsheet 'Installation-level allocations', available at website for 'Approved National Allocation Plan (2005–2007)'

the average of 1999–2003 emissions for each refinery. A value greater than one indicates annual emissions that are higher than average emissions during the pre-ETS period, and conversely for values less than one.

Most refineries had lower emissions than they had prior to the start of the ETS, but three installations – Pembroke, Dundee and Grangemouth – stand out due to their consistently higher emissions. All three of these installations were short with respect to their allowance allocations – which ranged from 6 to 9.2 per cent higher than their average emissions from 1999–2003 – and all three had unchanging crude input levels from 2003 to 2007. All the other refineries in the United Kingdom were long for the period as a whole and in nearly every individual year.

Neither the crude input data for the nearly complete sample of EU refineries nor the emissions trends among UK refineries suggest that allocation as such determines output (and therefore input) or emissions. If anything, the UK data would suggest an inverse relationship. One of the three UK refineries that were short was one of the two refineries that received a slightly lower allocation based on the United Kingdom's allocation rules, but the other two received allocations that bore the same relationship to the UK baseline as the refineries that were long.[12] Other explanations must be sought for the slight differences in *ex post* outcomes.

Allocation and coal plant utilization in Spain

The casual, visual evidence presented in figures 4.7 and 4.8 is not satisfactory from a rigorous statistical standpoint. A problem called endogeneity stands in the way of any attempt to test rigorously for a relationship between allocation and production, however. Free allocations to installations are typically based on past emissions, which depend on production, and current production is highly correlated with past production. Thus, any statistical test of whether current production depends on allocation will show a high correlation, but the inference that allocation is influencing current production would be false because of the strong serial correlation between past and current production. From a statistical standpoint, what is needed for a more thorough and satisfactory test of the relationship between allocation and emissions or output is some unique feature that distinguishes allocation from past production and other factors that might determine current production or emissions. Such a feature does figure in the rules for allocating EUAs to coal plants in the Spanish electricity sector, and it can be used to perform a more rigorous statistical test of the relationship between allocation and current production.

The allocation of EUAs to Spanish coal-fired electricity-generating plants was based upon past production, but it was adjusted to award more allowances to coal plants with lower emission rates than average and fewer allowances to plants with higher than average emission rates (Del Rio 2007). Moreover, the formula for the adjustment contained a quadratic term that increased the reward according to the distance between the historical emission rate for the individual plant and the average for all coal-fired units. Thus, if allocation had an influence on current production, lower-emitting units should be producing more and higher-emitting units producing less.

---

[12] Allocations in the United Kingdom were based on 'relevant emissions', which were determined by dropping the year with the lowest emissions from the 1999–2003 average. All but two refineries received an allocation that was 6.7 per cent higher than relevant emissions, and the allocations to the other two refineries were 5.0 per cent higher than their relevant emissions.

An important step in testing this relationship is to separate out the effect of the CO_2 price – which would encourage the use of lower-emitting units and discourage the utilization of higher-emitting units – from the allocation effect. As described by Reguant and Ellerman (2008), including a term for the CO_2 price in the estimating equation can do so, especially since the CO_2 price varied considerably over the period while the allocation did not. The price term would reflect the extent to which the varying CO_2 price created more or less of an advantage for the lower-emitting coal-fired units. In contrast, if allocation had an effect on production, there would be a constant advantage for the lower-emitting units. Thus, the test became whether a constant advantage for lower-emitting coal plants (and disadvantage for higher-emitting units) attributable to allocation could be detected separate from the varying advantage or disadvantage that would be created for these same units as the CO_2 price changed over the estimation period.

The results in Reguant and Ellerman (2008) support the Coasian assumption that allocation has no effect on production. This work is based on the daily utilization of thirty-six Spanish coal-fired units over the three years prior to the start of the EU ETS (2002–4), and for the first two years of the EU ETS (2005–6), for a total of 65,736 daily observations. A fixed-effects panel regression was completed, using the price of electricity, the megawatt-hour cost of EUAs,[13] a variable reflecting the relative liberality of the allocation to the plant and another variable reflecting the degree of subsidization of some of the coal plants. The base case regression results are presented in table 4.5.

The two estimating equations differ only in the inclusion or non-inclusion of a variable for the coal subsidy. The electricity price and the coal subsidy terms apply for all five years of the estimation period, whereas the CO_2 cost and allocation effects were operative only during the last two years. The results show that electricity prices, the CO_2 cost and the coal subsidy had a strong (more than 99 per cent probable) influence on the utilization of these plants. In contrast, the variable representing the relative liberality of allocation did not pass any test of statistical significance in this basic formulation, as well as in a number of variations testing for the robustness of the results. This

---

[13] The megawatt-hour cost of EUAs equals the EUA price times the observed plant-specific emission rate.

Table 4.5 *Regression results: the effect of allocation on Spanish coal plant operations*

	First equation	Second equation
Electricity price	0.045 (5.64)[1]	0.046 (5.64)[1]
Carbon cost	−0.043 (2.87)[1]	−0.043 (2.85)[1]
EUA allocation	0.104 (0.39)	0.055 (0.37)
Spanish coal subsidy		0.670 (2.85)[1]
Observations/plants	65,736/36	65,736/36

Notes: Robust t-statistics in parentheses clustered at the unit level.
[1]Significant at 1 per cent.
Source: Reguant and Ellerman (2008).

coefficient for the effects of allocation was always insignificantly different from zero. As such, it provides more rigorous statistical support for what would appear by casual visual inspection to be the case with refineries.

Investment effects of allocation: new entrant and closure provisions

Why the long-term effects are different

A novel but ubiquitous feature of the allocation rules in the EU ETS has created a potential further allocation effect: the provisions for new entrants and installation closures grant free allowances in some amount to new entrants or expanded capacity and require existing installations to forfeit their allowances if they cease operations. These provisions are unique to the EU ETS and they differ markedly from what has been the practice in cap-and-trade programmes in the United States for SO_2 and NOx emissions. In these programmes, new entrants receive no free allowances and facilities are not required to forfeit their existing allocations when they are closed.

These provisions are different from the usual fixed lump-sum allocations in depending on the actions of those who would receive or forfeit the allowances. For example, an operator of a facility that is about to be closed could be expected to keep the plant operating at minimum capacity as long as the revenues from the sale of surplus allowances is greater than the loss from ongoing operations. Similarly, investment in new capacity will be more attractive if accompanied by an endowment of allowances that reduces or perhaps even eliminates the need to purchase allowances to cover emissions from future production. In being contingent on current or future actions, the incentive effects triggered by these provisions are fundamentally different from those associated with the more usual fixed free allocations that are given to existing capacity.

There is some debate on exactly what the main effect of these provisions is. Ellerman (2007) argues that the most direct and obvious effect is to create overcapacity, which in turn (generally) decreases output prices and increases output. The effect of emissions markets is indirect and more ambiguous, as it depends on the emissions and production from the new capacity (and that kept operating as a result of closure provisions) and on the emissions of the production that is displaced by the excess capacity. He also points out that the effect of these provisions is to counter the effect of the CO_2 price on the investment decision and thereby to preserve the pre-CO_2 price investment criteria. Once the investment is made, the operational effects of the allocation will be the same as for existing capacity, since the new entrant endowment is fixed. The difference created by the new entrant provision is that the amount and type of new capacity will not fully reflect the CO_2 price.

Another line of analysis (Matthes, Graichen and Repenning 2005; Egenhofer *et al.* 2006; Neuhoff, Keats and Sato 2006) argues that the main effect of these provisions is on the pricing of carbon, and thus on the incentives provided for investing in coal-fired and gas-fired power plants. To the extent that the allowance endowments to be received differ according to the technology used and these differences are enough to tip the balance in the choice of technology, these effects will certainly occur. In this respect, it is worth noting that investments in new zero-emission capacity in electricity generation – whether nuclear or renewable energy – do not receive new entrant endowments, nor are there any endowments to be forfeited when existing capacity is shut down. Thus, whatever the effects of these provisions on the choice between new coal-fired and gas-fired capacity, they do provide some advantage to capacity that is CO_2-emitting in comparison with capacity that is zero-emitting. In addition, by offsetting the expected future cost of carbon for new investments and in creating some overcapacity, these provisions have the potential to slow down investment in lower-emitting new capacity and the turnover of capital stock.

All these theoretical effects are conditioned on whether the value of the allowance endowment to be received or forfeited is sufficient to make a difference in the eventual investment or closure decision. In the smooth and continuous world of standard economic theory, these provisions will always have some effect in creating overcapacity and distorting investment and closure decisions, but, in the more discrete world of actual decision-making, the question is always how these effects compare with and change the other factors that figure importantly in investment and closure decisions.

Can investment effects be detected?

Three years is too short a period and the observations too few to provide a sound empirical basis for assessing the effect of the new entrant and closure provisions on investment and closure decisions. An illustration of the problems confronting such an assessment can be provided by the electric utility sector, which is the sector most heavily impacted by the EU ETS and the sector about which the most information is available. This is also the sector in which the potential allocation effects would be the most important, since new power plants are relatively large emitters of CO_2.

Allocation rules and a CO_2 price are certainly not the only factors affecting decisions concerning investment and operations. Economic factors such as capital costs and expected fuel prices are paramount, and strategic considerations related to portfolio optimization, local siting and licensing requirements, and support mechanisms favouring some technologies are also important factors. Moreover, the first trading period of the EU ETS has seen large variations in power plant capital costs and fossil fuel prices, as well as electricity prices. Therefore, changes in investment plans that are contemporaneous with the start of the EU ETS may reflect factors other than CO_2 prices or the effects of allocation provisions.

Figure 4.9 presents a view of the evolution of planned investments in power plant capacity in the EU15, drawn from successive editions

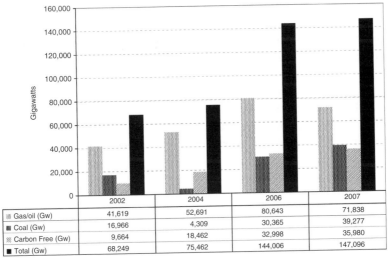

Figure 4.9 Planned investments in electricity generating capacity by type for the EU15, 2002–7
Source: Platt's PowerVision database (2002, 2004, 2006 and 2007 editions)

of the Platts PowerVision power plant database.[14] The years are chosen to reflect plans before the EU ETS was a reality (2002), on the eve of the system going into effect (2004) and for the last two years of the trial period (2006 and 2007). In order to focus on the effect of the EU ETS, capacity under construction is excluded, since it would already have been committed, and planned capacity additions are more reflective of expectations that would have included the effects of a CO_2 price and new entrant provisions.

Planned capacity additions are aggregated into three categories to reflect the main choices from a carbon standpoint: lower-emitting natural gas (and a very small amount of oil-fired capacity); higher-emitting coal; and carbon-free technologies, which include wind, bio-mass, solar, hydro, geothermal and nuclear. Several trends are clearly noticeable.

The total amount of planned capacity increased markedly in 2006 and 2007 (approximately 145 Gw) when compared with the pre-2005

[14] The Platts PowerVision database tracks planned investment by utilities and plants under construction. More information is available at www.platts.com/Analytic%20Solutions/POWERvision/index.xml.

plans (68 Gw in 2002 and 75 Gw in 2004). This increase must be placed in the context of the widely recognized need for investment in power generation capacity (between 20 and 40 Gw per year) to 2020 to replace ageing capacity. As a result, European countries have been entering a new investment cycle since the beginning of this decade, and the increase in construction plans from 2002 to 2007 is part of this cycle. In addition, the trial period years were characterized by relatively robust economic growth, which would have accelerated investment plans.

Other trends are clearly visible in the composition of the projected new capacity. Gas-fired plants account for 50 per cent or more of the new capacity in every year, although that share has been decreasing as coal and carbon-free capacity figure more largely in investment plans. The steady increase in carbon-free capacity (almost entirely wind) is not surprising given the carbon price, the higher cost of fossil fuels and the other incentives to increase the renewable energy capacity provided by many EU15 countries.

The surprising feature of the investment mix is the changing expectations concerning investment in new coal-fired capacity. In 2002, when the EU ETS was still only a proposal, approximately a quarter of the planned capacity additions were coal-fired. By 2004, when the ETS had been approved and a CO_2 price was an imminent reality, plans for additional coal-fired capacity dropped by three-quarters and constituted only 6 per cent of total planned capacity. In 2006 and 2007, however, plans for coal-fired capacity returned to being about a quarter of planned new capacity despite the CO_2 price. The explanation is, to a large extent, the unexpectedly high prices for natural gas and crude oil in these years. As shown by figure 4.10, the competitive position of natural gas in relation to coal worsened from 2004 to 2008.

In 2004 the highly efficient combined-cycle gas turbine (CCGT) form of gas-fired generation was closely competitive with coal and both were cheaper than the carbon-free alternatives. By 2008 CCGT applications were the most expensive form of new capacity, as calculated by this analysis. As can be readily seen by the section of the column representing fuel cost, the increase in natural gas prices more than offsets the advantage that carbon-pricing created for lower-emitting generating capacity.

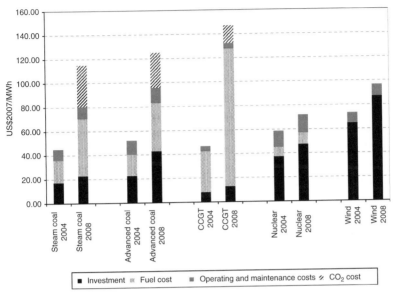

Figure 4.10 Evolution of European generating costs, 2004–8
Source: Authors' estimates

It is possible that the allocation rules gave a further impetus to the increase in plans for coal-fired generation, but, as illustrated by figure 4.10, changes in other factors – in this case fuel prices – are sufficient to explain the reversal of what seemed in 2004 to be the effect of CO_2 pricing on the choice of technology.

Concluding observations

The free allocation of allowances to affected installations inevitably raises questions concerning the effect that the allocation itself has as distinct from that of the associated CO_2 price. There can be no doubt that allocation has an effect, but this effect is not always what is argued or as important as asserted.

A first effect is almost trivial. How allowances are distributed to installations is a major determinant of the extent and direction of trading for compliance purposes. Although random factors and unexpected abatement account for some of the differences between allocations and emissions, the extent and direction of trading in the EU ETS was largely determined by the differentiation in the quantity of allowances available to different member states and to different sectors within member states.

Free allocation also has obvious financial effects. Installations facing a requirement to surrender allowances equal to emissions are better off financially if they receive allowances for free than if they do not. The significance of the value of the allocation in relation to other factors – and whether this value can be captured – can be questioned, but there should be no doubt about the existence of this financial effect.

A tougher question is whether free allocations have operational effects. Here a clear distinction must be made between the short and the long term: short-term effects impact production and emissions from existing capacity, while long-term effects influence decisions about investment in and abandonment of capacity. With respect to the short term, the available evidence supports the classical Coasian assumption that fixed lump-sum allocation has no effect on production or emissions. The competitive position of installations may be affected by the carbon price, but that is another matter, distinct both analytically and practically from the allocation effects.

With respect to the long term, the novel new entrant and closure provisions create a new allocation effect, which is to neutralize to some extent the effect of the CO_2 price on investment and to preserve the status quo as regards investment critieria. The first three years of the EU ETS cover too short a period of time and provide too little evidence to perform any rigorous test of whether the incentives to increase and to maintain capacity contained in the new entrant and closure provisions have had an effect. From what can be observed to date, however, it would appear that what holds for the financial effects applies here too: they exist but they are probably less important than other factors influencing investment and closure decisions.

The EU ETS has also given birth to a new issue, harmonization, based on the observed differences in installation-level allocations and a belief that a more harmonized allocation based on technical considerations would reduce, if not eliminate, them. These differences exist for a variety of reasons, ranging from unavoidable random variation in the factors determining production to the explicitly purposeful in the different treatment that may be given to different countries and sectors within a country. In addition, it seems at least possible that the heterogeneity among installations is such that no two are alike. While much is made of these differences, there is no basis for supposing that their effects extend to the operational aspects of production that determine the competitive position of firms. Moreover, the only way to eliminate the financial effect of these differences is to end free allocation.

5 | *Market development*

Introduction

In market-driven economies, giving parity of esteem to environmental endowments means introducing market prices for these assets that reflect their scarcity. Once the appropriate prices are in place, those who use these endowments have continuing and automatic incentives to use them parsimoniously and to find new and less expensive ways of doing so.

Thus, a critical issue in any cap-and-trade approach is whether this market price develops and whether participation in the market is broad enough to support the assumption of least-cost attainment of the environmental goal. These questions are particularly important when the facilities concerned are endowed with free allocations of allowances. In the case of free allocation, agents may not recognize the opportunity cost of using a freely allocated allowance to cover emissions and may simply consider their allocations as so many commands from the regulator to limit emissions to a specified level or to pay a required penalty. Facilities endowed with more allowances than their emissions would feel no need to abate and would simply surrender the required number of allowances and disregard the remainder. Facilities endowed with fewer allowances than needed to cover emissions would abate but only to the level of their allocation, or to the penalty price level, whichever would lead them to incur a lower marginal cost. In the absence of a market, this behaviour would be rational, but the marginal abatement cost (MAC) would vary and the environmental goal would not be achieved at least cost.

This chapter analyses how the market for emissions allowances developed during the first trading period of the EU ETS. The first section describes the borrowing and banking rules that conditioned the market during the first trading period. Section two describes the development of market institutions: the players, types of transactions, trading platforms and transaction volumes. Section three analyses the evolution of the CO_2 price as expressed by EUAs. The question in this section is whether pricing was rational: whether it could be explained in terms of the external conditions that were anticipated to influence emissions, abatement and therefore allowance prices. Section four addresses the extent of participation in this market using available data on the national origin of allowances surrendered for compliance. The final section concludes.

A self-contained first period with full intra-period 'banking' and 'borrowing'

The set of rules concerning the use of allowances within and between compliance periods was a defining feature of the EU ETS during the trial period. There is complete flexibility in the use of EUAs within a given multi-year compliance period. EUAs are issued for a given compliance period, and once placed in accounts they can be used for meeting annual compliance requirements for any year in the period. Not all the period's allowances are available to installations at the beginning of a compliance period, however. In its guidance for the preparation of first-period national allocation plans, the Commission recommended that first-period allowances be allocated in equal annual instalments, and all countries except Denmark chose to do this.[1] Still within a given trading period, installations are able to save, or 'bank', allowances for use in future years.[2] EUAs that were placed in accounts for 2005 and 2006 and that were not used for compliance in those two years could be 'banked' for use in 2006 and 2007. Similarly, installations were in fact able to engage in limited borrowing due to the timing of the allowance issuance and surrender timeline, as illustrated in figure 5.1.

The timeline shows that member states must issue allowances to installation accounts before 28 February, that installations must submit verified reports for the preceding year's emissions by 31 March and that they must then surrender allowances equal to these emissions

[1] Denmark front-loaded the annual allotment by placing 40 per cent of the EUAs allocated to installations for the period in their accounts in 2005 and 30 per cent in each of 2006 and 2007.
[2] From a legal standpoint, the terms 'banking' and 'borrowing' have no meaning within a compliance period in the EU ETS; they refer instead to the transfer of allowances between compliance periods.

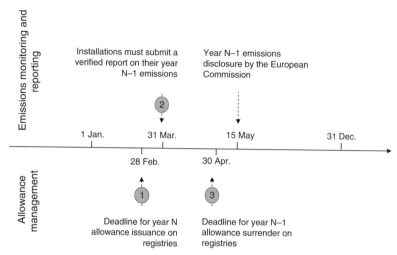

Figure 5.1 The EU ETS timeline: emissions reporting, allowance delivery and allowance surrender
Source: Authors

by 30 April. As a consequence of the overlap between the issuance and surrender dates, installations have the allowance issuance for two years in their accounts prior to surrender for the past year's emissions. Thus, an installation that was short in the previous year can 'borrow' from its allocation for the following year.

While complete flexibility in the use of issued allowances obtains within a compliance period, the rules concerning the use of allowances between compliance periods are more complicated. The EU ETS Directive prohibits any borrowing from one period for use in another. The rules concerning inter-period banking are more flexible. The directive mandates that banking be allowed between the second and subsequent trading periods, but banking between the first and second periods is left to the discretion of member states. All member states except France and Poland chose to prohibit banking from the first to the second period so as not to complicate compliance with their Kyoto Protocol obligations from 2008 to 2012.[3] In its 2006 guidelines for

---

[3] Since EUAs are not recognized as credits under the Kyoto Protocol, any first-period EUAs carried over and used in the second period would have meant either that non-ETS installations would have been required to reduce more or that the government would have had to purchase Kyoto credits to offset the banked first-period EUAs.

second-period NAPs, however, the European Commission required that any allowances banked from period 1 to period 2 be deducted from the period 2 allocation. This requirement led France and Poland formally to remove the possibility of banking, and the first period became completely self-contained.

The inability to bank or borrow allowances between the first and second trading periods had definite implications for the pricing of EUAs. In the absence of any mechanism for equating first- and second-period prices, each period's EUAs became separate goods with prices that would have no necessary relation to the other. Moreover, a binary end-of-period outcome was guaranteed for the first period. A surplus of allowances in the first period implied a zero end-of-period price as the certainty of that outcome was revealed. Conversely, a shortage implied an end-of-period price equal to the penalty for non-compliance, €40/tonne, plus the price of the second-period EUA that would be taken from the next year's allowance issuance – the cost incurred by installations unable to acquire allowances to cover their emissions.

Since the outcome for the first period would not be known initially, EUA prices could be expected to evolve as the passage of time resolved various uncertainties or other events revealed information to market participants concerning the likely outcome. As explained by Ellerman and Parsons (2006), the independent second-period price could be used in conjunction with the first-period price to calculate the market's estimate of the probability that the first period would be long, using the following formula:

$$\text{Probability (surplus)} = 1 - \frac{\text{First-period price}}{\text{Second-period price} + €40 \text{ penalty}}$$

In the absence of any information, an initial estimate of the probability of a surplus would have been 50 per cent – essentially the same as a coin toss. As observed in figure 5.2, from the time that a second-period price was first quoted in late September 2005, the probability of a surplus, as implied by EUA market prices, was slightly higher, but not by much. Initially it was around 65 per cent, but it decreased to 55 per cent just prior to the first release of information on verified emissions, in late April 2006. This data release caused a marked adjustment of expectations, which raised the implied probability of a

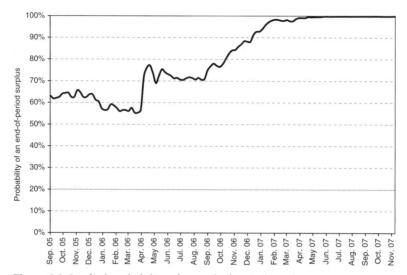

Figure 5.2 Implied probability of an end-of-period surplus
Source: Derived from Point Carbon News, *Carbon Market Europe* data

surplus to between 70 and 80 per cent, where it remained for several months before beginning a steady increase to 100 per cent, as more time passed and the winter of 2006/7 proved warmer than usual. The release of verified emissions data for 2006 in May 2007 – that is, for the second third of the total demand for the trial period – confirmed that the period would be in surplus, and the probability remained virtually at 100 per cent for the last year of the first compliance period.

The self-contained first period also implied higher volatility for first-period prices and higher volatility as the period came to an end. When banking and borrowing are possible over an infinite horizon, the price effect of temporary deviations from expected outcomes, such as those caused by weather, will be spread over the entire banking or borrowing horizon. For instance, the price impact of higher than expected emissions during a colder than usual winter would be offset by the expected warmer than normal winters in future years. The shorter the horizon the greater the impact that a single event would have on current prices, since the probability of a future offsetting event is lower. Consequently, the first period's truncated horizon implied greater volatility in first-period prices.

Institutional development

Markets can take many different forms, but their institutional development can be described in terms of the trading parties involved, the types of transactions or trading media that develop, the specific products that are exchanged and the volume of transactions.

The players in the EUA market

There are two types of participants in allowance markets: the compliance players, or 'naturals', who have a regulatory obligation to surrender allowances; and the financial intermediaries, who facilitate the compliance trades made by regulated entities but who have no compliance obligations themselves. For the latter group, allowances have no value other than as a means to earn income by providing services – facilitating trades or managing risk – to the first group.

The real compliance actors: firms

While registry data are available only on an installation-by-installation basis, many installations are owned by the same firm. The limited ownership information available in the registries can be combined with other publicly available data to group installations according to the firms that own them. Trotignon and Delbosc (2008) group this data for more than 6,300 installations that accounted for 94 per cent of the EUAs allocated over period 1. The authors define ownership as a 50 per cent or greater share in an installation, affiliate or subsidiary.

As observed in figure 5.3, the firm with the most allowances (RWE, an electric utility in Germany) received 6 per cent of the total allocation. The ten companies with the largest allowance allocations accounted for 33 per cent of the allocation total; 74 per cent of the total allowance allocation was distributed among 100 firms.

When allowances are aggregated from the level of installations to that of firms, the allowance allocation appears more concentrated. In figure 5.4, the grey line shows allowance concentration among installations; the black line shows allowance concentration after allowances are aggregated at the level of the firms that own the individual installations. The increase in concentration occurs because many of the largest installations, typically in the power and iron/steel sectors, are owned by the same company.

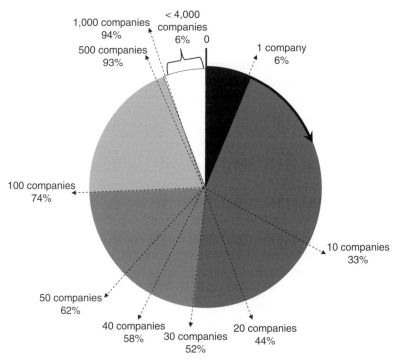

Figure 5.3 Allowance allocation to firms in period 1
Source: Trotignon and Delbosc (2008)

While there is a high degree of concentration at the firm level, an analysis using the Herfindahl–Hirschman Index (HHI) shows that it does not pose any threat to market power. This index is calculated by squaring the market share of each competing firm (expressed as a percentage) and then summing the resulting numbers.[4] The twenty firms receiving the largest allowance allocations for the first trading period, and accounting for 44 per cent of the EU-wide cap, are listed in table 5.1, along with relevant allocation and emission data for these firms.[5] Because the primary determinant of EUA market power is uncertain – it

[4] For example, for a market consisting of five firms with shares of 30, 30, 20, 10 and 10 per cent, the HHI is 2,400 ($30^2 + 30^2 + 20^2 + 10^2 + 10^2 = 2,400$).
[5] The firms with the largest allowance shares are a German electric utility, RWE, with 6.37 per cent of allocated allowances; Endesa, a Spanish electric utility, with 7.22 per cent of the gross deficit among short installations; and Arcelor-Mittal, with 7.62 per cent of the gross surplus at long installations. The share of the twentieth firm was 0.91 per cent of the total.

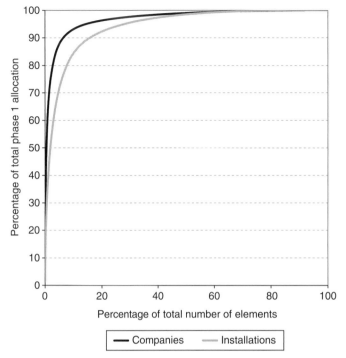

Figure 5.4 Effect of company aggregation on allocation concentration in period 1
Source: Trotignon and Delbosc (2008)

could lie in the size of the original allowance allocation, a firm's allowance surplus or its allowance deficit – HHI indices were calculated for each. All three indices revealed a low degree of concentration in the EUA market: 136, 94 and 228 respectively (Alberola 2008).[6]

Financial intermediaries

A salient feature of the EU ETS is the high degree of participation by financial intermediaries that have facilitated trading among affected

---

[6] Markets with an HHI greater than 1,800 points are considered to be concentrated and those with values between 1,000 and 1,800 points are considered to be moderately so. See 'The Herfindahl–Hirschman index' on the United States Department of Justice website, at www.usdoj.gov/atr/public/testimony/hhi.htm (accessed 17 February 2009).

Table **5.1** *Number of installations and allowance positions for the twenty firms with the largest allowance allocations in period 1*

Firm	Approximate number of installations	Total period 1 allocation (Mt)	Total period 1 emissions (Mt)	Period 1 net position (Mt)
RWE	74	397.7	427.2	−29.5
Vattenfall	87	254.7	244.3	10.4
Arcelor-Mittal	59	242.1	182.3	59.7
E-ON	207	230.3	256.1	−25.8
Endesa	40	173.3	207.6	−34.3
Public Power Corp. SA	29	156.2	156.0	0.2
Enel	45	154.5	182.4	−27.9
EDF	73	153.8	166.3	−12.5
BOT	3	153.3	150.5	2.8
CEZ Group	19	126.7	119.7	7.0
Electrabel (Suez)	50	93.8	110.4	−16.6
Corus Group	12	91.9	79.7	12.2
Total	33	72.8	65.9	6.9
Shell	44	72.4	64.4	8.0
Evonik New Energies GmbH	57	70.7	77.1	−6.4
Eni Group	63	68.4	70.7	−2.3
Lafarge	48	66.7	64.0	2.7
PKE SA	10	63.5	61.0	2.5
DONG Energy	35	58.0	61.4	−3.4
Dalkia	249	57.0	43.8	13.2

Source: Derived from CITL data.

installations and developed derivative products, such as futures, options and swaps, to help affected firms manage price risk. While trading for compliance purposes among affected firms is the fundamental underpinning of the scheme, many transactions are motivated by purely financial considerations. The distinguishing characteristic of these transactions is that they do not necessarily involve an actual transfer of allowances. For instance, a forward contract that has been purchased as a hedge may be, and often is, sold before its maturity if the risk that is being hedged has disappeared by that time.

The role of financial intermediaries is particularly important for small and medium-sized companies and for individual installations that do not have the internal capacity to understand and analyse the functioning of the carbon market. By facilitating the access of more participants to the markets and by offering risk management services, financial intermediaries increase the liquidity of the market and contribute to the emergence of a reliable price signal.

Financial intermediaries can be classified in two groups: brokers and traders. Brokers are involved in pure intermediation services. They facilitate market access for firms for which direct participation would be too time-consuming and inefficient. Brokers act on behalf of their clients, finding counterparties, negotiating deals and executing orders. They typically work on the over-the-counter (OTC) market, but they may also use an exchange to execute an agreed-upon trade. Distinguishing characteristics of brokers are that they do not buy and sell allowances on their own account and that their income comes from commissions on the services that they provide, often expressed as the spread between the negotiated purchase and sale prices. In the carbon market, the main brokers are either specialized subsidiaries of large brokerage houses operating in other financial markets, subsidiaries of investment banks that include carbon in their service offers, or specialized carbon market intermediaries.

Traders buy and sell allowances with their own funds, hoping to make a profit on the difference between purchases and sales. They improve market liquidity by providing the immediate counterparty to any entity wishing to buy or sell. Many banks have opened carbon desks that trade on their own accounts and also provide other related services to their clients. Some companies with ETS installations, mostly in the power and refining sectors, have developed carbon-trading activities, often as part of their existing trading activities in electricity and energy commodities. EDF trading, Total trading and Shell trading are examples. These trading entities are often also involved in the management of their own installations' accounts, and may also provide the same services for other companies. In this case, they perform the same role as pure financial intermediaries. Trading may also be conducted by subsidiaries of brokerage companies that wish to diversify their activities.

Types of transactions

Three types of transactions and trading platforms have emerged in the EUA market: bilateral trades, over-the-counter trading and organized exchanges. Their sequential development has marked the increasing maturity of the market.

Bilateral transactions

Bilateral transactions are carried out directly between two parties and without the use of intermediaries. These types of trades are typically characterized by a high degree of market knowledge and communication between the trading parties. Bilateral transactions tend to be large in size, and their prices are not disclosed. At the beginning of the EUA market bilateral trades were the most frequent transactions, and they have remained common between major energy desks. An increasing number of bilateral trades are now concluded through 'clearing' services offered by exchanges, however: buyers and sellers indicate to the exchange the volume and value of the agreed-upon transaction, and the exchange then executes the trade. In addition to convenience, this solution allows the trading parties to benefit from the guarantees offered by the exchange in the case of default by either party.

Over-the-counter transactions

OTC transactions are carried out by intermediaries that facilitate trading between various entities. The chief distinction between an OTC transaction and a bilateral transaction is that a party wishing to buy or sell on the OTC market does not have to find a counterparty and negotiate the deal. The party wishing to trade simply contacts the intermediary, and the latter either undertakes the task of finding a counterparty (the role of a broker) or buys or sells on its own account (the role of a trader). In OTC transactions, counterparty risk – the possibility that the opposite side of the deal will not deliver – is present. OTC trades appeared early in the EUA market, and since the summer of 2005 they have represented more than 70 per cent of all EUA transactions.

The details of an OTC transaction – the negotiated price and traded volumes – are not available to other market participants. Some exchanges and brokers have participated in establishing OTC price transparency, however. The European Energy Exchange (EEX) provided an early index of forward carbon prices, the European Carbon Index.[7] Later, the primary provider of comprehensive information on OTC trades became the news and analysis group Point Carbon, which now competes with other traditional financial information providers, including Reuters. In addition, other OTC carbon indexes have been developed, including that developed by the London Energy Brokers' Association (LEBA).[8]

Transactions on organized exchanges

A new phenomenon associated with the EU ETS, absent in earlier emissions trading systems, is the appearance by mid-2005 of organized exchanges dealing in emissions allowances. Organized exchanges offer continuous trading hours and eliminate the counterparty risks for the buying and selling entities. Five exchanges have developed trading activities for EUAs, and they are listed in table 5.2. The majority of these exchanges also clear transactions that have been agreed upon bilaterally or through a broker.

Exchanges have developed three main trading services. First, they have established electronic platforms through which buyers and sellers can enter their orders and execute trades anonymously. Second, they execute OTC and bilateral transactions through a clearing process, which assures confirmation, settlement and delivery in a prompt and efficient manner. Finally, they have established a block trade facility, which enables large EUA transactions to take place off the exchange, usually between two very sophisticated parties. Unlike smaller transactions, orders for block trades do not have to be reported to the market, so long as they meet or exceed a minimum volume threshold.

---

[7] Published on each trading day from 25 October 2004 to 30 November 2005, the European Carbon Index was a volume-weighted average price of the OTC forward-trading activities with delivery before 30 April 2006.

[8] Formed in 2003, LEBA represents the brokers in the wholesale OTC market and the exchange for liberalized European energy markets.

Table 5.2 *Carbon credit exchanges operating during period 1*

		ECX	BlueNext	NordPool	EEX/Eurex	EXAA
Country		United Kingdom	France	Norway	Germany	Austria
City		London	Paris	Oslo	Leipzig	Vienna
Contracts available from	EUA spot	NA	24 Jun. 05	24 Oct. 05	9 Mar. 05	28 Jun. 05
	EUA futures	22 Apr. 05	21 Apr. 08	11 Feb. 05	4 Oct. 05	NA
	EUA options	13 Oct. 06	NA	NA	14 Apr. 08	NA
	CER futures	14 Mar. 08	2 Jun. 08	NA	6 Feb. 08	NA
	CER options	13 May 08	NA	NA	NA	NA
OTC clearing		Yes	Yes	Yes	Yes	No
Trading model		Continuous	Continuous	Continuous	Fixing	Fixing
Trading days		From Monday to Friday	From Monday to Friday	From Monday to Friday	From Monday to Friday	Fixing Tuesday
Hours		7:00–17:00	8:00–17:00	8:00–15:30	9:00–17:30	14:00
Minimum contract size		1,000 t	1,000 t	1,000 t	1 t	1 t
Registry		Environmental Agency	Caisse des Dépôts (Seringas)	Dutch emission authority (NEa)	DEHst (German emissions trading authority)	Emission Certificate Registry Austria (ECRA)
Clearing		London Clearing House (LCH. Clearnet)	London Clearing House (LCH. Clearnet)	NordPool Clearing ASA	Eurex Clearing AG	APCS (Austrian Power Clearing and Settlement AG)
Delivery		Day + 3	Trading day	Day + 3	Day + 2	Day + 1
Members		91	76	108	120	22

Source: Compiled from exchange websites as of June 2008.

Trading products

EUA contracts on exchanges may take many different forms, including spot contracts, futures, options and swaps with different delivery dates. At the end of the first trading period this same range of contract types was developed for a new asset: the certified emission reduction credit. CER credits are generated through emission reduction projects undertaken as part of the Clean Development Mechanism established by the Kyoto Protocol. These products and their relation to the EUA market are discussed in more detail in chapter 9.

Cash or spot contracts

Cash or spot contracts are executed for trades that are physically delivered between twenty-four and forty-eight hours after they are negotiated. The spot market enables producers that have or expect to have surplus allowances to turn their unused EUAs into cash immediately, while allowing those that expect emissions to exceed their allocation to buy allowances at any time prior to the annual surrender dates. The first spot contracts for period 1 allowances were executed in early 2005, when EUAs were first placed in registry accounts, and continued until the end of the 2007 compliance process in April 2008.

Forward or futures contracts

Forward and futures contracts are concluded for a given future delivery date, volume and price. 'Forward' contracts are concluded bilaterally. 'Futures' contracts are offered by marketplaces in standardized conditions that allow daily trading. The convention has developed of making annual EUA futures contracts deliverable in December each year; thus, the contracts are typically called Dec. 05, Dec. 06, etc.

Forward and futures contracts offer firms an alternative to the spot market and give them the opportunity to lock in future prices. For instance, a firm with excess allowances could either sell those allowances immediately in the spot market or contract in the forward market to deliver them at a later December maturity. A firm would do one or the other depending on factors including the prices offered in the spot and forward markets and the interest that could be earned on the proceeds from an immediate sale. On the other side of the market, a firm that anticipates it will need additional allowances for a current or future compliance year would make a similar calculation, purchasing spot or futures contracts as needed.

Forward and futures contracts are particularly valuable for locking in profits on forward sales of products that create carbon liabilities. For example, electric utilities often contract to deliver a certain amount of power in the future at a specified price. In order to protect its expected profit, a power company uses futures to hedge the risk of fluctuations in the price of allowances and fuel between the time the contract (and price) is agreed and when the power is to be delivered. For instance, if the price of the power is 100, of which 10 is profit, and the electricity price assumes a CO_2 cost equal to the current EUA price of 20, the power company can protect itself against future fluctuations in the price of EUAs either by purchasing current spot EUAs and holding them or by contracting for future EUA delivery in the forward market, typically at a similar price with a slight mark-up for the interest cost. In doing so, the company protects itself from having to buy more expensive EUAs in the future. If the company were not to take these steps and decided to wait until the power is delivered, a future price of 30 would eliminate the company's expected profit. The company would also give up the possibility of doubling its profit should the EUA price fall to 10. Electric utilities typically undertake these hedging operations because, apart from their trading desks, they regard themselves as generators and sellers of power and not speculators on allowance or fuel price movements.

More exotic contracts: swaps and options

The growing maturity of the EUA market is reflected in the growing importance of products that help companies manage price risk, including swaps and options. Swaps, in which one asset is substituted for another, are designed to enable companies to profit from price differences between contracts, such as those between spot and near-futures contracts or between two futures contracts with different maturity dates. As is discussed in more detail later in chapter 9, swaps between EUAs and CERs first appeared in 2007, and they have become a very popular way to exploit the price difference between period 2 allowances and CERs, since both assets may be used for compliance in period 2.

Options are contracts drawn up between two parties whereby one grants to the other the right, but not the obligation, to buy an allowance (call option) or to sell an allowance (put option) at a specified price plus an associated premium. EUA option contracts satisfy the

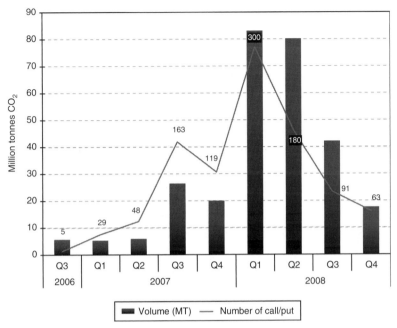

Figure 5.5 The development of EUA options trading
Source: Derived from ECX data

need to transfer the risk of financial exposure to those willing to accept it. For example, a firm that is not sure of its allowance needs for the year, or one that does not want to commit to purchasing allowances it may not need in the future, can buy a call option that will give it the ability to purchase allowances at a set strike price at a future date. The buyer is protected from having to pay more than the agreed price plus the option premium, while the seller assumes the risk of having to deliver allowances at what might be a below-market price at the time of delivery. By the same token, because buying this option does not obligate a buyer to take delivery, the buyer preserves the option to purchase allowances at a lower price on the market should the EUA price fall below the option's strike price. In this case, the buyer would bear the cost of the premium paid for the option, and the seller would gain the premium in return for having borne the risk of having to deliver allowances at a below-market price.

As shown in figure 5.5, the volume of option trading has grown since 2006 to a trading volume peak of 300 Mt in the first quarter of

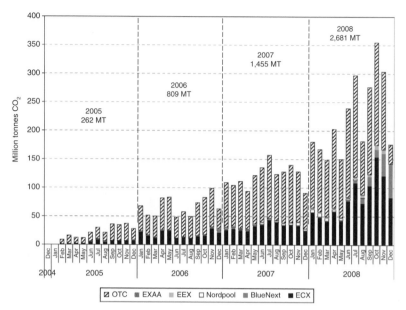

Figure 5.6 EUA trading: transaction volumes by platform
Source: Derived from Point Carbon data and exchange websites

2008. The economic crisis in 2008 led to a trading slowdown; as of the last quarter of 2008, option trading volume had declined to 63 Mt.

Transaction volumes

The volume of transactions on the EUA market has increased steadily since the inception of the EU ETS. Some bilateral forward transactions took place before 2005, but more substantial trading got under way only in that year, once EUAs had been placed in registry accounts. As is shown in figure 5.6, the volume of EUA trading increased four- to fivefold from the first to the last quarter of 2005, more than tripled between 2005 and 2006, increased another 75 per cent from 2006 to 2007 and rose by a further 84 per cent from 2007 to the end of 2008.

Another sign of the growing maturity of the market is the increasing importance of exchanges: they began trading in the first half of 2005 and were responsible for about one-third of transactions in early 2008. In addition, due to their low counterparty risk, exchanges benefited from the economic crisis at the end of 2008: during the last quarter of that year more than a half of EUA transactions were concluded through exchanges.

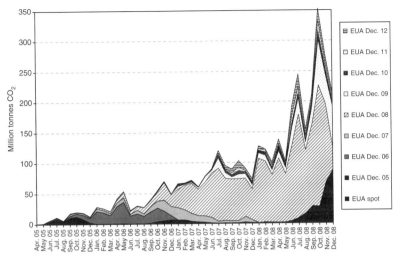

Figure 5.7 Trading in EUA futures: contract volumes during period 1 and period 2
Source: Derived from ECX, EEX and BlueNext data

Figure 5.7 presents the types and volumes of products traded on exchanges from mid-2005 to mid-2008.

The volume of spot transactions is barely visible until late 2008. As indicated by the barely perceptible, darkest shading, spot trading increased somewhat in late 2006 and early 2007, but otherwise the first period was dominated by trading in futures. Moreover, the most traded futures contract in any given year is the one for that year. Thus, in 2005 the bulk of the trading concerned the December 2005 contract, and for the most part in 2006 trades were for the December 2006 contract. Trading in the December 2007 contract began almost at the outset of the market and became more important in the latter half of 2006 and in 2007. It was also during late 2006 that market attention shifted to the second trading period, and the vast majority of transactions in 2007 were for the December 2008 contract.

Figure 5.7 also shows that most of the trading activity concerning first-period contracts occurred during 2006. The decline in trades for first-period products during 2007 suggests that short installations had provided for much of their expected needs prior to 2007 and that the demand for hedging was also less. The increase of spot transactions in late 2006 and early 2007 also provided a cheap alternative.

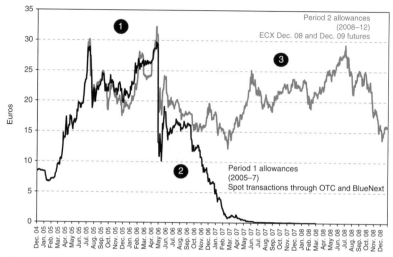

Figure 5.8 Evolution of EUA prices, 2005–8
Source: Updated from Alberola (2008)

EUA price development

The essential features of EUA price development can be analysed by examining the two products traded on the market in period 1: period 1 spot contracts and period 2 contracts with December 2008 maturities. Although most of the first-period trading took place in futures, their prices were always close to the current spot price, and the latter provides a continuous indicator throughout the first period. By definition, the only second-period contracts were futures, and the earliest and most frequently traded one was the Dec. 08 maturity. Following Alberola, Chevallier and Chèze (2008), the evolution of EUA pricing can be usefully divided into the three stages shown in figure 5.8.

Great uncertainty in the initial stage (January 2005–April 2006)

The first period of price development was characterized by significant uncertainty concerning the demand for allowances. At the launch of the EU ETS, on 1 January 2005, EUAs began trading at €8, but during the next six months they rose in price to over €20 and stayed there through April 2006, with surges to and slightly above €30. During this stage first- and second-period prices moved in a similar fashion, but second-period prices generally remained lower than first-period prices. Given the limitations on banking and borrowing between the two periods, this relationship indicated that the first period was expected to be shorter than the second period.

Another important factor during this initial stage was the imbalance in market participation between firms that were short and those that were long. EU15 power companies, which were short and therefore allowance buyers, were more present in the market during this stage than were the owners of installations that were potential sellers. The reasons for this imbalance are twofold. First, registry set-up was delayed in some eastern European countries in which significant surpluses existed. For instance, the registry of Poland, a member state with one of the largest allowance surpluses, was not operational until July 2006. As a consequence, many long installations that had surpluses, or expected to have them, were not able to trade.

The second reason for the imbalance of buyers and sellers was the asymmetry that always exists between long and short installations. Installations with long positions are under no compulsion to sell – unlike companies with short positions, which must acquire allowances to cover their emissions, unless they are able and willing to borrow from the next year's allocation. Companies with long positions can take a wait-and-see attitude, and many industrial firms appear to have done so during this stage, when experience was being gained and price uncertainties were high. For industrial firms in general, the CO_2 price did not have as large an effect on the variable cost of their final output as it did for power companies, and this circumstance may have caused many potential industrial sellers to take a much more passive attitude towards market participation in this first stage of the market.

The information shock and the calibration of expectations (April 2006–October 2006)

The second stage of the EUA market was ushered in with the release of information in late April 2006 indicating that emissions had been lower than expected in 2005. This was the first information that enabled market participants to calibrate their expectations of allowance demand with the actual emissions levels of the installations included in the EU ETS.[9] As market participants recognized that the

[9] Various estimates of emissions were made in the allocation process, but the data were poor and the process rushed, as explained in chapter 3.

allowance market would be longer than expected, prices for both first- and second-period allowances dropped dramatically. During the course of just one week the first-period price fell by 50 per cent and the second-period price fell by 33 per cent. First- and second-period prices were both affected because the uncertainty about the magnitude of the emissions covered by the ETS concerned both periods.

First- and second-period prices continued to track each other during this second stage of price development, but the relationship between the two prices reversed. The second-period price rose above the first-period price, because expectations had shifted concerning the relative shortage of allowances in the two periods. A shortage in the first period was considered less likely (but still possible, as evidenced by a still significant first-period price), and it became reasonable to assume that the first-period emissions cap would be less constraining than the second-period cap, even though the second-period cap was not yet known.

The total disconnection between first- and second-period prices (October 2006 onwards)

The third and final stage of EUA pricing during the first trading period was characterized by a complete separation between the prices of first- and second-period allowances. In October 2006 first-period EUA prices began a steady, six-month-long decline as the end of the first period approached and it became evident that weather, fuel prices and other conditions would not create an increased demand for allowances during 2007. In February 2007 first-period EUA prices fell to under €1, and they ended the year at €0.02. In contrast, the prices for second-period EUAs fluctuated around €15 before rising to a range of €20 to €25, where they remained for about a year until late 2008, when the second-period EUA price returned to €15 in response to the economic downturn.

A comment on second-period pricing

Period 2 allowance pricing contrasts markedly with the pricing for period 1 allowances. While first- and second-period prices fluctuated in a similar manner during the first two pricing stages of the first trading period, second-period prices never sank to zero and remained between €13 and €30 until the end of 2008. The separation between period 1 and period 2 EUA prices from October 2006 onwards was driven mostly by the inability to bank or borrow between the first and second trading periods.

An important determinant of the extent of separation in prices was the availability of information about the level of the second-period emissions cap. When second-period EUAs first began to trade, in the autumn of 2005, there was no information about the level of the second-period cap. All that could be presumed was that the cap would be at least equal to the first-period cap, and probably lower. The Commission's first guidance concerning the second-period cap, issued in December 2005, confirmed the expectation that the cap would be lower in the second period than in the first by stating that the target would be 6 per cent lower (European Commission 2005c).

The first release of verified emissions data, four months later, dramatically changed expectations concerning the stringency of the first-period cap and raised the question of whether a second-period cap that was 6 per cent lower than that of the first period would be constraining enough. The revised guidance, issued in November 2006, clarified that the second-period cap would indeed be lower by establishing 2005 verified emissions, which were almost 7 per cent below the first-period cap, as the point of reference for cap-setting (European Commission 2006b). This guidance created a brief jump in the second-period EUA price at the end of 2006. The steady price increase to above €20 began only when the European Council announced in March 2007 that EU-wide emissions would be reduced to 20 per cent below 1990 levels by 2020. Although the Council's announcement of the 2020 target did not directly address the level of the second-period cap, the greater scarcity it implied for the post-2012 period, coupled with the ability of installations to bank allowances from the second period onwards, drove demand for period 2 allowances up, along with allowance prices.

Carbon price drivers

As in any other commodity market, EUA prices are driven by the expected balance between supply and demand. The first-period price has been the object of several published papers seeking to determine the main drivers of the EUA price and its effect on other

prices: Mansanet-Bataller, Pardo and Valor (2007), Alberola, Chevallier and Chèze (2008), Bunn and Fezzi (2007) and Alberola and
Chevallier (2009). Generally, these papers have found that EUA prices
have responded to: (1) data releases and regulatory decisions;
(2) energy prices; and (3) weather conditions.

Data releases and regulatory influences

As already noted, the release of data at variance with expectations
can have a significant effect on prices. Similarly, political decisions
concerning the stringency of the current or future EU-wide emissions
cap may impact EUA prices, as can be observed in the increase in
second-period prices during 2007. In addition, decisions and announcements by regulators – within both the member states and
the European Commission – have had effects on market players'
behaviour. Two papers, those by Alberola, Chevallier and Chèze
(2008) and Alberola and Chevallier (2009), focus on these factors.
Both confirm the importance of the late April 2006 release of data in
creating a 'structural break' in EUA pricing. The second paper also
finds that several regulatory announcements concerning cap levels
and banking have had statistically significant effects on first-period
EUA prices.

Energy prices

Energy prices are important short-term drivers of EUA demand, due
to the ability to shift the supply of electricity between natural-gas-
fired and coal-fired power plants. For any given pair of power plants
on a network, the marginal cost of fuel-switching from higher-carbon
energy sources (such as coal) to lower-carbon sources (such as natural
gas) is determined by the prices paid for fuel used in generation and
the efficiency with which each of the competing power plants con-
verts fuel into electricity. Power plant efficiencies are not observed,
but fuel prices are, and all researchers have found that fluctuations
in energy prices had a significant effect on EUA prices during the
trial period.

The first paper published on EUA prices, by Mansanet-Bataller,
Pardo and Valor (2007), examined 2005 data alone, finding that
EUA prices in the first year of the EU ETS responded (with a lag) to
changes in crude oil and natural gas prices, as well as to extreme

variations in temperature. This paper was important in empirically establishing that factors that would be expected to influence CO_2 prices were indeed doing so at a time when there was some doubt about the rationality of EUA pricing. Alberola, Chevallier and Chèze (2008) and Alberola and Chevallier (2009) confirm the significance of energy prices using a longer time series (to April 2007) and a somewhat different formulation for the energy price variables. Bunn and Fezzi (2007) used a structural, co-integrated vector autoregressive model to show that carbon prices are essentially exogenous in the United Kingdom and that they have a significant influence on both natural gas and electricity prices in the United Kingdom. As established by previous research, they also find that gas prices affect CO_2 prices, and they observe that an indirect effect of the EU ETS has been to strengthen the effect of natural gas price changes on electricity prices.

Weather conditions

EUA prices have also been influenced by unexpected variations in temperature, rainfall and wind through their effect on energy demand and supply. Cold winter weather, for example, increases the need for heating by electricity or fuel, whereas warm summer weather leads to higher electricity demand for cooling. Warm summer weather also heats the water sources used to cool nuclear power plants, and thus reduces the amount of power that can be generated from nuclear sources. Rainfall, wind speeds and sunshine hours affect the share of power that can be generated through carbon-free sources, including hydropower, wind and solar.

Both Mansanet-Bataller, Pardo and Valor (2007) and Alberola, Chevallier and Chèze (2008) find that unseasonable temperatures have had an effect on first-period EUA pricing. During the winter of 2005/6 lower than average temperatures increased energy demand and had a positive impact on EUA prices, as did higher than average temperatures during the summer of 2006. Conversely, higher than average temperatures during the winter of 2006/7 resulted in a lower energy demand than anticipated and contributed to the fall in the first-period price that was occurring at this time. The variations in European temperature that had these effects are illustrated in figure 5.9.

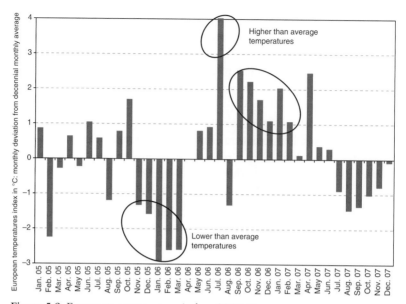

Figure 5.9 European temperature index, 2005–7
Source: Derived from Mission Climat of the Caisse des Dépôts data

The relationship between EUAs of different maturities

Another test of the rationality of markets is the relationship between
the prices of the same commodity that is to be delivered at different
times. In a mature market, these relationships should reflect the characteristics of the commodity being traded. Emission allowances have
some unique characteristics. Unlike commodities such as oil or grain,
they incur neither storage costs nor transport costs. Like financial
assets, allowances are mere bookkeeping entries that can be electron-
ically transferred instantly and at very low cost. Furthermore, they are
not needed for compliance until some time after the emissions creating
the compliance obligation have occurred.

As on financial asset and commodity markets, players on the EUA
market are able to engage in intertemporal arbitrage by simultaneously
buying and selling EUAs of differing maturities in the spot and forward
markets. As a result, the prices for EUAs being delivered at various
dates would be expected to differ only by the risk-free interest rate plus
any premium for systemic risk associated with the returns on EUAs held
as assets. For example, if the allowance price of a futures contract is
lower than the current spot price plus the cost of carry (the interest

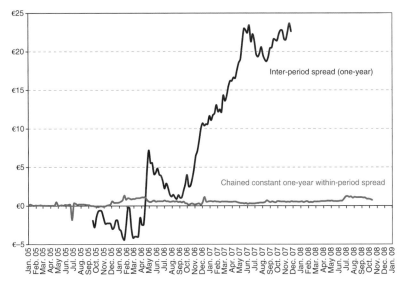

Figure 5.10 Within-period and inter-period EUA spreads, 2005–8
Source: Derived from ECX data

forgone by purchasing an allowance and holding for some period), market participants can be expected to buy futures and to sell spot contracts until the future price is equal to the spot price plus the cost of carry, and vice versa if the price relationship is reversed.

The following relationship expresses the equilibrium condition between the cost of carry, future and spot prices:

$$S_t = F_T e^{-r(T-t)}$$

with S_t equal to the spot price at time $t = \{0, 1, 2, \ldots T{-}1\}$, $T = \{1, 2\}$ representing contracts with different future delivery dates, F_T equal to the future price of a contract with delivery at time T, and r equal to the interest rate (Working 1949; Brennan 1958). This condition states that the only cost of buying an allowance (or any other similar asset) at time t and delivering it at time T is the forgone interest.

The time relationships between EUAs of various maturities demonstrate that the rules governing the intertemporal use of allowances matter. Figure 5.10 displays two differences in EUA pricing according to the time of delivery.

The relatively stable line gives the price premium for within-period deliveries that are one year apart. For example, in calendar year 2005 the premium is the price difference between the December 2006 and the December 2005 contracts, and in 2006 the premium is the price difference between the December 2007 and the December 2006 deliveries. In 2007 the nearest within-period deliveries were those for December 2009 against December 2008, and, accordingly, the price premium between those contracts is shown for the years 2007 and 2008. Note that the within-period price premium is nearly always positive, as would be expected given a positive risk-free interest rate and commodities that are essentially the same.

The highly variable price relationship between contracts from different periods (such as that between the December 2007 and December 2008 maturities) shows that period 1 and period 2 allowances are not perfectly substitutable, however, and, indeed, that they are essentially different goods. Apart from brief periods, the inter-period premium was always either significantly lower (until April 2006) or significantly higher (from April 2006 onwards). The rising premium between contracts for first- and second-period allowances after April 2006 is a clear indication of the effectiveness of the rules that prevented banking between the periods. Had it been possible to use first-period allowances for compliance during the second period, this premium would have been similar to the within-period one-year premium.

Another reflection of the differing rules governing the intertemporal use of EUAs is the contrasting effect of the release of verified emissions data in late April 2006 on the within-period and between-period spreads. In the space of a month the between-period spread experienced a change of almost €10, from a discount of €2.45 (on 7 April) to a premium of €7.20 (on 5 May). Over the same period the within-period premium remained positive, and in fact declined somewhat (from €1.10 on 7 April to €0.55 on 5 May).

Volatility

The volatility of allowance prices is a concern that is often raised about cap-and-trade systems, despite the fact that the prices in all markets exhibit volatility, and financial instruments exist that allow market participants to hedge against potentially unfavourable future price developments. This concern about volatility can be better understood as a concern about excess volatility – that is, more

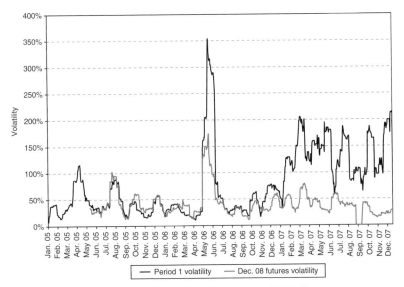

Figure 5.11 Historical volatility of EUA contracts, 2005–7
Source: Derived from ECX, BlueNext and Point Carbon data

volatility than would customarily be encountered in other asset and commodity markets.

Volatility is typically measured as an annualized historic volatility (AHV): the standard deviation of financial returns on assets, computed over a window of a pre-specified number of past trading dates. As illustrated in figure 5.11, period 1 and period 2 prices exhibited considerable variation in volatility from 2005 to 2007.

The figure shows the moving fifteen-trading-day volatility for benchmark first- and second-period EUA prices. Two notable features are evident. First, the period surrounding the first release of verified emissions data in late April 2006 and the subsequent price collapse was a time of markedly high volatility. Nevertheless, the peak volatility of second-period allowances was considerably less than that of first-period EUAs (175 versus 300 per cent). This difference is attributable to fact that the between-period banking constraint had a greater impact on period 1 prices than on period 2 prices. The second feature of note is the increase in first-period volatility as the period drew to a close. As first-period allowance prices fell under €1/tonne, even small price fluctuations reflecting normal market variations had a significant upward impact on observed volatility.

EUA volatility can also be compared to that of associated energy commodities such as natural gas, crude oil, coal and electricity. The volatility associated with these energy markets is, and has long been, an everyday fact of life for the same installation operators that were required to deal with CO_2 prices beginning in 2005. Table 5.3 compares the volatilities of these different markets, presenting concurrent quarterly volatilities calculated in the same manner as the monthly volatilities displayed in figure 5.11.

The last row of table 5.3 summarizes the range of observed quarterly volatilities for these related assets. The quarters exhibiting much higher EUA volatilities due to the idiosyncrasies of the EU ETS (such as the first release of verified emissions data and the low first-period prices in 2007) have been excluded to create greater comparability with the circumstances prevailing in other markets. By this measure, EUA volatility is comparable to that for other energy commodities and generally greater than the volatility of coal and crude oil but less than that for natural gas and electricity.

Ex post evidence of the extent of trading

While the existence of a market indicates that at least some owners of affected facilities are participating, little is said about the extent of market participation by firms that received free allowances. The CITL registry accounts into which EUAs are initially deposited and among which they may be transferred would provide one source of information about trading for compliance purposes. For instance, any surrendered allowance that was not originally allocated to a particular installation implies a trade. Similarly, registry accounts with no transfers would indicate no trading and some diminution of the efficiency attributes of the cap-and-trade system.

Unfortunately, these data can be observed only with a considerable lag, since complete information about transfers and holdings at the account level is not made public until five years after a given compliance year. Thus, complete information about the EUA transfers made in 2005 and the origin of the allowances surrendered for 2005 compliance will not be publicly available until some time in 2011. Information on 2006 compliance will not be available until 2012, etc.

One useful piece of information is immediately available in the CITL, however: the registry of origin for every surrendered allowance

Table 5.3 *Carbon and energy price volatility, 2005–8 (percentages)*

| | | Carbon | | Natural gas | Crude oil (Brent) | Coal | Electricity | |
| | | EUA spot price | EUA futures Dec. 08 price | Month ahead | Month ahead | Month ahead | Futures, month-ahead base | Futures, month-ahead peak |
		BlueNext	ECX	Zeebrugge	ICE	CIF ARA	Powernext	Powernext
2005	Q3	57	62	55	31	14	35	50
	Q4	29	38	121	28	13	42	64
2006	Q1	29	35	122	27	21	78	97
	Q2	152	92	64	25	14	43	65
	Q3	39	28	128	24	22	43	42
	Q4	53	40	138	26	9	96	105
2007	Q1	140	53	84	32	8	53	54
	Q2	159	44	123	21	15	92	133
	Q3	137	35	85	22	17	52	60
	Q4	263	22	71	29	28	97	117
2008	Q1	30	35	28	44	17	35	39
Summary		29–57	22–62	28–138	21–44	08–28	35–95	39–133

Sources: Derived from Reuters and BlueNext data.

is stated. This piece of information provides a tracer that can be used to evaluate the extent of trading among member states. If an installation in one member state surrenders EUAs that were initially issued in a registry outside that member state, a transfer has taken place. While this tracer is only a partial indicator – for instance, it does not allow for a determination of whether allowance transfers took place between installations in the same member state – it nevertheless provides a useful indicator of the extent of trading during the first period of the EU ETS.[10]

Trading relationships between EU ETS installations

One indication of trading activity is the number of trading relationships indicated by the registries of origin of surrendered EUAs. The existence of a non-domestic EUA in an installation's account communicates two pieces of information: (1) the installation surrendering the allowance acquired it somehow from an installation in another member state; and (2) an installation in another member state sold or otherwise transferred the allowance to the installation surrendering the allowance. Thus, this information confirms both the existence and direction of a cross-border transfer. Figure 5.12 shows the number and direction of these cross-border flows for the 25 EU member states that participated in the first trading period.

Each diamond represents a member state. The location of a diamond on the vertical axis indicates the number of member states from which the member state in question imported at least one EUA. The location of the diamond on the horizontal axis indicates the number of member states to which the member state in question exported at least one EUA. In the case of Greece, for example, Greek installations surrendered EUAs that were initially issued to installations in eleven other member states. Conversely, installations in twelve member states outside Greece surrendered at least one EUA that was originally issued in Greece. Thus, it could be said that Greek installations imported from eleven other member states and exported EUAs to twelve other member states.[11]

---

[10] This section draws heavily from Trotignon and Ellerman (2008), to which the reader is referred for a more extensive discussion and analysis of the surrender data.

[11] All the same, the vast majority (99 per cent) of EUAs surrendered in Greece were also issued in Greece.

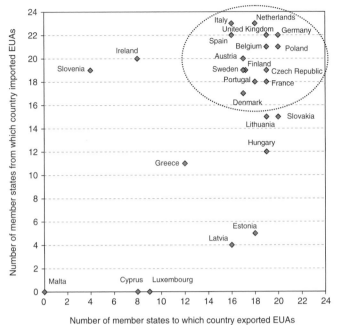

Figure 5.12 Cross-border flows, 2005–7
Source: Trotignon and Ellerman (2008)

The location of the member state plots in figure 5.12 provides one indication of the extent of participation in the EU-wide market. In general, the further to the upper right-hand corner a member state is located the greater the number of trading relationships that were developed by installations in that member state. Malta, whose registry was not online until 2007, and which had only two installations, both of which had a surplus in all years of the trial period, neither imported nor exported any EUAs. Cyprus and Luxembourg were two other member states that did not import any EUAs from other member states despite having installations that were short in at least one year. Allowances from these two countries were surrendered in eight and nine other member states, respectively, however.

By far the most interesting feature of figure 5.12 is the cluster of member states in the upper right-hand corner. The theoretical maximum would be a score of 24 on both axes; the non-participation of Malta in flows in either direction and of Cyprus and Luxembourg in imports, however, implies a practical maximum score of 23 on the vertical axis and 21 on the horizontal axis. Italy and the Netherlands in fact receive the maximum score on the vertical axis, indicating that Italian and Dutch installations surrendered EUAs issued in every other member state except Malta. As it turns out, allowances from no member state were surrendered in all twenty-one member states that imported EUAs for compliance. Nonetheless, three member states – Germany, Poland and Slovakia – exported to twenty member states. The fourteen member states included within the circle, which account for 90 per cent of all the allowances issued in the EU ETS, imported and exported EUAs for compliance from and to at least fifteen other member states. Four of these fourteen member states were net importers, yet they also exported EUAs for compliance to a significant number of other member states. The other nine member states were net exporters, but they were importing EUAs for compliance from an equally large number of trading partners.

A truly international market

The explanation for this phenomenon is that the EUA market is EU-wide. This may seem obvious, but it is different from what is often assumed and modelled: that international flows occur only after domestic markets have cleared. Short and long installations existed in all member states, and most installations used intermediaries in this EU-wide market to acquire needed EUAs or to dispose of unused ones. A prime example is provided by a comparison of the flows observed in the United Kingdom, the member state that was the largest net importer, with those of Poland, which was the largest net exporter of EUAs. UK installations surrendered allowances from twenty-two other member states and UK allowances were surrendered by installations in nineteen other member states. For Poland, the comparable numbers are virtually identical: twenty-one member states from which EUAs were imported and twenty to which EUAs were exported. In both these member states, with very different net positions, short installations were purchased from an EU-wide market and long installations sold into the same EU-wide market. Since there were longs and shorts in both countries, the diversity of origins and destinations is similar. The only difference is that there were more shorts importing a greater amount in the United Kingdom and more longs selling larger surpluses out of Poland.

Table 5.4 *Average percentage of non-domestic EUAs surrendered by short and long installations, period 1*

Year	Short installations	Long installations
2005	17	2
2006	30	2
2007	46	15
First period combined	33	7

Source: Derived from CITL data.

The absence of national markets can be observed readily by comparing the cross-border flows with the aggregate short positions as revealed by the annual reporting of emissions and allowance allocations. The registry data for the EU ETS reveal that approximately 3,000 of the 11,000-plus installations covered by the EU ETS were short in one or more years, and that their cumulative short for the three years was 650 million EUAs. Assuming that all these installations used all the allowances allocated to them before acquiring others, 650 million is the minimum level of EUA transfers that would be required for the short installations to be in compliance. If the further assumption were made that national markets cleared first – that is, that short installations within the member state purchased EUAs from long installations in the same member state before engaging in import or export – the required amount of cross-border flows for the trial period would be 90 million EUAs. In fact, this total was 354 million EUAs, four times higher than what would have been required if there were some mercantilist entity ensuring that all domestic allowances were used before trading occurred, or about 55 per cent of the sum of all the short positions. By implication, 45 per cent of the transfers, or about 300 million EUAs, involved domestic EUAs, although those transfers can only be inferred since the data cannot yet be observed.

Table 5.4 provides an indication of the *ex post* distribution of installations surrendering non-domestic allowances, according to whether the installation had a short or long position for the year and the period as a whole.

Two features are clearly evident. First, non-domestic EUAs are far more likely to be used for compliance at short installations than at long ones. This is not surprising; short installations are the potential buyers in the EUA market and the data do not indicate what happened to surplus allowances at long installations. By the logic of compliance trading, it can be surmised that the non-domestic surrendered allowances originated at long installations. Even so, it is notable that some non-domestic EUAs are surrendered by long installations.

The second feature of note in table 5.4 is the increasing incidence of non-domestic EUAs surrendered in each successive year. This probably indicates some increasing participation in the market, but, as pointed out by Trotignon and Ellerman (2008), it also reflects the resort to borrowing from the forward allocations for compliance in 2005 and 2006. While borrowing was an alternative compliance method in 2005 and 2006, it was not for 2007. The inability to borrow for the next year's allocation, which was in a different compliance period, meant that all earlier borrowing had to be paid back no later than 2007 and the only alternative was to acquire allowances in the market.

Finally, the percentages given in table 5.4 for the short installations show only the use of non-domestic EUAs. The data do not indicate how many of the domestic EUAs surrendered were issued to the installation and how many were acquired from other domestic installations. Thus, these percentages are not complete indicators of market participation, but they do show the minimum levels of the extent of trading for compliance and the likely trend in market participation.

Conclusions

There can be no doubt that a CO_2 price exists in Europe. Both anecdote and empirical data indicate that this price is incorporated into business decisions concerning operations in the near term and investment in the long term. At the beginning of the EU ETS, many participants in the scheme may not have recognized that CO_2 emissions had a cost, and there are probably some who still do not fully understand the implications of the EU ETS for their operations. Their number has diminished steadily, however. To maintain otherwise simply ignores the evidence provided by the increasingly available empirical data. The general recognition by ETS participants that carbon is no longer free, and that it will continue to be costly in the future, is a major achievement after only three years.

During the first period of the EU ETS the market price of EUAs increased by three to four times before losing a half of its peak value in less than a week, and finally sinking to zero. While this would seem to be a sign of a dysfunctional market, in fact it is not. If nothing else, the behaviour of the first-period allowance price demonstrates that market design and information matter. The self-contained nature of the first period meant that first-period pricing was always going to be unusual. The second-period price is much more important for the longer term, and it has exhibited behaviour similar to that which would characterize prices for most other commodities. More importantly, first- and second-period prices both reflected the changes in external factors that would be expected to influence actual conditions of supply and demand in the EUA market, which suggests that EUA pricing has been rational.

Participation in a market is always hard to gauge, but the existing indicators, which are similar to those used for any market, show increasing transactions, liquidity and sophistication in products. This development has been progressive but rapid. What started out in late 2004 and early 2005 as a small number of bilateral and over-the-counter transactions among creditworthy institutions trading something that did not actually exist have now multiplied twentyfold, along with the development of exchanges and more sophisticated financial instruments aimed at meeting the needs of all owners of facilities included in the EU ETS. A particularly interesting aspect of the development of the EUA market is the high degree of participation indicated by the cross-border flows of EUAs for compliance purposes. This pattern of trading is consistent with an EU-wide market in which allowances issued by all member states are equally valid and which the owners of affected installations use to turn allowance surpluses into cash or to purchase allowances to avoid more costly internal abatement. This behaviour is what would be hoped for in a cap-and-trade system. It augurs well for the second period, in which the informational deficiencies and programme design issues that made the first trading period unusual will no longer exist.

In summary, the conditions are present for efficient or least-cost attainment of the European Union's goal of limiting CO_2 emissions. There is a common price that reflects the changes in external factors that will determine the price for any given cap; the arbitrage conditions that characterize mature markets are present; and participation in the EUA market has grown steadily from its inception.

6 | *Emissions abatement*

Introduction

The objective of a cap-and-trade system is often expressed as reducing emissions by a given amount, but no cap-and-trade system can guarantee any given reduction. All that is assured is that the cap, the absolute limit on emissions over some relevant period of time, will be observed. The actual reduction of emissions, or abatement, will depend on what emissions would otherwise have been, given all the conditions prevailing at that time except the price on emissions, or what is called counterfactual emissions. For instance, if economic growth is stronger (or weaker) than expected, counterfactual emissions would be higher (or lower) than expected, and the reduction in emissions required in order to stay within the cap would be commensurately greater (or smaller). What is assured by the cap is that the level of emissions will be limited regardless of all the other conditions that may obtain. Instead, it is the price and the quantity of abatement that will vary.

Abatement is a matter of particular interest in the EU ETS because emissions during the trial period were significantly lower than the cap. This slack condition is frequently referred to as over-allocation, which implies that the cap was set too high, often with the further implication that there was no abatement.[1] This slack condition is an *ex post* condition, however, and, in the EU ETS, a significant CO_2 price prevailed for almost two years until the slack condition became widely recognized. During this time the owners of affected facilities had an incentive to abate emissions. The question therefore remains: did these owners and operators reduce emissions in response to the carbon

---

[1] Ellerman and Buchner (2008) provide a definition of over-allocation and provide estimates of the amount of over-allocation and where it may be considered to have occurred.

price that they faced? To the extent that they did, the observed end-of-period surplus was larger than it would otherwise have been.

Since abatement depends on the counterfactual, which can only be estimated, complete certainty concerning the amount of abatement can never be obtained and any reasonable estimate will be a range. Nevertheless, when the estimates are made *ex post*, many of the factors that determine emissions are known. Examples are the level of economic activity, energy prices and the weather, to mention only the most obvious. As a result, some of the uncertainty that surrounds *ex ante* estimates of abatement can be removed.

The presentation of data and the discussion in this chapter proceeds in three parts. First, a top-down macro estimate of abatement is presented based on the observed level of economic activity and of emissions for the European Union as a whole and for Germany. This broad-brush approach cannot be very exact, but, for something as important as a price on CO_2 emissions, it can reveal whether the aggregate data suggest that some new factor was operating. The next section focuses on the electric utility sector, in which most of the abatement was expected to occur. It relies on plant-specific simulation modelling of the dispatch (the order in which plants are called on) of the European electrical system, using observed demand, plant availability and energy prices to gauge the effect of a CO_2 price. Econometric evidence concerning abatement in the UK power sector is also presented. The succeeding section of the chapter provides anecdotal evidence drawn from the trade press and other sources. Such evidence cannot be taken as definitive, but it does serve to illustrate plans and specific responses to the CO_2 price. As with other approaches, whether the announced actions are attributable solely to the CO_2 price can be questioned, but the accumulation of such evidence serves to illustrate what is indicated by the more statistical approaches. The final section concludes.

Macro estimates

This approach assumes that the level of economic activity is a major determinant of CO_2 emissions and that the relationship between the levels of emissions and economic activity that can be observed in a recent past period, when there was no CO_2 price, would have continued into the present period. The projection of that past relationship between emissions and economic activity into the period under analysis based on observed levels of economic activity creates the estimate of counterfactual emissions. This estimate can then be compared with the actual level of emissions during the period when a CO_2 price prevailed.[2]

Various factors, such as weather, energy prices and changes in economic activity within specific sectors, will alter the relationship between emissions and economic activity from year to year, but averaging and the use of aggregates will tend to cancel out annual variations and errors. The more difficult problems are identifying any changes in the underlying relationships that may have occurred and taking account of persistent changes in some other factor, such as energy prices. Qualitative judgements and more detailed modelling can help to alleviate these concerns, but the underlying problems of the validity of the assumed relationships and of omitted variables always remain.

Forming a counterfactual estimate of EU ETS emissions for the European Union as a whole, or for a specific member state, is complicated by the same problem that afflicted the allocation process: lack of data. The sectors and installations to be included in the EU ETS were not known before the scheme was implemented, so no data were collected on them specifically. Consequently, the analyst must depend on various proxies that can be constructed from two data sources: (1) the greenhouse gas inventory data that are reported annually with a considerable lag under the UNFCCC, known as the common reporting format (CRF) data; and (2) the data specifically collected during the allocation process to form the baselines that were used to set emissions caps and to determine how member state emissions totals would be distributed to sectors and installations.

The CRF data are available in most instances from 1990 onwards. The reporting of these data by gases, sources and sectors makes it possible to create a proxy for the emissions that were eventually included in the ETS. An extensive comparative analysis of the CRF data and verified ETS emissions data for 2005 finds that the fuel-specific emissions and oxidation factors are highly consistent and that the main inconsistencies arise from general differences in the coverage

---

[2] An early attempt to provide estimates of counterfactual emissions and abatement based on 2005 and 2006 data was made by Ellerman and Buchner (2008).

of emissions in the two reporting systems (Herold 2007). In particular, the ETS does not include installations under a certain size, and the scope of what is defined as an installation and as an installation's emissions are less broad in the ETS than in the CRF reports. As a result, when compared across sectors for any member state, verified emissions are always less than the emissions recorded in the CRF data by about 15 per cent for the European Union as a whole (Herold 2007). Thus, for the purposes of forming a counterfactual, the CRF data can be used to form a proxy of what would become ETS emissions. With appropriate adjustment, this proxy can be spliced to the verified emissions data to provide a longer data series that can be used for an analysis of the pre-ETS trend in carbon intensity. The construction of this proxy is explained in box 6.1.

The second source of data is that collected during the allocation process. These data can be used for specific member states, but the years for which data were collected are not always consistent among member states, with the result that aggregates for the EU15 or EU25 cannot be formed. In addition, these data are often viewed with some suspicion, because of the time pressure under which they were collected and concerns about upward bias introduced because the parties providing the data received allocations based on the same data. All the same, the data were checked at the time for consistency with other previously existing data, and several member states – particularly Germany – have gone back after the fact and verified the original data submissions. Although errors were found both in the on-the-spot checking and the later verification, observers report surprisingly little evidence of systematic bias or falsification.[3] The public availability of these data and their comparability for the purposes of aggregation to an EU-wide level constitute bigger problems.

An EU-wide estimate

Figure 6.1 provides the CRF data for CO_2 emissions for the economy as a whole and the reconstructed ETS proxy for the EU25.

---

[3] See the contributions in Ellerman, Buchner and Carraro (2007) for accounts of and judgements concerning the verification efforts during the allocation process. Judgements concerning later verification efforts in Germany are based on personal communications with personnel at the Öko-Institut in Berlin.

Box 6.1 Calculation of the EU ETS counterfactual

(1) Common reporting format data for CO_2 emissions for the following
    Intergovernmental Panel on Climate Change (IPCC) sectors are ex-
    tracted and summed to obtain a raw ETS proxy:
    (a) combustion: energy industries (1.A.1);
    (b) combustion: manufacturing industries and construction (1.A.2);
    (c) combustion: other transportation (1.A.3.E);
    (d) combustion: other stationary sources (1.A.5.A);
    (e) fugitive emissions from fuels: oil and natural gas (1.B.2);
    (f) industrial processes: mineral products (2.A), except subsectors 5
        (asphalt roofing) and 6 (road paving with asphalt); and
    (g) industrial processes: iron and steel production (2.C.1).
(2) The ETS proxy is then rescaled to verified ETS emissions by multiply-
    ing the sums obtained in step one for the years 1990 to 2004 by the
    ratio obtained by taking the average relationship that verified emis-
    sions bear to the raw ETS proxy in 2005 and 2006, the only years for
    which the data overlap.
(3) This rescaled proxy for the years 1990 to 2004 is then spliced with
    verified emissions for 2005–7 to create a single series reflecting ETS
    sector emissions from 1990 to 2007.
(4) A GDP index for the EU25 is constructed by summing constant-price
    GDP indices for the twenty-five member states for 1995 to 2007, each
    weighted by its 1995 share of EU-wide GDP as calculated in inter-
    national dollars on a purchasing power parity basis by the IMF.
(5) The average rate of improvement in the CO_2 intensity of the ETS
    sectors from 2000 to 2004 is calculated based on the relative changes
    in ETS sector emissions and the EU-wide GDP index.
(6) Counterfactual ETS sector emissions are calculated, starting in 2005,
    by multiplying the previous year's ETS sector CO_2 emissions (step 3)
    by the observed rate of change in GDP for the year (step 4) and the
    average annual rate of CO_2 intensity improvement over the 2000–4
    period (step 5).
(7) Data sources are the IMF's World Economic Outlook database for the
    GDP data, the EEA's GHG Data Viewer for the CRF data and the EU's
    CITL database for ETS verified emissions.

The axes on the right- and left-hand sides of figure 6.1 are scaled so
that the economy-wide and ETS sector emissions lie on top of each
other to reveal the similarity of their movements. The evolution of EU
economy-wide CO_2 emissions prior to 2005 can be broken down into

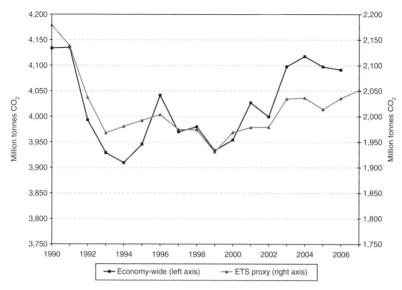

Figure 6.1 EU economy-wide and ETS sector CO_2 emissions, 1990–2007
Sources: Derived from EEA greenhouse gas data viewer and CITL data
(see box 6.1)

three distinct phases, roughly corresponding to successive half-decades. The first phase extends from 1990 to 1995 and is a period of falling emissions. The second phase, in the latter half of the 1990s, is one of stable emissions, and the third phase, from 2000 to 2004, is one of rising emissions. ETS sector emissions – which are about a half of economy-wide CO_2 emissions – experience these same trends, although there is still some continuing decline in emissions in the late 1990s and the increase in the early 2000s is not as pronounced.

Table 6.1 provides a summary of the annualized changes in GDP, CO_2 emissions and CO_2 intensity (emissions per unit of GDP) during each of the last two of these three phases.[4]

EU25 GDP has been increasing steadily since 1995, but there was a marked slowing of the rate of growth in economic activity from 2000 to 2004, reflecting the effect of the 2002 recession. Despite slower economic growth, 2000–4 was a period of rising CO_2 emissions, because the rate of improvement in CO_2 intensity had slowed since

[4] A lack of data in the IMF database for some of the eastern European member states before 1995 makes the construction of an aggregate EU25 index for the period 1990 to 1995 difficult.

Table 6.1 *Annual rates of change in GDP, CO_2 emissions and intensity, 1995–2007 (percentages)*

Period	GDP	CO_2 emissions		CO_2 intensity	
		Economy-wide	ETS sectors	Economy-wide	ETS sectors
1995–2000	3.00	0.06	−0.24	−2.94	−3.24
2000–4	1.83	1.00	0.85	−0.83	−0.98
2004–6	2.69	−0.30	−0.02	−2.99	−2.71
2004–7	2.78	NA	0.25	NA	−2.53

Note: See box for explanation of EU GDP index.
Sources: Derived from EEA greenhouse gas data viewer, CITL and the World Economic Outlook database (October 2008 edition), available at www.imf.org/external/pubs/ft/weo/2008/02/weodata/index.aspx.

2000 by about two percentage points for both economy-wide and ETS sector emissions. The cause of this change in the relationship between CO_2 emissions and GDP levels is not known, but the trend immediately preceding the start of the EU ETS (a rate of improvement in carbon intensity of about 1 per cent per annum) seems the most appropriate one to use in developing projections of counterfactual emissions for the first years of the EU ETS. Figure 6.2 shows the comparison between a projection of emissions assuming the continuation of this trend and actual emissions under the EU ETS. The difference is abatement.

The scale is truncated in figure 6.2 to emphasize the trends and the annual changes. Actual emissions are shown in the solid shading, abatement in the striped sections, and counterfactual emissions in 2005–7 are the sum of actual emissions and abatement. Counterfactual emissions would have continued to rise during the ETS years, much as emissions have since 2000, while actual emissions in these three years exhibit a distinct flattening. In 2005 CO_2 emissions decline perceptibly as the EUA price is incorporated into production decisions, after which emissions continue to increase in response to continuing economic growth, albeit on a lower trajectory, reflecting the effect of the CO_2 price. The cumulative abatement for the three years of the EU ETS is indicated as about 210 million tonnes.

More attention should be given to the cumulative estimate than to the increasing annual amounts that are shown on figure 6.2. The projection of counterfactual emissions assumes that each of these

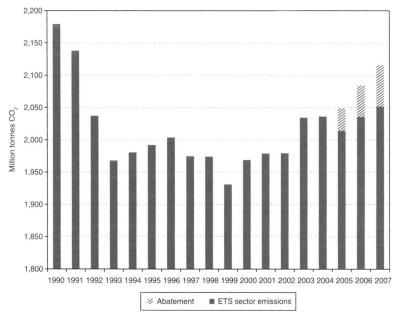

Figure 6.2 EU ETS sector emissions, EU25, 1990–2007
Sources: Derived from EEA greenhouse gas data viewer, CITL and World Economic
Outlook database (2008)

years was average with respect to other factors influencing emissions.
In actuality, CO_2 intensity would have varied around the assumed
constant 1 per cent per annum improvement, depending on weather
and other factors. Since actual emissions for 2005–7 reflected the
effect of these variations while the projected counterfactual does not,
the actual abatement in any year would be greater or smaller than
shown depending on these factors. For instance, counterfactual emissions were probably higher in both 2005 and 2006 because of adverse
weather conditions from a carbon standpoint (colder winters and
hotter summers) and higher natural gas prices relative to coal prices.

A second factor that would have affected the annual amounts was
the CO_2 price, which was relatively high in 2005, lower on an average
annual basis for 2006 and virtually zero for most of 2007. This factor
alone should have caused actual CO_2 emissions to rise quite aside from
continuing robust growth in economic activity. In theory, if all abatement were completely reversible then actual emissions in 2007 should
have been close to counterfactual emissions. While some abatement is
reversible, however (e.g. the dispatch of generating plants), other forms

Table 6.2 *Annual growth in GDP and industrial and electrical output, 2004–7 (percentages)*

	2004–5	2005–6	2006–7	2004–7
GDP	2.2	3.2	3.0	8.6
Electricity	1.4	0.6	−0.6	0.4
Industry (except construction)	1.2	3.8	3.4	8.9
Cement	2.5	4.1	0.1	7.1
Iron and steel	−2.7	7.1	0.5	4.3

Note: Eurostat does not provide indices for the EU25 in 2007. Therefore, the percentage changes in the last two columns for industrial and electrical output are for the EU27.

Sources: Compiled from Eurostat data and EU25 GDP index (see box).

of abatement (investment and other actions taken to improve energy efficiency) are not. With CO_2 prices clearly expected to be higher in 2008 than during most of 2007 (as signalled by the 2008 futures prices), firms would have undertaken these abatement actions despite the temporarily low CO_2 prices at the end of the trial period.

One can speculate on the amount of abatement that may have occurred in each year – and presumably there was more in 2005, when prices were higher than in 2007 – but to do so is to go beyond the precision that this type of estimate permits. A more reasonable approach to consider is simply that the available evidence suggests that CO_2 emissions in the European Union were reduced by some 200 million tonnes over the three years of the trial period. When compared with total verified emissions of 6,100 million tonnes, this indicates a reduction of about 3 per cent.

This abatement estimate depends importantly on the assumption that ETS sector emissions are driven by observed growth in GDP. GDP includes much else beyond the output of the sectors included in the EU ETS – the service sector and agriculture, for instance – and it is quite possible that the increase in economic activity in the sectors included in the EU ETS was less than that for the economy as a whole. Table 6.2 presents a comparison of the annual growth rates during the trial period for constant-price GDP and for various indicators of real output in sectors covered by the EU ETS.

Individual components can vary considerably from the GDP growth rate, and one is never sure that these indices are any more representative of the factors determining production and emissions, especially for the electricity sector, in which emissions per unit of output can vary considerably depending on fuel and CO_2 prices. Nevertheless, the comparison presented in table 6.2 suggests that the GDP components included in the ETS may have grown at a slower rate than aggregate GDP. If it were to be assumed that an appropriately constructed index of real output in the ETS sectors would show rates of growth approximately one-half percentage point lower than that for total GDP, the estimate of the abatement would be approximately 150 million tonnes for the period as a whole.

Other factors also have an effect on emissions, and they should be taken into account in any estimate of counterfactual emissions. This is particularly true of the electrical sector, for which both weather and the relative prices of the fossil fuels used to generate electricity can have a large influence on emissions. The next section of this chapter, which addresses the electrical sector specifically, takes both these factors into account through simulation modelling. The important point for the less detailed estimates being presented here is that both these factors worked to increase emissions during the trial period. The price of crude oil and of natural gas relative to that for coal was much higher than expected in the years prior to 2005, and this changed relationship led to more generation from coal-fired generation than would have occurred otherwise. A positive carbon price would still have an effect of reducing emissions, but actual emissions reflect the effect of both the CO_2 price and the less favourable relative fuel price ratio. Including the latter would increase the estimates of counterfactual emissions and abatement. In addition, the weather was not particularly favourable from a carbon emissions standpoint. The first two years of the trial period were characterized by a succession of colder than usual winters and hotter than usual summers, and these factors would have had an effect on observed emissions that should also be incorporated into the counterfactual estimate. On balance, it is reasonable to think that other factors operative during the trial period would have increased counterfactual emissions and led to greater abatement than would otherwise be indicated.

Taking everything into account, the initial estimate of 210 million tonnes may be taken as a reasonable central value. This implies abatement of about 3.5 per cent, and a reasonable range might be plus or minus 1.5 per cent or between 120 and 300 million tonnes for the three years of the trial period. In the end, the case for abatement rests upon the fact that observed emissions show a perceptible flattening following the introduction of the EU ETS despite robust economic growth and other factors that would have caused emissions to increase. There could be yet other factors that might have caused the observed change in emissions, but a price for CO_2 emissions is the most obvious explanation.

The geographic distribution of abatement

Application of this same approach to the estimation of a counter-factual and of abatement at lower levels of aggregation reveals that most of the inferred abatement occurred in the EU15 and almost none occurred in the ten new member states that participated in all three years of the trial period. Figure 6.3 presents the results of calculations analogous to those in figure 6.2 for the EU15 and the mostly eastern European new member states of the EU10.

The trend in ETS sector emissions is very different in eastern Europe from what it is in the EU15. Emissions fell sharply in the EU15 in the years immediately following 1990 because of the incorporation of the former East German state and the reform of coal support mechanisms in Germany and the United Kingdom. The decline in emissions in the east is less abrupt but longer-lasting as a result of the ongoing restructuring of the energy sectors in these countries. When the 2000–4 trend in the relationship between GDP and ETS sector emissions is projected through 2005–7 based on actual GDP growth in these two regions, most of the abatement occurs in the EU15. The indicated abatement for the EU15 is 195 million tonnes, or about 4 per cent of EU15 emissions, while the comparable figure for the east is 25 million tonnes, or about 2 per cent. Less abatement in the east is consistent with anecdotal evidence that, while some firms in the new member states did take the opportunity cost of EUAs into account, most did not (Fazekas 2008b). Nearly all installations in the new member states were allocated more allowances than they needed to cover emissions, and they may have continued operating as before and sold their surplus allowances or even left them in the registry accounts.

Germany is the largest and most complex economy in the European Union, and it can be seen as a microcosm of the expanded Union because of the inclusion of the former East Germany. It is also one of the few member states to have verified and published the pre-2005

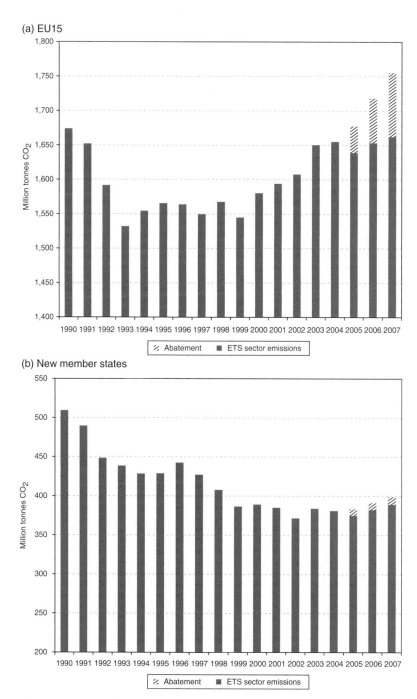

Figure 6.3 Counterfactual emissions and abatement in the EU15 and the new member states, 1990–2007
Sources: Derived from EEA greenhouse gas data viewer, CITL and World Energy Outlook database (2008)

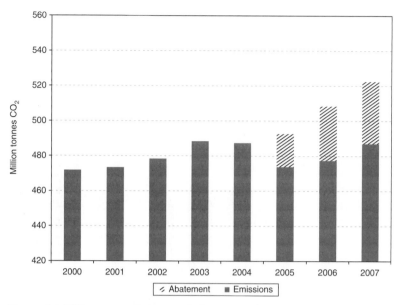

Figure 6.4 ETS sector emissions and abatement, Germany, 2000–7
Source: Ellerman and Feilhaver (2008)

emissions data from ETS installations, in this case back to 2000. Therefore, it is possible to construct a longer and continuous data series for Germany's ETS sectors that does not need splicing with some proxy for which there are, inevitably, definitional differences. Using the same methodology as described above for the European Union as a whole, namely projecting the 2000–4 relationship between GDP growth and emissions into the trial period years to form a counter-factual, the magnitude of the emission reduction potentially attributable to the EU ETS can be estimated. Figure 6.4 presents the ETS sector trends for Germany since 2000 in a manner exactly analogous to that depicted in figure 6.2 for the EU25 as a whole.

The total abatement over the three years of the trial period is 86 million tonnes, about 40 per cent of the estimate for the EU25 as a whole.[5] This share is larger than that of Germany's share of EU15 emissions, which is about 30 per cent, but it is reasonable to assume (as is discussed in more detail below) that Germany's share of abatement would be greater than the EU15 average due to the high share of

---

[5] When the same calculation is done using the CRF proxy data, the abatement estimate is 74 million tonnes.

coal-fired power plants in its electricity sector (approximately 50 per cent of generation). This estimate implies an emission reduction in Germany in the order of 6 per cent.

The availability of 2000–4 data by installation in Germany also allows for sector-specific projections to be made. Figure 6.5 presents these data, in which the German ETS installations are split between the power sector (panels (a) and (c)) and the industrial or non-power sector (panels (b) and (d)), and the calculations are shown both as emissions (panels (a) and (b)) and as CO_2 intensities (panels (c) and (d)). In the case of the power sector, the calculations are based on total electrical output. For the industrial sectors, the intensity is calculated based on constant-price gross value added as reported in the German national income statistics.

These pictures of abatement and the resulting intensities also reveal something about the manner of abatement. The greater flexibility in dispatching electricity-generating plants of differing CO_2 intensity per unit of electricity produced makes the economics of abatement depend far more upon the current price of CO_2 than is the case for other forms of abatement. As shown by panels (a) and (c) of figure 6.5, these calculations indicate more abatement by the power sector in 2005 and 2006, when CO_2 prices were relatively high, than in 2007, when they were near zero. Panel (c) also shows that power sector CO_2 intensity was falling steadily in the pre-ETS period and that the rate of improvement increased markedly in 2005 and 2006, when a price for CO_2 was added.

In contrast, most industrial processes do not have the flexibility that is inherent in any electrical system, and abatement in this sector tends to take the form of improvements in energy efficiency or changes in production processes that are not as easy to reverse. Consequently, the pattern of abatement shown in panels (b) and (d) of figure 6.5 is more cumulative, as firms make the investments in improved efficiency and other adjustments in response to the actual and expected CO_2 prices. As a result, the low CO_2 prices experienced in 2007 would have had less effect on abatement in this sector than in the power sector.

When these separate calculations of abatement are made and summed, the total for Germany in the three years of the trial period is 71 million tonnes, split about equally between the power and industrial sectors. This estimate is 15 million tonnes, or 17 per cent, less

(a) Power sector emissions

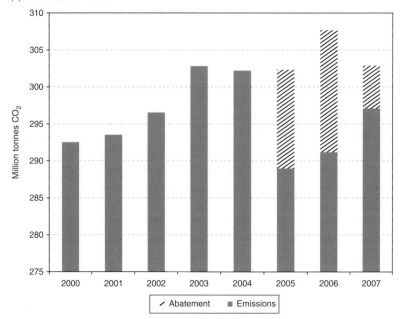

(b) Industrial sector emissions

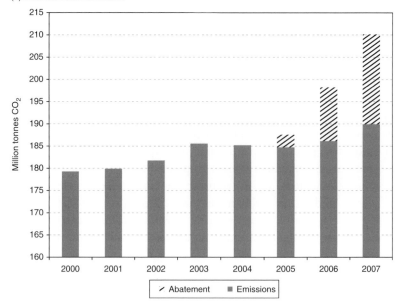

Figure 6.5 Sector trends in emissions, intensity and abatement, Germany, 2000–7
Sources: Derived from EEA greenhouse gas data viewer, CITL and German government statistics

(c) Power sector intensity

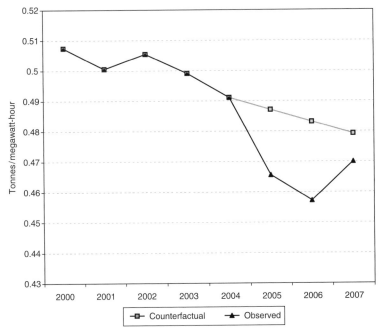

(d) Industrial sector intensity

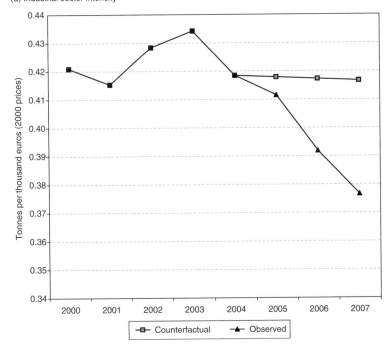

Figure 6.5 (*cont.*)

than the aggregate estimate first presented, but this difference illustrates the range in estimates that can be expected. The important point is that all show abatement in some magnitude.

An interesting and important further implication of these calculations is that the emission reduction accomplished by the industrial installations was as large as that in the power sector, which is generally viewed as having a greater ability to reduce emissions. Since power sector emissions were approximately 880 million tonnes and industrial sector emissions 560 million tonnes, the percentage abatement implied is 4.1 and 6.3 per cent, respectively.

Abatement through fuel-switching

Fuel-switching refers to the ability of power plants with lower emission rates per unit of output, typically fired by natural gas, to substitute within the electrical grid for higher-emitting power plants, typically coal-fired. Electricity is produced by a number of plants, all of which generate electricity and provide varying amounts of power to the electrical grid, from which customers draw the electricity they consume. The amount of electricity generated and supplied by a particular plant depends on the load, or demand, which varies considerably on a daily, weekly and annual basis, as well as on the relative cost of generation at that plant. The order in which plants are called on, or dispatched, depends on the variable cost of generation, which mainly reflects fuel costs, the efficiency of the plant in converting fuel to electricity and, since the beginning of the EU ETS, the price of CO_2. The introduction of the CO_2 price would cause the cost of higher-emitting units to increase more than that of lower-emitting units, which would lead in turn to some reshuffling of the order in which plants are dispatched. While most switching will be from coal to natural gas units, the potential for switching within fuels to exploit differences in plant efficiencies should also be recognized.[6]

[6] In theory, more efficient plants would always be dispatched ahead of less efficient ones and there would not be any possibility for within-fuel-switching. In practice, differences in the cost of delivering the same fuel to different plants on the grid and congestion on certain transmission lines in the electrical grid can cause less efficient plants to be dispatched ahead of more efficient ones, thereby creating these possibilities for further abatement.

Fuel-switching has often been thought to be the main form of abatement because it requires no additional investment and because adjustments in the dispatch order are frequently made in response to commonly occurring changes in the cost of fuels delivered to particular plants. When internalized, the price of CO_2 emissions is just another form of fuel cost that should have the same effect as an increase in the price of coal delivered to various plants. Thus, it requires no investment and no change in normal operating procedures, and the obvious differences in emission rates among existing power plants would seem to leave plenty of scope for this form of abatement.

While fuel-switching is an important form of abatement, it is not the only form of abatement, as just noted in the discussion of abatement by sectors in Germany. Because CO_2 emissions are so inextricably tied to energy use, there is a tendency to believe that the opportunities for CO_2 emission reduction are limited to fuel-switching in the power sector, with very few opportunities in other sectors. This belief extends the fixed coefficient between CO_2 and energy to energy use and tends to ignore or to minimize the potential for energy efficiency improvements, which in other contexts are widely believed to exist and to be underexploited.[7] The effect of the CO_2 price is simply to cause at least some of these opportunities for increased energy efficiency to be adopted. Furthermore, as explained below, the possibilities for fuel-switching may not be as great as commonly assumed.

The highly variable potential for fuel-switching

Fuel-switching assumes the existence of both available unused capacity that is lower-emitting and of higher-emitting capacity that is in use. If either is absent, there is no potential for fuel-switching. Moreover, the extent of fuel-switching will depend largely on the magnitudes and substitutability on the grid of plants for which these features apply. Both depend heavily on load and relative fuel prices.

Let us consider load first. Obviously, if, at some particular hour, the load is such that all lower-emitting capacity is committed, there can be

---

[7] A growing body of research indicates the large potential for energy efficiency improvements. Nonetheless, a significant portion of this potential is not realized because of barriers in the energy market. See IEA (2007a) for a discussion on how to cope with one of the most pervasive barriers to energy efficiency: principal–agent problems.

no fuel-switching. There is nearly always some capacity held in reserve, but at peak hours the amount of these reserves is clearly less. Conversely, if load is so low and the dispatch order is such that none of the higher-emitting units are in production (for instance, if zero-emitting nuclear and hydro generation is dispatched first), there are also no opportunities for fuel-switching.[8] More generally, anything that causes higher-emitting capacity to be less utilized or lower-emitting capacity to be more utilized will reduce fuel-switching possibilities. Thus, in the typical diurnal cycle of a system in which lower-cost, higher-emitting coal units are dispatched ahead of higher-cost, lower-emitting natural-gas-fired units, more fuel-switching will occur in response to a CO_2 price at night, at weekends or – in the case of winter-peaking systems, as in most of Europe – in the summer, when demand is low and more gas-fired units are uncommitted.

Fuel prices also affect the potential for fuel-switching. For instance, if gas prices were low enough to invert the dispatch order so that gas plants would be run all the time and coal plants would be used to meet daily demand, there would be no potential for abatement through fuel-switching. At the opposite extreme, natural gas prices could become so high relative to coal prices that no fuel-switching would occur within the range of expected CO_2 prices.

All these heuristic examples illustrate that the amount of abatement to be expected through fuel-switching in response to any given CO_2 price is highly contingent on load and relative fuel cost, or, more generally, the amounts of committed higher-emitting capacity and available but unused lower-emitting capacity. Figure 6.6 presents a three-dimensional graphic representation of these relationships for the European electrical system.

The vertical dimension of the figure shows the amount of abatement produced by a price of €60 per tonne for different combinations of load and relative fuel prices. Abatement is expressed as kilotonnes per hour and it applies for the European electrical system as a whole. The horizontal axes represent the range of power output that characterizes the interconnected European electricity grid, and the relationship between natural gas and coal prices is presented as a ratio with the coal price as the denominator. The EUA price in figure 6.6 is higher

---

[8] In Europe, however, this does not occur. At times of lowest load, a significant share of the electricity generation remains coal- or lignite-fired.

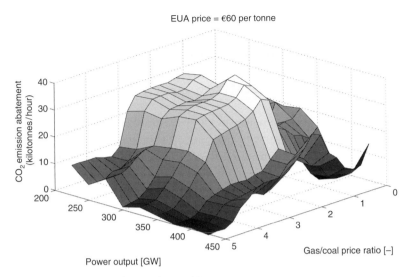

Figure 6.6 Fuel-switching relationships
Source: Delarue, Ellerman and D'haeseleer (2008)

than what has been experienced in the EU ETS, but it illustrates the essential relationships more clearly than lower prices.[9]

The characteristic relationship between the CO_2 price, the relative fuel prices and the load is that of a hill or mound of abatement that occurs when the load is not too low or too high and when gas prices are not too low or too high relative to coal prices. As any of these conditions is approached, the quantity of abatement falls off rapidly, with the result that relatively high levels of abatement occur only for those combinations of middle values that characterize the higher elevations of the hill, which tend to resemble a plateau. Particular characteristics of the electricity system create interesting ridges and valleys in this topography, especially at lower CO_2 prices, and the exact lie of the land – including the height of the plateau – depends on the CO_2 price, but the essential feature is the highly variable quantity of abatement associated with any given price of CO_2.

If the load and relative prices were unchanging over considerable periods of time, the amount of abatement associated with a given CO_2

---

[9] As the CO_2 price declines, the terrain becomes less regular than shown in figure 6.6, although the essential features remain. Delarue, Ellerman and D'haeseleer (2008) give examples at lower prices.

price would be indicated by a fixed point on this surface. In the course of any one day, however, the load is moving back and forth across the plateau and perhaps descending down one side or the other. If the relative price ratio is towards one of the extremes, this traverse might be at the lower elevations. Moreover, since relative prices vary on a daily basis, the traverse due to the load is occurring on different parts of the plateau for days in any given week, month or year. Finally, and not least, the CO_2 price, which also varies from day to day, determines the height of the plateau as well as the details of its topography. Abatement over any period of time is the sum of the hourly abatement resulting from traverses over the terrain that is determined by prices and demand.

Simulation modelling of abatement through fuel-switching

Figure 6.6 is illustrative, and it reflects the relationships embodied in the simulation model that produced it. In this case, the simulation model is one developed at the Catholic University of Leuven in Belgium, called E-Simulate, which encompasses most of the countries included in the EU ETS, divided into ten zones with interconnections. The power sector is modelled at the plant level and with hourly demand and dispatch. When zonal demand and prices are imposed exogenously, the model solves for the least-cost dispatch of existing capacity subject to technical constraints on plant utilization and zonal interconnections, and produces estimates of plant-level generation and emissions. Running E-Simulate with actual data for 2005 and 2006 with and without the actual CO_2 price produces the estimate of abatement.[10]

The output of such a model can also be portrayed linearly as a function of time using actual values for fuel and CO_2 prices and load.

---

[10] For more complete descriptions of the model, see Voorspools (2004), Voorspools and D'haeseleer (2006) and Delarue, Voorspools and D'haeseleer (2008). All of the EU25 are included in E-Simulate except the three Baltic countries, Greece, Cyprus, and Malta; and the model includes two non-EU countries, Switzerland and Norway, that are tightly integrated into the European grid. The emissions involved in the included non-EU countries and the excluded EU member states are not significant in relation to the totals for the entire system.

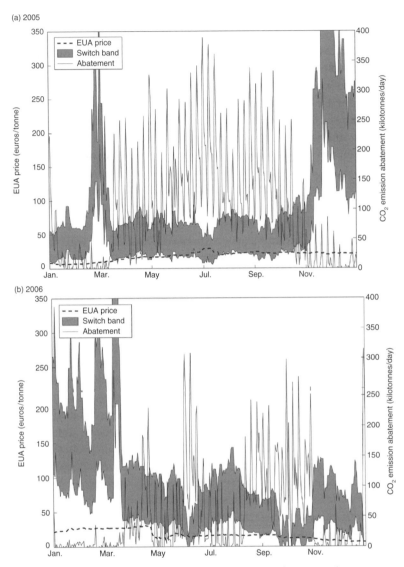

Figure 6.7 Abatement, CO_2 prices and conditioning factors in the EU power sector, 2005 and 2006
Source: Delarue, Ellerman and D'haeseleer (2008)

Using those that applied during the first two years of the EU ETS, this linear representation is given in figure 6.7.

The two panels provide data on abatement, CO_2 prices and fuel prices for 2005 and 2006, respectively, all expressed as daily values.

The dashed line towards the bottom of each panel gives the EUA price and the dark band indicates the range of EUA prices within which most switching would be expected to occur given the prices of gas and coal on that day. The lower end of this band indicates the EUA price at which an efficient gas plant would displace an inefficient coal plant and the higher end indicates the EUA price at which an inefficient gas plant would displace an efficient coal plant.[11] When the lower end of this switching band exceeds the EUA price, as occurs occasionally, little switching can be expected. These are times when the natural gas price in Europe is too high relative to the coal price to justify fuel-switching. The highly jagged line is daily abatement, expressed on the right-hand-side axis, as the sum of abatement over the twenty-four hours for which the fuel and EUA prices prevailed. The jagged nature of the line reflects the weekly cycle between weekdays, when there is more demand on the system and less potential for fuel-switching, and weekends, when there is less demand and more potential for abatement through fuel-switching. As can be seen, this amount varies not only according to the fuel and EUA prices but also depending on seasonal variations in demand and other factors that might influence the load.

The impact of seasonal load and the dependence upon fuel and CO_2 prices is readily evident in the quarterly figures provided in table 6.3.

In any given year, and regardless of the abatement estimate, about three-quarters of the annual abatement occurs during the second and third quarters because these are the quarters when demand is lower. Abatement can be higher or lower in any given quarter depending on other factors. For instance, abatement was much lower in the first quarter of 2006 despite a significantly higher EUA price because the price of natural gas was much higher in 2006 than in 2005. Similarly, abatement increased in the fourth quarter of 2006 over what had been experienced in 2005 despite a lower EUA price because the price of natural gas was significantly lower in 2006 than in 2005.

In table 6.3, two estimates of abatement are provided, labelled STA for the use of the model in its standard form and CAL for the use of the model after it had been calibrated to actual results obtained in

---

[11] Note that this band gives only an indication of what CO_2 prices should be to trigger a significant amount of coal to gas fuel-switching. Fuel-switching can also occur at even lower levels of CO_2 prices – e.g. between very inefficient coal plants and very efficient gas plants – or between other fuels than coal to gas.

Table 6.3 *Quarterly and annual abatement in the EU ETS through fuel-switching, 2005 and 2006*

(a) 2005	Q1	Q2	Q3	Q4
Average generation (TWh/day)	8.7	7.4	7.4	8.2
Average gas/coal price ratio	2.6	2.1	2.1	5.2
Average allowance price (euros/tonne)	9.0	18.4	23.2	21.9
STA abatement (Mt)	6.2	22.4	26.9	6.3
CAL abatement (Mt)	3.4	12.6	16.0	3.5
(b) 2006	Q1	Q2	Q3	Q4
Average generation (TWh/day)	8.8	7.5	7.4	8.2
Average gas/coal price ratio	4.8	2.5	2.3	2.0
Average allowance price (euros/tonne)	26.1	19.0	15.9	9.4
STA abatement (Mt)	1.1	11.2	12.8	10.0
CAL abatement (Mt)	0.7	6.2	6.9	5.3

Note: TWh = terawatt-hours.
Source: Delarue, Ellerman and D'haeseleer (2008).

2003 and 2004. The standard, or non-calibrated, version of the model produced an estimate that was almost twice as large as the calibrated version. The reason for the lower estimate in the calibrated run was the lower utilization of coal plants, and greater use of gas plants, in 2003 and 2004 than the model would have predicted using standard operating assumptions for the power sector (Delarue, Ellerman and D'haeseleer 2008). Whether one or the other estimate is more appropriate depends on whether one believes that the conditions holding back coal use from what the model predicted for 2003/4 were temporary (plant outages) or more permanent (environmental constraints on utilization or poor maintenance). To the extent that these conditions disappeared in 2005/6, more coal use would occur in the counterfactual and more abatement in response to the EUA price. The variation in these estimates underlines their sensitivity to assumptions about load and availability, and, more generally the need for using ranges in making estimates of abatement.

The zonal nature of E-Simulate also allows total estimated abatement to be broken out by zones, which correspond to single member states or groups of neighbouring countries depending on the degree of

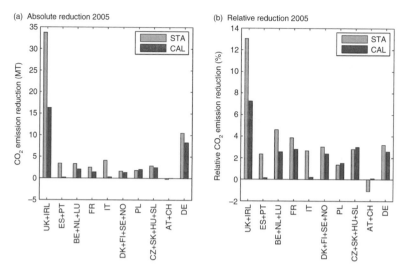

Figure 6.8 Geographic distribution of abatement from fuel-switching in the EU power sector, 2005

Note: UK+IRL=United Kingdom and Ireland. ES+PT=Spain and Portugal. BE+NL+LU=Belgium, the Netherlands and Luxembourg. FR=France. IT=Italy. DK+FL+SE+NO=Denmark, Finland, Sweden and Norway. PL=Poland. CZ+SK+HU+SL=Czech Republic, Slovakia, Hungary and Slovenia. AT+CH=Austria and Switzerland. DE=Germany

Source: Delarue, Ellerman and D'haeseleer (2008)

integration of the electrical grid. Figure 6.8 presents these data for 2005, which is similar in the distribution of abatement among zones to that observed in 2006.

Most of the abatement through fuel-switching, whether in the calibrated or standard run, occurs in two zones: the United Kingdom and Ireland (UK+IRL) and Germany (DE). The United Kingdom and Germany are the two countries with the largest amount of coal-fired capacity and they both have significant amounts of natural-gas-fired capacity. The United Kingdom accounts for the largest amount of abatement – about 50 per cent of the EU total from fuel-switching – because it has more gas-fired capacity. For the same reason, abatement from fuel is larger relative to power sector emissions than in any other zone. It is also evident from figure 6.8 that most of the reduction in coal use in the calibrated runs of E-Simulate is located in the United Kingdom.

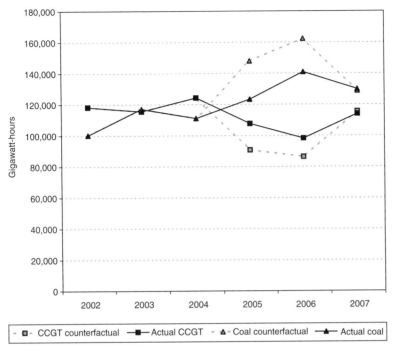

Figure 6.9 Coal-fired and CCGT generation in the United Kingdom, 2002–7
Source: Compiled by the authors based on unit notification data from Elexon,
purchased through EnAppSys Ltd, Elexon's data purveyor; available at www.elexon.
co.uk/marketdata/default.aspx

Abatement in the UK power sector

The UK power sector provides a good illustration of the importance of
establishing an *ex post* counterfactual, because coal-fired generation
was higher in 2005 after the start of the ETS than it was in 2004 and
earlier years, and combined-cycle gas turbine (CCGT) generation was
lower. If all conditions apart from the presence of a CO_2 price had
been the same in 2005 as in 2004, an increase in coal-fired generation
and decrease in gas-fired generation would have suggested that the
CO_2 price had little effect. In fact, conditions were not the same in
2005 as in 2004, and in particular the price of natural gas rose
significantly in 2005 in relation to that for coal. In an econometric
study of the relationship between power plant utilization and fuel and
CO_2 prices in the UK power sector, McGuinness and Ellerman (2008)
show that, in the absence of a CO_2 price, coal-fired generation would
have been even higher and gas-fired generation even lower. Figure 6.9

Table 6.4 *Regression results: effect of EUA price on UK power sector dispatch*

Independent variables	Separate fuel price and EUA terms	Additive fuel price and EUA terms
UK electricity demand (MWh)	-2.18 E^{-09}	-2.31 E^{-11}
	1.15 E^{-09} (1.89)	1.22 E^{-09} (0.02)
Coal dummy times UK	8.61 E^{-09}	3.51 E^{-09}
electricity demand	1.90 E^{-09} (4.54)	2.03 E^{-09} (1.73)
Nuclear generation (MWh)	-3.53 E^{-08}	-2.96 E^{-08}
	7.33 E^{-09} (4.81)	6.40 E^{-09} (4.62)
Fuel price ratio (coal/gas)	0.5037	0.4333
	0.0371 (13.58)	0.0351 (12.33)
Coal dummy times fuel	-1.1278	-0.9851
price ratio	0.0601 (18.76)	0.0493 (18.68)
CO_2 price term	0.0082	0.4969
	0.0008 (9.70)	0.0413 (12.03)
Coal dummy times CO_2	-0.0169	-1.1239
price term	0.0012 (14.03)	0.0671 (16.76)
F (7, 1572)	112.15	115.31
R^2	0.3406	0.3468

Notes: Values in parentheses are the t-statistics. The CO_2 price term is expressed in euros in the separate specification and converted to equivalent additional fuel cost in the additive specification.
Source: McGuinness and Ellerman (2008).

shows the actual evolution of coal- and gas-fired generation in the United Kingdom from 2002 to 2007 compared to the modelled estimate of what generation would have been without the CO_2 price.

This representation of the effect of the CO_2 price was obtained through the use of fixed-effects panel regression techniques to estimate the relationship between monthly coal and CCGT plant utilization and average monthly fuel and CO_2 prices for twenty-nine CCGT and sixteen coal-fired plants from 2005 to 2007. These results indicate that the CO_2 price caused coal plant utilization to be 16 to 18 per cent lower than it otherwise would have been and CCGT plant utilization to be 19 to 24 per cent higher.

McGuinness and Ellerman (2008) find strong statistical evidence that the EUA price affected dispatch decisions independently of the fuel prices. Their regression results are presented in table 6.4.

In this regression, the coal dummy serves to distinguish the effect of the indicated independent variables on coal and CCGT plants. Thus, the coefficient for the variable without the coal interaction term is that applicable to CCGT units, and the sum of that coefficient and the one for the corresponding interaction term applies to coal plants. For instance, the relative price term, which is defined as the cost of coal per megawatt-hour (MWh) divided by the similar cost of natural gas, has opposite effects. In both specifications, the coefficients applicable to the CCGT plants are positive, indicating that CCGT generation increases as the relative price of coal rises. The sum of these coefficients and those for the coal interaction terms are negative, indicating that coal-fired generation decreases. Both the fuel price and CO_2 terms have the expected directional effects and they are statistically significant at a high level of confidence.

These regression results can be used to predict actual emissions and, when run without the CO_2 price, to predict counterfactual emissions. Because these estimates are based on statistical probabilities, confidence intervals can also be placed around the central point estimates of the amount of abatement. Table 6.5 shows these results for the two specifications.

These results indicate that the quantity of abatement through fuel-switching in response to the CO_2 price in the UK power sector can be placed between 13 and 20 million tonnes in both 2005 and 2006 with 95 per cent confidence. While the point estimate for abatement in 2007 is positive, the 95 per cent confidence interval includes the value of zero and therefore it is not possible to affirm that abatement occurred in 2007. Given the low price for CO_2 in 2007, this result is not surprising. Moreover, the estimates for 2005 and 2006 are similar to those for the United Kingdom in figure 6.8, which were obtained through simulation modelling.

Anecdotal evidence

Anecdotal evidence of CO_2 emission reductions abounds but it is not always clear that the reason for the observed reduction is the CO_2 price created by the EU ETS. The general enthusiasm for emission reductions is such that observed reductions in emissions are celebrated, and increases deplored, without much attention being paid to the other factors that may have contributed to the observed phenomenon. All the same,

Table 6.5 *Estimates of abatement from fuel-switching in the UK power sector, 2005–7*

Year	Estimated abatement	Minimum	Maximum
(a) Specification with separate fuel and CO_2 price terms			
2005	16,283,047	13,164,569	19,401,524
2006	17,443,888	14,186,694	20,701,081
2007	678,596	(2,200,414)	3,557,606
(b) Specification with additive fuel and CO_2 price terms			
2005	18,007,296	14,808,847	21,205,746
2006	17,022,066	13,735,100	20,309,031
2007	1,138,599	(2,115,616)	4,392,813

Source: McGuinness and Ellerman (2008).

some of these reports provide good prima facie evidence of responses to the EUA price, and at the very least they provide context for what can be inferred from the more rigorous analysis just presented.

A good example is provided by the abundance of articles in the trade press concerning reductions of emissions in the Spanish electric utility sector, as 2008 emissions totals are reported and compared to those for the corresponding quarters in 2007 (Point Carbon 2009). Net generation in both Spain and Portugal rose in 2008 compared with 2007, but CO_2 emissions were lower by 4.6 per cent in Portugal and 16.7 per cent in Spain. This report and earlier ones attribute the reduction in emissions to fuel-switching. In Portugal, the main coal-fired plant reduced output by 14 per cent while generation at the major gas-fired unit increased by 24 per cent. In other reports, the Spanish utility Iberdrola reported a reduction in coal-fired generation of 63 per cent and an increase in gas-fired generation of 52 per cent in the first three quarters of 2008 when compared to the comparable year-ago period (Point Carbon 2008c). Earlier, another Spanish utility had reported a 42 per cent reduction of coal-fired generation and a 38 per cent increase in gas-fired production in the first half of the year (Point Carbon 2008b).

These comparisons between 2008 and 2007 are particularly welcome, because the CO_2 price was significantly higher in 2008 than in 2007 while the relationship between natural gas and coal prices was little changed. In addition, the reduction in emissions is not attributable to increased renewable energy, which did not manage to replace the hydro output that had been reduced due to a drier than usual year in 2008. This context suggests strongly that the cause of the reduction in emissions and the observed fuel-switching was the EUA price. Although the circumstances surrounding many similar reports are not as clear, these reports and what is known about other relevant factors indicate that the abatement effects that can be simulated for the European electrical system as a whole and verified by econometric analysis in the United Kingdom are a more general phenomenon.

A less immediate but no less important form of abatement is the upgrading of power plant efficiency, particularly at coal-fired power plants. A prime example is provided by the very large (6 GW) Drax coal-fired power plant in the United Kingdom, which is one of the five largest-emitting sources in the European Union (20 million tonnes in 2005). In early 2007 the management of the privately owned Drax power station announced two 'strategic carbon abatement projects', consisting of a £100 (€150) million investment in upgrading turbines and another £80 (€120) million for a fivefold increase in biomass co-firing capacity (Drax Group 2008). The turbine upgrade, which was one-third complete as of mid-2008, provides a 5 per cent improvement in the efficiency of converting coal to electricity (from 38 to 40 per cent efficiency) and comparable reductions in CO_2 emissions and coal consumption. Construction of the expanded biomass co-firing facility has begun, and when completed in mid-2010 it will lead to 10 per cent reductions in CO_2 emissions and coal use, as well as the creation of renewable energy obligation certificates.[12] When all the turbine upgrades have been made and the biomass co-firing capability has been completed, CO_2 emissions will be 15 per cent lower than they otherwise would have been. It is evident that the payback for this investment is not only in CO_2 cost savings but also in fuel cost savings and renewable energy credits. The role of each cannot be determined with

---

[12] Renewable energy obligation certificates, also called 'green certificates', encourage the generation of renewable energy by setting a quantitative objective. The distributors (or the power producers, depending on the applicable regulations) are required to offer a certain proportion of renewable energy as part of the electricity they sell (or generate). To document their compliance, they are required to purchase green certificates from the producers of renewable-resource-generated electricity. One green certificate generally corresponds to 1 MWh of renewable energy. This system is in use in the United Kingdom, Poland, Italy, Sweden, Belgium, Bulgaria and the Netherlands.

the information available, but the timing of the investment and management's explanation of the projects leaves little doubt that carbon abatement is a major consideration.

A similar example of abatement occasioned by the EU ETS is provided by ČEZ, the main electric utility in the Czech Republic, in an unusually detailed accounting of the costs and savings of its actions in response to the EU ETS in 2005 (ČEZ undated). In this east European example, ČEZ calculated a reduction of 4.78 million tonnes, or 13 per cent of counterfactual emissions, in 2005: 3.3 million tonnes from forgone export sales to Germany and 1.48 million tonnes from efficiency improvements. The former reduction occurred because the prospective profit on the export sales, €8.5/MWh, would have been less than the market value of the EUAs saved by not activating the marginal coal-fired generation, which would have resulted in about 1 tonne of emissions per megawatt-hour of power supplied. From a system-wide standpoint, the emissions associated with the power used in Germany to replace ČEZ's exports would have to be taken into account, with the result that the net reduction was probably somewhat less than the tonne of CO_2 abated by ČEZ. This example illustrates both the redistribution of production created by the introduction of the EUA price and the recognition of the opportunity cost of freely allocated allowances by a company that had a surplus of allowances.

The energy efficiency improvements undertaken by ČEZ were the result of accelerating planned upgrades. Implementing these upgrades sooner cost €21 million, but allowance sales enabled ČEZ to recoup these costs and earn a profit of €7.7 million in 2005. These measures included the reconstruction of feeding pumps, cooling pumps and boilers, the replacement of a turbine and general improvements in maintenance and plant operation. Over the longer term, ČEZ's 'action plan for CO_2 reduction' anticipates a general three- to four-year acceleration of its plans for power plant renewal, which it specifically attributes to the EU ETS (ČEZ undated). ČEZ estimates that this plan will cost €317 million – specifically stated as the cost of the time value of money associated with the acceleration of planned investments – which will yield CO_2 emission reductions of about 3 million tonnes annually.

These examples from Drax in the United Kingdom and ČEZ in the Czech Republic are anecdotal and unusual only in the detail with which they are presented. They are nonetheless illustrative of the abatement actions that would be expected and that are usually reported simply as planned upgrades or improvements without much attention to what the motivating factor is. These examples are also illustrative of the longer-term response that requires some investment and that goes beyond simple fuel-switching within the limits of existing capacity. Interest in improving energy efficiency as a means of reducing CO_2 emissions is not limited to the off-the-shelf improvements that are reported above for Drax and ČEZ. The German utility RWE recently announced a 32 per cent increase in its research and development budget 'mostly to improve efficiency and cut emissions from its fossil-fuel-fired power plants' (Point Carbon 2008d). Although research and development expenditure does not necessarily translate into improved energy efficiency, this report is indicative of the focus of the longer-term efforts that go beyond fuel-switching.

Larger percentage reductions can be anticipated as newer, more efficient coal plants are built. As an example, in June 2008 RWE and the Polish utility Kompania Weglowa announced a joint venture to build an 800 MW coal-fired plant in Poland by 2015 that would have an efficiency of 46 per cent, instead of the usual 33 to 35 per cent efficiency that characterizes existing coal-fired plants in Poland (Point Carbon 2008a). This improvement in efficiency is equivalent to a 25 per cent reduction in CO_2 emissions. Of course, existing plants may be upgraded by 2015 so that their efficiency then is higher than what is stated in the announcement of these plans, and the efficiency of the new plant might not be as high as hoped, but this example provides further illustration of the ways in which carbon emissions will be reduced, even without considering a switch to lower-emitting fuels or other means of generating electricity.

Improvements in energy efficiency as a means of reducing CO_2 emissions is not restricted to the electric utility sector. In mid-2007 SAB Miller, the world's second largest brewer, with plants in Spain, Italy, the Czech Republic, Poland, Hungary and Slovakia, reported a 12 per cent improvement in the carbon intensity of its operations through energy efficiency measures taken with respect to coal and natural gas combustion at its breweries (Point Carbon 2007a). As with other energy efficiency measures, the cost savings include fuel costs as well as emissions costs, and as a result it is difficult to know how much of the emission reduction can be attributed to CO_2 costs and how much to the higher energy costs, especially those for natural gas, that were experienced in 2006. This conflation of motives is also reported by

Lacombe (2008) in his survey of refinery managers. A frequent response to questions about the effect of the CO_2 price was that energy efficiency improvements were being undertaken not only because of the CO_2 price but also because of the significantly higher costs for crude oil, which is the primary variable-cost item in a refinery. Nevertheless, most interviewees reported that they recognized the new CO_2 cost component and took it into account in optimizing refinery operations.

The cement sector provides abundant anecdotal evidence of abatement in company announcements and products. Abatement in this sector takes three forms: (1) energy efficiency and associated CO_2 savings as described above; (2) fuel-switching, usually in the form of increased use of biomass and waste-derived fuels; and (3) the increasing use of various additives – most notably ground granular blast furnace slag, pulverized fly ash and limestone – as partial substitutes for clinker, the CO_2-intensive but essential ingredient of cement. A notable example of the latter was the announcement by CEMEX UK of the receipt of regulatory approval for the construction of a new grinding and blending facility at the Port of Tilbury in Essex for the manufacture of blended cements. The main product from this 1.2 million tonne facility, which was scheduled to come online in 2008, will be CEM-III, a blend of traditional cement and blast furnace slag, which will have 50 per cent fewer CO_2 emissions for each tonne of blended cement produced because of its reduced clinker content (CEMEX UK 2007).

The increased use of these less CO_2-intensive but lower-grade cements also depends on changes in regulatory standards that will allow a finer matching of applications and the type of product. Walker (2007) provides a good description and analysis of the interplay between company experimentation with new blends and consideration of changes in standards that would permit their greater use. As in many other instances, it is not always possible to identify the exact effect of the CO_2 price created by the EU ETS. Experimentation with the use of these blends had begun before the EU ETS, and renewable energy mandates also contribute to the increased use of biomass and waste-derived fuels. Nonetheless, the announcements and publicity found on any cement company's website never fail to mention the CO_2 emission reductions, and there can be little doubt that the CO_2 price has provided added impetus for the adoption of these changes.

Not the least of the advantages of the abundant anecdotal evidence of abatement is an increased appreciation of the many different ways in which CO_2 emissions are being reduced. Even a cursory survey, such as provided above, shows the considerable flexibility that exists in production and use. The overall picture is far more complex and widespread than the view that short-term abatement is limited to fuel-switching between coal and natural gas in the electric power sector or to producing less output.

Conclusions

Abatement was modest during the first trading period of the EU ETS, which is in line with the modest ambition of the cap set for the trial period. All the same, there should be no doubt that emissions were reduced as a result of the EU ETS. The EU ETS produced a relatively high price for CO_2 during half the trial period, and firms did respond to that price. More importantly, that price and the clear indication that it would continue caused firms to incorporate the CO_2 price into their investment decisions and to search for new ways to reduce CO_2 emissions.

While anecdotal evidence abounds, and rigorous tests for abatement can be performed when data permit, the strongest evidence of the effectiveness of the EU ETS is that CO_2 emissions in the EU ETS sectors stopped growing after the start of the system despite continued robust economic growth and developments in relative fuel prices that would have otherwise led to higher emissions. The rough estimates that have been developed here suggest that the EU ETS created emission reductions of between 2 and 5 per cent, or between 120 and 300 million tonnes for the three years of the trial period.

A clear distribution of this reduction in CO_2 emissions by geography and sector also emerges from the data. The western EU15 member states, which account for 80 per cent of the ETS emissions, appear to have accounted for a larger proportion of the reductions that can be attributed to the EU ETS. Anecdotal and other evidence suggests that emission reductions did occur in the eastern European new member states, but most of the reduction in carbon intensity observed in eastern Europe must be attributed to the ongoing restructuring of those economies and of their energy use.

The most interesting feature of the sectoral distribution of abatement is that it was not restricted to the electric power sector, which would seem to have the greatest capability for short-term abatement through fuel-switching. Both crude statistical approaches and anecdotal evidence imply that industrial facilities subject to the EU ETS have undertaken a number of measures to reduce emissions per unit of output in both the short term and the long term.

Fuel-switching within the electricity sector was probably the dominant form of emission reduction occasioned by the EU ETS, but less of it occurred than expected, because the high prices for natural gas during most of the trial period made this form of abatement more expensive. The other forms of abatement that have appeared during the trial period are more pervasive but less easy to model and to demonstrate conclusively. The most important and widespread has been improvements in energy efficiency, both in industrial facilities and in existing power plants. This should not be surprising. There has always been some dissonance between the beliefs, on the one hand, that little abatement of CO_2 emissions can be obtained beyond fuel-switching and, on the other hand, that further improvements in energy efficiency can be achieved. The CO_2 price provided a needed incentive, which was further enhanced by the contemporaneous increases in price for all forms of energy. Abatement measures go beyond improved energy efficiency, however. The increased use of biomass and waste-derived fuels in combustion is a clear response to the CO_2 price, although in some member states such measures also respond to local mandates of varying forms and effectiveness.[13] These measures can be seen as a form of fuel-switching, but similar substitutions can also be observed in other parts of the production process, notably in the introduction of substitute materials – often by-products of other industrial processes – to reduce the CO_2-intensive clinker requirements in producing cement.

While abatement during the trial period has been modest, it takes time for the effects of a CO_2 price to sink in and for investments to bear fruit. Even without considering the higher prices that future, more stringent caps would imply, more abatement can be expected over the longer run. The abatement observed during the trial period was the easiest to achieve and required the least lead time.

---

[13] Such mandates may include the avoidance of landfill (e.g. for used tyres) or the safe disposal of biohazards (e.g. meat and bonemeal).

7 | Industrial competitiveness

Introduction

The impact of the EU ETS on competitiveness is an issue that emerged months ahead of the launch of the scheme in 2005. Following the conclusion of the first trading period, the debate is as heated as ever – all the more so because rhetoric continues to supersede evidence. Various proposals for border adjustments and other trade measures have now emerged in official debates, and the global economic slowdown is unlikely to make them go away.

The purpose of this chapter is to clarify the primary issues in the competitiveness debate and to share the evidence to date about the impact that the EU ETS has had on the competitiveness of industry. The discussion addresses the impacts observed during the first three years of the EU ETS, and is thus an examination of how the competitiveness of EU installations evolved over the short term.

Competitiveness is a notion that is most useful when applied at a relatively microeconomic level. Krugman, in his article 'Competitiveness: a dangerous obsession' (Krugman 1994), warns against the view that nations, like companies, compete against each other, and that their economic problems are attributable to a failure to compete in global markets. Krugman's advice is all the more relevant for an analysis of the EU ETS, whose effects are felt almost exclusively by a subset of economic activities. How, then, does one define competitiveness at the microeconomic level? The OECD offers a pragmatic definition: '[T]he ability to produce high-quality, differentiated, products at lowest possible cost, to sustain market shares and profitability' (OECD 1996b). Alexeeva-Talebi, Böhringer and Moslener (2007) define competitiveness as a firm's 'ability to sell' – to maintain or increase volumes – and its 'ability to earn' profits.

In the context of international climate policy, these notions have a different ring when envisaged in the near term as well as in the longer term, as all economies will need to transition to a low-GHG path. This transition will require the supply of new technologies, practices and know-how. There may be rewards for those companies and sectors that have embarked early on this journey, as their ability to earn and sell in these new conditions will be enhanced. It is important not to lose sight of this aspect of the climate and competitiveness debate, and also to recognize that some activities will stand to gain, and others will lose. Seeking to preserve the status quo – the way industrial activities are conducted today – would not only be a denial of the rapid and significant change required to mitigate climate change, but would also make future mitigation efforts more costly.

With the above definitions in hand, one can proceed to the central question of this chapter: how has the first trading period of the EU ETS affected the competitiveness of various industrial sectors? Furthermore, what does this suggest for the future?

First, the root of the potential problem: through the EU ETS, the European Union has introduced a price on the greenhouse gas emissions of some industrial sectors, in an attempt to force emitters to internalize a negative externality of their operations. To date, the European Union is the only region of the world in which a carbon price is applied on such a scale. Firms outside the Union that compete in similar markets hence benefit from a price distortion, as their price systems do not reflect the costs of climate change. In theory, non-EU competitors should increase their market shares on world markets.

In addition to the loss of market share, pricing carbon inside the European Union may lead to another problem: carbon leakage. Leakage is defined here as the ratio of increased emissions in one region as the result of an emissions constraint introduced in another. If carbon leakage were to occur, the environmental target set by the ETS would be undermined by the relocation of industrial activities, and their emissions, outside the region. Two phenomena may be associated with relocation: (1) a company may choose to expand production outside the European Union instead of inside the Union, or (2) a company may see its market share, both inside and outside the Union, decline as more competitive production is deployed outside the Union.[1]

---

[1] The study of the impacts of the EU ETS on competitiveness is, and will remain, plagued by the difficulty of establishing a proper counterfactual scenario (i.e. what would have happened in the absence of a policy): how does one detect, in the rapid industrial production growth outside the European Union,

Which, of all the activities covered by the EU ETS, are the ones a priori most prone to international competition due to carbon prices? This question is well answered by the literature: energy-intensive and trade-exposed industrial activities, including cement, glass, iron and steel, paper and pulp, petrochemicals, refining and aluminium (Reinaud 2005a; Hourcade, Demailly, Neuhoff *et al.* 2008). The power generation sector is to a large extent not exposed to international competition, although electricity imports from the Russian Federation – where carbon constraints do not apply directly – could change this situation.

Accordingly, this chapter focuses on those sectors that produce the majority of non-power GHG emissions covered by the EU ETS, and that may thus be the most vulnerable to competitiveness impacts: cement, iron and steel, oil-refining and aluminium. In what follows, we first describe the basic production and market features of these diverse sectors, consider their exposure to the carbon constraint, analyse possible cost impacts and provide results from both models and empirical observations regarding the impact of the EU ETS on international trade flows and leakage.

Cement

How cement is produced

A typical European plant produces between 2,000 and 3,000 tonnes of cement per day on a continuous basis. The best available technique for producing cement is based on the 'dry' process, illustrated in figure 7.1. In the initial step, calcium carbonate (in the form of limestone or chalk) and silica sand are processed into a fine powder, the raw meal. Other minerals are included to improve subsequent processing. The raw meal is then preheated and calcined (oxidized) in so-called cyclones by a counter-current stream of flue gases. Calcium carbonate decomposes into lime, emitting CO_2 in the process. In the third step, the calcined materials are fed into a rotary kiln, where they are heated further by the combustion gases. The output of this process is a sintered (made solid by heating) granular intermediate known as clinker. The final step (milling and blending of additions) takes place after the clinker has been cooled.

the actual effect of the Union's ambitious climate policy and the resulting relocation of industry?

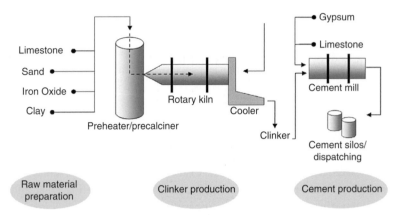

Figure 7.1 Schematic of dry process cement production
Source: Adapted from Walker (2006)

CO₂ emissions and opportunities for abatement

Cement production results in CO_2 emissions from three separate sources: the process of decarbonation of limestone; combustion of fuel in the kiln; and indirectly through electricity use (Reinaud 2005a). The quantity of process CO_2 emissions associated with a tonne of Portland cement – the most common type of cement for general use – depends on its percentage of clinker content. The quantity of fuel-derived emissions depends partly on the clinker concentration, but also on thermal efficiency and the choice of fossil fuel. On average, the production of a tonne of cement emits some 0.7 tCO_2 (tonne of carbon dioxide), excluding emissions from electricity generation.

Kiln operators have four primary options for reducing their CO_2 emissions: improving process energy efficiency, using substitute fuels for combustion, reducing clinker content and employing carbon capture and storage (CCS) technology. The latter is in principle an attractive option, as the concentration of CO_2 in the kiln flue gases is roughly twice that in flue gases from coal-fired power stations.[2] However, technical, regulatory and economic barriers to the use of CCS remain.

---

[2] The British Cement Association is assessing the feasibility of CCS in cement installations, together with the IEA Greenhouse Gas R&D Programme.

Economic environment

The demand for cement is driven mainly by its application in concrete. In some countries (notably Spain and Ireland), a buoyant construction sector over the decade up to 2007 led to a consumption boom and an increasingly tight local production capacity. In Ireland, this has triggered investment in three new clinker kilns. In contrast, the Spanish market growth has stimulated investment in grinding plants, and growing imports of non-EU clinker. In some other countries, notably Germany, cement demand has been either static or even declining, resulting in overcapacity.

Despite the commodity nature of cement, European markets are generally national or subnational, partly reflecting the high cost of transporting product by road. Some blended cement is transported between EU member states, but relatively little is imported from outside the European Union. The national markets are typically characterized by oligopoly competition between multinational clinker producers. This may be due to the capital-intensive nature of clinker production, whereby profitable operation requires a stable, high gross margin to be achieved over the variable costs. Market prices can vary widely between adjacent countries and sometimes between regions in a country. This does not appear to result from differences in variable cost, however, including a potential CO_2 cost. Figure 7.2 shows little change, if any, in the market price of cement following the introduction of the EU ETS but, rather, a continuation of existing trends and cycles.[3]

Evaluation of the impact of the EU ETS on the competitiveness of the European cement industry

Ex ante studies

Since the origin of the process that led to the EU ETS, the European cement industry has warned that the ETS would threaten its competitiveness, in light of its high CO_2 content and low value added per tonne of product.[4] Only a few studies on competitiveness and

---

[3] Note that Ponssard and Walker (2008) arrive at the same conclusion using monthly data.

[4] For example, the industry organisation Cembureau wrote in 2005 that 'the unilateral initiative of the EU to launch its ETS is leading to major problems of competitiveness for the EU cement industry and will not succeed in reducing

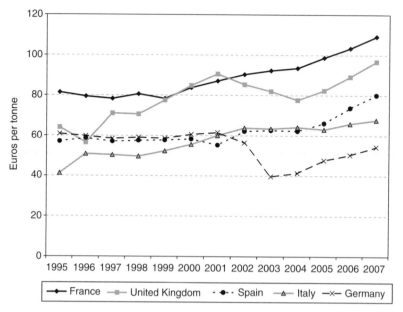

Figure 7.2 Annual average cement market prices, selected EU15 countries, 1995–2007

Source: Eurostat's External Trade database, available at ec.europa.eu/eurostat

leakage, based on partial equilibrium models, attempt to isolate the potential impacts of the EU ETS on the cement industry, and their results differ widely.

Ponssard and Walker (2008) develop a stylized model of the European cement industry, with an explicit treatment of transportation costs and Cournot competition in two markets: a coastal market and an inland market. They further assume no barriers to trade apart from transportation costs and a full auctioning of allowances. Ponssard and Walker find a high leakage rate (around 70 per cent). This result assumes negligible emission reductions per tonne of clinker, however, and no reduction of clinker content in cement. Their model may therefore overestimate leakage rates.

Szabó *et al.* (2003, 2006) build a large-scale world model of the cement industry and find a lower leakage rate (29 per cent) assuming

global CO_2 emissions. On the contrary, the ETS may be an incentive to import cement/clinker from countries with no carbon constraints with, as a result, relocation of production CO_2 emissions and additional CO_2 from shipping.'

an ETS covering the EU15 alone and allowance allocation based on grandfathering. They do not explicitly represent the transportation costs, but model the market shares of the domestic versus foreign producers as a function of national capacities and production costs, which result in some barriers to cement trade.

Demailly and Quirion (2006)[5] use a large-scale world model of the cement industry, but, like Ponssard and Walker (2008), they assume that domestic and foreign cement are perfect substitutes and explicitly represent the transportation costs. They find a leakage rate of about 40 per cent, assuming emission trading in the EU27 and lump-sum allocation. Imports from non-EU countries rise from 3 per cent of EU consumption to 13 per cent, while EU exports are halved. If allowance allocation were proportional to cement output (i.e. updated, output-based allocation) rather than fixed, however, the leakage rate would drop to less than 10 per cent: imports and exports would remain almost unaffected. The updated, output-based allocation would work as a production subsidy, and deter relocation.

In all, two assumptions drive the magnitude of leakage rates in *ex ante* studies: barriers to international trade other than transportation costs and the allocation method. Hourcade, Demailly, Neuhoff *et al.* (2008) argue that barriers to trade are significant. In addition, the allocation method used for the first period of the EU ETS (see chapter 3) has similarities to an output-based allocation, in that the new entrant reserve and closure rules allow allocation to follow production capacity to respond to changes in production output. Assuming no trade barriers, lump-sum allocation or full auctioning necessarily leads to an overestimated leakage rate and impact on cement trade due to the ETS, at least during its first and second periods.

Ex post analysis

In contrast to these *ex ante* analyses, an *ex post* assessment of the impact of the EU ETS on cement trade flows reveals a limited impact during the first trading period. EU27 net imports (imports minus exports) of cement and clinker grew slightly in 2005 and 2006 – the

---

[5] Demailly and Quirion (2009) find a lower leakage ratio when they assume a climate policy in all annex B countries apart from the United States, instead of only in the European Union. The annex B countries are the thirty-nine emissions-capped industrialized countries and economies in transition listed in annex B of the Kyoto Protocol.

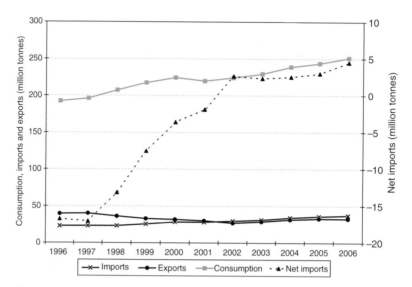

Figure 7.3 Cement and clinker trade flows and cement consumption, EU 27, 1996–2006
Source: Derived from Cembureau (1997, 2008) data

first two years of the EU ETS – after two years of relative stability (see figure 7.3). This growth is very limited in comparison with the evolution of net imports between 1997 and 2002. Furthermore, the growth in imports and slight reduction in exports can also reflect a tightening of domestic capacity in times of growing demand.

To test the relative influence of consumption and of the EU ETS on EU net imports, a simple econometric test, whose results are displayed in table 7.1, was performed for the EU27 as a whole and for a sample of member states. Two models were compared. In model 1, consumption is the only determinant of net imports, while, in model 2, net imports are explained by consumption and the annual average price of EU allowances. If the ETS has had a positive influence on net imports, the EUA price should have a positive and statistically significant coefficient.[6]

To overcome unit root problems, the models are estimated on first differences, using ordinary least squares (OLS). The estimation period

---

[6] Another regression was run using the one-year-ahead forward price for EUAs, as some cement prices are negotiated in advance on an annual basis. This variable was not significant except in France, although in this case the explanatory power of the model was very low (adjusted $R^2 = 0.16$).

Table 7.1 *Regression results: influence of consumption and carbon prices on EU net cement imports*

	Model 1			Model 2			
	R^2	Adj. R^2	Consumption coefficient	R^2	Adj. R^2	Consumption coefficient	EUA price coefficient
EU27	0.50	0.45	0.29**	0.52	0.39	0.30**	NS
Germany	0.28	0.25	0.20***	0.28	0.23	0.20***	NS
France	0.01	−0.02	NS	0.03	−0.04	NS	NS
United Kingdom	0.45	0.43	0.40***	0.48	0.44	0.40***	NS
Italy	0.36	0.33	0.20***	0.36	0.31	0.19**	NS
Spain	0.34	0.32	0.41***	0.36	0.31	0.43***	NS
Portugal	0.58	0.57	0.57***	0.59	0.57	0.56***	NS

Notes: *** and ** represent 1 and 5 per cent significance levels, respectively. NS indicates that the variable is not significant, even at 10 per cent.

Source: Authors.

is 1976 to 2006, except for Portugal (1976–2005) and the EU27 as a whole (1996–2006). Consumption, imports and exports are obtained from Cembureau (1997, 2008).

With the exception of France, an increase in cement consumption significantly increases cement and clinker net imports. A 1 tonne increase in consumption entails an increase in net imports ranging between 0.25 tonnes (Germany) and 0.57 tonnes (Portugal). On the other hand, the EUA price is never statistically significant even at the lenient threshold of 10 per cent, except in the United Kingdom, but here the coefficient, unexpectedly, has a negative sign. To compare the explanatory power of the two models, the adjusted R^2 is displayed, which accounts for the different number of independent variables in both models. It turns out that, except in the case of the United Kingdom (but with the above-mentioned caveat), the first model brings a higher adjusted R^2, and hence has a larger explanatory power.

Conclusion: no observed impact on the cement sector during the first trading period

To sum up, the data available to date do not reveal an impact of the ETS on cement trade during 2005 and 2006, the first two years of the first trading period. Several factors can explain this lack of evidence. First, various trade barriers may protect domestic production from foreign competition. This would be consistent with large price differences between member states. Cement producers may then be able to pass on the opportunity cost of EUAs without suffering from international competition. A second explanation may be linked to the generous level of allocation to European cement producers.

Looking forward, the first explanation implies that shifting from a grandfathered to an auction allocation mode would not drastically affect the European cement industry. Economic simulations stressed the importance of location, however: cement producers on the coast would be more exposed to competitors from unconstrained regions. The second explanation – no cost pass-through – brings a more cautionary message, since the 2005–7 period would say relatively little about the ability of producers to pass on the cost of carbon in cement prices. The evidence on the rate of pass-through in this sector (10–30 per cent) does not allow for a conclusion about the sector's ability to pass on cost: firms may have included cost on an average-cost rather than marginal-cost basis, or delayed pass-through as a result of contractual lags. Alternatively, capacity constraints in the home market could lead to prices being effectively set by importers, limiting the ability to augment prices (Walker 2006).

Furthermore, besides the short-run impact on trade flows that was examined here, the EU ETS may have a negative longer-run impact by reducing investment and production capacity – although today's practice of new entrant reserves could mitigate this effect. The long lags involved suggest that no impact can be observed at this relatively early stage, however.

Iron and steel

How steel is produced

There are two main routes to produce crude steel, as illustrated in figure 7.4. The basic oxygen furnace (BOF) route uses mostly coal, iron ore and recycled steel (known as scrap) as inputs. The electric arc furnace (EAF) or 'secondary' route uses electricity, scrap and, in some countries, direct reduced iron. In 2006 the BOF route accounted for 59.5 per cent of EU25 output, as compared to 40.5 per cent for EAF.[7]

The output of both production routes is liquid steel, which is then turned into semi-finished products through the casting process. These are further processed by hot- or cold-rolling into two main categories of steel products: flat and long products. These products then undergo various finishing processes to meet the desired product shape and quality.

BOF steel production is very capital-intensive. The minimum economic scale is high, resulting in high entry barriers (Reinaud 2005a). Annual capacity for installations in the BOF route ranges between 1 and 20 million tonnes. Vertical integration is the rule: many producers control an important part of the raw material chain, and most are integrated downstream into first-transformation products (sheets, panels, profiles and tubes) and steel distribution.

The EAF route consists of much smaller production units, from 0.5 to 3 million tonnes of annual capacity (Reinaud 2005a). It offers several advantages over the integrated route: production flexibility;

---

[7] In 2006, 65.5 per cent of the global steel production came from the BOF route, 32 per cent from the EAF route and 2.4 per cent from open-hearth furnaces, an outdated technology found in Commonwealth of Independent States (CIS) countries and India.

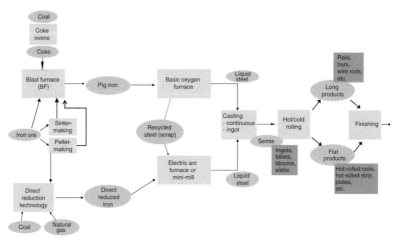

Figure 7.4 Schematic of iron and steel production
Source: Authors

the ability to meet specific product qualities for particular end markets; and location near demand markets, facilitated by the small unit size. Constraints on scrap availability in certain regions and product quality (if produced from scrap) nonetheless limit the contribution of the EAF route.

CO_2 emissions and opportunities for abatement

The level of energy and CO_2 intensities of steel mills depend on the production route, the energy cost and the availability and quality of raw materials. As a result, the best performance cannot be achieved in all circumstances.[8] Assessing performance is further complicated by the complex set of energy and material flows; the materials that are used and produced by an installation can greatly affect its observed energy consumption and related CO_2 emissions. For example, one steel mill may purchase its coke or its electricity, while another may produce both (IEA 2007b; Baron *et al.* 2007; Tanaka 2008). As a result, energy use and CO_2 emissions may vary considerably for installations with similar output structures, unless coherent measurement

[8] A large share of the observed differences in energy intensities and CO_2 emissions at the plant and country level are explained by variations in the quality of the resources that are used and the cost of energy, which determines the cost-effectiveness of energy recovery technologies (IEA 2007b).

methods are used. This is of great importance, as the allocation of allowances is based on direct emissions.

The majority of CO_2 emissions in the BOF route come from pig iron production in the blast furnace, from pig iron transformation in the basic oxygen furnace and from coke-making (Reinaud 2005a). Coke is used as a chemical reducer and as a source of energy. Coke-making produces a large amount of coke oven gas, which is used as a fuel in other segments of the process or is recovered in power stations. The blast furnace also emits gas, which is used as fuel in power generation and heat production. Integrated steel mills may therefore cover most of their electricity needs and purchase the remainder from the local power grid. In some cases, the coke oven and blast furnace gases are sold to power companies.

A typical Western BOF steel mill emits about 1.95 tCO_2 per tonne of semi-finished steel.[9] The plant also consumes on average 140 kWh of electricity per tonne of semi-finished steel. This electricity consumption reaches between 244 kWh/tonne of steel for hot-rolling and 384 kWh/ tonne of steel for cold-rolling.

Electric arc furnace plants also emit process emissions, although in a much smaller quantity than the integrated route.[10] In Europe, direct emissions reach 0.23 tCO_2 per tonne of semi-finished steel (see www.eurofer.org). This route also uses on average 600 kWh/tonne of semi-finished steel, reaching between 700 and 840 kWh of electricity to produce a tonne of crude steel depending on how the molten steel is rolled.

With the CO_2 intensity of steel-making estimated above, a BOF operator faces an opportunity cost of €50 per tonne of steel, at an EUA price of €25/tCO_2. This represents about 10 per cent of the prevailing market price for typical products in western European countries in 2005.[11] Note that steel prices have increased greatly since 2006, and

---

[9] This emission rate is representative of the average European BOF mill as covered by the EU ETS. It includes electricity generated on-site and considers full recycling of the blast furnace gas. This figure does not take into account the emissions from electricity produced off-site and consumed on-site (representing approximately 10 per cent of the total electricity needs in BOFs).

[10] Direct emissions in the EAF route come from three sources: the use of graphite electrodes, the use of burners (if the EAF uses primary energy and not just electricity as an energy source) and from directly injecting coal dust into the scrap.

[11] In December 2005 prices for hot-rolled coils reached €500/tonne and reinforcing bars €480/tonne.

as a result the theoretical CO_2 cost burden should diminish. The EU ETS also has an indirect effect on the economics of both production routes, particularly on the EAF route, through its effect on electricity prices. This effect appears to be an order of magnitude smaller than the opportunity cost linked to direct emissions in the BOF route.[12] In the EAF case, the absence of uniform electricity prices and the general practice of buying electricity via forward contracts make such costs difficult to assess (Reinaud 2007).

Several emission reduction opportunities are available at all stages of the production process (coke-making, blast furnace, BOF, EAF and finishing). Specific investments can improve energy intensity, such as the additional recovery of gases emitted in the blast furnace route and their use for electricity and heat. Other investments can allow by-passing one production process (see Baron *et al.* 2007 or IEA 2007b for details).[13] Some investments are limited by the availability of products and by the limited incentives provided by the allocation level in the first period, however. Further, it is not clear whether industry is taking into account the opportunity cost associated with free allowances.

Emissions intensity (emissions per unit of output) has decreased steadily since at least the early 1990s, dropping from 1.27 tCO_2 per tonne of steel in 1990 to 0.95 in 2006, implying an average drop of 1.8 per cent per year (see figure 7.5).[14] The main part of the decrease has been due to a progressive switch from BOF to EAF. Had the emission factors been constant for each route (1.8 tCO_2 per tonne in BOF, 0.24 in EAF), the aggregate emission ratio would have decreased by 1.0 per cent a year due to this change in technique alone. Additional improvements in each route add up to an additional 0.8 per cent decrease in average

---

[12] For example, an EAF mill consuming 0.6MWh of electricity per tonne and facing a 10 per cent electricity tariff increase would incur additional variable costs of 1.2 per cent (or €1.9 per tonne). Calculations are based on data provided by Reinaud (2005a).

[13] CCS technology for this sector is not yet commercially available and the financial incentives during the first period of the EU ETS would not have been sufficiently high to justify an investment.

[14] CO_2 emissions data are taken from the UNFCCC (2008) inventories (categories 1A2a and 2C1) and production data from International Iron and Steel Institute (IISI) (2007).

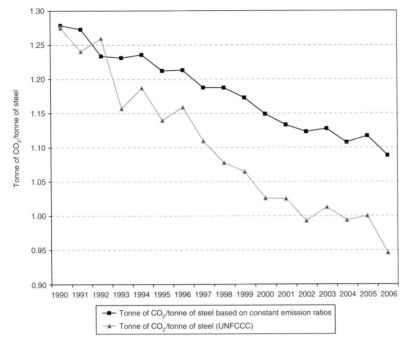

Figure 7.5 Emissions per tonne of steel, EU15, 1990–2006
Note: Emissions include on-site emissions but not indirect emissions from electricity purchases
Sources: Derived from UNFCCC data and IISI production data

emissions per year. In all, 54 per cent of the improvement in emissions intensity can be attributed to the switch to EAF.

Emissions intensity increased in the first year of the ETS, but decreased sharply in 2006. In all, emissions intensity decreased by 2.4 per cent per year between 2004 and 2006, of which 36 per cent was due to the switch from BOF to EAF. Emissions intensity thus decreased slightly more rapidly than the long-term average (1.8 per cent). This may be due to the ETS, but the change is too small to allow concluding with certainty that the ETS triggered additional reductions in the first two years of period 1.

The global economic environment of the steel sector

Prices of all major steel products increased dramatically from 2004 to 2007, reflecting important changes in industry structure and global market dynamics.[15] This sector has experienced considerable consolidation over the last fifteen years, with the creation of Arcelor in .52002, its merger with Mittal Steel in 2006 and the acquisition of the UK company Corus by India's Tata Steel in 2007.[16] Concentration in the steel sector remains low nonetheless: the top fifteen crude steel producers accounted for a mere 37 per cent of world production in 2006, with ArcelorMittal and Tata–Corus accounting for 9.5 per cent and 1.9 per cent, respectively. Concentration is high at the European level, however, where the top five producers account for 90 per cent of total production.

Between 2000 and 2006 Chinese crude steel production increased by 232 per cent, and its global share grew from 15 to 34 per cent. The production in the EU25 increased by just 6 per cent over the same period, and its share in global output declined accordingly from 22 to 16 per cent (IISI 2007). The Chinese steel sector triggered a sea change not just in the steel trade but also in raw material markets. The prices of coking coal, coke and scrap were two to three times higher in January 2008 than a year earlier, while prices for iron ore fines were 66 per cent higher (figure 7.6), which led the Chinese government to seek to temper steel output and control exports.

Steel is a widely traded commodity. In 2007, 40 per cent of steel production (i.e. over 300 million tonnes of steel) was traded globally, as compared to 26 per cent in 1990. China, once the largest importer of steel products, has since 2005 become the primary exporter. China is now the largest exporter of steel to the European Union (30 per cent of EU27 imports in 2007), having overtaken Russia and Ukraine (see www.eurofer.org).

Evaluation of the impact of the EU ETS on the competitiveness of the European steel industry

Ex ante studies
Numerous studies have examined the potential impacts of unilateral carbon policy on the competitiveness of the iron and steel sector. Some

---

[15] There is no common price indicator for steel as there is no central marketplace for steel products. Prices are mainly set on a bilateral basis and are reported in specialized publications (Baron *et al.* 2007).

[16] Note that these massive direct investments (€26 billion for Arcelor, €6.4 billion for Corus) in the European steel sector indicate that, in spite of the EU ETS, European steel factories are seen as profitable by their competitors.

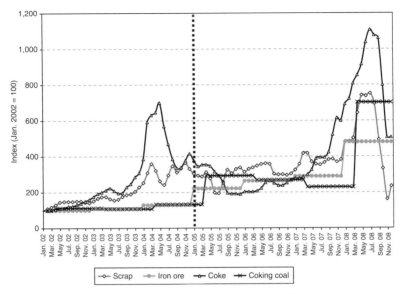

Figure 7.6 Prices of raw materials in the steel sector, 2002–8
Source: Derived from OECD (2008)

model the impacts of a CO_2 tax applied uniformly to the sector in a country or set of countries (Gielen and Moriguchi 2002; OECD 2003; Hidalgo, Szabó, Calleja *et al.* 2003), others study the impacts of an emissions trading scheme resembling the EU ETS (Carbon Trust 2004; Reinaud 2005a; Hourcade, Demailly, Neuhoff *et al.* 2008; Demailly and Quirion 2008). The estimated impacts include profit and market share loss and carbon leakage.

Gielen and Moriguchi (2002) model the impacts of several CO_2 tax levels applied in both Japan and EU15. With a tax rate of $42/tCO_2 (€46/tCO_2 using January 2002 exchange rates), production is halved in 2020 in Japan and Europe. Significant structural changes occur, such as increasing scrap availability as steel products reach the end of their lifespan, leading to a gradual shift from BOF to EAF routes. Emissions decline by 120 Mt in 2030. The bulk of this reduction comes from a reduction in steel output, however, compensated for by increased imports. The CO_2 leakage rate reaches 70 per cent by 2030.

OECD (2003) tests the impacts of a CO_2 tax at $25/tCO_2 (€24/tCO_2 using January 2003 exchange rates) applied in the OECD countries or in thirteen European countries (the EU15 minus Finland and Sweden).

The tax applies equally to steel and power generation. BOF steel and EAF steel are treated as similar products, but steel products from different regions are treated as imperfect substitutes. An OECD-wide carbon tax would reduce OECD steel production by 9 per cent. This effect is more pronounced for CO_2-intensive BOF mills (12 per cent) than for the EAF route (2 per cent). Lower steel production in the OECD countries would be partly offset by increased volumes in non-OECD regions. The tax would trigger a reduction of 120 Mt CO_2 inside the OECD, partly offset by a 53 Mt increase outside the region – i.e. a leakage rate of 44 per cent in this sector.

Demailly and Quirion (2008) quantify the impact of the ETS for the iron and steel industry, assuming a CO_2 price of €20, testing the robustness of the results against various assumptions: the abatement cost curve, trade and demand elasticities, pass-through rates and allocation rules. The leakage rate is very robust to the choice of the parameters for the first three assumptions and more sensitive to assumptions on pass-through rates and allocation rules. The authors test pass-through rates ranging from 0.5 to 1.0 in the EU market and from 0.25 to 0.75 in the rest of the world. They model three allocation methods: no updating (lump-sum allocation), output-based updating every five years and emissions-based updating every five years. The leakage rate is lower with output-based updating and with lower pass-through rates. Over the 243 combinations of parameters tested, the leakage rate varies from 0.5 to 25 per cent, with a low median value of 6 per cent. These results are much lower than the above, possibly because the model does not include feedback effects described in other studies, including the decrease in coal and iron ore price and the increase in scrap price triggered by CO_2 reduction measures taken in Europe.

The above studies show that the estimated leakage rate varies greatly with modelling assumptions: tax versus allowance; price elasticity; product differentiation between regions; transport costs and other trade barriers. The leakage rate is also sensitive to the level of pass-through of the carbon cost, as well as to the allowance allocation mode.

Ex post analysis

Figure 7.7 shows that the EU25 became a net importer of steel in 2006 for the first time since at least 1995, although net imports amounted to only 1 per cent of EU production. Was this change a consequence of the ETS? Probably not: EU net imports actually decreased during

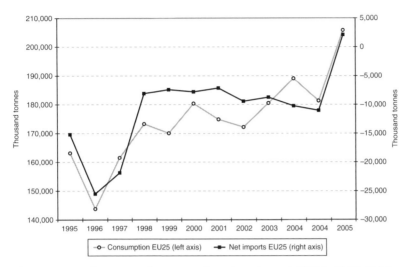

Figure 7.7 Net imports and consumption of crude steel, EU25, 1995–2006
Source: Derived from data in IISI (2005, 2007)

2005, while EUA prices on the spot market increased by 152 per cent between January and December of that year. In fact, net imports increased following a surge in consumption in 2006 (see figure 7.7). This is confirmed by an increase in the utilization rate (the ratio of production to capacity) observed in 2006, from 83 to 90 per cent.[17] Had the rise in net imports been driven by a decrease in price competitiveness, the utilization rate would have decreased. The explanation for the 2006 rise in net imports is undoubtedly a shortfall in domestic production capacities vis-à-vis domestic demand.

To test the relative influence of consumption and of the EU ETS on EU net imports in a more systematic way, monthly data were submitted to a simple econometric test, the results of which are presented in table 7.2. Volume data are provided by Eurofer (www. eurofer.org), for net imports as a whole and separately for long and flat products. Value data are provided by Eurostat's external trade database (ec.europa.eu/eurostat). Two models are compared. In model 1, consumption (in volume) is the only determinant of net imports, while, in model 2, net imports are explained by consumption and

---

[17] Authors' calculation based on production data from IISI (2007) and capacity data from OECD (2008a), for the subset of countries for which data were available.

Table 7.2 *Regression results: influence of consumption and carbon prices on EU net iron and steel imports*

	Model 1			Model 2			
	R^2	Adj. R^2	Consumption coefficient	R^2	Adj. R^2	Consumption coefficient	EUA price coefficient
Flat products (volume)	0.22	0.21	0.07***	0.29	0.24	0.08***	NS
Long products (volume)	0.17	0.15	0.04***	0.18	0.13	0.04***	NS
All products (volume)	0.25	0.24	0.11***	0.3	0.25	0.11***	NS
All products (value)	0.30	0.29	0.10***	0.30	0.28	0.10***	NS

Notes: *** represents 1 per cent significance level. NS indicates that the variable is not significant, even at 10 per cent.
Source: Authors.

the monthly average price of EU allowances. If the ETS had a positive influence on net imports, the EUA price should have a positive and statistically significant coefficient. To overcome unit root problems, the models are regressed on first differences, using ordinary least squares. The estimation period is January 2003 to December 2007.

It turns out that, in all cases, an increase in steel consumption increases net imports. A 1 tonne increase in consumption entails an increase in net imports from approximately 0.04 tonne (long products) up to approximately 0.11 tonne (all products in volume). In contrast, the EUA price is never statistically significant, even at the lenient threshold of 10 per cent.

Conclusion: no observed impact on the iron and steel sector during the first trading period

The above analysis does not allow us to identify an effect of the EU ETS on the competitiveness of the European steel industry at present. Neither does it suggest that this should remain so: the sector was, on the whole, massively over-allocated in the period from 2005 to 2007, and the price of carbon collapsed near the end of the period. It is not clear, under such conditions, that steel companies decided to treat EUAs as a new cost factor that would eventually be reflected in steel market prices. In addition, the global steel market has been very dynamic over the last four years, with surges in input and product prices. Had CO_2 played a role in European steel product prices, it would probably have been overwhelmed by other factors at play in the sector today.

In all, the effects of the EU ETS have been negligible on the immediate competitiveness of the EU steel industry. Simulations suggest that this may change as producers face a real carbon constraint and need to balance abatement costs, compliance costs via the purchase of allowances, and lower output of most CO_2-intensive products, substituted by imports.

Oil-refining

How oil is refined

Oil refineries process crude oil into a variety of petroleum products, from gasoline and light transportation fuels to road tar and bunker

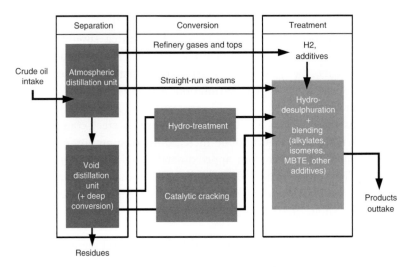

Figure 7.8 Schematic organization of a complex refinery
Note: MBTE = methyl tertiary butyl ether
Source: Adapted from Favennec (2001)

fuel. The role of the refinery is to isolate the different streams of petroleum products from crude oil, to remove the impurities and to convert and blend the different compounds so as to create outputs with valuable properties (Muehlegger 2002). Refiners are constrained in two ways when it comes to their mix of refined products. First, their choice of crude oil intake determines the natural yield of the refinery, and hence the relative quality and quantity of the different streams that compose the end products. Second, the initial choice of refining units and the subsequent decisions on their operational parameters affect how streams are isolated and blended into final products. Figure 7.8 presents the scheme of a modern complex refinery, equipped with advanced conversion capabilities.

There are three major types of refineries.[18]

- Hydroskimming refineries (HSKs): the simplest refinery structure, based on atmospheric and void distillation with very limited conversion capacity.
- Semi-complex refineries: hydroskimming refineries with additional deep conversion units, which transform the heaviest portions of the

[18] For more on refinery types and the different refinery units, see Lacombe (2008).

Table 7.3 *Sources of oil refinery CO_2 emissions*

Source	Fraction
Oil and gas fuel firing of furnaces and boilers	65%
Regeneration of cracker catalyst	16%
Flares	<3%
Methane steam reforming to make hydrogen	2%
Incineration and effluent processes	1%
Power	13%

Source: Gale and Freund (2001).

distillation products into fuel oil streams that are redirected into the plant's blending and conversion units. Examples include visbreaker (VB) and delayed coker (DC) units.

- Complex refineries: deep conversion refineries with additional conversion and treatment capacity. Units such as fluid catalytic crackers (FCCs) and hydrocracking units (HCUs), the most versatile conversion units, allow refineries to transform light and heavy fuel streams efficiently from the distillation process into the desired output mix.

CO_2 emissions and opportunities for abatement

There are three main sources of CO_2 emissions in oil-refining: (1) heat, steam and power needs; (2) process emissions; and (3) flares and effluents (see table 7.3). In European refineries, most heat and steam needs, and on average 55 per cent of the power needs of the plants, are met by burning fuel oil coming from the distillation units in boilers and furnaces. Process emissions are produced through the necessary regeneration of catalysts and through the burning of the coke accumulated during their operation. Other process emissions include those linked to chemical processes, such as hydrogen production from methane. Last, refineries may not always have proper outlets for refinery gas and liquefied petroleum gas (LPG), which may then be burnt in flaring towers. Greenhouse gases may also simply leak along the various circuits of the refinery.

Academic journals, as well as technical and policy reports, describe a range of options to reduce greenhouse gas emissions from refineries. Lacombe (2008) provides a detailed summary of the different options for abatement discussed in the literature, while Worrell and Galitsky (2005) provide a complete guide to potential energy-saving options in refineries. Among the options, refineries may choose to reduce the amount of wastes that are flared; they may switch from fuel oil to cleaner energy sources, such as natural gas or refinery gas; or they may improve the efficiency of their heat and power use by refining various industrial processes.

Well-known and closely controlled sources of CO_2 emissions make refining a prime candidate for carbon capture and storage. Because of the process control and optimization culture of refinery operatives and the existing capability for liquid- and gas-handling, refineries could leverage their expertise to accelerate the deployment of CO_2 recovery pipelines and systems. CO_2 streams in refineries stem mostly from the combustion of a fuel/ambient air mixture, however, and hence have a low concentration that is suboptimal for carbon capture.

Economic environment

Three macroeconomic trends dominated the economic environment of oil refineries as the EU ETS was introduced: a widening global trade imbalance linked to the shift towards diesel in Europe, a surge in crude oil prices that largely trumped any other driver of refining profitability, and a dearth of resources available for abatement investment.

A major constraint on energy efficiency improvements has been the widening imbalance between gasoline and diesel consumption in the European Union and the United States. Figure 7.9 presents the net imports of gasoline and diesel into the European Union, expressed as a percentage of gasoline production and of diesel production inside the Union. Official data are given for the EU25 area until 2005 and for the EU27 area in 2006 and 2007. The figure reveals that the European Union consumes more diesel than it produces and produces more gasoline than it consumes, with the gap steadily widening since 2000.

Combined with the fact that the United States consumes more gasoline than it produces, the European demand for diesel creates a trade imbalance on the global petroleum products market: the European Union exports the excess gasoline it produces in order to serve the needs of the United States and imports diesel to meet its own

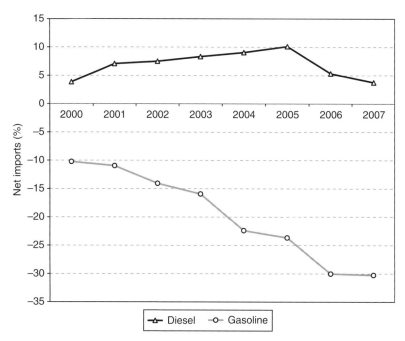

Figure 7.9 Net imports as a percentage of domestic production in the European Union, 2000–7
Source: Adapted from Eurostat (2008b)

demands. This imbalance in demand is unlikely to decrease significantly in the future, and it forces refineries to operate out of their optimal configuration, which entails higher carbon emissions. This poses significant challenges for the competitiveness of the EU refining industry under a carbon constraint.

Another factor that weakened the abatement incentives created by the EU ETS was the surge in prices that unfolded during the first period of the scheme. Figure 7.10 presents the evolution of refinery margins in the European Union, computed on the basis of the market prices of a barrel of Brent and of petroleum products, based on the theoretical output mix for cracking and hydroskimming refinery types. It shows that cracking margins, a good indicator of the profitability of advanced refineries in the European Union, reached an historic high during the period.

The surge in crude oil prices from around $30 per barrel in 2004 to up to more than $100 at the end of 2007 and its impact on

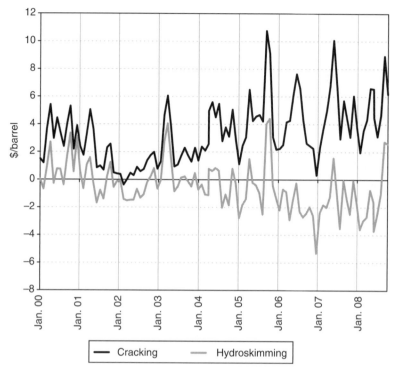

Figure 7.10 Evolution of EU refinery margins, 2000–8
Source: IEA (2008)

refinery margins trumped all other economic developments. While a higher crude price translates into an added incentive for energy efficiency, it also means that the carbon price incentive per barrel is weaker, and that carbon costs are a smaller portion of net margins. Qualitative evidence from a series of interviews also suggests that the high margins that prevailed at the time meant that refiners did not care as much about carbon costs as they would have under financial pressure.

Finally, several structural constraints combine to complicate and delay any in-depth response to the introduction of a carbon price. After years of low margins and low growth, the industry suffers from underinvestment. The size of the experienced workforce has plummeted, which puts an additional strain on capital stock renewal. Tightening sulphur content requirements also entails higher

CO_2 emissions, on account of the drastically increased utilization of treatment units.

Evaluation of the impact of the EU ETS on the competitiveness of the European refining industry

Ex ante simulations

The most authoritative *ex ante* study to date of the competitiveness impact of the CO_2 constraint on EU refining is that of Reinaud (2005b). It builds on a microeconomic model of European refineries developed by an oil and gas consultancy to assess the changes in costs stemming from different scenarios. Table 7.4 reports a summary of the results from the study, and the impact of carbon costs on refinery margins.

Reinaud concludes that 'the opportunity cost of CO_2 allowances is not trivial for the refining industry' (Reinaud 2005b: 10). These costs are fully offset under the present grandfathering system, but could become more important if allowances were to be auctioned.

Smale *et al.* (2006) investigate *ex ante* the effect of the EU ETS on petroleum prices. Based on an oligopolistic model of refineries in Europe, they find a cost pass-through rate that would lead to a 0.4 to 0.6 per cent increase in firms' profits.

Ex post analysis

The available quantitative evidence suggests that the EU ETS has had little measurable impact so far. A first aspect of *ex post* competitiveness impact assessment is the issue of short-term carbon leakage materialized by trade flow changes, and specifically by potential losses of market share on the part of intra-ETS companies to extra-ETS companies.

To account for short-term carbon leakage, Lacombe (2008) tests for the presence of structural breaks in the trends of the time series of deseasonalized net imports of gasoline and diesel. The time series are reported in figure 7.11, and the regression coefficients are reported in table 7.5.

As evidenced by figure 7.11 and table 7.5, breaks in the series are indeed detected, but they are not statistically significant, and the net import trends tend to converge towards a stabilization of the EU25 global trade imbalance, suggesting that carbon leakages are not yet a discernible threat. In the long run, carbon leakage may still be an issue if the scheme creates a structural profitability differential

Table 7.4 Ex ante *estimates of the impact of direct and indirect costs of CO_2 on refinery margins*

Configuration[1]	Emissions	Direct carbon cost	Impact on refinery margins
	Tonne CO_2 per tonne of crude	\$/tonne CO_2	\$ barrel
North-west Europe: Belgium, France, Germany, Ireland, Netherlands, United Kingdom			
HSK	0.078	1.93	−1.77
+VB+FCC	0.149	3.68	2.58
+VB+HCU	0.129	3.19	−1.42
+DC+HCU	0.131	3.26	5.46
+VB+FCC+HCU	0.154	3.82	4.69
Mediterranean Europe: Greece, Italy, Portugal, Spain			
HSK	0.079	1.96	−2.46
+VB+FCC	0.144	3.57	2.65
+VB+HCU	0.131	3.26	4.16
+DC+HCU	0.133	3.29	3.51
+VB+FCC+HCU	0.149	3.7	4.94
Central Europe south: Austria, Czech Republic, Poland, Slovakia, Slovenia			
HSK	0.083	2.12	−0.33
+VB+FCC	0.141	3.5	5.08
+VB+HCU	0.149	3.7	6.05
+VB+FCC+HCU	0.153	3.79	4.42
Central Europe north: Denmark, Finland, Norway, Sweden			
HSK	0.083	2.12	−0.33
+VB+FCC	0.141	3.5	4.51
+VB+HCU	0.149	3.7	5.4
+VB+FCC+HCU	0.153	3.79	4.35

Notes: [1]KSK: Hydroskimming; VB: Visbreaking; FCC: Fluid Catalytic Cracker; HCU: Hydro Cracking Unit; DC: Delayed Coker.
Source: Reinaud (2005b).

between EU and non-EU refineries, which would curb the growth of refining capacity inside the European Union. A last element of competitiveness analysis hence consists of understanding what the impact of the EU ETS has been on the profitability of refineries.

The high variability of refinery plant design and the strategic nature of operating cost information make production cost data difficult to

Table 7.5 *Chow test for structural break in January 2005 in the trends of deseasonalized gasoline and diesel net excess demand*

Hypothesis	Structural break in January 2005 for net gasoline excess demand	Structural break in January 2005 for net diesel excess demand
F-statistics	$F\,(2,\,88) = 2.07$	$F\,(2,\,88) = 0.78$
P-value	$\Pr > F = 0.1319$	$\Pr > F = 0.4638$

Source: Lacombe (2008).

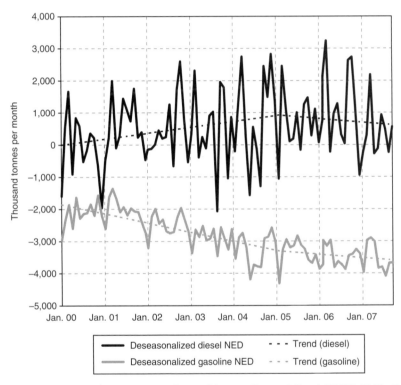

Figure 7.11 Trends in net excess demand for gasoline and diesel, EU25, 2000–7
Source: Lacombe (2008)

gather. Table 7.6 presents an estimated average cost structure of refineries under simplifying hypotheses (detailed in Lacombe 2008). These results largely confirm the *ex ante* results of Reinaud (2005b): in the margin environment prevailing in 2008, a full auctioning of

Table 7.6 *Refining cost structure under the EU ETS*

Cost item	Expenditure	
	€ per bbl processed	€ per tonne processed
Electricity	0.10	0.75
Chemicals and catalysts	0.10	0.75
Labour and maintenance	0.55	4.00
Materials and others	0.20	1.50
Capital depreciation	0.20	1.50
Total transformation costs	1.15	8.50
Added cost of electricity	0.02	0.15
Net cost of allowances	−0.04	−0.30
Total cost after EU ETS (period 1)	1.13	8.35
Full cash cost of allowances	0.59	4.30
Projected total cost with full auctioning	1.72	12.75
Comparison: crude purchase	80	585
(of which: consumed in refinery)	2.70	19.80
Comparison: transformation margin	3.30	24.40

Sources: Lacombe (2008), from European Commission, McKinsey & Company and Ecofys (2006).

allowances at €20/tCO$_2$ would represent a cash cost equivalent to 1 per cent of the cost of the crude oil processed, while margins are currently closer to 5 per cent.

Ex post studies of carbon allowance cost pass-through have so far failed to exhibit a causal link between the introduction of the scheme and any clear change in prices. As carbon costs have so far been very limited for refineries and refinery margins have stayed high, no significant detrimental effects of the ETS on profitability have been noticed during the period. The topic nonetheless calls for scrutiny during the next stages of the scheme, as competitiveness issues may arise when allowances are no longer allocated for free.

A survey of the refining industry: perspectives on competitiveness
Lacombe (2008) conducted a series of interviews of executives and managers at refineries and the downstream headquarters of four major European oil and gas companies whose footprints total

36.9 per cent of the recorded emissions from refining in the European Union. Although the answers to this survey are hard to back by precise quantitative evidence, they show a clearer and more differentiated picture of the impact of the EU ETS on the EU refining industry than inferred from the quantitative evidence available to date.

An important conclusion from the series of interviews is that some abatement potential remains in the refining sector. The price of carbon was widely recognized as a factor that added to the incentives for energy efficiency created by high fuel costs. This led to an emphasis on 'leak-plugging' activities, with some notable successes. No significant changes in price and production were measurable during this first period, however, because the EU allowance price was too low to trigger capital stock renewal; one interviewee described the mechanism as a 'computer simulation of a carbon market'. Clearly, this situation would change under full auctioning of allowances.

The trading scheme was instrumental in helping the oil-refining sector to build the monitoring capacity needed to tackle the carbon constraint and price, without leading to substantial costs. This proved to be more difficult than foreseen, however. Three years after the introduction of the scheme and four years after the legislative debate, engineers at modern, state-of-the-art refineries were still battling with flow measurement devices to decrease the uncertainty of CO_2 emissions reporting. Others quoted the sheer complexity of the industrial refining facilities as a factor that delayed the completion of verification.

The survey revealed that some participants had internalized CO_2 costs. They have made business units liable for their CO_2 emissions, while retaining allowances at the headquarters. This has removed potentially flawed incentives linked to free allowances, as it ties business unit results to abatement without exposing companies to the full cost of carbon and related competitiveness effects.

Conclusion: no observed impact on the refining sector during the first trading period

In all, the EU ETS has so far had minimal impacts on the competitiveness of the EU refining sector, which also benefited from fairly high refinery margins in these years. This recent experience may be a poor indication of the scheme's future impact on the competitiveness of the refining sector, however, especially as the cap becomes more binding and free allocation is phased out. As is the case for other sectors, three years is too short a time to make definitive judgements; nonetheless, the disparity between *ex ante* expectations of competitive impact and the impact observed to date is noteworthy.

Aluminium[19]

How aluminium is produced

The production of primary aluminium consists of three steps: bauxite mining, alumina production and electrolysis. One hundred tonnes of bauxite produce twenty to twenty-five tonnes of primary aluminium, which is extracted from alumina in reduction plants (smelters) through electrolysis. Two main types of smelters are used: the Hall–Héroult system and the Søderberg cell. The majority of global primary aluminium production uses the former, and, in Europe, Søderberg units account for some 10 per cent of the total capacity (European Aluminium Association [EAA]: see www.eaa.net). By 2010 the share of the latter technology should decrease to 6 per cent of total EU capacity, as it is less efficient in its electricity use than the Hall–Héroult system.

The secondary aluminium sector recycles process scrap or used aluminium products. There are no differences in quality between an aluminium product entirely made of primary metal and a product made of recycled metal. The output of both primary and secondary production routes is molten aluminium, further processed and combined into ingots of various shapes. Other finishing processes are applied based on consumers' needs. The aluminium production pathway is illustrated in figure 7.12.

CO_2 emissions and opportunities for abatement

The aluminium sector contributes 1.4 per cent of the world's total GHG emissions – of which 0.6 per cent is direct emissions from the aluminium plants and 0.8 per cent is indirect emissions from electricity generation (Marks 2007). The largest source of both direct and indirect greenhouse gases in the production of aluminium comes from primary smelting operations (IAI [International Aluminium Institute]

---

[19] This section is based closely on Reinaud (2008b).

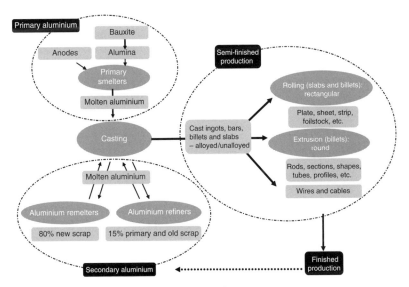

Figure 7.12 Schematic of aluminium production
Source: Reinaud (2008a)

2007). Direct emissions from smelting are CO_2 emitted during electrolysis, which uses carbon anodes, and two perfluorinated carbon compounds, CF_4 and C_2F_6, which are emitted when the process is out of balance. In Europe, direct emissions from primary aluminium production are estimated at 2.4 to 2.8 tCO_2 equivalent per tonne of aluminium (see table 7.7).[20]

Primary aluminium production is about twenty times as energy-intensive as aluminium-recycling (IEA 2007b). Indeed, electrolysis is the most energy-intensive step in the production of aluminium. Primary aluminium-smelting consumes large quantities of electricity: electrolysis uses 15.3 MWh per tonne (MWh/t) on average globally; the EU27 average is lower, at 14.8 MWh/t. Secondary aluminium consumes only about 5 per cent of the electricity needed to produce primary aluminium, however. Downstream, rolling and extruding consume 4.5 per cent of the electricity needed in primary smelting; hence the focus here on primary aluminium-smelting.

Several options are available to reduce greenhouse gas emissions from aluminium production. Blending recycled metal with new metal

[20] The share of perfluorocarbon (PFC) emissions in total direct CO_2e emissions ranges between 28 and 31 per cent.

Table 7.7 *Direct emissions from primary aluminium production*

	Primary		Rolling	Extrusion	Remelting
	Anode produced on-site	Purchased carbon anode			
Average 2005 emissions (tCO$_2$/t primary aluminium)	2.79	2.39	0.135	0.155	0.184

Source: Authors' communication with the EAA.

allows considerable energy savings, although this is limited by the availability of scrap. Second, the existing Søderberg processes could be replaced by Hall–Héroult – the former uses about 15 to 18 MWh/t, as compared to 13 to 16.5 MWh/t for the latter. Finally, the enhanced use of process heat could allow for further savings.

Economic environment

The primary aluminium sector is not directly covered by the EU ETS in its first and second commitment periods. Aluminium-related prices are set at the London Metals Exchange (LME), and these prices are global, with a few price premiums based on product and location. Primary aluminium prices increased by 82 per cent between 2003 and 2006, to reach $2,500/tonne (€2,075/tonne using 2006 exchange rates). This increase was driven by supply-demand dynamics as well as the high prices of raw materials (i.e. alumina and electricity) and freight costs. Chinese smelters are the main drivers in the aluminium and alumina market.[21] Chinese demand is estimated at approximately 33 per cent of global demand; and the country's consumption grew by 37 per cent in 2007 alone (ENAM Research 2007), matched by an increase in production.

---

[21] Russia ranks second, after China, with some 12 per cent of production capacity as of 2004. Over the long term, the aluminium industry in OECD countries is feeling the pressure not just from the growing Chinese output but also from new capacity in the Middle East, which benefits from low fossil-fuel-based electricity costs.

Aluminium is heavily traded: 77 per cent of total output is traded internationally. Its high value per tonne means that transport costs weigh little in the final price; further, production is traditionally located near low-cost electricity capacity. The latter is a major element in the choice of location; proximity to markets much less so, in contrast to commodities such as cement.

In 2006 the European Union produced 14 per cent of the world's primary aluminium, as compared to 22 per cent in 1980. Total output, however, grew by 33 per cent, from 3.5 Mt in 1980 to 4.7 Mt in 2006, with most of that growth occurring before 1999. Since then production has increased only by 5 per cent, while consumption has grown by 40 per cent. The shortfall was met by imports into EU27 countries; the region became a net importer in 2000.

The bulk of primary aluminium imports into individual EU countries originate from outside the European Union: the volume of intra-EU trade was only 60 per cent of the imports from non-EU countries in 2006. Eight countries account for 85 per cent of imports into the Union (see figure 7.13).

Evaluation of the impact of the EU ETS on the competitiveness of the European aluminium industry

Ex ante studies

While the primary aluminium sector is not directly covered by the EU ETS in its first and second commitment periods, the sector is in theory vulnerable to the EU ETS due to its high electricity intensity. Studies have shown that the cost of the EU ETS can be high at the margin for aluminium (Reinaud 2005a; European Commission 2006b). These marginal costs could have a pronounced effect on decisions to increase output in, or imports into, the region. An allowance price of €20/tCO$_2$ would increase operational (i.e. variable) costs in a primary smelter by 9 to 30 per cent depending on the electricity intensity of the primary smelter (Reinaud 2008a).

Ex post assessments

Reinaud (2008b) considers two indicators of changes in the competitiveness of an activity: profit margins driven by costs and prices, and trade flows.

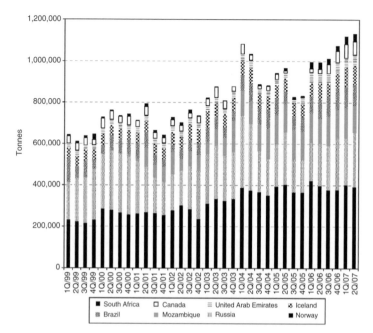

Figure 7.13 Main sources of primary aluminium imports into the EU27, 1999–2007
Source: Reinaud (2008b)

High LME prices have allowed European primary aluminium smelters to benefit from operational margins in the order of 49 per cent, compared to 20 per cent on average in 1999. Nonetheless, it costs more to produce a tonne of primary aluminium in Europe than in many other regions. What is true today was also true in 1999, a few years before the introduction of the ETS.

The primary aluminium sector in the European Union, whose emissions are not capped in the present EU ETS, still stands to lose profit margins and, possibly, market shares, as electricity prices have increased following a constraint on generators' emissions (see annex for more details on the effect of the EU ETS on electricity prices in Europe). In theory, a 10 per cent increase in electricity costs would imply a cost increase of $50/tonne (€39/tonne using November 2008 prices) of primary aluminium for an average European smelter (or 3 per cent of the total operating costs).

European smelters' electricity costs increased (on average) slightly more rapidly than in the rest of the world (Reinaud 2008b). This

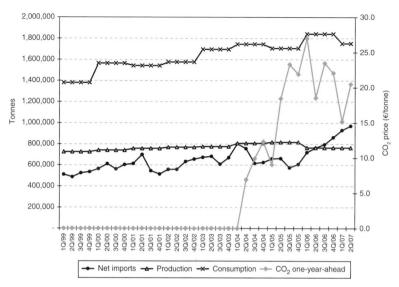

Figure 7.14 Evolution of net imports, production and consumption of primary aluminium and evolution of CO_2 prices, EU27, 1999–2007
Sources: Derived from Point Carbon data and private communication with the EEA

increase occurred despite a rather low proportion of smelters that acquire electricity on the markets. As of 2006 82 per cent of Europe's primary smelting capacity was operating under long-term electricity contracts. Beyond this distinction, large price differences exist for smelters within countries: for example, an estimated difference of €23/MWh between the highest and lowest prices in the Netherlands, €22/MWh in Germany, €21/MWh in the United Kingdom and €25/ MWh across eastern Europe.[22] These differences have grown significantly since 1999, when they were in the €2–17/MWh range. These growing differences may be interpreted as signs that some long-term contracts expired; this is reported to be the case in the Netherlands and for some German smelters.

Figure 7.14 shows that net imports of primary aluminium have risen more rapidly since 2005 (by 25 per cent in total in 2005/6). This can be explained partly by an increase in consumption but also by the closure of some 6.5 per cent of the European Union's production

---

[22] That same year the average European price paid by smelters was approximately €30/MWh.

Table 7.8 *Regression results: influence of consumption and carbon prices on EU net primary aluminium imports*

Model 1			Model 2			
R^2	Adj. R^2	Consumption coefficient	R^2	Adj. R^2	Consumption coefficient	EUA price coefficient
0.54	0.52	0.64***	0.54	0.51	0.61***	NS

Notes: ***represents 1 per cent significance level. NS indicates that the variable is not significant, even at 10 per cent.
Source: Authors.

since 2005.[23] The owners of the smelters that were shut down reported that the closures were motivated by the companies' inability to secure power contracts, rising electric energy prices in the region and the weak dollar. Is this a sign that the closure was caused by the CO_2 cap, and not by electricity prices in Europe? At this stage of the analysis, it is not possible to draw this conclusion.

A simple econometric analysis was used to test the relative influence of consumption and of carbon prices on EU net imports for the EU27 as a whole.[24] The results are displayed in table 7.8. In the first model, consumption is the only determinant of net imports; in the second model, net imports are explained by consumption and by the monthly average price of EU allowances. The underlying assumption is that, as CO_2 prices rise, so do electricity costs, and, with them, the incentive to import primary aluminium instead of producing it in the European Union with too low a profit margin.[25] The models were tested

[23] Three smelters closed, in Germany, Hungary and France. In addition, one smelter in Switzerland also closed as the result of high European electricity prices. Note that Switzerland's electricity prices are correlated to prices in Germany and France.

[24] Such models were not run with electricity prices as explanatory variables, because there is no single indicator for EU-wide electricity prices (Reinaud 2007) and there is no definitive information on how electricity prices translate into costs for this sector. The $/€ exchange rate and price premiums for Europe were tested, but they were not statistically significant in explaining changes in trade flows.

[25] In continental Europe, if smelters are no longer under long-term supply contracts, the general practice is to sign one-year-ahead electricity contracts (Reinaud 2007). The electricity suppliers hedge their position by buying CO_2 allowances on the forward market.

between the first quarter of 1999 and the second quarter of 2007 for the EU27 as a whole.

An increase in aluminium consumption has a direct impact on net imports: the simple model suggests that a 1 tonne increase in consumption entails a 0.64 increase in net imports. The statistical results reveal no effect to date of the EUA price in the European Union on net imports of primary aluminium, however.

Reinaud (2008b) further tests whether net trade flows incurred any structural change upon the introduction of the EU ETS, finding that there has been no measurable structural change in trade flows between 1999 and 2006.

The absence of statistical evidence of a direct effect of CO_2 prices on aluminium trade flows is not surprising. There are a number of reasons as to why the impacts during the period under review would have been difficult to observe: the prevalence of long-term electricity contracts; a high cycle for demand for aluminium and correspondingly high prices on the London Metals Exchange, which should alleviate concomitant increases in costs, including those related to CO_2; high levels of imports following an increase in consumption and no additional production capacity coming online in the European Union; and, finally, aluminium smelter direct emissions were not covered by the EU ETS in this period.

This should certainly not be taken as definitive evidence that increased electricity prices caused in part by the EU ETS have had no impact on aluminium smelting. Some smelters have definitely suffered from increases in electricity prices following the end of their long-term contracts. What remains unclear, however, is how quickly such a phenomenon will develop and lead to an additional increase in aluminium imports compared to what would have happened in the absence of the EU ETS.

The impacts of a carbon price may be felt when prices move as global supply comes online over the next few years. Moreover, by 2010 power supply contracts will have expired for 65 per cent of EU capacity. By 2016 no smelter will benefit from a power contract concluded before the European Union embarked on electricity market reform. Combined with the full auctioning of EU allowances to power generators after 2012, and more ambitious mitigation objectives, the sector should incur higher electricity costs, all other things being equal.

Finally, the EU ETS may also include the aluminium sector's direct emissions of CO_2 and PFCs after 2012. At current levels of more than 2 tCO_2e per tonne of aluminium, the inclusion of aluminium in the EU ETS could add a non-trivial cost. On the other hand, international best practices record much lower PFC emissions than the average reveals, with PFC emissions near 0.1 tCO_2e per tonne (Porteous 2007). The additional cost to the sector will depend largely on its ability to move to best practices in PFC emissions. The pressure through electricity prices is likely to remain, however, as breakthrough technologies are not on the horizon yet. If the sector's direct emissions were covered, acquiring allowances to cover all emissions from additional production would push costs up by 45–46 per cent (depending on whether the carbon anode is produced on-site or off-site).

Conclusion: no observed impact on the aluminium sector during the first trading period

As is the case for the other sectors examined, we find no statistical evidence that the EU ETS has triggered additional imports from countries without a carbon cost. As was true for cement, iron and steel, and refining, the observed changes in imports and EU production appear to be more a continuation of past trends in the industry than specific responses to the imposition of a carbon price.

In the case of aluminium, however, three factors make it harder than usual to detect the effect of the ETS. First, EU smelters have benefited from relatively high profit margins as a result of high aluminium prices, which doubled profit margins in the European Union and overwhelmed any effect of the EU ETS. The high prices were even enough to cause one smelter in Germany, closed in 2005, to reopen in 2007.[26] Second, most smelters still benefit from electricity supply contracts that shelter them from any immediate impact of higher electricity costs due to a CO_2 price. Third, not all, or even most, of the increase in electricity costs can be attributed to the inclusion of the

---

[26] It should also be noted, however, that the smelter that reopened was written down in the books (i.e. fully depreciated) of the previous owner (a global aluminium operator) and then sold to local investors, who reopened it on the back of high aluminium prices, a short-term electricity position (including the decline in the ETS permit price), German government assistance to maintain employment, and almost zero capital exposure. This combination of factors provided the opportunity for strong positive cash flow for the new owners.

new CO_2 price. Fuel prices were notably higher during the trial period, and disentangling the contribution of CO_2 costs is not easy.

Competitiveness impacts and leakage: only preliminary conclusions

Policy discussions around the revision of the EU ETS and various legislative proposals for cap-and-trade systems in the United States, among others, confirm the importance of competitiveness concerns in the political economy of such systems.

This chapter has provided a comprehensive analysis of the competitiveness impacts of the EU ETS on a diverse set of activities seen as the most vulnerable to a carbon constraint because of their high level of CO_2 emissions per output or their exposure to indirect costs, from electricity in particular. The analysis exposes great differences and some common features across these activities. Cement has a low value per tonne, and is not transported easily on land; coastal production may be at risk, provided there is excess capacity in the rest of the world. Iron and steel are much more traded and therefore exposed to international competition – but they too appear to have been little affected. The refining sector, not unlike steel, has enjoyed growing margins that diminished the effect of any carbon cost introduced by a free allocation of CO_2 allowances. Aluminium, not covered by the EU ETS, ought to have felt the pinch of higher electricity prices, yet most smelters still enjoy long-term contracts with their suppliers, and, when they do not, they have been able to surf the wave of high international aluminium prices.

Using 2005–6 trade data (imports to and exports from the European Union), no statistical evidence of a change coinciding with the introduction of the EU ETS can be found. Had the scheme had an impact, the Union would have increased imports of cheaper substitutes from unconstrained regions and exported less to the rest of the world. While this has been a general trend for some of these sectors (aluminium and steel), the additional impact of the EU cap-and-trade system has not been felt to date. These results are in stark contrast with *ex ante* analyses, which projected negative effects from a unilateral constraint on emissions from these industries. The first trading period may be a poor indicator of what is to come, however: CO_2 prices were new and volatile; many installations in these sectors were granted allowances in excess of their actual emissions; and two to three years of observations say little, if anything, about where companies will take their next investments.

Monitoring trade flows, in combination with other observations on prices, is important to expose any impact of the European Union's climate policy on the competitiveness of these sectors vis-à-vis the rest of the world. Concerns about competitiveness and leakage have not diminished, and, as countries move towards more ambitious mitigation commitments, it is likely that the debate will only grow. Without calling for undue trade protection, policy-makers will need to consider measures to ensure that industry in the European Union has a fair chance of developing the low-CO_2 production patterns that will both establish the feasibility of a low-carbon economy and enable EU industry to remain competitive.

8 | Costs

Introduction

No concept is more debated before the adoption of an environmental programme, and less discussed afterwards, than cost. Typically, a number of *ex ante* analyses of cost can be found, albeit of varying quality, but few or no *ex post* evaluations. Part of the problem is that cost can be defined in a number of different ways and from a variety of perspectives. This chapter starts with a discussion of the varying concepts of cost as typically found in analyses, including the important economic distinction between costs and transfers. The next section discusses the several published *ex ante* studies that have presented some aspects of cost for the first period of the EU ETS. The following section takes an *ex post* perspective and offers several estimates of what the cost of the EU ETS during the trial period might reasonably have been. The next section addresses an aspect of cost that is often overlooked: transaction costs. These are not the direct costs that are occasioned in reducing emissions but the more indirect costs that are incurred in preparing for and participating in the programme. In this instance, the results of a survey of the transaction costs incurred by Irish installations included in the EU ETS are reported. The final section concludes.

Defining cost

A first important distinction is that between costs and transfers. Strictly speaking, costs reflect resources – labour, capital, energy, etc. – that are devoted to producing a good or service and, thereby, are not available for other uses. In this context, the resources used in reducing emissions are costs, since these resources are not available for producing the conventional goods and services that were produced before the cap-and-trade programme was initiated, and that would be produced in the absence of the programme. Transfers do not diminish the goods and services available for other uses, but only redistribute them. These transfers are the scarcity rents that are created by the carbon constraint and embodied in the value of allowances in a cap-and-trade programme. They are the cap-and-trade analogue to the revenues generated by a tax on carbon. These transfers have been pejoratively called 'windfall profits' when paid to corporations and are usually (but not always) viewed more benevolently when received by the government through auctioning the allowances. However the allowances are distributed, the price on carbon implies that those who consume a lot of carbon-intensive goods and services will have less to spend on other goods and services, while the recipients of these transfers will have more to spend. By the common analogy with a pie, costs shrink the pie while transfers rearrange the slices.

A simple way to think about the net effects is to imagine auctioned allowances with the revenues returned fully to households on a per capita basis. Individuals leading a more carbon-intensive life than average would pay more than they receive, and they would have to reduce their consumption of conventional goods and services. On the other hand, those leading a less carbon-intensive life would receive more than they pay, and would thus be able to increase their consumption. The end result of this equal per capita distribution of the scarcity rent is that conventional goods and services would be redistributed in some small way from more carbon-consumptive households to those using less carbon. Other distributions of the transfers created by the scarcity rent would result in other net effects. For instance, free allocation benefits primarily shareholders of the corporations receiving the allowances. In this case, the redirection of conventional goods and services would be from all consumers to those consumers who are also shareholders of the corporations receiving free allowances.[1]

These two concepts – their approximate magnitudes, and their relation to emissions and abatement – can be simply illustrated as in figure 8.1.

The horizontal axis represents emissions, with the value 100 expressing business-as-usual (BAU) emissions. The vertical axis is the marginal cost of reducing emissions, or, alternatively, the price of

---

[1] It bears noting that the government is also a beneficiary of free allocation, through the taxation of corporate profits.

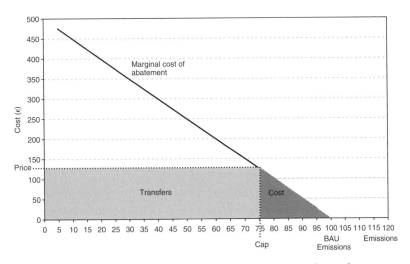

Figure 8.1 Relation between emissions, abatement, cost and transfers
Source: Authors

allowances, in some monetary unit. The downward-sloping line shows the relation between a given emissions constraint and the marginal cost of abatement, or, equivalently, the price of allowances. For instance, a cap that would reduce emissions by 25 per cent, to 75 on the horizontal axis, would produce an allowance price of 125 on the vertical axis, at the point labelled 'Price'.

An efficient programme of emission reduction would make all reductions up to this price, as represented by the triangle labelled 'Cost', which represents the direct expenditures for labour, capital and intermediate products that would be needed to reduce emissions. The rectangular area, labelled 'Transfers', represents the value of the remaining emissions, as embodied either in the value of allowances freely allocated to various legal entities in a cap-and-trade programme or as revenues flowing to the government if a tax instrument is chosen or allowances are auctioned. The sum of the transfer rectangle and the cost triangle represents the redistribution of goods and services that are occasioned by the price of the newly regulated emissions.

As is readily evident in figure 8.1, the transfers are much greater in magnitude than the resource cost of abatement when the ambition of the cap and the implied abatement are modest. As is also readily evident, as the cap is reduced, the cost triangle increases steadily, while the transfer rectangle may increase or decrease initially (depending on the slope of the marginal abatement cost curve), but eventually it will diminish and even disappear if emissions are reduced to zero.

While, from the standpoint of society as a whole, transfers can be viewed with relative indifference, the same is not necessarily so for the consumers, citizens and voters who are on the sending and receiving ends of the transfers. The entities that are now required to pay for these rights to emit will regard these payments as costs, however they may be defined by economists. For them, distinguishing between cost and transfer is a distinction without a difference. Consequently, it is not hard to understand that, while much of the debate about cap-and-trade programmes invokes cost, most of the controversy actually concerns transfers.

Within the definition of cost, several concepts of cost are commonly encountered. The one most frequently used, the allowance price or the marginal cost of abatement, is, properly speaking, not a cost at all but an indicator of cost. As just noted, the tighter the cap the higher the marginal cost or price, and the greater the cost, all else being equal.

A more complete measure is total abatement cost, often expressed as some fraction of GDP, which can be interpreted as the area represented by the triangle in figure 8.1. The inadequacy of marginal cost as an indicator of total cost can also be readily grasped by reference to this figure. The slope (and convexity) of the MAC curve determines total cost for any given level of abatement and corresponding marginal cost. For any given level of abatement or marginal cost, there could be many different shapes of the MAC curve that would yield very different figures for total cost.

Yet another cost concept, associated with computable general equilibrium models and also often expressed as a percentage of GDP, is welfare cost. General equilibrium models take other secondary pricing and distributive effects into account, unlike partial equilibrium analyses, which ignore these effects. Technically, welfare cost is the loss of consumer and producer surplus after the entire economy has fully adjusted to the carbon constraint and the effects of the carbon price. Welfare cost is the most complete and theoretically correct cost concept; it requires more elaborate modelling than is often available to those developing cost analyses, however, and under most circumstances the magnitudes of welfare cost and total abatement cost will be similar.

Table 8.1 Ex ante *estimates of the EUA clearing price for period 1*

Study	Model	ETS clearing price (€/allowance)
Böhringer *et al.* 2005	PACE-SIMAC	0
Kemfert *et al.* 2006	GTAP-E	2.00
Reilly and Paltsev 2006	EPPA-EU	0.50–0.85
Jourdan de Muizon 2006	GTAP-ECAT	0.50

Ex ante evaluations of the costs of the EU ETS

Anyone seeking *ex ante* estimates of the total cost of the EU ETS during the trial period will search in vain. The most that can be found are estimates of the marginal cost or price of allowances, and four of these analyses (Böhringer *et al.* 2005, Kemfert *et al.* 2006, Reilly and Paltsev 2006 and Jourdan de Muizon 2006) agree that this price would be very low, as illustrated in table 8.1.

The relative paucity of cost estimates for the trial period is under-standable: almost all attention was focused on the subsequent 2008–12 period, when the EU ETS would be an important part of the policy package for meeting the European Union's Kyoto obliga-tions. The whole point of the trial period was to prepare for this subsequent, more serious engagement. Thus, when cost estimates are provided, they are for 2010 or 2012, and in some cases for 2020. The motivation of these analyses also varies, usually depending on when they were completed. The early studies (generally those completed before 2005) tend to focus on the cost savings from emissions trading as part of the European Union's climate policy mix for meeting its Kyoto obligations.[2] Typically, the cost savings were those to be obtained if emissions trading occurred among the then EU15 rather than each member state taking actions independently to achieve their targets under the European burden-sharing agreement. Since the trial period was not yet a reality for these very early analyses, the studies tended to model emissions trading as economy-wide, or, if recognizing the sectoral nature of the EU ETS, they assumed that the ETS totals

[2] For example, Capros and Mantzos (2000), Institute for Prospective Technological Studies (2000), Sijm *et al.* (2002) and COWI (2004).

and the measures adopted in the non-ETS sectors would result in the same marginal costs.

Once the trial period was established and the NAP1 process completed, analytic attention shifted to the implications of the NAP1 totals for the costs of meeting the European Union's emission reduction obligations under the Kyoto Protocol for 2008–12.[3] All the later studies point out that, if the NAP1 totals for the ETS sectors were continued into the second period, a more than proportionate reduction and higher marginal costs would be implied for the non-ETS sectors, since the ETS would then be a cap within the Kyoto cap. Some of these studies (Böhringer *et al.* 2005 and Jourdan de Muizon 2006) make estimates of first period prices, but the focus is always on the 2008–12 period, and few further results, such as total cost, are reported for the trial period.

The four studies cited in table 8.1 that provide *ex ante* marginal cost estimates for the trial period largely share the objectives of showing cost savings and pointing out the implications for Kyoto compliance. Kemfert *et al.* (2006) use the NAP1 allocations as the allowed emission levels to demonstrate the gains from EU-wide trading when compared with cases in which trading was restricted to sectors within member states or was not allowed at all. Böhringer *et al.* (2005) and Jourdan de Muizon (2006) assume EU-wide trading but focus on showing that the NAP1 cap levels implied a more expensive level of abatement from the non-ETS sectors if maintained into the second trading period.

Although written at a time when actual EU ETS prices were much higher than what the models were predicting, none of the previous studies commented on this disparity. Reilly and Paltsev (2006) focus squarely on what then appeared to be a serious empirical challenge to the accuracy of these state-of-the-art analyses. They note that survey estimates of the first-period price gathered by Point Carbon from market participants prior to and at the start of the EU ETS were higher than estimated by modelling studies – a median estimate of €5.50 in late 2003 and €7.00 in early 2005 – although still much below the actual level prices for more than half the first period. Their paper is devoted to a discussion of alternative explanations of the observed high prices, such as unusual weather, higher than expected

---

[3] For example, Böhringer *et al.* (2005), Klepper and Peterson (2005), Peterson (2006) and Jourdan de Muizon (2006).

natural gas prices, errors in modelling estimates of key parameter values, etc. They find that none of these could explain the observed high prices and cautiously suggest that the prices observed in this early market may not reflect fundamentals, at least as represented in the computable general equilibrium models used in these studies.

The four studies of the trial period predict very low marginal costs (and, consequently, total costs), because all find that the EU-wide cap in the first period was either non-restrictive (Böhringer *et al.* 2005) or only very slightly so, requiring emission reductions at most of a few percentage points. These turned out to be accurate judgements, although, in seeking to explain the discrepancy between these predictions and observed prices for the trial period, the differences between these modelling simulations and reality must be kept in mind. The solutions presented by these models assume complete knowledge, full participation, full and instantaneous adjustment and profit-maximizing behaviour by all participants at all times, not to mention correct specification of all the parameter values in the model.

While useful for purposes of illustrating particular policy choices, these assumptions should not be thought of as realistic descriptions of the conditions that characterize actual markets. In reality, the information that is relevant to price formation – such as weather, energy prices and the level of economic activity – is revealed only as time elapses. As a result, prices reflect expectations as much as actual current conditions, and, as illustrated in April 2006, these expectations can shift quickly when information that differs from expectations becomes available. In addition, as was stressed in the previous chapter on the EUA market, not everyone participates from the beginning. Moreover, all the adjustments that will be occasioned by a carbon price occur immediately in the models, which present equilibrium conditions that will occur in reality only after some time. Finally, and as will be discussed presently, not all participants are the assiduous profit-maximizers that economists assume; or, perhaps more commonly, regulatory and other institutional details are such that the incentives are aligned somewhat differently from what they are assumed to be.

Ex post evidence

The actual evolution of prices in the EUA market complicates forming even a rough estimation of the total costs of abatement, even if we

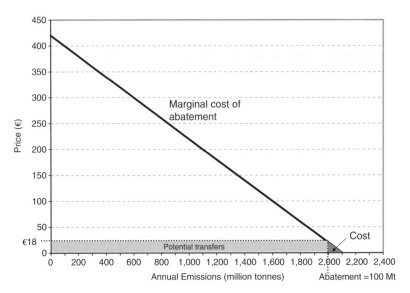

Figure 8.2 Illustration of EU ETS costs and transfers, 2005 and 2006
Source: Authors

accept that many of the other conditions assumed in models are present. For instance, the significant price that existed for the first two years would have occasioned some abatement, and the allowances thereby freed up in 2005 and 2006 would have added to the surplus existing at the end of the first period. Nevertheless, and again if the standard assumption of economics are accepted, enough data are available to make some rough estimates. Figure 8.2 is a reproduction of figure 8.1 scaled to the annual emissions and the euro prices applicable to the EU ETS. There are two observed values, the price of EUAs and the level of verified emissions, that can be applied in conjunction with the abatement estimate presented in chapter 6 to develop an estimate of total cost using the underlying economic logic that is represented by the geometry of figure 8.1.

For these purposes, a stylized representation of the trial period can be adopted. For two years there was a significant EUA price and abatement occurred. Then, because of the inability to bank surplus allowances into the second trading period, the price during the third year was effectively zero, and abatement would also have been nil. Although the evolution of price in 2005 and 2006 was different, the average price for the two years was remarkably similar: €18.11 in

2005 and €17.54 in 2006.[4] Chapter 6 presents estimates of abatement that suggested that, in these years, the quantity of emissions abated annually was between 40 and 100 Mt of CO_2. As a stylization, we adopt a price of €18 for each of these years and assume annual abatement of 100 Mt, as illustrated in figure 8.2. The implied area of the cost triangle is €0.9 billion. If the amount of annual abatement was only 50 Mt, the MAC curve would be steeper than shown in figure 8.2, and the implied cost would be €0.45 billion. Conversely, if the abatement were as much as 150 Mt, the MAC curve would be less steep, and the implied cost €1.35 billion. Compared to an annual GDP of 13 to 14 trillion international dollars (as used by the IMF) for the European Union in each of these years, even €1.35 billion is a trivial amount (approximately 0.0125 per cent at an exchange rate of $1.30/€1).

This same approach can be (and often is) used to estimate the potential value of the transfer rectangle in figure 8.2. As can be readily seen, it is considerably larger than the cost triangle for what is estimated to have been an emissions reduction in the order of 5 per cent during the first period of the EU ETS. The potential transfer is approximately €36 billion per year, but care should be taken in assuming that all these transfers were made. To the extent that the CO_2 cost was not passed through to final consumers, transfers did not occur.

Sijm, Neuhoff and Chen (2006) have estimated that the level of pass-through of CO_2 costs in the relatively liberalized wholesale electricity markets in the Netherlands and Germany was 60 to 100 per cent; pass-through into retail rates is not always straightforward, however. As has been noted a number of times throughout this book, there is considerable evidence that at least some firms were not able to pass on the opportunity costs of free allocation. In the electricity sector, the regulation of retail electricity rates and long-term electricity contracts (Reinaud 2007) often limit pass-through. The Spanish electricity sector is one example. Most retail electricity prices were capped, with the result that neither CO_2 costs nor increases in fuel costs could be passed on, at least immediately. Although regulated utilities expect to recover the deferred fuel costs in the future, the retail price caps in Spain do not allow 'windfall profits' from the free

---

[4] Based on the Thursday closing prices reported weekly by Point Carbon in *Carbon Market Europe*.

allowance allocation to be included in retail rates. Instead, the value of free allowances is deducted from other costs that electricity utilities would otherwise be allowed to recover through future price increases. A similar inability to recover the opportunity cost of free allocation may have occurred for at least some industrial participants because of international competition that did not allow the added CO_2 cost to be passed on. There is also anecdotal evidence that at least some firms with allocations greater than emissions do not recognize the opportunity cost of freely allocated allowances and therefore have passed none of the scarcity rent through to consumers (Fazekas 2008b with respect to Hungary, and Lacombe 2008 with respect to refiners).

These same qualifications also urge caution in considering the costs observed in the first period of the EU ETS as representative. The approximate pairing of a presumed marginal cost of €20 and abatement of about 5 per cent from a business-as-usual emissions scenario suggests that costs will be significantly higher as the cap is tightened. For instance, if the cost relationships illustrated by figure 8.2 are accurate, a 50 per cent reduction of emissions would indicate a marginal cost of abatement and an allowance price of about €200. There are two reasons for thinking that the cost relationships observed in the first period of the EU ETS may not be representative.

The first is that only short-term actions could have been undertaken during the three years of the first period. Many abatement actions require a change in the capital stock, which involves investment and some time lag. Given the very tight schedule for the implementation of the EU ETS and the uncertainties surrounding cap levels and prices, the only abatement responses that could reasonably be expected to have taken place during the trial period are those that did not involve changes of the capital stock. It is clear that these short-term abatement actions were undertaken – especially in the electricity sector, in which the decision was often no more than electing to run one plant instead of another – but the full response to a carbon price of €20 has not been observed.

A second reason is that the abatement response observed in the first period is inertia, in the form of failing to internalize the opportunity cost of freely allocated allowances. To the extent that this failure was due not to regulatory or contractual considerations but to perceptual and managerial deficiencies, less abatement would be undertaken. About two-thirds of the installations in the EU ETS received more allowances than needed to cover emissions, and the owners of these installations can more easily continue to operate as before, or defer abatement actions that would be profitable, than can operators who are in a short position. Anecdotal evidence abounds to support opposite contentions concerning the internalization of opportunity costs, indicating both that the owners of many installations did internalize these costs and that many others did not.

Point Carbon's annual surveys of EU ETS participants provide one measure of the extent of this inertia (Point Carbon 2007b, 2008e). The survey completed in early 2006 indicates that only 15 per cent of participants were taking actions to reduce CO_2 emissions. By early 2007 the percentage of participants acting to reduce emissions or planning such action had increased to two-thirds, and it remained at this level until the early 2008 survey. Taking action to reduce CO_2 emissions is not exactly the same as internalizing the cost of allowances (for some firms, no economically justifiable emissions reductions may exist), but it is a close proxy. As such, the actions reported in 2007 and 2008 suggest that a significant share of participants may not be internalizing the opportunity cost of allowances and that further emission reductions at a price of €20 can be expected in the future.

Transaction costs

The direct costs for abatement are not the only costs associated with executing environmental policies, including cap-and-trade systems. Transaction costs – the resources required to set up these programmes, to meet compliance requirements and to trade – can also be significant. Transaction costs are mostly fixed overhead costs, although those associated with trading also have efficiency implications, as pointed out by Stavins (1995). Transaction costs are usually assumed to be small in relation to the direct abatement costs, but there are few actual studies of these costs. To address this issue, researchers at University College Dublin conducted a detailed and intensive survey of the transaction costs that Irish firms participating in the EU ETS faced during the first trading period (Jaraite, Convery and Di Maria 2009). The results of the survey are reported in this section.

The following discussion focuses only on the transaction costs incurred by firms, but it must be understood that governments also incur transaction costs. The European Commission incurred costs associated with the creation and maintenance of an EU ETS team in

Brussels and the establishment of the central registry. In addition, each EU member state had to identify the nation's potential CO_2 emitters, decide how to distribute allowances among participants, monitor and verify emissions, set up and maintain allowance registries, conduct an allowance auction if necessary, communicate and negotiate with the European Commission and enforce the provisions of the directive.

Transaction costs are incurred at the firm level in setting up a monitoring scheme, reporting emissions, hiring an emissions verifier every year and trading allowances. Some of these costs occur only at the initial stage of the policy implementation; the costs associated with emissions monitoring, reporting and verification procedures are continuing costs, however. The costs related to allowance trading are variable, as they depend on the number of trades conducted and/or the volume of each trade.

In order to analyse the transactions costs of firms empirically during the first trading period, all Irish companies covered by the scheme during 2005 to 2007 were asked to complete a survey. While Ireland is not a representative EU member state in some respects – the ETS share of its CO_2 emissions is low (around 30 per cent) and it has a rapidly growing service economy and industrial output that is concentrated primarily in non-energy-intensive sectors – it is in others. With the exception of metal-processing, Ireland is home to all the sectors covered by the EU ETS; a number of firms have multiple installations subject to the ETS; and installations vary in size, thereby allowing an understanding of whether transaction costs differ between installations of different size.

Survey methodology

The survey of Irish firms consisted of two stages: (1) a mail survey and (2) face-to-face interviews. In stage 1, a questionnaire was sent to all seventy-two companies that operated the 106 installations covered in the first period of the EU ETS.[5] Twenty-seven

[5] A questionnaire was sent to all companies that had greenhouse gas permits before 31 March 2004. New planned developments were thus included, as their timing for compliance was the same as for existing installations. For each company, the form was sent to the account-holder of the permit. All contact details are provided in the CITL database. Four of the seventy-two companies contacted had closed down and are not participating in the second phase of the EU ETS. Since they had to comply fully with the EU ETS's procedures during the 2005–7 period, however, they were contacted as well.

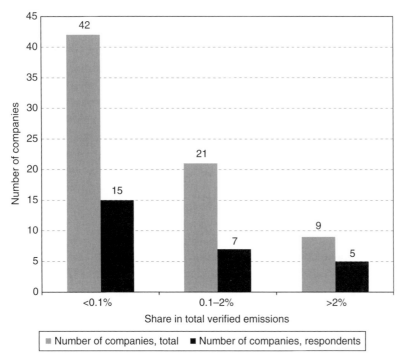

Figure 8.3 Distribution of verified emissions across Irish companies in the EU ETS, 2005–7
Sources: Jaraite, Convery and Di Maria (2009), derived from CITL and Irish EPA data

companies[6] completed and returned the questionnaire over an eight-week period (7 July 2008 to 1 September 2008), with an understanding that no individual companies would be identified in the research results. These twenty-seven respondents represented 39.7 per cent of all sixty-eight Irish companies and 69.9 per cent of the total allowance allocation for 2005 to 2007. According to the level of the respondents' verified emissions, they were grouped into three categories: large (with a share larger than 2 per cent of the Irish total of 22.3 million EUAs annually), medium (0.1 to 2 per cent) and small (up to 0.1 per cent) (see figure 8.3). In stage 2, representative responses were identified by sector and scale, and face-to-face interviews were conducted.

[6] Two respondents, each with multiple installations, provided incomplete answers. One company reported answers for only one of its installations, the other for two out of its three installations.

Applying the classification suggested by McCann *et al.* (2005), transaction costs of firms were grouped into three categories: (1) early-implementation costs – i.e. costs that were incurred before 1 January 2005; (2) monitoring, reporting and verification costs – i.e. costs that were experienced annually; and (3) trading costs, which depended on the number of trades and the trading volume. The first two categories of costs were relevant for all firms in the scheme, whereas the third category was significant only for firms that entered the CO_2 trading market. Early-implementation costs are almost all fixed costs, MRV costs are periodic costs and trading costs are variable costs incurred only with trading.[7]

Findings

Early-implementation costs
The fixed set-up costs were divided into three categories: (1) internal costs, (2) consultancy costs and (3) capital costs. Twenty-five of the respondents (92.6 per cent) experienced some internal costs consisting of time and staff commitment. Twelve firms (44.4 per cent) incurred consulting costs and seven (25.9 per cent) incurred capital equipment costs. Only five firms responded that they experienced all three kinds of costs, while two firms answered that they incurred none of these costs in implementing the EU ETS rules.

Respondents ranked their early-implementation activities according to the costs they experienced. Most judged the measurement of baseline emissions and learning about the functioning of the EU ETS to be the most costly early-implementation procedures, while applying for allowances and delivering a monitoring and reporting plan were the least costly.

Figures 8.4 and 8.5 summarize the early-implementation costs faced by respondents, expressed as average euros per firm and per tonne of verified CO_2 emissions over the three years of the trial period.

Figure 8.4 shows that most of the fixed early-implementation costs were incurred by large firms. On average, their set-up expenditures were ten and thirty times higher than those of medium-sized and small

---

[7] As an alternative to this classification, Betz (2005) divides transaction costs between one-time costs (early implementation) and ongoing costs (MRV costs and trading costs).

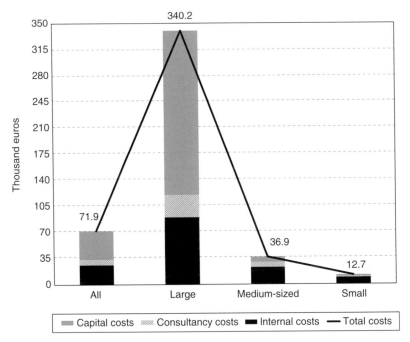

Figure 8.4 Average early-implementation costs per firm, by firm size
Sources: Jaraite, Convery and Di Maria (2009)

firms, respectively. When costs are expressed per tonne of CO_2 emissions emitted, however, the costs are significantly higher for small respondents. For instance, the average early-implementation costs were €0.03/tCO_2 emitted for large firms, whereas they were seventeen times higher (€0.51/tCO_2) for small firms.

These findings are not unexpected, and they are consistent with other research studies (Schleich and Betz 2004; Betz 2005) and with concerns expressed by the European Commission about the unequal distribution of administrative costs across EU ETS participants of different sizes (European Commission 2008a). The composition of early-implementation costs also differs among firms by size. Capital costs were the major component of the total early-implementation costs for large firms, while internal costs among small and medium-sized firms were larger than their capital and consultancy costs combined.

The higher capital costs for large firms are probably explained by monitoring requirements. Large installations are subject to more stringent monitoring and reporting requirements than small installations

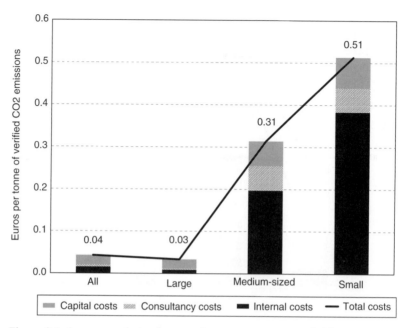

Figure 8.5 Average early-implementation costs per tonne of CO_2 emissions, by firm size
Sources: Jaraite, Convery and Di Maria (2009)

and they often have multiple and complex emission points, both of which would lead to the installation of expensive monitoring equipment. With fewer and less complex emissions points, small and medium-sized firms would have been able to track emissions by using low-cost fuel meters. The relatively low consultancy costs faced by firms in all size categories may imply either that sufficient consultation support was acquired at no cost from the governmental bodies responsible for the scheme's implementation[8] or that there was no need to engage with external consultants.

Monitoring, reporting and verification costs
As MRV procedures were mandatory for all operators in the EU ETS, all respondents incurred some MRV costs in the first period of the

---

[8] This phenomenon could be considered as a reallocation of transaction costs from private to public organizations. This burden-shifting is welcome, in principle, if regulators are more efficient than private entities in acquiring and providing information.

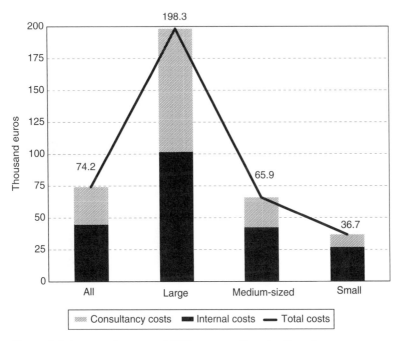

Figure 8.6 Average three-year MRV costs per firm, by firm size
Source: Jaraite, Convery and Di Maria (2009)

EU ETS. MRV costs consist of internal (staff) costs and consulting (verification) costs, and are generally assumed to accrue annually, as MRV procedures are undertaken on an annual basis.

The magnitude, distribution and composition of the MRV costs are presented in figures 8.6 and 8.7.

As is the case for the early implementation costs, most of the MRV costs are incurred by large firms, but costs per tonne of CO_2 regulated are significantly higher for small firms. Moreover, as shown in figure 8.7, the disparity in MRV costs is particularly large: €0.02/tCO_2 for large firms and seventy-six times this level (€1.51/tCO_2) for small firms. The composition of the MRV costs differs from that of the early-implementation costs, in that the share of the consultancy costs in the total MRV costs is larger than in the early-implementation costs. For large companies, the shares of internal and consultancy costs were approximately equal, while internal costs dominated consultancy costs at medium-sized and small firms.

Both the higher share of consultancy costs at larger firms and survey responses provide some evidence that small firms were

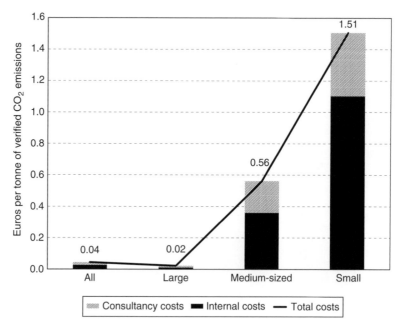

Figure 8.7 Average three-year MRV costs per tonne of CO_2 emissions, by firm size
Source: Jaraite, Convery and Di Maria (2009)

interested in compliance only and that larger firms were more likely to go beyond compliance and to manage emissions with an eye to minimizing cost. Small firms may have had little financial capacity to hire consultants for purposes other than compliance and they appear to have engaged outside help only for required verification. In contrast, large firms seem to have been concerned not only with compliance but also with reducing allowance costs. For instance, one large company reported that the external consultant helped not only to perform the necessary MRV procedures but also to identify potential abatement opportunities. Moreover, as shown in figure 8.8, larger firms spent proportionately more on monitoring, and they appear to monitor their emissions more frequently, on a weekly or monthly basis, as would be required for managing emissions cost-effectively. Survey responses also revealed that most of the companies had not monitored emissions before the launch of the EU ETS and that participation in the scheme had influenced most of the companies' day-to-day operations.

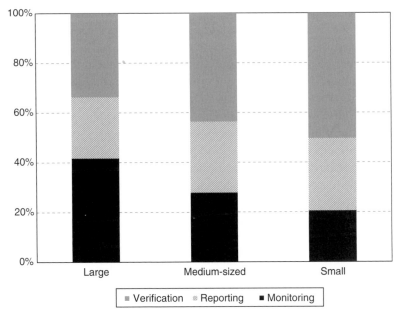

Figure 8.8 Breakdown of total MRV costs, by firm size
Source: Jaraite, Convery and Di Maria (2009)

Trading costs

In contrast to implementation and MRV costs, trading costs are variable, as they depend on the volume of allowances traded.[9] Out of twenty-seven respondents to the Irish survey, eleven firms traded some allowances in the first period of the EU ETS: six sold allowances and five purchased allowances. Interestingly, three of the five that bought allowances held allowances in excess of their verified emissions at the end of the first period. The remaining sixteen respondents did not sell or buy allowances at all. Seven of these firms held significant surplus allowances at the end of the trading period.

The sixteen firms that did not trade allowances were asked why they chose not to participate in the market. Fourteen firms responded, and they reported that they had been able to meet their CO_2 obligations without engaging in trading. None of the respondents reported

---

[9] This dependency might not be perfect, as trading transaction costs might have a fixed component as well. For instance, brokerage commissions might consist of a fee per trade (fixed component) and a fee depending on a volume of trade (variable component).

that CO_2 abatement was cheaper than buying allowances or that trading was too expensive. In addition, none of the respondents mentioned transaction costs as a factor that discouraged trading. These comments also reveal operators' uncertainty about the first-period allocation and their recognition of the first-period allowance price collapse. One firm noted that it maintained an allowance surplus because it was unsure of the extra allocation it was to receive from the new entrants' reserve for an expansion of capacity. Other respondents commented that the allowance price was too low at the end of the period, when the surplus was evident, to bother with trading. Some respondents considered transferring allowances to affiliated installations outside Ireland that were under common ownership, but they did not do so because the outside operators also had allowance surpluses.

The eleven respondents that did engage in trading (six sold and five bought) were asked what their trading partner companies had been. Four firms responded that they had traded only with other Irish installations inside their own business group, and one firm traded with domestic and foreign installations in the same business group. Another respondent that was over-compliant traded both with installations inside its business group and via financial institutions. The other five (including two over-compliant respondents) traded with financial institutions, mainly commercial banks. Some of the firms that performed allowance trades within their domestic business group regarded this action as a transfer, not as a trade.

Seven respondents were involved in direct bilateral trade with the counterparty and the other four traded indirectly through an intermediary. The reasons for these different choices were mixed. Among respondents trading directly, two said that trading volumes had been too small to trade via a third party, while another noted also that it was cheaper to engage in direct rather than indirect trade. Another respondent traded directly because it wanted to learn how to trade and another stated that there had been no need to engage a third party because direct trading was not a complex process.

Three companies chose indirect trading because they had no in-house trading capacity and because indirect trading was a quicker process than direct trading. One over-compliant respondent in the power sector added that indirect trading was chosen because it provided a more transparent process for cost accounting in rate-making proceedings. This respondent added that low brokerage fees made

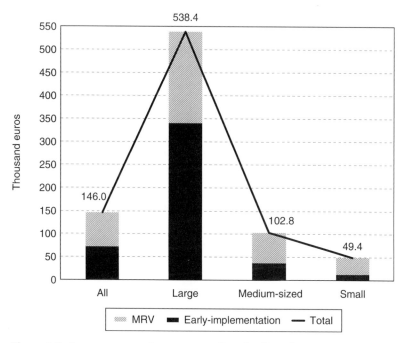

Figure 8.9 Average transaction costs per firm, by firm size
Source: Jaraite, Convery and Di Maria (2009)

indirect trading an attractive option. As remarked in an earlier survey by Convery and Redmond (2007), brokerage fees per tonne of CO_2 traded declined from €0.10 in January 2005 to €0.06 in August 2006; and the EUA prices in 2007 suggest even lower fees at the end of the first period.

These responses do not suggest that the transaction costs associated with trading were determining in firms' decisions about whether or not to trade. An inclination among smaller firms in particular to use allowances for compliance only, caution at the beginning of the period and the low allowance prices at the end of the first trading period seem to be the primary reasons for non-participation in trading.

Summary of first-period transaction costs

Figures 8.9 and 8.10 summarize the burden of all transaction costs by firms with small, medium-sized and large emissions allowance allocations during the first trading period. The cost distribution shows,

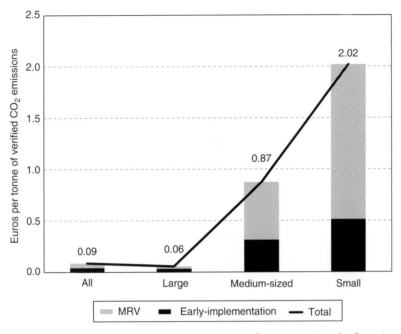

Figure 8.10 Average transaction costs per tonne of CO_2 emissions, by firm size
Source: Jaraite, Convery and Di Maria (2009)

again, that most of the transaction costs were borne by large firms, but that transaction costs per tonne of CO_2 emitted were much higher for smaller operators. Additionally, the composition of transaction costs shows that, while early-implementation costs were more significant for large respondents, ongoing MRV costs were more considerable for medium-sized and small firms.

With some caution, these figures can be used to obtain rough estimates of the transaction costs associated with the first period of the EU ETS. Trotignon and Delbosc (2008) have undertaken an analysis of CITL installation data in conjunction with other publicly available information on group installations according to the firms that own them. They were able to assign 6,345 of the 11,106 installations in the CITL database to 1,137 firms, which accounted for 93.5 per cent of the EUAs issued in the first period. Table 8.2 splits this EU-wide firm-level database into large, medium-sized and small firms using the same size criteria that were applied in the survey of Irish firms. The last three columns multiply EUAs by the corresponding

Table 8.2 *Estimate of total EU ETS transaction costs*

Firm size	Number of firms	EUAs (first-period totals)	Early-implementation costs	MRV costs (three-year totals)	Total
		(Million EUAs)	(Million euros)		
Large	361	5,634	169	113	282
Medium-sized	488	204	63	114	178
Small	288	6	3	9	12
Unidentified	NA	403	124	226	351
Total	NA	6,247	360	462	822

Source: Jaraite, Convery and Di Maria (2009).

per tonne costs in figures 8.5 and 8.7 to arrive at estimates for the EU ETS as a whole.[10]

The combined costs for initial set-up and for three years of monitoring, reporting and verification are roughly equal to the annual direct abatement costs of €900 million, as given in the stylized estimate presented earlier in this chapter. Slightly less than a half of this amount was incurred initially, on a one-time basis, and the ongoing MRV costs are around €150 million a year, approximately one-sixth of the annual direct abatement costs. Over time, the share of MRV costs will surely diminish, as learning by doing and increased competition among verifiers reduces this component of transaction costs and a tightening cap raises direct abatement costs. Evidence of lower MRV costs was provided by one-quarter of respondents in the Irish survey, which stated that these costs decreased over the three years of the EU ETS. All the same, set-up costs that are equal to one-half of initial annual abatement costs, and ongoing MRV costs of even less than one-sixth of the direct abatement cost are significant.

---

[10] The extrapolation of costs to an EU-wide basis is based on costs per tonne, which are more likely to be similar to those observed elsewhere in the European Union than the costs per firm because of size differences between firms in Ireland and the rest of the Union. The extrapolation is based on EUAs allocated instead of verified emissions, but the two are very highly correlated (>90 per cent).

The distribution of transaction costs on a per tonne basis by size of firm has implications for the point of regulatory obligation – that is, where the surrender of allowances is performed. At a cost of €0.05/tonne for the large firms, which account for most of the CO_2 emissions in the EU ETS, the transaction costs involved in setting up a programme to limit CO_2 emissions seems reasonable. The problem lies in the small firms with significantly fewer emissions, which face relatively high transaction costs per tonne.

A provision of the amendments to the EU ETS for the post-2012 period, which will allow installations with fewer than 10,000 tonnes of emissions to opt out of the programme, is aimed at remedying this disproportion in cost. The opt-out is conditioned on the installation being subject to equivalent measures and continuing to report emissions, however. Consequently, opting out will not reduce the ongoing MRV costs, which small firms must continue in order to maintain their qualification for the opt-out. The dilemma here – the varying incidence of transaction costs between firms according to emissions volume – illustrates a fundamental point: fixed costs are lowest where they can be spread over a large number of the appropriate units of account. The only way to remove these relatively high transaction costs for small firms, while still requiring them to implement the same or equivalent measures, would be to place the MRV obligation upstream – on the carbon content of fuels entering the system – so that the carbon charge would be included in the fuel price. This would also ensure internalization of the climate externality regardless of how allowances are allocated.

Conclusions

The costs associated with the emissions abatement achieved through the EU ETS are imperceptible – much like the similarly controversial trade effects that were considered in the preceding chapter. A cost that is on the order of one-hundredth of 1 per cent of GDP is lost in the noise.

What is observed in the trial period with respect to trade effects and abatement costs does not present the complete picture, however, simply because the time has been too short to make any judgement about longer-term effects. Nevertheless, the implications of the longer term are distinctly different. While it is possible that the long-term trade effects on investment will be greater than what can be observed now, investment and change in the capital stock will make average and marginal costs lower than those associated with short-term responses – which is all that can be observed in the first trading period.

It is also important to distinguish between the cost to the economy as a whole and the far larger transfers among economic agents that are occasioned by a carbon price. To label the latter as redistributive is not to denigrate their importance. No cap-and-trade programme can be enacted without dealing equitably with these redistributive effects.

Although the treatment of direct cost in this chapter has been illustrative at best, considerable attention has also been given to the results of a survey of Irish firms concerning the nature and magnitude of transaction costs associated with the EU ETS. Everyone recognizes that these costs exist, but they are rarely investigated and often ignored. These results show that, at least at the start of the programme, these costs can be as large as half the initial abatement costs, and that they can constitute a significant ongoing cost. The results also show that the incidence of these costs is highly unequal between firms ranked by size. On a per tonne basis, the burden on small firms is about fifty times greater than that on large firms. This result raises the important questions of the point of regulatory obligation and of the entities upon which the costs for monitoring, reporting and verification should be imposed.

9 | Linkage and global implications

Introduction

At its launch in 2005 the EU ETS covered approximately 40 per cent of all European Union greenhouse gas emissions through caps on CO_2 emissions from energy-intensive sectors in the then twenty-five member states. It did not limit non-CO_2 emissions from the ETS sectors, nor did it regulate emissions from agriculture, housing, waste management or transportation. Nevertheless, the emissions initially covered by the ETS represented 11 per cent of emissions from developed nations and 4 per cent of emissions worldwide.

In order to enhance its environmental impact and its cost-effectiveness over time, the EU ETS was designed to be enlarged. The directive establishing the scheme included provisions to extend the programme's coverage by enabling member states to add further installations, economic sectors and non-CO_2 gases (the opt-in). Additionally, the linking directive established a connection between the EU ETS and the Kyoto Protocol. This provision not only gave EU ETS participants permission to use Kyoto project credits for their compliance, but also outlined a framework by which the EU ETS could connect directly with cap-and-trade programmes in nations not covered by the scheme.

To date, the discussion of how the EU ETS might link with other nations has been largely normative. This chapter seeks to provide empirical evidence of how these links have been achieved in practice, and how the scope of the trading scheme was enlarged during the trial period. The first section explores how the reach of the EU ETS has grown due to an increase in the number of installations, sectors and nations covered by the scheme. Section two explains the link between the EU ETS and the Kyoto Protocol, and how ETS installations may use credits generated through the Kyoto-based mechanisms – the Clean Development Mechanism and Joint Implementation – for a portion of their compliance. Sections three and four discuss the central role that the EU ETS plays in driving demand for credits generated through CDM and JI projects, and in turn how the trading scheme is helping launch emissions reduction projects in countries around the world and in the non-trading sectors inside the European Union. The final section concludes.

Enlarging the scope

Including additional installations, sectors and gases

The permanent opt-in provision

Article 24 of the EU ETS Directive, 'Procedures for unilateral inclusion of additional activities and gases', enables member states to expand the coverage of the ETS by 'opting in' activities, installations and greenhouse gases not originally covered by the scheme.

During the first trading period, member states were able to add installations in sectors covered by the ETS that operated below defined capacity limits. For an opt-in proposal to be approved, the European Commission required the host country to provide a precise assessment of its potential impacts on the internal market and its possible effects on cross-border competition, and a report on the proposal's environmental integrity, including the reliability and accuracy of the planned monitoring and reporting system. Only five member states chose to take advantage of the opt-in provision during the first trading period (see table 9.1). Austria, Finland, Latvia, Slovenia and Sweden all added combustion installations with capacities below 20 MW, with Finland and Sweden each adding over 200 installations. The addition of these installations expanded the scope of the EU ETS by approximately 2 Mt CO_2 in the first trading period.

Since 2008 the opt-in provision has been expanded: member states may add installations from sectors not covered by the EU ETS, and they may also add emissions of greenhouse gases other than CO_2. Only the Netherlands has chosen to exercise this option, however (see table 9.2). It has included several facilities that emit nitrous oxide (N_2O) from the chemical industry, collectively extending the ETS cap a further 6 Mt CO_2e/yr during the second trading period.

In all, the opt-in provision of the EU ETS Directive has enlarged the scope of the EU ETS by approximately 6 Mt CO_2e, or 0.26 per cent.

Table 9.1 *Opt-in summary for period 1*

Member state	Number of installations 'opted in'	Description	Annual allocation (ktCO$_2$e)
Austria	1	GHKW Mistelbach Hospital.	3
Finland	221	District heating plants with a capacity of 20MW or less that operate in district heating networks in which one or more installations fall under the scope of the EU ETS.	At least 125
Latvia	27	Combustion installations that were included in Latvia's NAP as mandatory participants with a rated thermal input exceeding 20MW, but that subsequently fell out of the scope due to improvements in data.	Around 150
Slovenia	15	Small energy conversion facilities (at least 15MW).	?
Sweden	274	Installations having a rated thermal input of 20MW or less that operate in district heating networks in which one or more installations fall under the scope of the EU ETS.	Around 1,750
Total	538 (5% of all installations covered by the EU ETS)		At least 2,000

Note: ktCO$_2$e = kilotonnes of carbon dioxide equivalent.
Source: Compiled from European Commission decisions.

Despite a greater degree of opt-in in period 2, the provision remains little used. Obstacles to using the opt-in provision seem to be threefold. First, small installations that are added may incur high transaction costs for monitoring, reporting and verifying their emissions. Second, member states wishing to include large installations may face domestic political obstacles to doing so; installations may

Table 9.2 *Opt-in summary for period 2*

Member state	Number of installations 'opted in'	Description	Annual allocation (ktCO$_2$e)
Netherlands	6	N$_2$O emissions from nitric acid production	5,600

Source: European Commission (2008b).

agree to be included only if they believe they can realistically achieve emissions reduction goals without large additional costs or if they have political incentives to do so. Third, emissions of greenhouse gases other than CO_2 are not always easy to monitor, and may require costly new reporting and verification protocols. In some cases, as with landfill gas projects, it is easier to measure captured emissions than it is to monitor diffuse non-point source emissions. These sorts of projects may thus be better executed through the Kyoto Protocol's project mechanisms than through the EU ETS's opt-in provision.

The temporary opt-out provision

Article 27 of the EU ETS Directive, 'Temporary exclusion of certain installations', allowed member states to opt certain installations out of the EU ETS during the first trading period. Opt-out was allowed only if the concerned installations were subject to emissions constraints, monitoring and reporting rules and penalties similar to those imposed by the EU ETS. No such opt-out is allowed during the second or subsequent trading periods. The opt-out provision was no more than a temporary option designed to facilitate the implementation of the EU ETS. It gave installations already subject to constraints additional time to ensure that they could make a smooth transition into the EU-wide scheme.

As illustrated in table 9.3, Belgium, the Netherlands and the United Kingdom chose to exclude 570 installations with annual emissions of approximately 38 Mt CO_2 during period 1. The United Kingdom exercised the opt-out for by far the greatest number of installations, as it had implemented its own domestic emissions trading scheme in

Table 9.3 *Opt-out summary for period 1*

Member state	Number of installations 'opted out'	Description	Annual allocation (ktCO$_2$e)
Belgium	22	Emergency generators in nuclear power stations, thermal power plants in buildings, natural gas transport and military installations.	Around 275
Netherlands	152	Installations that emit less than 25 ktCO$_2$e/year, installations subject to long-term energy efficiency agreements, benchmarking covenants and obligations under the Netherlands Environmental Management Act.	Around 7,800
United Kingdom	396	Installations participating in the UK-ETS and climate change agreements.	Around 30,000
Total	570		Around 38,000

Source: Compiled from European Commission decisions on period 1 NAPs.

advance of the EU ETS. From 2005 to 2007 the United Kingdom excluded a total of 396 installations, responsible for 30 Mt CO$_2$ per year. Each of these installations, as well as those excluded by Belgium and the Netherlands, were reincorporated into the EU ETS at the start of the second period in January 2008. The United Kingdom discontinued its domestic emissions trading scheme at the end of 2006.

Integrating a new sector: the inclusion of aviation during the second trading period

The integration of aviation in the EU ETS is by far the largest and most ambitious expansion of the scheme since its inception in 2005. From 2012 onwards emissions from all airlines flying into and out of EU airports will be constrained by way of the Aviation Trading Scheme

(ATS), which will be linked to the EU ETS. This programme will expand the European emissions cap by 15 per cent. It will cover an estimated 300 Mt CO_2 per year by 2012 – an annual emissions total greater than that of any member state but Germany.

The European Commission began considering how to regulate aviation emissions in 2005. In September that year the Commission published a communication that presented an aviation emissions trading scheme as the most feasible way forward, but also discussed other options, including a tax on jet fuel (European Commission 2005b). In December 2005 the EU Environment Council adopted conclusions that were broadly supportive of the Commission communication, and the European Parliament confirmed its support in a July 2006 report. This was followed in December 2006 by a legislative proposal from the Commission, which marked the beginning of the iterative legislative process between the Parliament and Council. This process concluded in October 2008, when member state governments gave their final approval for the creation of the Aviation Trading Scheme, to be linked to the EU ETS.

The ATS and the EU ETS will be linked by a trading gateway: airlines will be able to purchase EUAs from the EU ETS, but they will not be able to sell aviation allowances (AAs) on the ETS market. Starting in 2012, the ATS will cover the emissions of all flights that arrive at or depart from European airports, with a *de minimis* exemption for small or exceptional flights. The 2012 emissions cap will be set at 3 per cent below the average emissions of covered airlines from 2004 to 2006 and at 5 per cent below this average from 2015 onwards.

The integration of aviation into the EU ETS presented some new problems. International flights, which represent around two-thirds of aviation traffic in the EU27, are not covered by the Kyoto Protocol, so there is no mandatory international target for those emissions. In addition, aviation emissions sources are by definition mobile, and emissions take place both inside and outside Europe.

The EU decision to include in its ATS the emissions from flights between EU and non-EU nations was motivated by two factors. First, the European Union wished to take a leadership role in the face of what it regarded as a failure by the International Civil Aviation Organization to limit aircraft emissions effectively. Second, the extension of the cap to extra-EU flights can be seen as a border tax adjustment, as is increasingly advocated for traded goods. The latter has led to protests by non-EU companies that now find their emissions from flights to and from the EU27 included in the EU emissions cap.

The European Union could have chosen to regulate other transportation sector emissions – such as those from road transport, which have a negligible international component – before addressing aviation. The road transport sector is a complicated sector to regulate in the Union, however. First, the car manufacturing lobby is very strong (especially in Germany), and opposes additional emissions constraints. Second, member states already have varying fuel taxation regimes and are loath to introduce alternatives that might diminish this important fiscal resource.

The question of emissions from the maritime sector, which are comparable to if not greater than those from aviation and are expected to grow even more rapidly, is currently under discussion at the International Maritime Organization (IMO). The European Commission has announced that European maritime transport could be included unilaterally in EU ETS if no IMO consensus is reached.

Expanding the geographic scope of the scheme

The scope of the EU ETS has also been enlarged through an expansion in the geographic coverage of the scheme. Romania and Bulgaria became new EU member states in 2007 and, accordingly, have been required to participate in the EU ETS from 2007 onwards. The nations of the European Economic Area (EEA) – Norway, Iceland and Liechtenstein – also agreed to join the scheme and began participating in the ETS in January 2008. The process of including these new partners in the European trading scheme, conducted during the first trading period, has enlarged the coverage of the EU ETS by 133 Mt CO_2e per year.

Bulgaria and Romania: new member states and trading partners

The accession of Bulgaria and Romania to the European Union on 1 January 2007 has been the most important geographic expansion of the EU ETS to date. As new EU members, the countries have been obligated as part of the *acquis communautaire* to adopt CO_2 emissions limits and participate in the EU ETS. Bulgaria and Romania's emissions caps were set at 42.3 Mt and 74.8 Mt, respectively, in 2007, thus enlarging the coverage of the EU ETS by approximately 117 Mt CO_2, a little over 5 per cent, in the last year of the first period.

Although Bulgaria and Romania's entry into the EU ETS is an important expansion of the geographic scope of the scheme, the effective entry of these two countries into the trading scheme has been delayed. Romania launched its allowance registry in April 2008, the last month of period 1 trading, thereby giving its installations only a short time to submit their first-period allowances. The launch of Bulgaria's registry was delayed even further: it did not become functional until October 2008. As a result, Bulgarian installations were unable to participate in first-period trading.

Bulgaria and Romania undoubtedly faced technical obstacles and resource shortages that contributed to these delays. Their problems were similar to those experienced in the other new member states, with the difference that they had only one year to get their ETS systems up and running, while the other new member states had had three. The experience of Bulgaria and Romania suggests that one year may not be a long enough period of time for overcoming some institutional obstacles.

Incorporating the nations of the European Economic Area
The incorporation of Norway, Iceland and Liechtenstein into the EU ETS extended the scheme's cap by a further 21 Mt CO_2e per year, or 1 per cent.[1] These three states make up the EEA, a group of countries that participate in the single European market but which are not EU members themselves. Their incorporation into the EU ETS was the result of extensive negotiations between the European Commission and the EEA states, which began after the ETS Directive was adopted in 2003.

Initially, the ETS Directive was not regarded as relevant to the EEA countries, as these states are separate parties to the Kyoto Protocol and not part of the EU coalition that lobbied for a collective emissions

---

[1] Most of this expansion is due to the incorporation of Norway in the EU ETS. According to the Norwegian Ministry of the Environment, CO_2 emissions from covered installations in Norway totalled 18 Mt in 2005 and are projected to rise to 21 Mt by 2010. While twelve Icelandic installations were originally identified as falling within the scope of the ETS Directive, they were exempted from participation in the EU ETS because they were determined to be already implementing emissions reduction measures of equal stringency to those mandated by the EU ETS. Liechtenstein has only two installations subject to the ETS, which together produce 18,000 tonnes of CO_2 emissions per year.

reduction target at Kyoto. Norway – the only EEA state planning its own emissions trading initiative at the time – thus planned to launch its own domestic ETS and to link it to the EU ETS by way of the linking provisions outlined in article 25 of the ETS Directive.

Norway launched its ETS in 2005, the same year that the first period of EU ETS trading began. The Norwegian ETS was designed to harmonize with the EU ETS, with the exception that some Norwegian installations already subject to CO_2 taxes – including offshore oil and gas facilities and onshore pulp and paper and fishmeal processors – were not covered by the scheme. Instead, emissions from these facilities were addressed by way of a CO_2 tax ranging from approximately €10 per tonne of emissions for the wood-processing and fishmeal industries to €40 per tonne for the petroleum industry (Ministry of Finance 2006).

The European Commission rejected Norway's plan to connect with the EU ETS by way of the ETS Directive's linking provisions. It maintained that, since the ETS Directive affects the ability of players to compete in the single European market, all members of the market, including the EEA states, had to adopt the same emissions trading rules. An agreement between the Commission and the EEA states was reached on 26 October 2006, with Norway, Iceland and Liechtenstein agreeing to adopt the EU ETS Directive in its entirety. In return, the Commission granted the EEA states a number of concessions, the most significant of which was exempting the EEA states from article 10 of the directive, which limits to 10 per cent the proportion of allowances that may be auctioned (European Economic Area Joint Committee 2007). This derogation allowed Norway to avoid having to allocate allowances for free to offshore petroleum installations for which inclusion in the ETS was a partial replacement for a pre-existing carbon tax.

To bring its trading system into conformity with the EU ETS Directive, Norway had to incorporate into its ETS several facilities that were not included from 2005 to 2007. Twenty pulp and paper installations were added to the scheme, as well as eight fishmeal and fish oil facilities. Twelve mineral-processing installations were also added, including two cement plants. In addition, Norway included the entirety of its petroleum sector in its post-2007 ETS, adding all its offshore oil and gas installations as well as a few onshore facilities that had not been included from 2005 to 2007.

In order to integrate these new facilities into the ETS, Norway chose to modify its existing CO_2 tax policy. First, Norway eliminated the CO_2 tax levied on onshore facilities subject to emissions quotas – including the pulp and paper and fishmeal industries – and decided to allocate allowances to this sector free of charge. Second, Norway reduced the CO_2 tax for the petroleum industry, including offshore installations, but required this sector to purchase all its allowance requirements on the market from 2008 onwards. This policy change was designed using a projected 2008 allowance price of approximately €20/tonne so as not to change the total cost of CO_2 emissions for the offshore sector and to ensure a continuous revenue stream from this sector (Ministry of the Environment 2008).[2]

In its national allocation plan for 2008–12, Norway proposed a total allowance allocation of 14 Mt CO_2 per year, 4 Mt below the 2005 emissions recorded from covered installations (18 Mt), and 7 Mt below projected emissions for 2010 (21 Mt). With a 22 per cent reduction from the 2005 emission level, Norway will have a cap at least as demanding as the most demanding member state total among the EU27.

Synthesis: a 22 per cent expansion of the EU ETS cap by 2012

Between 2005 and 2012 the scope of the ETS will be expanded by approximately 22 per cent (see figure 9.1). The inclusion of the aviation sector in 2012 will account for the largest part of this expansion. The agreement to include this sector was negotiated relatively quickly, thanks in large part to the Commission's confidence in emissions trading as an effective policy tool and to the absence of member-state-specific taxes on aviation fuel. This bodes well for the future inclusion of the maritime sector in the trading scheme. An EU-wide agreement on ground transport emissions will probably prove more difficult to broker, however, as fuel providers are subject to a variety of taxation schemes across member states, which will make upstream allowance trading difficult.

---

[2] The CO_2 tax for the offshore petroleum industry was reduced from the 2007 level of approximately Nkr.340 (€43) per tonne of CO_2 to a level of Nkr.180 (€23) per tonne in 2008. This reduction corresponds to Nkr.160 (€20) per tonne of CO_2, which was the 2008 forward allowance price quoted on Nord Pool/ECX in the autumn of 2007.

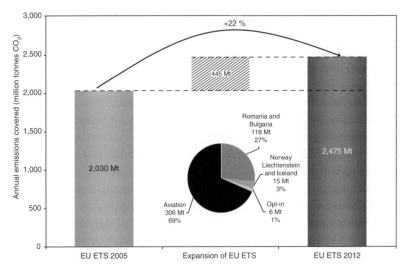

Figure 9.1 Expansion of EU ETS coverage
Source: Authors

The addition of Romania, Bulgaria and the countries of the European Economic Area has also played an important role in the expansion of the coverage of the EU ETS. The difficulty that Bulgaria and Romania faced in launching their registries was a product not only of scarce resources but perhaps also of a lack of political will. The Kyoto Protocol did not impose a requirement on either nation to make an emission reduction, but the EU ETS imposes a real emission constraint on both of them. The inability to apply the political leverage provided by EU accession in negotiations with countries outside Europe foreshadows the difficulties that may be encountered in convincing other growing economies (such as China and India) to agree to binding emissions reduction targets in the future.

Norway's inclusion in the EU ETS demonstrates the feasibility of integrating pre-existing greenhouse gas emissions control systems and shows what must be done to reach this result. Norway had previously implemented both a carbon tax and a national emissions trading scheme before it joined the EU ETS in 2008. The harmonization of these two programmes required Norway to include more installations to make the scope of the two systems more similar, and the European Union granted a waiver from one of its requirements in order to accommodate a unique circumstance: a pre-existing carbon tax. The accommodation allowed the installations subject to the tax to be incorporated into the trading regime while maintaining the revenue stream coming from the CO_2 tax. As such, it shows that emissions trading and carbon taxes can co-exist and that the choice of a tax does not preclude participation in a cap-and-trade programme. This is an important lesson for countries that are currently developing their own GHG mitigation strategies and may feel constrained to choose just one of these policy options.

The opportunity of countries to exercise the opt-in for installations not covered by the scheme was little used and has thus played a less significant role in the expansion of the EU ETS. Although there are opt-ins in the EU ETS, nearly all of them were implemented in the context of district heating systems that already had some of their systems mandatorily included in the ETS and for which it was easier to monitor emissions for the heating system as a whole. Otherwise, small installations are particularly difficult to include because the costs of measuring and monitoring emissions tend to exceed the savings from any emission reduction.

Using project-based mechanisms to establish links: the rules

The EU ETS Linking Directive

Project-based mechanisms established by the Kyoto Protocol offer another opportunity to enlarge the impact of the EU ETS. The Linking Directive, passed as an amendment to the ETS Directive in 2004, enables European installations to use emissions offset credits generated by the Kyoto mechanisms – the Clean Development Mechanism and Joint Implementation – to meet a portion of their emissions reduction obligation. In doing so, the Linking Directive not only lowers the cost of ETS compliance for European industry but also extends the price signal of the EU ETS to types of activities not originally covered by the scheme. These projects also familiarize these activities with emissions trading and help to develop many of the institutional prerequisites that prepare the way for later broader participation by host countries in a global trading regime.

The project-based mechanisms allow annex I signatories to meet part of their Kyoto Protocol obligations with credits generated as a result of certain types of emissions reduction projects. The main difference between the two mechanisms is that CDM projects, which generate certified emission reduction credits, are undertaken in non-annex I countries while JI projects, which generate emission reduction units, are implemented in annex I countries.[3] In addition, CERs can be generated for emission reductions occurring as early as 2000, whereas ERUs can be issued only for emission reductions occurring in 2008 or later. Both CDM and JI projects must be registered with the UNFCCC and their emission reductions verified prior to the issuance of the appropriate credit.

Different rules apply for the use of Kyoto project credits in the first and second trading periods. During the first trading period there was no quantitative limit on the number of CERs that could be used by operators to meet their ETS obligations. Few CERs were expected to be issued before April 2008, however, and none were used for compliance during period 1, due both to the higher price offered for their use in the second period and to the delay in the launch of the International Transaction Log, the accounting link between the CDM registry and the EU ETS. This link was not activated until October 2008, well into the second trading period. During the second trading period, as discussed in chapter 3, the use of CERs and ERUs for compliance is subject to member state limits expressed as percentages of allocations (see table 3.7). When taken together, these limits would allow the use of about 1.4 billion JI/CDM credits over the five years of the second trading period, or about 13.4 per cent of the EUAs issued. The post-2012 amendments to the ETS Directive allow any CERs or ERUs falling within member state limits and not used during the second trading period to be carried over into the post-2012 period, but otherwise the use of project-based credits appears likely to be substantially less.

The probable reduced use of project-based credits after 2012 is part of a 'graduation' policy that aims to encourage countries hosting these projects to establish fully fledged cap-and-trade programmes that

---

[3] Annex I of the Kyoto Protocol lists the signatory countries that have agreed to accept binding limits on their emissions (generally OECD nations and economies in transition in eastern Europe and the former Soviet Union). Non-annex I countries are those signatories that have no emission limitation obligations (generally developing countries) but that have agreed to certain reporting requirements.

could be linked to the EU ETS as further steps in building a broader global system. The same post-2012 amendments broaden the scope of cap-and-trade programmes with which mutual recognition might be extended to include subnational and sector-specific systems. As is the case with Norway, mutual recognition between the two systems would not carry any limit on trading or use of the other's allowances for compliance. In the absence of such linkage, the type of project-based credits and the quantity that can be used for compliance in the EU ETS will depend on the outcome of the Conference of the Parties to the Kyoto Protocol in Copenhagen in late 2009 and on internal deliberations within the European Union.

The role of the EU ETS in the world carbon market

The ability to use CERs and ERUs for compliance in the EU ETS has made the price of EUAs the reference price for the world carbon market. This market includes a wide variety of products and markets, many of which have no direct relation to one another. For instance, the separate markets for verified emission reduction credits (VERs) and for the allowances issued to participants in the voluntary trading system organized by the Chicago Climate Exchange (CCX) are sub-markets with little if any relation to the EU ETS. By far the largest component of the world carbon market, however, both in volume and value, is that associated with the Kyoto Protocol, including the EU ETS. This Kyoto complex consists of three distinct but linked products: assigned amount units, certified emission reductions/emission reduction units and European Union allowances.

- **AAUs:** the allocations to the annex I nations that are signatories to the Kyoto Protocol.
- **CERs and ERUs:** project credits from non-annex I and annex I signatories (respectively) of the Kyoto Protocol; in practice, the supply of CERs is much greater than that of ERUs, so the market for these similar products is often simply called the CER market.
- **EUAs:** allowances issued under the EU ETS, which are AAUs that have been renamed and allocated to the owners of affected installations.

Although some minor additional sources of demand exist, the two main sources of demand for these three products are:

- **the governments of annex I parties,** which have been issued AAUs and must surrender AAUs, CERs or ERUs equal to their economy-wide emissions during the first commitment period (2008–12); and
- **the owners of installations** included in the EU ETS, who have been issued EUAs (matched one to one with AAUs from the issuing member state) and who must surrender EUAs or CERs/ERUs subject to the limits indicated above.

Since both these markets can use CERs or ERUs for compliance, these credits provide the vital link between the Kyoto/government market and the EU ETS market (Delbosc and De Perthuis 2009). Moreover, because it was the EU ETS that created the first effective demand for carbon-trading and the potentially abundant supply of AAUs, usable only in the Kyoto/government market, the EU ETS has become the market of preference for all JI and CDM project credits.

Initial project developments were motivated by the prospective demand in the government market, but, ever since the EU ETS Linking Directive was adopted in 2004, operators have known that they would be able to use Kyoto credits in some amount for compliance. From the time that an EUA price first appeared and was higher than the expected prices in the Kyoto/government market, operators of facilities subject to the EU ETS became prominent investors in CDM projects. Similarly, developers of CDM projects looked to the EU ETS as the preferred market in which CERs and ERUs would not have to compete with AAUs, whether 'greened' or not, which provide a cheaper alternative for compliance with the Kyoto Protocol.[4] Although this latter market is not well developed, prices are expected to be lower because of the availability of surplus AAUs, primarily from eastern Europe and the former Soviet Union.

The existence of the quantitative limit on CER/ERU use in the EU ETS creates the possibility, if not the likelihood, that prices for EUAs and CERs/ERUs will be different. If there were no limit, or if the supply of CERs/ERUs were less than the limit, then the price of EUAs and CERs would be identical and all CERs and ERUs would be sold into the EU

---

[4] The term 'greened' AAUs refers to surplus AAUs, often pejoratively called 'hot air', for which the selling governments have promised to invest the sales revenues in green projects. These programmes are also called 'green investment schemes'.

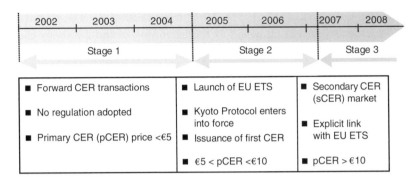

Figure 9.2 Three stages of CER market development
Source: Authors

ETS market. If the supply of CERs and ERUs is greater than the limit on their use in the EU ETS, however, the prices of EUAs and CERs/ERUs will separate and the latter will be lower than the EUA price. The degree of price separation will depend not only on the demand for EUAs, now bumping up against the EU-wide cap and the fully subscribed JI/CDM import limits, but also on the balance of supply and demand in the government market, which will depend – among other things – on the availability of AAUs and the willingness of governments to purchase them for compliance with obligations under the Kyoto Protocol.

The CER market

CER trading is split into two market segments. The first segment is a primary market, in which project developers sell forward contracts for CERs representing emissions reductions that their projects will achieve in the future. Primary CERs bear project risks, including whether or not a project will be successfully registered, if it will achieve emissions reductions and if CER credits will actually be issued and delivered to the credit purchaser. The second market segment is a secondary market, in which participants trade CER credits that have already been issued or whose expected issuance has been guaranteed by a counterparty, such as a financial institution. Delivery of secondary CERs is assured, and thus they do not bear the same project-related risk as primary CERs.

The development of the CER market has occurred in three stages, as illustrated in figure 9.2.

(1) **The early days of the primary CER market (2000–4).** The primary
    CER market was launched at the beginning of the 2000s by the
    World Bank and the Dutch government. The World Bank's Proto-
    type Carbon Fund brought together a number of pioneer invest-
    ors, which included both states subject to Kyoto constraints and
    proactive European and Japanese businesses wishing to build
    carbon credit portfolios. The Dutch government established its
    own accounts for purchasing ERUs and CERs: the emission reduc-
    tion unit procurement tender (ERUPT) and the certified emis-
    sion reduction unit procurement tender (CERUPT). The first
    transactions took place at approximately €2.6 per tonne of
    CO_2e. Other funds then formed and enlarged the demand. This
    stage of development was characterized by a very high degree of
    regulatory risk, as the entry into force of the Kyoto Protocol
    remained uncertain.

(2) **The primary CER market matures (2005–6).** The price of primary
    CERs gradually increased – notably in 2005, after the launch of
    the EU ETS and the entry into force of the Kyoto Protocol – and
    the first CERs were issued. Credit prices varied between €5 and 10
    per tonne of CO_2e, in accordance with the inherent risks of the
    projects and the respective calendars for payment and delivery of
    CERs. As of early September 2008, almost 184 million primary
    CERs had been issued (see figure 9.3).

(3) **Secondary CER trading takes off (mid-2007).** Secondary CER
    trading soared in 2007 – the last full year of period 1 – and
    contracts for CER futures from project developers were negoti-
    ated for an average of €$10/tCO_2e$. As of early September 2008,
    more than 282 million secondary CERs had been exchanged in
    over-the-counter trading and on marketplaces in both spot and
    futures transactions. As indicated by the greater number of sec-
    ondary CERs traded when compared with the number of CERs
    issued, some of the futures trades represent CERs not yet issued
    but guaranteed, usually by some financial institution.

CER price relationships

Table 9.4 presents the evolution of prices, expressed as annual aver-
ages, of the two types of CERs and the EUAs for which already issued
or secondary CERs are a fully equivalent substitute up to the JI/CDM
limits for ETS installations.

Table 9.4 *Average annual carbon asset prices*

€ per tonne	2002	2003	2004	2005	2006	2007	2008 (1st half)
Primary CER[1]	2.6	4.3	4.2	5.5	8.7	9.8	>10
Secondary CER[1]	–	–	–	17.5	14.2	16.3	16.8[2]
EUA Dec. 08[3]	–	–	–	20.6	18.5	20.1	23.6

Sources: [1]Capoor and Ambrosi (2008).
[2]Reuters secondary CER price index.
[3]ECX.

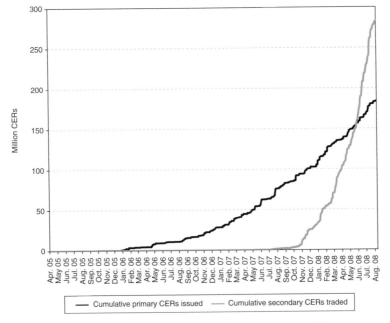

Figure 9.3 Cumulative volume for primary and secondary CERs
Sources: Derived from UNEP (United Nations Environment Programme) Risoe Centre, ECX, LEBA and Nord Pool data

The two spreads between these three related carbon assets have attracted market participants who wish to take advantage of the lower price asset and bear the risk associated with it. The first spread is that between secondary and primary CER prices, which can be seen as the project promoter margin. Given that information is scarce on primary

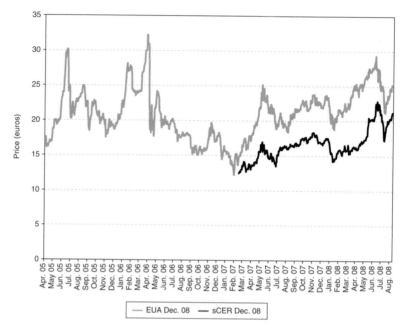

Figure 9.4 Price of EUAs December 2008 versus secondary CERs December 2008
Sources: Derived from Reuters and ECX market data

CER prices and liquidity is low, this spread should be interpreted with caution. Furthermore, the spread is highly sensitive to the way emission reduction contracts are structured (such as who bears the risk of non-delivery, etc.), where the projects are undertaken (country risk and foreign exchange risk) and project-specific risks (institutional risks, with CDM board approval rates varying upon the kinds of projects and methodologies). Project developers are interested mainly in this spread.

The second spread is that between the EUA price and the secondary CER price, which is depicted by figure 9.4 as a comparison between the December 2008 maturities for EUAs and for secondary CER futures since they were first introduced in early 2007.

To date, this spread has reflected the risk that an installation may not be able to use a secondary CER for compliance in the EU ETS. This risk takes many forms. Initially, there was a risk that the ITL–CITL connection would not be completed in time to allow delivery. This link was finally completed in October 2008, although announcements of its successful test run and pending completion during the summer of 2008 decreased this spread considerably. A second risk is regulatory and relates to the uncertainty surrounding whether the JI/CDM limit will be reached. The third risk concerns delivery, mostly whether futures contracts are backed by already issued CERs and the extent to which the associated counterparty guarantees can be relied upon. The spread between secondary CERs and EUAs has attracted compliance buyers in the EU ETS who have sought to minimize their own compliance costs through 'CER swaps', which consist of selling EUAs and purchasing secondary CERs to the extent allowed by the JI/CDM limits that are applicable to the installations belonging to the entity conducting the swap.

This second spread also depends upon conditions in the Kyoto/ government market, where CERs also have value. It is conceivable that demand there would be so great, or supply so little, that the price in this market would rise to equivalence with EUAs. Much depends on the willingness of buyer governments to purchase AAUs, of which there is a considerable surplus held by most Kyoto signatories in eastern Europe and the former Soviet Union. Since surplus AAUs have no cost, the demand for them and the resulting price constitute the floor for CER prices, plus perhaps some premium for perceived higher quality.

The other side of the CER market: emissions reductions in developing nations

The growing market for CERs, driven primarily by demand from EU ETS installations but also by nations seeking credits for Kyoto compliance, has significantly increased the number of emissions reduction projects outside the European Union. According to the information available in the UNEP Risoe CDM/JI pipeline analysis and database, more than 4,300 CDM projects are under development with an abatement potential of 2.9 Gt (gigatonnes) CO_2e. An analysis of this database, which takes into account a number of risks associated with project planning and implementation, as well as new projects that will enter the pipeline before the end of 2012, has estimated that 2.0 billion tonnes of this potential will be realized by 2012 (Leguet and Elabed 2008).

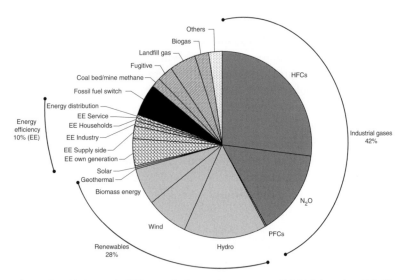

Figure 9.5 Estimated CER supply by project type until 2012 (total = 2.0 Gt CO$_2$e)
Source: Derived from UNEP Risoe Centre database

Relatively few types of projects are being developed, with non-CO$_2$ greenhouse gases of high global warming potentials and very low abatement costs taking a large share, as shown by figure 9.5.

Ten types alone are expected to generate 90 per cent of the potential CERs before 2012. The incineration of HFCs and N$_2$O should yield more than 40 per cent of all emission reductions achieved through the CDM by 2012, and the capture and destruction of methane should account for more than 10 per cent of the abatement. More diversified technologies to avoid emissions of CO$_2$ are also present: renewable energy projects should account for roughly one-third of emissions abatement, and energy efficiency for one-tenth of the projected emission reductions. Transport and agro-forestry projects account for only a small number of the CDM projects being developed.

The geographic origin of the CERs being produced by these projects is also relatively concentrated (see figure 9.6).

As of mid-2008 seventy countries had submitted at least one CDM project to the UNFCCC Secretariat, but roughly 80 per cent of the potential CERs generated by 2012 by projects in development will come from the Asia-Pacific region and 10 per cent from Latin America.

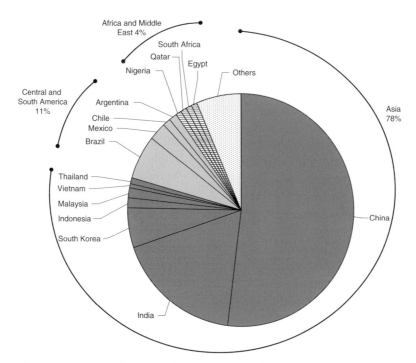

Figure 9.6 Estimated CER supply by country until 2012 (total = 2.0 Gt CO$_2$e)
Source: Leguet and Elabed (2008)

Around a half of the abatement appears likely to take place in China, 18 per cent in India and 6 per cent in Brazil. By 2012 five countries alone – China, India, Brazil, South Korea and Mexico – are expected to account for more than 80 per cent of the abatement due to CDM projects. At the opposite end of the spectrum lies sub-Saharan Africa, with only 3 per cent of the potential credits. The bulk of these projects are hosted by just four countries: Nigeria, South Africa, Côte d'Ivoire and Kenya.

The predominance of China on the seller side of the CDM market is largely attributable to the country's size and attractiveness, and to the early start it took by developing large projects based on the inciner-ation of industrial gases. In 2007 it accounted for three-quarters of all CDM transactions, according to the World Bank (Capoor and Ambrosi 2008).

A surprisingly large number of small-scale projects (projects that abate less than 60,000 ktCO$_2$ per annum) are being developed in

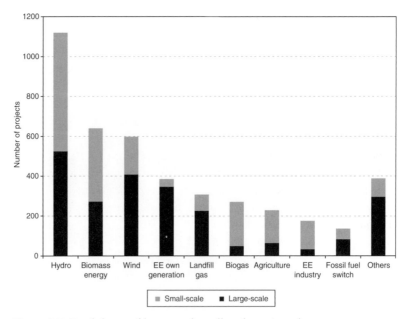

Figure 9.7 Breakdown of large- and small-scale projects by type
Source: Leguet and Elabed (2008)

the renewable energy sector: wind, solar, hydro and biomass (see figure 9.7).

Of the 190 small-scale wind projects being developed in the world, 170 are hosted by India; 364 of the 596 small-scale hydro projects are hosted by China; and, of the 367 small-scale biomass projects, 226 are Indian, fifty Brazilian and twenty-eight Malaysian. The concentration of these projects in a few countries emphasizes the importance of a favourable regulatory, technical and economic environment in the host country and shows that clusters of small-scale projects can be at least partly financed through the CDM as a result of the demand and price created by the EU ETS.

Expanding emissions coverage in developed nations and inside the European Union

Demand stemming from the EU ETS has also enabled member states to launch emissions reduction projects through the Joint Implementation framework. These projects may be located in industrialized countries outside Europe, and they may also be within other EU member states if the projects are to reduce emissions from sectors not already covered by the EU ETS. This second possibility offers an opportunity for European member states to use the price signal observed on the EU ETS to achieve additional emission reductions within their borders, and it may generate additional emission reductions inside the EU during the second period of the ETS.

The expected volume of ERUs to be generated by JI projects is considerably less than that of CERs: approximately 300 million tonnes CO_2e as opposed to 2 billion tonnes. The geographical origin of the ERUs produced by these projects is presented in figure 9.8.

By far the largest source of ERUs is expected to be Russia (with ninety projects) and the Ukraine (twenty-seven projects). These projects have the potential to abate 247 Mt of emissions by 2012, and are focused on a small number of technologies, chiefly preventing methane leakage from pipelines, coal mine methane capture, energy efficiency improvements and the incineration of industrial gases with high global warming potential. Nine of the eastern European new member states are the second major source of JI projects.[5] At least fifty-four projects are under development in eastern Europe and could abate 47 Mt CO_2e between 2008 and 2012 (UNEP Risoe Centre on Energy, Environment and Sustainable Development [URC] database). The bulk of the abatement would take place through a reduction in N_2O emissions at nitric acid production plants (32.3 Mt CO_2e); the remainder would be abated through renewable energy projects (10.8 Mt), energy efficiency programmes (2.0 Mt), the capture of fugitive methane from the fossil fuel industry (0.9 Mt) and landfill gas capture (1.2 Mt). Some of these projects have a direct or indirect influence on EU ETS emissions, which had to be taken into account in the second-period NAPs to avoid double-counting.

JI projects are also being set up in some western European countries. France, Germany, Spain and Denmark have set up procedures to host JI projects on their territory and Germany and France are known to be effectively hosting JI projects. In Germany, six projects have been approved by the government with an emissions abatement potential of 11.7 Mt CO_2e (URC database). In France, thirty projects are being

---

[5] Slovenia, Malta and Cyprus are the only new member states that are not currently hosting JI projects. Malta and Cyprus cannot host JI projects, as they are not Annex B countries as defined by the Kyoto Protocol.

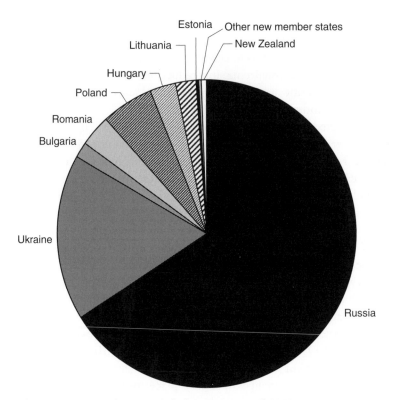

Figure 9.8 Potential ERU supply by country until 2012
Note: Total = 0.3 Gt CO_2e JI projects outside Europe and in the EU12
Source: Derived from UNEP Risoe Centre database

developed with an estimated abatement potential of 5 Mt CO_2e between 2008 and 2012 (André, Bodiguel and Leguet 2008). In both countries, several energy efficiency programmes are programmatic, meaning that credits are earned for a programme of activities rather than a single project. In order to avoid double-counting, activities that would have a direct or indirect effect on ETS emissions are excluded, such as projects involving small boilers below the ETS size threshold or that produce renewable heat or reduce the consumption of fossil-fuel-fired heating systems. When the latter are replaced by electrical heat pumps, CO_2 emissions are reduced with no compensating increase in CO_2 from electricity consumed, since the latter is already capped. These projects effectively extend the scope of the ETS into non-ETS sectors, albeit in a small way.

Beyond the short-term benefits of the ERUs produced by these projects, they have important longer-term effects. They reveal innovative ways of abating emissions and provide policy-makers with useful information that can be used to set baselines and develop monitoring, reporting and verification protocols, which may be used to adopt stricter regulations or to include whole new sectors in the EU ETS at a later date. The role of these 'domestic projects' was recognized in the post-2012 amendments to the ETS Directive, which call for harmonizing the rules governing these projects after 2012. This provision could facilitate a significant expansion in the sectors and emissions covered by the EU ETS.

Conclusion: what are the next steps?

The first trading period of the EU ETS has planted the seeds of what may one day become a global carbon market. Two achievements are of particular note: (1) the scope of the programme has been successfully expanded, through the addition of additional gases, sectors and trading partners; and (2) the ETS has established a carbon price signal that has led to the development of emissions reduction projects in sectors and countries not covered by the trading scheme.

This first achievement speaks highly to the design of the EU ETS Directive, which has permitted the inclusion of additional activities, ranging from opt-ins to the aviation sector, beginning in 2012. The opt-in provision has enabled member states to increase the scope of the coverage within their own borders if they choose to do so. In addition, the scope of emissions trading has been increased through the establishment of the Aviation Trading Scheme, which is linked to the EU ETS and is expected to expand further as proposals to include the maritime sector and the aluminium and chemicals industries are acted upon in future years. While the incorporation of Bulgaria and Romania in the European Union in 2007 was more important in terms of emissions covered than Norway, their participation was a condition of accession, whereas Norway's was not. Norway's accession to the EU ETS provides the first empirical evidence of how independent emissions trading schemes can be successfully incorporated.

From a global market perspective, the second major achievement of the EU ETS has been to establish a carbon price signal that is internalized by market players around the world. Demand for carbon allowances by installations subject to the EU ETS has driven the development of emissions reduction projects far outside European borders, and in sectors not covered by the trading scheme. Although the continued success of these activities depends on political and institutional decisions, there is little doubt that demand from the EU ETS has spurred emissions reductions outside Europe that probably would not have occurred in the absence of the trading scheme.

At the conclusion of its first trading period, the EU ETS has proved itself to be an environmental market with truly global implications. The next challenge will be to determine how the European Union's trading scheme can be successfully linked with those launched by other major economic players, including the United States, Australia and Canada. The Kyoto project mechanisms also offer an indirect route towards linking these schemes.

10 | *Conclusions*

Doubt is an uncomfortable position; certainty is absurd.　　　Voltaire

While conclusions ought not to be riddled with doubt, definitive judgements on the EU ETS seem out of place, given that the first trading period offers only three years of experience and observations. Policy is often formed on less, however, and the absurdity of certainty can apply to both sides of any proposition. Thus, we hope that the reader will share the discomfort, and appreciate the tentativeness, with which the following conclusions are proposed.

CO_2 emissions are no longer free

The importance of this conclusion rests not in the price, which ranged from a few cents to more than €30, but in the changes in institutions and thinking that have characterized the trial period of the EU ETS. From being seen as a quixotic and, for some, dubious initiative, the EU ETS has become an accepted fact and centrepiece of European Union climate policy. More importantly, the fact that greenhouse gas emissions have a price has become embedded in the thinking and, more particularly, in the decision-making process for production and investment affecting the sources of more than a half of European CO_2 emissions.

When emissions trading was first formally suggested by the European Commission in May 1999, the European Community comprised fifteen member states with a very diverse set of policies and inclinations regarding climate policy, not to mention attitudes towards the idea of mobilizing markets to address climate change. Nevertheless, in surprisingly few years, a trial trading period was developed and applied to twenty-seven countries with a population of close to 500 million, embracing twenty-three languages, varying institutional capacities and economic structures, and considerable diversity as regards familiarity with markets generally, and the application of markets to environmental policy in particular.

This bold public policy experiment required all twenty-seven member states to bring their understanding and capacities from close to zero, in many cases, to the level of adequacy needed to set up registries, measure baseline emissions, implement monitoring, reporting, verification and enforcement systems, decide how and to whom to allocate allowances and, most surprisingly, agree on aggregate limits for each member state. In view of the institutional and even cultural vacuum that existed with respect to the use of emissions trading, political systems, bureaucracies and business communities were stretched to the limits and beyond in meeting all these requirements. Inevitably, there were of course delays and setbacks, but, all in all, the challenge was successfully met.

By the end of the trial period the understanding had emerged that CO_2 emissions could no longer be treated as a free good and that the EU ETS would be a permanent feature of EU institutions. It may be too much to claim that all participants have fully internalized the cost of CO_2 emissions into their operations, but it seems clear that most have and that the number that have not is becoming progressively smaller. While using a carbon market as a primary instrument for climate change policy has always had and continues to have its detractors, the overall effect of the trial period has been to create a working system that is understood and accepted by all key players.

Allocation is controversial

The historical evidence we have interrogated is unambiguous: there would have been no EU ETS unless allowances in the trial period had been allocated for free. This issue was fully debated, as is appropriate for an issue involving the creation of valuable rights and their distribution, but the outcome was the same as it had been in all earlier cap-and-trade systems. The controversy did not go away, however, and the pendulum has now swung in favour of auctioning, at least for the power sector. This change is a product of two forces that became evident during the pilot period. The first is the reaction to the increased profits that resulted from the inclusion of the opportunity cost of the free allowances in the prices charged for electricity in member states in which markets were deregulated. The second influence was the experience with the allocation process itself, which member states found to be time-consuming and politically and administratively difficult, and the belief that auctioning (and the distribution of the resulting revenues) will be easier.

The controversy concerning allocation was not limited to the question of who is to receive the scarcity rent created by the limit on CO_2 emissions. The tougher question concerns the effect of allocation (as distinct from the CO_2 price) on operations and investment. Here the theoretical arguments are abundant and clear, but rigorous empirical evidence of the predicted effects is scant. In theory, fixed, lump-sum allocations will have no effect on operational or investment decisions. The EU ETS has introduced a novel feature into allocation, however, that theory would predict to have a clear effect on capacity: the award of free allowances to new CO_2-emitting plants and capacity expansions and the forfeiture of free allocations when CO_2-emitting facilities are closed. These new entrant and closure provisions both decrease the expected cost of new capacity and increase the cost of shutting down existing (and perhaps inefficient) older capacity. Unfortunately, the short experience to date and the long-term nature of investment decisions do not yet allow a good empirical verification of the effects of the new entrant and closure provisions on capacity, not to mention on the choice of technology or emissions.

A liquid and sophisticated market emerged

A cap-and-trade system is an efficient means for regulating emissions only if a market emerges to provide a single price signal to all covered installations and to facilitate the allowance trading that is needed to equalize the marginal costs of the abatement required to comply with the cap. A market for EUAs emerged as soon as the EU ETS became operational, and it has since grown steadily in volume and sophistication. A very broad and deep trans-frontier market for CO_2 now exists, with widespread participation across countries, sectors and firms and with many and varied financial intermediaries serving buyers and sellers. Although it will never be possible to know with certainty that the emission reductions are being achieved at least cost (because the underlying structure of abatement costs are known only to each participant), the conditions for this result – a single price and widespread participation – are present. As targets become more ambitious in the future, this platform will be crucial in helping Europe meet objectives at minimum cost, and this in turn will advance competitiveness.

The emergence of this market has also demonstrated two other points. The first is that market design affects market behaviour. The self-contained nature of the trial period – created by the inability to trade with the subsequent trading period – made EUA prices during the trial period more volatile, and this feature alone largely explains the zero price at the end of the first period. Poor information about the scope of the emissions included in the EU ETS at the start compounded these effects and also contributed to the unusual evolution of price that was observed. The quick reaction of EUA prices to the revelation of reliable information through the release of verified emissions data for the first year also showed that the EUA market is no different from other markets in reacting quickly to new information and the resulting changes in expectations.

The EUA market has also demonstrated that its effects extend beyond the installations covered by the EU ETS. Although project credits were not a factor in the trial period, the EUA market also provided the price signals concerning the second compliance period that greatly encouraged project development, notably the signals offered in developing countries under the provisions of the Clean Development Mechanism. Before the EU ETS this market had languished; but allowing installations to meet some of their requirements by the purchase of project-based allowances immediately raised their value and the willingness of developers and intermediaries to supply the market.

Abatement occurred

Expectations concerning emissions abatement for the trial period were modest – slightly below business-as-usual emissions – with the focus in these initial years on getting the EU ETS up and running. Significant emission reductions would be achieved in future periods. Nevertheless, the EU ETS experienced relatively high initial prices, and all the evidence demonstrates that these prices resulted in emission reductions during the trial period. For the European Union as a whole and for most member states, the aggregate CO_2 emissions of EU ETS facilities were lower in 2005 than in 2004, despite robust economic growth and developments in the pricing of coal and natural gas that counteracted what would otherwise have been the effect of the EUA price. These latter developments increased carbon intensity in these years, but, as can now be shown rigorously, it would have increased even more without the CO_2 price. A reasonable estimate is that emissions were lower by 2 to 5 per cent as a result of the EU ETS.

Most of the modest emission reduction occurred in the electric utility sector, in which existing power plants found that the hierarchy of dispatching output from lowest to highest cost was changed once carbon cost had been internalized. Abatement was not restricted to the electric power sector, however. Other noticeable incremental sources of reduction included the use of biomass as feedstock and the use of slag from the steel industry in the production of cement. It is too early to know the effects on investment decisions, and no systematic evidence exists in the pilot period that innovation was stimulated beyond the organizational changes that focused managers' attention on this new constraint. There is a renewed focus on accelerating progress on carbon capture and storage, however, in tandem with the Commission proposals, which foresee the allowance price as a key incentive to make such a process commercially viable.

Competitiveness and cost effects were small

Fears to the contrary notwithstanding, the effects of the EU ETS on the competitive position of EU industry are imperceptible to date. Imports of CO_2-intensive goods, such as cement, iron and steel, did not increase any more than they had in the past, and European production continued at and even exceeded previous levels. This was also a period of relatively robust economic growth in the European Union and of some remarkable shifts in world commodity markets, but, overall, our observation is that production and trade patterns were not greatly affected by the CO_2 price. This result, which seems puzzling when viewed in the context of the fears expressed on the subject, is easier to understand when the CO_2 price is placed in perspective. It is only one price among many prices, not to mention other non-price factors – such as location or government policies – that determine production and trade patterns, and all these other prices and factors remain as important as ever.

Three important qualifications must be made, regarding the period of observation, the range of prices experienced and the effect of free allocation. The long-term effects cannot be expected to be fully observed in three or four years, although non-CO_2 prices and other factors also matter in the long term. In addition, the highest CO_2 price observed was €30, and only for a brief period – much less than the prices that modelling exercises indicate as needed to effect a major reduction of greenhouse gas emissions. Finally, the ample supply of free allowances received by most industrial installations removed the immediate financial sting of the EU ETS. Although this intended bias may not have been conducive to a full consideration of the CO_2 cost by these entities, they may not have incorporated the CO_2 price into their output-pricing decisions, either for strategic reasons or because the pricing of their products is truly global. This subject deserves more research, both theoretical and empirical.

The cost of the EU ETS, in terms of resources diverted to abatement, was small by any estimate and in line with the modest abatement achieved. What the trial period demonstrated is that far greater concern was focused on the transfers implicit in the scarcity value of emission allowances. Even these were small in relation to the EU economy as a whole (about four-tenths of 1 per cent), and how much of this newly created scarcity rent was actually captured is a continuing matter of debate, but the concern of participants and observers alike was directed more to these actual and potential transfers than to the macroeconomic cost of the programme. Some highly focused research on transaction costs shows that the average costs of setting up and operating the scheme and of conducting trades were very modest, but that they increased substantially per tonne for the smallest operators.

Whatever the level of Voltairian discomfort one might feel in these conclusions, there is one in which certainty does not seem absurd. The EU ETS is a path-breaking public policy experiment with implications that will extend far beyond the European Union. It has provided a laboratory and an example that has been, and will continue to be, studied by those who consider similar measures, not least in the United States. It is also the potential cornerstone for a much larger global regime. For this, the architects of and participants in the EU ETS can take justifiable pride; but they also bear the responsibility that goes with being pioneers: to show what can be done without discouraging others from following.

Annex: The interaction between the EU ETS and European electricity markets

JAN HORST KEPPLER, UNIVERSITY
PARIS-DAUPHINE[1]

Introduction

The launch of period 1 of the EU ETS in January 2005 coincided with a particularly turbulent period in Europe's electricity markets. Two directives of the European Commission, Directive 2003/54/EC (internal electricity market) and Directive 2005/89/EC (security of electricity supply), advanced the objective of complete liberalization of electricity and gas markets in the European Union. In parallel, Europe experienced an intense process of industrial concentration, with a de facto transnational oligopoly emerging around EDF, E.ON, Enel-Endesa, RWE and GDF Suez. Coupled with the intrinsic short-term inelasticity of electricity demand, the absence of storage and electricity's importance as an essential good for households and industry, the establishment of wholesale markets outside national regulatory oversight and the movement towards concentration have repeatedly given rise to suspicions of the abuse of market power. To top it off, western and central Europe experienced severe cold snaps, in the winters of both 2004/5 and 2005/6, which, in conjunction with low hydro-power levels, led to dramatic high price spikes during the first phase of the EU ETS.[2]

There is objectively a close connection between electricity and carbon markets, and this annex explores it. The introductory remarks above should, however, draw attention to the fact that electricity prices had plenty of reason to be both unusually high and volatile during period 1, in particular during the crucial period stretching from

---

[1] I would like to thank Richard Baron, Barbara Buchner, Felix Matthes and Julia Reinaud for their helpful comments. Special thanks also go to Denny Ellerman, whose numerous valuable remarks greatly helped to improve the final version of this paper.
[2] On 27 July 2006, for instance, the price for an MWh of peak-load power on the day-ahead spot market reached a staggering price of €544.

the beginning of 2005 until spring 2006, quite independently of the newly introduced EU ETS. In addition, the European electricity market is not yet fully unified due to the saturation of certain physical interconnections at peak times and different regulatory regimes for retail prices in several EU countries. In the following, I concentrate on three points in particular: (1) the key features of the European Union's electricity market; (2) the connection (or relationship) between electricity and carbon prices during the trial period; and (3) the rents ('windfall profits') gained by electricity producers through the costless allocation of allowances and higher electricity prices.

Overview of the European electricity sector

The production mix

Figure A.1 provides an overview of the production mix of the European power sector in 2004 as well as two possible scenarios for its further development by 2030.[3] While currently still dominated by coal and nuclear, which each contribute roughly one-third of European electricity, the already important share of natural gas is set to grow strongly. The fastest-rising sources of electricity, however, are 'new' renewable sources such as wind, geothermal and photovoltaic solar energy. In March 2007 the European Union committed itself to produce 20 per cent of its energy from renewable sources by 2020, so substantial incentives to achieve this growth are likely to be put into place. The sites for the 'old' renewable source of large hydroelectric power, based both on reservoirs and run-of-the-river, are by and large exhausted, and its contribution will not be able to increase much further.

Several countries, notably Germany, Sweden and the Netherlands, have made commitments to phase out their production of nuclear power. Since doing so, however, the feasibility of this choice is increasingly being questioned, in particular in the context of the European Union's commitment also to reduce carbon emissions by 20 per cent by 2020.[4]

---

[3] The figure contains two scenarios developed by the International Energy Agency (IEA 2007c). The 'reference scenario' is a business-as-usual scenario extrapolating current trends. The 'alternative policy scenario' also includes declared policy objectives and announced policies.

[4] It should be noted that, in all three countries, the commitment to phase out nuclear power is weakening. In Germany, the Christian Democrats are committed to reverse the phase-out after the elections in 2009; in Sweden, a majority of the

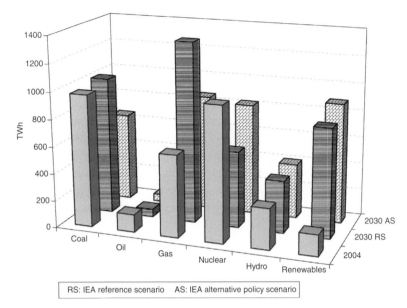

Figure A.1 EU25 power generation mix, 2004 and 2030
Source: IEA (2007c)

The most dramatic development, however, is likely to take place in the gas sector. Figure A.2 shows how Europe's gas consumption has approximately tripled in the past fifteen years. If the IEA's forecast holds true, it will roughly double again (now from a much higher base) in the next twenty-five years.

Despite worries about the ability of Europe's long-term gas suppliers, the three largest of which are Russia, Algeria and Norway, to support such increase in gas prices in the wake of record oil prices, gas has some important advantages that often make it the fuel of choice for private investors in Europe's liberalized electricity markets. First, combined-cycle gas turbines have low capital costs and high efficiencies, which allow for reduced risk and shortened payback times. Second, because of its higher price and hence marginal cost per kWh produced, gas is frequently the marginal fuel in power generation – i.e. the last unit to be fired up to produce electricity. Electricity prices are therefore frequently set by gas prices. For a private investor this constitutes an automatic hedge against price variations – an advantage

population is now in favour of nuclear; and the Dutch government recently decided to extend the operational life of the Borssele nuclear power plant, which was initially scheduled to be shut down in 2013, until 2033.

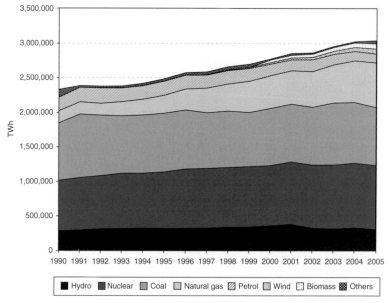

Figure A.2 The rising share of natural gas in EU25 power generation, 1990–2005
Source: Eurostat's Environment and Energy database, available at epp.eurostat.ec. europa.eu

that other fuels cannot match.[5] In terms of CO_2 emissions this is both a boon and a bane. Although gas produces roughly between one-third and one-half of the CO_2 per MWh of electricity compared to coal, it still produces substantially higher emissions than nuclear or renewables. The latter, however, are held back by high investment cost, which exposes investors to the volatility of electricity prices. Nuclear and renewables thus require some form of risk management, either in the form of private long-term contracts or implicit or explicit public guarantees for the value of their output.[6]

Contrary to the ultimate objective of the European Commission, the EU electricity market is not yet a 'copper plate', in which a point source of demand can be serviced with minimal transaction costs by any provider in the system, but a complex web of national markets, in which limited and varying interconnection capacity opens and closes

[5] See, for instance, Roques, Nuttal and Newberry 2006.
[6] For the study of a successful case of such risk management in the case of nuclear energy see Keppler 2005. Renewable energies, in addition to their exposure to price uncertainty, also need to cope, of course, with an absolute cost disadvantage. On the basis of average cost (not including price uncertainty), nuclear has always been able to hold its own.

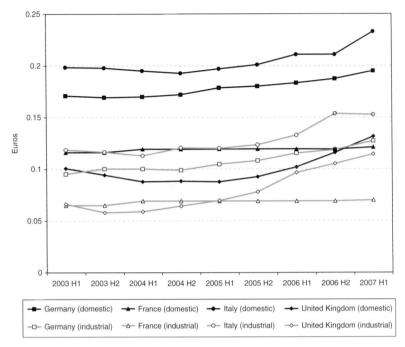

Figure A.3 End-use electricity prices in selected EU countries, 2003–7
Source: Eurostat's Environment and Energy database

markets in a matter of hours or less. In addition, prices for households and some industrial consumers are still frequently regulated; when they are not, the stability of transmission and distribution costs ensure that small consumers will be exposed to relatively minor variations in end-use prices. Consumers are therefore frequently shielded from developments in the wholesale power market.

Nevertheless, one can discern a common tendency over the past five years: prices in the European electricity sector have been going up (see figure A.3), both in the wholesale market (not pictured here) and also for households and industry.

So far, however, these price rises have failed to dent fast-rising electricity demand, at least until 2006 (see figure A.4). Demand has proved to be stable not only in the household and services sectors but also in industry in general, as well as in the steel and aluminium (non-ferrous metals) industry. Although this may seem surprising, on account of the fact that the latter two industries consume large amounts of electricity and are hence vulnerable to higher electricity

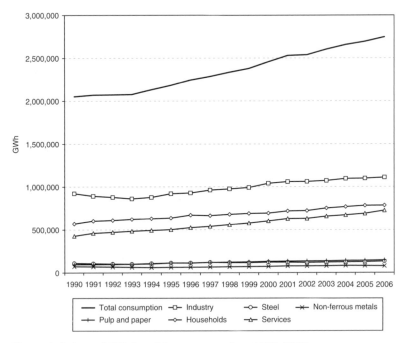

Figure A.4 Annual EU electricity consumption, 1990–2006
Source: Eurostat's Environment and Energy database

prices (the cost of electricity in aluminium production can reach up to 50 per cent of value added), many industrial companies actively manage short-term electricity price risk or are still benefiting from electricity contracts signed prior to the liberalization. For example, in the primary aluminium sector, only 18 per cent of EU capacity operated without long-term contracts in 2006 (see box A.1).

A small demand effect might be visible in the statistics concerning monthly electricity production to 2007. Demand responses typically manifest themselves with a lag, and the first nine months of 2007 indeed show a slight levelling off of total electricity production. Thus, while carbon prices were very low all through 2007, electricity prices stayed high, and we may see here the first impact on demand of the rise for electricity prices that began in 2003 and accelerated in 2005. Concerning the structure of supply, one should note that a number of support schemes for renewables have substantially increased production in these technologies.

**Box A.1   Electricity wholesale prices and industry costs:
what is the relationship?**

Electricity price increases do not necessarily translate into electricity cost increases for industry. To gauge the impact of CO_2 allowances on industry power prices requires, among other things, an analysis of contractual arrangements between industry and power suppliers in the different countries. Precise data on the type of supply contracts are often unavailable, however. Indeed, in liberalized energy markets, eligible customers are entitled to choose their energy supplier and contract among a range of possibilities.

How does the electricity cost faced by industrial energy users relate to the prices observed on electricity markets, and what is the role of CO_2 in industry electricity costs? For some sectors, long-term electricity contracts concluded before liberalization are still running. This is the case in the primary aluminium sector, in which only 18 per cent of the EU capacity operated without long-term contracts in 2006 (Reinaud 2008b). Although the details of these contracts are unknown, cost estimates indicate lower average electricity costs in these cases than for aluminium smelters acquiring electricity on the market. The extent to which smelters were actually exposed to higher electricity prices as a result of the EU ETS is limited. In some member states, moreover, agreements have been concluded, or are being planned, that promote new long-term partnerships between customers and energy suppliers. In such contracts, industry shares part of the investment risk with the electricity generator (e.g. Exceltium in France, Blue Sky in Belgium).

Finally, various other electricity pricing mechanisms are found across European countries if companies are not bound by long-term electricity contracts. End-user prices can be a mix of various market prices, as energy-intensive industries can purchase electricity by using a mix of instruments such as long-term contracts (especially for base-load) and forward contracts for the bulk of their consumption. Regulated tariffs in many European countries further distort the picture. The impact of carbon-pricing on end-users' costs is thus even more uncertain than the impact on generation costs. As a result, changes in electricity costs for energy-intensive industries cannot be estimated from day-ahead or forward electricity prices variations alone, even though supply contracts may sometimes be indexed to exchange prices.

Julia Reinaud, International Energy Agency

The special role of the power sector in the EU ETS

As far as the EU ETS is concerned, the European electricity sector is special in the sense that it constitutes by far its largest sector. Of the 2 billion plus allowances allocated annually in the trial period the electricity sector received somewhat over 40 per cent – i.e. 800 million allowances, significantly more than any other sector (Trotignon and Delbosc 2008). The peculiar situation of European power producers is also highlighted by the fact that the electricity sector was the *only* sector substantially short of allowances. Power producers thus emitted some 60 million tonnes more than their allotment in 2005 and some 80 million tonnes more in 2006. These figures need to be compared to the overall allowance surpluses of the EU ETS of around 80 million tonnes in 2005 and of around 40 million tonnes in 2006.

Allowance prices are, of course, set as a function of the total surplus or shortfall, and European power producers could – in principle – cover their shortfall very cheaply, when prices were hovering below 10 cents during most of 2007, given that full banking and borrowing were allowed during the three years of period 1. The need to search for cover for its structural short position, however, made European electricity producers by far the most active participants in the new EU ETS. Their large size in a still developing market also poses the question of market power. For instance, the largest single emitter – a large European power company – received 6 per cent of all allowances or about 120 million tonnes, more than many countries (Trotignon and Delbosc 2008). In other words, power production by and large determines the overall demand for carbon allowances and, in the interplay with exogenously set supply, their price. This does not imply that power producers had a coherent strategy to manipulate prices (see below for some econometric evidence to the contrary), but it does imply that events in the power sector are decisive for what happens in carbon markets.

How electricity markets work

As electricity is a non-storable commodity and its demand varies during the day, a certain amount of capacity has to be switched on and off during the day. This means that at certain times of the day, say between 6 a.m. and 8 p.m. in a country such as France, roughly 15,000 additional MW of capacity must be made available. Another 5,000 MW are needed between 6 p.m. and 7 p.m. in the evening, when factories and commuter trains are still running and TVs and household appliances are being switched on (see figure A.5).

The power generated twenty-four hours each day is referred to as base-load, while the additional power needed only intermittently is referred to as peak-load (between one-fifth and one-quarter of

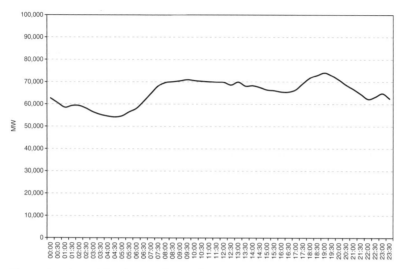

Figure A.5 French load-curve for Wednesday, 5 December 2007
Source: RTE (2007)

demand during daytime). Base-load technologies are nuclear, coal, CCGTs and intermittently working renewables, while gas- and oil-fired single-cycle turbines are peak-load technologies. The former have relatively high fixed and low marginal costs, while the latter have somewhat lower fixed costs and higher marginal costs.

In liberalized markets, at each point in time the price of electricity is set by the generating unit with the highest marginal cost (the last one being pressed into service to meet demand). This means that all other installations, those with lower marginal costs, are then earning infra-marginal rents, or what could be considered short-run surplus profits. This is not the place to discuss in detail the working of a liberalized electricity system.[7] Suffice it to say that (1) these infra-marginal rents are vital to finance the high fixed costs of base-load technologies with low marginal costs; and (2) under certain assumptions a competitive electricity market, in which marginal costs set the price at each instance, can bring about a generation mix that precisely covers the full cost of each type of plant.

The general role of CO_2 allowances in electricity prices

The introduction of the EU ETS has necessarily increased the marginal costs of the CO_2-emitting fossil fuels, coal, gas and oil, to the extent

[7] For a thorough and very readable introduction to the issue, see Joskow 2006.

that carbon allowances that constrain the total emissions of a sector imply putting a price on these emissions. This holds, independent of the question of whether allowances have been given to producers at no cost or have been acquired by the latter during an auction or on the market. Burning fossil fuels to produce electricity *always* incurs a cost for emitting carbon emissions. When the allowances surrendered for compliance were freely allocated to the installation, this cost is, in economic terminology, an 'opportunity cost' – the forgone revenue that would otherwise be earned by selling the unused allowance.

This somewhat counterintuitive fact can be explained quite easily by means of the following example. Think of a producer who generates 1 MWh of base-load electricity by burning 1 tonne of coal, which costs €50 (net of carbon). Since he will emit 1 tonne of CO_2 in the process, he will need to use one of the allowances he received for free. Say that this allowance would have fetched €12 on the EU ETS (the average price during period 1). Our producer will now need to sell his electricity at €62, even if the allowance did not cost him anything. Why? Because, by *not* producing the electricity (this is where the notion of opportunity cost comes in), he would have neither sold electricity nor bought coal, but he could have sold his allowance on the EU ETS, thus making a €12 profit. In order to produce electricity, he will thus demand the same profit of €12, or €62 per MWh.[8]

Crucially, a carbon price thus increases the marginal costs of fossil fuels, and electricity prices, as well as the infra-marginal rents for both fossil-fuel-based and carbon-free power producers. In other words, the carbon price increases the rents of all power producers. Below, I illustrate the magnitude and incidence of this increase of infra-marginal rents in electricity due to carbon-pricing.

[8] Even if the logic is surprisingly simple, it is far from universally accepted in public discussion, where fears persist that auctioning will raise electricity prices further. While the allocation method makes no difference to prices, it should be underlined that the question of free allocation versus auctioning makes an enormous difference to the total amount of rents that fossil-fuel-based producers receive. Auctioning is, in fact, a way to capture part of the carbon rents of fossil-fuel-based producers, but is neutral on prices. This confirms the microeconomic principle that rents are residuals – i.e. profits for which no effort has been forthcoming – and, by definition, have no impact on prices.

The formation of carbon and electricity prices

Before estimating the additional rents generated by the EU ETS for European power producers, I consider the interplay of both carbon and electricity prices. This is an area of ongoing research. Accordingly, I do not provide definite answers but present two main theories and their variants to explain the formation of carbon prices in interaction with electricity prices. In addition, I provide some econometric evidence on both the interplay of carbon, electricity and gas prices and the interplay of spot and future prices. This evidence indicates certain causal relationships without being able to answer the question definitively. In this context, it should not be forgotten that the EU ETS is a very young market in which certain structural relationships are *assumed* by traders (sometimes for only months at a time) without there being sufficient time to establish feedback loops through the real economy. In particular, the non-bankability of carbon allowances between period 1 and period 2 limited investment incentives.[9] The uncertainty driven by the short duration of period 1 also introduced a cost premium for investors, who had an incentive to keep their options open by delaying investment until there was more visibility about period 2 and period 3 options.[10]

The long-run carbon–electricity hypotheses

The hypotheses that postulate a relationship in which carbon prices determine electricity prices are based on economic assumptions in which carbon prices are exogenously determined by factors such as marginal abatement costs or political and institutional factors. At the same time, carbon allowances are considered an essential input into electricity production. Logically, the allowance price will thus drive electricity prices. There exist two principal forms of the long-term carbon–electricity hypothesis, both briefly presented below.

---

[9] The possibility of forward banking between periods 2 and 3 (2013–20) establishes de facto a thirteen-year time horizon for the validity of a carbon allowance. This should contribute greatly to the ability of the market to focus on long-term possibilities for generating carbon emission reductions. See also Keppler 2007b.

[10] For the effects of price and cost uncertainty on investment in the power sector, see IEA 2007d.

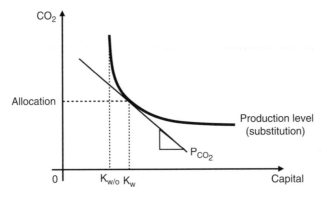

Figure A.6 Carbon emissions with factor substitution
Notes: $K_{w/o}$ = capital without carbon-pricing in the EU ETS and K_w = capital with carbon-pricing in the EU ETS
Source: Author

The first, the marginal abatement cost theory, has its foundations in basic microeconomic theory. A unit of electricity can be produced with different combinations of capital investment and fuel, which has an impact on CO_2 emissions (think for instance of a plant that is expensive to build but very efficient when operated, and another one that is cheaper to build but more expensive during operation). The choice of the investor will be determined by the relative prices of capital costs and the combined costs of fuels and emissions.[11] In order to simplify the argument, the price of fuels is considered to be constant. It then holds that, for any given level of electricity output, the higher the price of emissions the higher the amount of initial investment to lower the carbon emissions.

If capital (and these other inputs) and emissions can be substituted smoothly for each other, the isoquant in figure A.6, which indicates a given level of production, will be smooth and convex towards the origin. When authorities fix the level of allowances, this implicitly sets

---

[11] Strictly speaking, it is not only capital that can be substituted for emissions in order to produce an MWh of electricity. One might also think of substituting more expensive fuels with higher thermal content per tonne of carbon for cheaper fuels with a lower thermal content. The equivalent happened in the US market for SO_2 allowances, in which, after the introduction of the market for sulphur dioxide allowances, operators substituted cheap high-sulphur coal with more costly low-sulphur coal, which proved to be the most cost-efficient option for abatement.

the price of a carbon allowance that will indicate the additional capital investment needed not to emit the marginal emissions in question – hence the expression 'marginal abatement cost' or 'marginal cost of reduction'.

The second, the end-of-period hypothesis, sees expectations and the length of time remaining to the end of the allocation period as the key drivers of trial allowance prices (Ellerman and Parsons 2006). This hypothesis presents a special case applicable to the trial period, based on the inability to bank into or to borrow allowances from the second trading period. It argues that these constraints inevitably lead to either over- or under-allocation of allowances. If at the end of the trial period an aggregate short is revealed, the final price for first-period allowances will be the penalty price for not surrendering allowances (€40 plus the price of second-period allowances). If an aggregate long position is revealed, prices will drop to zero. Prices at each point in time will then correspond to the expectations of market participants concerning the possibility of either over- or under-allocation. The carbon prices thus established in return will be integrated into electricity prices.

There is little doubt that the end-of-period hypothesis was the relevant paradigm for the carbon market during 2007, when the gradually declining carbon price showed that the evidence for over-allocation was becoming ever more obvious for market participants. It is less clear, however, whether this confirms the long-term carbon–electricity hypothesis. Electricity prices in fact held up very well during 2007 both in the futures market and, after a slight drop in the first half of the year, also in the spot market, while carbon prices were approaching zero. This was partly due to rising coal prices, but partly also to autonomous developments in the electricity sector, such as decreasing capacity margins, the difference between installed capacity and peak demand, which is an indicator of tightness in the market.

The short-run electricity–carbon hypotheses

The short-term electricity–carbon hypothesis also comes in two forms. In the first form, the market power of operators creates scarcity rents in the electricity market that are subsequently captured in the price of carbon credits, which are, crucially, limited in number. This is possible only in the short run, when no additional carbon emission reductions are possible and no substitution of emissions with other factors exists. Given that capital and fuels are traded in competitive global markets, one may assume their price to be fixed. In this situation, the margin between the price of electricity (set by the interplay of demand and monopolistic suppliers) and its marginal cost (essentially fuel costs) will be captured in the price of the fixed number of carbon allowances. In other words, a carbon allowance is a ticket to gain monopoly profits in the electricity sector. In case the carbon market is competitive, the price of the ticket will be equal to the profit that can be obtained with it.[12]

An example can provide some intuition. In a power market with scarce capacity, electricity is sold at €70 per MWh before the introduction of a carbon-trading scheme. Variable production cost (net of carbon), however, is only €50, and producers make a €20 profit per MWh. Now a carbon-trading scheme is introduced in which the supply of allowances precisely matches the current production of each producer and no trading takes place.[13] In this situation, a new competitor, too small to influence industry output, tries to come into the market. Given that he does not possess any allowances himself, he will need to buy one. The question now is: how much would he be willing to pay (and how much would the incumbents ask of him)? The answer is €20 per allowance (assuming that precisely one allowance is needed to produce an MWh). If the profit per MWh had been €30, this would have determined the price of the allowance.

In the short-term electricity–carbon hypothesis, the divergence between electricity prices and variable costs (net of carbon – essentially fuel costs) are thus not due to the intrinsic value of carbon allowances (defined by the cost of abatement) but due to the monopoly power of the operators.[14] The price of these allowances is determined *ex post* by the spread between electricity prices and variable costs.

---

[12] For those interested in historic analogies, I point out that the price of an EUA in this case corresponds to a Ricardian rent, a residual whose value is set by demand rather than by the cost of production, or, rather, abatement in the case of carbon.

[13] The example would also work just as well if the amount of allowances was *less* than current production. In this case, scarcity in the carbon market would reinforce the monopoly power in the electricity market and consequently raise the prices of both electricity and carbon. The example would *not* work if allowances were larger than current production under scarcity, which would let their price drop to zero.

[14] Ellerman correctly points out, in a personal communication, that market power in the electricity market does not necessarily imply the lasting market dominance of a particular firm but the (rotating) short-run pricing power of different operators due to low capacity margins during peak-load operations.

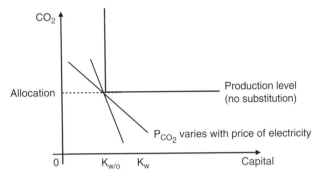

Figure A.7 Carbon emissions without factor substitution
Notes: $K_{w/o}$ = capital without carbon-pricing in the EU ETS and K_w = capital with carbon-pricing in the EU ETS
Source: Author

It should also be kept in mind that the notion of monopoly power in electricity is first and foremost a structural issue and not a moral or a legal issue. Competitive spot electricity markets at peak times are an economically unsustainable constellation: competition will equate price with marginal – i.e. variable – cost, which will not allow remunerating the fixed costs of peak-load installations. Operators thus usually find a way around competition, most commonly by investment retention (or the cocooning of existing capacity) in the face of rising demand.

At peak times, market power for the marginal producer is therefore practically inevitable, because of the inelasticity of demand and the need of the system operator to match demand with supply at every given second. Electricity prices higher than marginal costs therefore provide the scarcity rents that are captured in the prices for carbon allowances in fixed supply. If competition should push prices towards variable cost, producers will decommission plants in order to avoid losses, and thus again create intermittent scarcity (and temporary monopoly power) in the market.

The electricity–carbon hypothesis is based on the assumption that strictly no abatement or substitution is possible. In other words, it is strictly a short-run hypothesis applicable to the spot markets. In keeping with the framework introduced above, the graph of the isoquant would be kinked (see figure A.7), which implies indeterminacy of the carbon price on the basis of cost of production or abatement.

There exists, in addition, a strong technical rationale for this link between scarcity in electricity markets and higher prices for CO_2 allowances. If electricity prices rise due to increased demand, this encourages the use of additional 'peakers' (peak-load power generation technologies). These are frequently diesel-fired combustion turbines with carbon emission factors between 0.8 and 1 tonne of CO_2 per MWh. Increased electricity demand will thus translate into increased carbon demand and, ultimately, higher carbon prices. Causality will thus run again from electricity to carbon prices.

The short-run fuel-switching hypothesis

A second version of the short-term hypothesis sees fuel prices rather than electricity prices as the key driver of carbon prices. In this theory, the price differential between gas and coal determines the composition of power generation and hence the demand for carbon credits. There is some evidence that the gas–carbon link drives markets. Period 2 of the EU ETS, for instance, shows increased correlation between carbon and energy prices. The correlation for the December 2008 EUA future with the ICE (IntercontinentalExchange) gas future for the United Kingdom thus rose to 0.9 from January to May 2008, up from -0.3 in 2005, 0.2 in 2006 and 0.6 in 2007. The link with electricity (German base-load power) prices instead weakened from 0.5 in 2007 to 0.4 during the first five months of 2008 (Szabo 2008).[15]

The big question is whether such correlations are the result of industrial decisions to optimize the structure of the generation mix or whether they result from the decisions of disoriented traders in new markets who establish virtual correlations through a combination of herd behaviour and loss aversion. On the industrial side, the 'real' side of the economy, any link between carbon, coal and gas prices would need to show up in the form of coal-to-gas or coal-to-biomass fuel-switching once carbon prices had reached the threshold level of the 'switching price'. Deciding conclusively on this issue is difficult. Nevertheless, I draw attention to three important facts that will need to be heeded in any more definite assessment:

[15] Matthes points out, in a personal communication, that the weakening of the link between German electricity prices and carbon prices in 2008 might be due to the strong increase in the price of coal, which determines base-load electricity prices in Germany, whereas carbon prices are set Europe-wide by gas prices.

(1) There does not exist one single switching price throughout the EU ETS but a rather large price band inside which specific operators will find it profitable to substitute certain kinds of fuels (e.g. biomass for coal), or to change the dispatch order between coal and gas plants.[16]

(2) In most continental European markets, the EUA price during period 1 was too low to provide any incentives for switching from coal to gas on the basis of the average plant efficiencies that go into the calculation of the generic (average) 'switching price'.[17] The average 'switching prices' presented in the literature and calculated on the basis of the carbon emissions of the quantities of coal or gas needed to produce 1 MWh of electricity are also certainly a lower bound for the true cost of switching. Running and stopping a plant ('cycling', in industry jargon) is a costly operation causing additional operational costs, increasing the probability of failures and affecting plant life (Lefton and Besuner 2006).

(3) There is some evidence for the United Kingdom that carbon prices did contribute to different plant utilization rates and emission abatement (McGuinness and Ellerman 2008 and Delarue, Ellerman and D'haeseleer 2008). The United Kingdom is also the only market in which significant amounts of gas are used in base-load power generation, however. This is a necessary condition for switching from coal to gas, since switching needs to take place during base-load operations given that during peak-load operations *all* plants, with the exception of some costly oil or gas combustion turbines for back-up, are in operation anyway.

All this is to say that the statistical correlations between coal, gas and carbon prices do not necessarily imply corresponding developments

[16] Ellerman affirms correctly, in a personal communication, 'There does not exist one uniform "switching price" for the whole of Europe or even the whole of a European country but only a switching price for any given pair of plants.'

[17] According to the data of the Mission Climat of the Caisse des Dépôts (Mission Climat 2008), it was advantageous for operators on the so-called 'continental shelf' power markets (essentially France, Germany and the Benelux countries) to switch from coal to gas only for a few days in spring and summer 2007. This was when gas prices were seasonally low and coal prices had already engaged their historic climb to almost $200 per tonne due to strong Chinese demand. Ironically, during that time, the price for carbon allowances was already below €0.10. The situation changed dramatically in period 2, when fuel-switching became an economically viable option. A comparison of the generating mix between 2005–7 and 2008 should provide significant new insights.

on the ground, quite apart from the fact that the price of carbon allowances was rarely high-enough to induce a producer to switch from coal to gas. There is an added question connected to this issue of price correlations. Why should the price of carbon allowances (a perfectly storable good that is needed only once a year) react at all to transitory variations, such as changes in the prices of coal, gas, electricity or even the weather? Only permanent changes should, in principle, lead to changes in the price of carbon. If weather patterns after a cold snap return to normal, the demand for carbon credits over the whole period should not change. Only the most extreme supporters of the efficiency market hypothesis would argue that *all* short-term price variations are permanent.

In particular, one would expect the price volatility of easily storable carbon allowances to be lower than the price volatility for non-storable electricity. Markets for fuels would be expected to assume an intermediate position – less volatile than the electricity market but also less easily storable, and hence more volatile, than a carbon credit.

In conclusion, the theoretical formulation and empirical verification of the movements in carbon markets need to heed the fact that these markets are relatively new and untested, prone to government inter-vention and rumour. The very novelty of the carbon market had traders occasionally focus on 'virtual correlations', when herd behav-iour substituted for the still absent drivers from the real economy. In any case, saying that the coal–gas price differential was not high enough to induce fuel-switching does *not* imply that carbon-pricing had no impact on emissions. Given that carbon prices were included in the cost of electricity production and had an impact on demand, they contributed to emission abatement. The fact should also be underlined that the learning curve of market participants is very steep and carbon markets are professionalizing rapidly. While the econometric tests below on the relationship between carbon and electricity prices during period 1 provide valuable insights, there is little doubt that the results will be reviewed once sufficient data from period 2 are available.

The econometric evidence

In the econometric tests for the relationship between carbon prices and electricity prices, most tests related to the whole period, from 2005 to 2007, except when specific periods displayed noteworthy

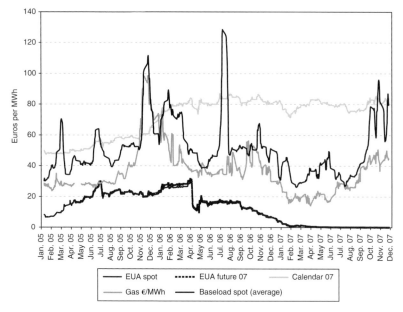

Figure A.8 Carbon, electricity and gas prices in Europe, 2005–7
Sources: BlueNext and EEX data

behaviour. In these cases, three specific periods were distinguished: January 2005 to April 2006 (period I), May 2006 to October 2006 (period II) and November 2006 until December 2007 (period III) (see figure A.8).[18]

Given that the primary focus was on the establishment of causal relationships, Granger causality tests were used after testing for stationarity of the time series (see box A.2 for an explanation of causality tests). The Philipps–Perron test confirmed that all time series were stationary (i.e. absence of unit root and constant mean), which allowed working with the original data rather than with first differences. The results of the different causality test are presented below.[19]

[18] For a discussion of the different periods, see also Alberola, Chevallier and Chèze 2007, as well as chapter 5 of this book.

[19] Slightly different time periods over which testing took place are due to the limited existence of markets (for instance, the market for EUA futures with settlement in December 2007 begins on 22 April 2005 and ends on 17 December 2007; the market for annual electricity futures, the calendar, for 2007 ends on 27 December 2006). Data on EUA futures come from the ECX market and data on electricity and EUA spot prices from the EEX market.

In the tests five different issues are focused on: (1) the link between carbon spot and forward prices; (2) the link between carbon and electricity futures; (3) the link between carbon and electricity spot markets; (4) the role of natural gas prices; and (5) the evidence for market manipulation during summer 2006.

(1) On the link between the spot price for an EUA and the price for the EUA December 2007 futures contract the tests provide a clear answer. The causality runs from the future to the spot market.[20]

Sample: 22/4/2005–17/12/2007

Lags: 2			
Null hypothesis:	Obs.	F-statistic	Probability
The EUA spot price does not Granger-cause the price of the EUA future contract (Dec. 07).	651	0.06930	0.93305
The price of the EUA future contract (Dec. 07) does not Granger-cause the EUA spot price.		95.8597	$3.5e^{-37}$

In other words, it is highly probable that during the whole of period 1 the EUA future market drove the EUA spot market. This is not really a surprising result, given that the forward market is about ten times larger than the spot market. The action was in the forward market.

(2) In the second step, the correlation between carbon and electricity prices in the one-year forward market was looked at, in particular the price of a EUA to be delivered in 2007 and the price of the

[20] Econometric tests produce positive statistical evidence by testing for and – if need be – by rejecting the 'null hypothesis', which is frequently formulated as a negative. In the following example, the hypothesis 'The EUA spot price does not Granger-cause the price of the EUA future contract (Dec. 07)' has a probability of 93 per cent and thus cannot be rejected. Instead, the hypothesis 'The price of the EUA future contract (Dec. 07) *does not* Granger-cause the EUA spot price' has a probability of almost zero ($3.5e^{-37}$), far below the critical 5 per cent threshold, and can thus be rejected. One can therefore conclude the opposite to hold true – i.e. 'The price of the EUA future contract (Dec. 07) *does* Granger-cause the EUA spot price'. Results whose opposite could be rejected with more than 95 per cent of probability are considered 'significant'. Analogous reasoning applies, of course, in all the other cases.

Box A.2 On Granger causality tests

Granger causality tests look at 'causality' in the sense of 'precedence' between time series. Named after the first causality tests performed by the winner of the Nobel Prize in economics in 1969, Clive Granger, they analyse the extent to which the past variations of one variable explain (or precede) subsequent variations of the other. Granger causality tests habitually come in pairs, testing whether variable xt Granger-causes variable yt and vice versa. All permutations are possible: univariate Granger causality from xt to yt or from yt to xt, bivariate causality or absence of causality.

Granger causality does not imply 'causality' in the colloquial sense of an unavoidable logical link, but in the sense of an intertemporal correlation. A more detailed introduction to the use of causality tests in energy economics can be found in Keppler (2007a).

---

one-year forward contract (calendar) for base-load delivery during 2007. Interestingly, the results change with the timescale (number of lags or days) considered, and this holds for all three periods. Thus, looking at the relationship over one day, the causality runs from the electricity market to the carbon market.

Sample: 03/01/2005–28/12/2007

Lags: 1			
Null hypothesis:	Obs.	F-statistic	Probability
The price of the EUA future contract (Dec. 07) does not Granger-cause the price of the 2007 calendar.	409	0.49067	0.48403
The price of the 2007 calendar does not Granger-cause the price of the EUA future contract (Dec. 07).		5.11058	0.02431

Looking at the relationship over two days, EUA futures have a somewhat stronger impact on electricity futures than vice versa, although the relationship could technically be qualified as bidirectional.

For three days or more there is, unsurprisingly, strong bidirectional causality.

The same reversal can be observed between the EUA spot market and the electricity future market.

Sample: 03/01/2005–28/12/2007

Lags: 2			
Null hypothesis:	Obs.	F-statistic	Probability
The price of the EUA future contract (Dec. 07) does not Granger-cause the price of the 2007 calendar.	408	20.9923	$2.1e^{-09}$
The price of the 2007 calendar does not Granger-cause the price of the EUA future contract (Dec. 07).		6.33263	0.00196

Sample: 03/01/2005–28/12/2007

Lags: 3			
Null hypothesis:	Obs.	F-statistic	Probability
The price of the EUA future contract (Dec. 07) does not Granger-cause the price of the 2007 calendar.	407	9.47790	$4.6e^{-06}$
The price of the 2007 calendar does not Granger-cause the price of the EUA future contract (Dec. 07).			$8.3e^{-09}$

Sample: 03/01/2005–28/12/2007

Lags: 1			
Null hypothesis:	Obs.	F-statistic	Probability
The EUA spot price does not Granger-cause the price of the 2007 calendar.	486	2.03215	0.15465
The price of the 2007 calendar does not Granger-cause the EUA spot price.		5.59012	0.01846

Sample: 03/01/2005–28/12/2007

Lags: 2			
Null hypothesis:	Obs.	F-statistic	Probability
The EUA spot price does not Granger-cause the price of the 2007 calendar.	485	16.1700	$1.6e^{-07}$
The price of the 2007 calendar does not Granger-cause the EUA spot price.		2.94679	0.05346

In other words, the carbon market seems slow to react, but once a price signal has been incorporated it will drive the price of the calendar (the contract for electricity delivery over one year). This differs from the relationships between other energy markets. Relationships between gas and electricity prices or between spot and forward electricity markets show up after one day. The carbon market shows its relationship with the electricity forward market after two, or even three, lags, as if relationships still needed time to be established.

(3) The spot market for electricity is clearly driven by carbon prices, however. This is somewhat surprising, as it might have been expected that the link from electricity prices to carbon prices would have been stronger in the spot market than in the forward market. The empirical evidence is unequivocal, however. There is a short-term link from the electricity future market to carbon markets, which is then transmitted into the spot market (even though the link is strongest after the first day and declines subsequently). One explanation could be that the market for the calendar, the most liquid and most heavily traded among all the markets considered, is also the most efficient one and the one that assimilates new information the most rapidly.

Sample: 03/01/2005–28/12/2007

Lags: 1			
Null hypothesis:	Obs.	F-statistic	Probability
The EUA spot price does not Granger-cause the price of base-load electricity (day ahead).	738	13.9524	0.00020
The price of base-load electricity (day ahead) does not Granger-cause the EUA spot price.		0.03145	0.85930

(4) Finally, the relationship between the gas market and electricity markets is unequivocal, with causality running from the gas market to the electricity market.[21] The causality is stronger in the spot market than in the forward market, and it strengthens during the winter and declines during the summer.

---

[21] The cost of producing an MWh of gas-based electricity was calculated on the basis of the price in the Zeebrugge spot market.

Sample: 03/01/2005–28/12/2007

Lags: 1		
Null hypothesis:	F-statistic	Probability
The cost of gas per MWh does not Granger-cause the price of the 2007 calendar.	4.34532	0.03782
The cost of gas per MWh does not Granger-cause the price of peak-load electricity (day ahead).	53.3826	$8.6e^{-13}$
The cost of gas per MWh does not Granger-cause the price of base-load electricity (day ahead).	59.0139	$6.3e^{-14}$

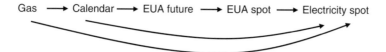

Figure A.9 Causality relationships between the carbon, electricity and gas markets
Source: Author

Summarizing the causality relationships

The results of the different causality tests can now be summarized in a single graph that is easy to assimilate, figure A.9. In order to simplify, the figure concentrates purely on the relationships after one period (one day), keeping in mind that longer periods establish more complicated bilateral links. Gas drives the calendar as well as electricity spot prices directly. The calendar drives CO_2 allowance prices, both forward and spot, especially in the immediate aftermath of new information. The EUA forward market reacts here more quickly and pulls the EUA spot market along. EUA prices then reinforce the impact on electricity spot prices.

Market manipulation

The close interaction of relatively illiquid carbon markets and huge electricity markets in connection with massive price increases has generated suspicion about the incentive for manipulating carbon markets for the benefit of electricity producers. Market participants, for instance, mentioned the possibility that operators artificially held carbon prices high in summer 2006 to support forward prices in the much larger electricity market (see the APREC website for the 2007 workshop meeting 'The ex-post evaluation of the European CO_2 market', held in Paris in April: www.aprec.net/uk_evaluation.php). Other experts suggested looking at the correlation between carbon prices and electricity forward sales in order to test for manipulation during the critical period (see the APREC website for the 2008 workshop meeting on the same topic, held in Washington, DC, in January). The econometric evidence for the period in question (May to October 2006) does not provide evidence for any market manipulation. The one-day causality still runs from the calendar to the carbon markets, and after two days the causality between carbon and electricity markets is *less strong* during this particular period when compared with the whole of period 1 (see below). Market volumes during 2006 are also about 25 per cent *less* during the period from May to October than during the equivalent period of 2005, while manipulation would have been associated with increased activity.

Sample: 02/05/2006–31/10/2006

Lags: 2			
Null hypothesis:	Obs.	F-statistic	Probability
The price of the EUA future contract (Dec. 07) does not Granger-cause the price of the 2007 calendar.	120	3.54794	0.03198
The price of the 2007 calendar does not Granger-cause the price of the EUA future contract (Dec. 07).		2.25937	0.10903

There is no evidence therefore for market manipulation. The relative stability of carbon markets during summer 2006 must be attributed to European carbon markets waiting for new indications after the mini-crash at the end of April that year. This indication came in autumn 2006, with the temporary decline of the oil price – a trend that carbon prices eagerly adopted until evidence had accumulated that the market would be long, which led to the very low prices of 2007. During that period – i.e. after October 2006 – spot electricity prices also declined, but prices for electricity forward delivery remained stable. This confirms the econometric evidence of the causality test that the price of the calendar is relatively independent of the carbon price, but that the latter does have an impact on electricity spot prices.

Rents generated by the EU ETS for European power producers

The question of pass-through

This section begins with a comment on the lively discussion about 'pass-through' that captured the attention of commentators at the beginning of period 1. The term 'pass-through' refers to the percentage of the carbon allowance price that is included in the electricity price. Numerous ad hoc conjectures were formulated to come to terms with the intuitively appealing and politically sensitive notion of pass-through, many of which stood neither the test of theory nor that of time. The first point that needs to be made is that there is no theoretical foundation for pass-through rates lower than one in a competitive market. As explained above, the principle of opportunity cost ensures that the holder of a carbon allowance will always try to recuperate the full market value of the allowance, independently of whether he or she uses it in electricity production or sells it separately.

Sijm, Neuhoff and Chen's widely cited paper (2006) is occasionally considered to provide rationales for the alternative view that cost pass-through under competition might be less than 100 per cent. The three main arguments concern (1) voluntary constraints and suboptimal behaviour, (2) changes in the merit order due to fuel-switching (an argument also made by Reinaud 2003) and (3) the fact that the returns for certain carbon-intensive infra-marginal producers will not change if marginal (price-setting) producers are using low-carbon or carbon-free technologies.

The first argument cuts both ways – i.e. producers may also use carbon-pricing to pass through otherwise unwarranted price increases, and should be abandoned. The second argument would apply only to the limited amount of fuel-switching observed by McGuinness and Ellerman (2008) in the United Kingdom. The third argument is an argument about rents rather than about electricity prices. It also has limited empirical pertinence, given that carbon-free technologies such as nuclear and hydro are used in base-load, when coal often sets the marginal price, and carbon-intensive gas- or oil-fired combustion turbines frequently set prices in peak-load.

The question of whether pass-through rates under competition can differ from 100 per cent is largely a definitional one, hinging on the question whether the term 'pass-through' is a relevant notion for infra-marginal (not price-setting) producers. If the key question remains the impact of carbon-pricing on electricity prices (rather than its impact on operators' rents; see below), then the 100 per cent pass-through hypothesis indeed remains the theoretically most solid option for competitive markets.[22]

Price increases due to the integration of the price of carbon allowances at *less* than the full value of allowances are instead entirely feasible under imperfect competition. This is not an unreasonable assumption, especially at times of peak demand. Reflecting the high inelasticity of electricity demand and asymmetric incentives prevailing in competitive electricity markets, which tend to promote under- rather than overcapacity, the exercise of some form of market power at certain times of the day is the norm rather than the exception.[23] Otherwise, producers would be unable to cover the fixed costs for peak-load capacity.

If allowance is therefore made for some form of market power in electricity markets, pass-through rates lower than 100 per cent are logical. A profit-maximizing monopolist will not fully pass on an increase in marginal cost, since it will lead to too great a loss in demand. Taking this into account, he or she will only partly pass on any increase in his or her marginal cost, so as to protect his or her revenue. Figure A.10 shows the relationship in a very intuitive manner.

The trouble (in terms of communicating the subject to the general public) with this reasoning is only that, in this case, the difference between cost (net of carbon) and price will still exceed the value of the

---

[22] The empirical evidence of pass-through rates between 60 and 117 per cent cited by Sijm, Neuhoff and Chen (2006) should be regarded with caution. First, the authors themselves point out that OLS estimations were used with autocorrelated time series. Second, the question of the counterfactual (what would electricity prices have been in the absence of carbon-pricing?) is not addressed. Increases in the price of electricity due to carbon-pricing are thus indistinguishable from increases due to changes in market power, weather, demand or other factors. Third, the question of market power (which would explain pass-through rates lower than 100 per cent) is never addressed.

[23] Frequently this market power is exercised through investment retention in the face of rising demand. In addition, electricity production continues to exhibit increasing returns to scale due to substantial indivisibilities such as technical competence, in particular when operating nuclear power plants, financial savvy and the ability to spread risks over different geographic markets. The volatility and risk of electricity markets in the wake of liberalization has probably increased rather than decreased the optimal size of an operator, and thus heightened the possibility of exercising market power.

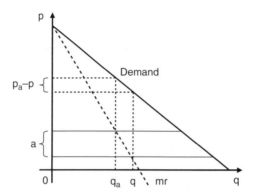

Figure A.10 Decreased pass-through due to monopoly power
Notes: q = quantity; p = price; mr = marginal revenue; a = cost of allowance
(carbon permit); q_a = quantity with allowance; p_a = price with allowance;
p_a–p = price increase due to the allowance
Source: Author

carbon allowance. This is because of the fact that the monopolist will, of course, exploit his or her monopoly power. There is also the fact that counterfactuals – i.e. prices in the absence of allowance trading – are very difficult to establish. The result is that the debate on pass-through, in order to stay rigorous, needs to return to the original question of what the impact of carbon prices is on electricity prices. Analysing the impact of carbon-pricing changes on scarcity and the infra-marginal rents of operators in the electricity sector requires a different approach, and this is explored below.

Rents and windfall profits

In order to calculate the amount of 'windfall profits' – i.e., the additional profits due to carbon-pricing, gained by producers – one needs first to define on a conceptual level the different types of rent in order to clarify a discussion marred by inconsistencies and confusion. This confusion reflects the inability to separate clearly three different issues affecting the EU power sector: (1) the liberalization of European power markets; (2) electricity price increases due to higher fuel costs; and (3) additional rents from carbon-pricing with or without auctioning. The discussion is concerned exclusively with the third point.

The question of windfall profits, or rents gained by power producers as a result of the introduction of the EU ETS, is complex enough by itself, however. In fact, there exist three different types of rent that electricity producers obtained during period 1 of the EU ETS. The first kind of rent, type I, is by far the most important one and concerns the additional profits earned by power producers due to higher prices once the cost of allowances has been integrated into electricity prices. This affects the 'infra-marginal' rents habitually earned by base-load technologies with low marginal costs during the operation of higher-cost peak-load technologies, which set the price (see below the section 'Calculating type I rents' for more detail).

Base-load power producers thus gain large rents due to carbon-pricing once the price of allowances has been included in the price of electricity (see the discussion on pass-through and opportunity costs above). If allowances are allocated freely, such rents are obtained both in carbon-free (nuclear and renewables) and in carbon-intensive (coal and gas) base-load power production. This reflects the fact that neither group experiences any cost increases with the price increase of their output: carbon-free producers do not need to buy allowances, and carbon-intensive producers can satisfy their commitment by means of the costless allowances they have received. With full auctioning, carbon-intensive producers would lose the windfall profits from carbon-pricing, while the carbon-free producers would continue to enjoy them.

A second kind of 'windfall profit' consists of the informational rent earned by the recipients of large quantities of allowances in a market with imperfect information. It is conceptually of a less clear-cut nature but it has received some attention in public discussions. Its empirical estimates are also particularly uncertain. Last but not least, the gains from asymmetric information are probably confined to the peculiar price dynamics of period 1 and should disappear once the major actors in the market have engaged in the necessary learning processes.

This informational rent is due to the fact that the over-allocation during period 1 should have produced a zero or very low price from the start. Instead, average EUA prices from 2005 to 2007 were around €12 per tonne. Recipients of allowances would, in principle, have been able to gain large trading profits from first selling their allowances to financial players and speculators without allocations of their own and then covering their own needs at the end of period 1 at prices close to zero. This hypothesis, for which there is some anecdotal evidence but no proof, is based on the argument that recipients of allowances, especially large power companies, had an informational advantage over the whole of the market that allowed them to reap such one-off trading profits. The numbers reported below for the type II rents are an upper bound under the (unrealistic) assumption that all electricity companies were able to engage profitably in such intertemporal arbitrage; real trading profits were certainly much smaller, but cannot be assessed because of the private nature of this information.

A third type of 'rent' was much discussed during period 1 but is of lesser practical significance and applies only to trading systems with free allocation of allowances. It arises from the fact that carbon-intensive emitters receive large amounts of allowances at the beginning of the production period that constitute real financial assets at no cost until they are used during routine electricity production. Until their use in production, these allowances constitute 'capital'. If one assumes a linear decrease of this 'capital' during the allocation period – typically a year – half the value of the allowances can thus be used, for instance, as collateral in obtaining funds at lower interest rates.

Although seductive in theory, there are several practical limits to this argument. First, it assumes that intertemporal arbitrage of the value of allowances is costless (given that allocation comes in spikes at the beginning of each year). Second, it assumes that banks would accept such a volatile asset as carbon credits as collateral; so far, no real-world cases have been reported. Third, the asset of a carbon allowance is a non-interest-bearing financial asset, which further reduces its attractiveness. The impact of this type III rent is therefore relatively low, and there is no attempt here to calculate it. Table A.1 summarizes the three types of rent.

A calculation of the order of magnitude of the annual type I and type II rents obtained by different power producers in the European electricity sector during period 1 of the EU ETS is now provided. Clearly, the calculations for type I rents (changes in infra-marginal rents due to carbon-pricing) are conceptually more important (given that the argument also extends to period 2 and full information) and are, despite the remaining uncertainties, empirically more reliable.[24]

---

[24] Nevertheless, the calculation of type I rents was made possible only by making a number of assumptions, the most heroic of which is that the European Union constitutes a single unified power market. This is, obviously, not yet the case, given that interconnection capacities between different regions can be limited.

Table A.1 *Types of rent in power markets due to carbon-pricing*

Type of rent	Free allocation	Auctioning
Type I: changes in infra-marginal rents due to carbon-pricing (estimated).	Applies to both carbon-intensive and carbon-free base-load producers.	No longer applies to carbon-intensive base-load producers; still applies to carbon-free base-load producers.
Type II: intertemporal trading profits due to asymmetric information (estimated).	Significant during period 1, will decrease with better overall information.	Will fade away in period 2 with better knowledge.
Type III: EUAs as financial assets (not estimated).	Potential gain for carbon-intensive producers.	No longer applicable.

Calculating type I rents

In order to understand the nature of the type I rents due to changes in relative costs after the introduction of carbon-pricing obtained by power producers, one needs to be aware that electricity produced by installations that have marginal costs lower than the technology with the highest marginal costs *always* earns rents even without carbon-pricing. For decades such inevitable rents existed; they were well understood by experts and attracted little public attention. Such infra-marginal rents are also necessary to finance the fixed costs of base-load power generation in the long run. The key issue pertaining to the introduction of the EU ETS, however, is that carbon-pricing alters the relative marginal costs of different technologies and thus impacts (usually raises) the infra-marginal rents. The different infra-marginal rents before and after carbon-pricing will provide the type I rents – the additional gains of power producers due to carbon-pricing.

This does not limit the relevance of the exercise, however. These calculations constitute, in fact, a *lower bound* for the real infra-marginal rents obtained by operators. During period 1, prices for the year-long power contract (calendar), the most liquid future contract, were around €55 per MWh on the German EEX power exchange. This is considerably higher than the marginal cost (inclusive of CO_2) for natural-gas-based electricity, €38, which is driving the bulk of the results in these calculations.

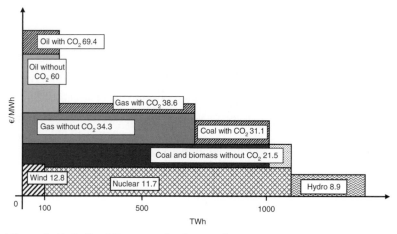

Figure A.11 Stylized European load-curve for 2005
Source: Author's calculations

Figure A.11 provides an indication of the marginal costs with and without taking into account the cost of CO_2 emissions for coal-fired, gas-fired and nuclear power generation (all numbers are calculated on the basis of IEA [2007b] and IEA/NEA [Nuclear Energy Agency] [2005], as well as on the basis of the average carbon spot price of €12 for an EUA during the 2005–7 period according to the French carbon exchange Bluenext). The terminology is explained in box A.3.

Once the marginal costs with and without CO_2 allowances, as well as the respective production volumes, are known, one can calculate the total amount of rents. A rent in this context is the difference between the market price (set by the fuel with the *highest* marginal cost) and the marginal cost of each fuel. Of course, the marginal fuel does not earn any rent. Total rents for each fuel are obtained by integrating the respective areas for each fuel under the load-curve.

One remark of caution is of order: rents are nothing intrinsically bad. They are part and parcel of the working of a well-functioning electricity sector. Remember that power plants need to earn rents above their marginal costs in order to finance their past fixed costs and their future investments. What is of interest in this discussion is the amount of *additional* rent gained by European power producers due to the introduction of carbon-pricing. Table A.2 provides the results of the following calculations.

> ## Box A.3 Understanding load-curves
>
> The load-curve depicted in figure A.11 provides a very crude approximation of the production profile of the European electricity sector in 2005, which produced a total of 3,276 TWh. The horizontal axis provides the total amounts of electricity produced by each technology and the vertical axis its marginal cost, both excluding and including (where applicable) the cost of carbon emissions. The cost of carbon emissions is equal to the average allowance price of €12 during period 1. In this exercise, which is concerned with orders of magnitude, competition is assumed and thus a 100 per cent pass-through of carbon allowances into the electricity price. This exercise does not therefore include scarcity rents from the exercise of monopoly power.
>
> The generating technologies with the lowest marginal costs (wind, nuclear and hydro) are technologies that run best in an uninterrupted manner, and they are referred to as base-load technologies (bottom row). Coal and biomass (and in some European markets, such as the United Kingdom, gas) can be considered mid-load technologies (second row), whereas gas and oil are originally peak-load technologies (third and fourth row).[25] The latter are characterized by low fixed costs and high variable costs. The height of the marginal costs determines the 'merit order' – i.e. the order in which different technologies are switched on in times of need.
>
> Merit order curves, or load-curves, are usually depicted in terms of hours of operation per year on the horizontal axis, with a maximum of 8,760 hours per year. In order to calculate total rents in the electricity sector, however, which are a function of hours of operation multiplied by capacity multiplied by the hourly rent, it is easier to work with the total electricity produced (hours of operation multiplied by capacity) rather than to convert the data into hours of operation by dividing it through capacity.

(a) *Infra-marginal rent without* CO_2: the normal rents generated by the electricity system in the absence of any carbon-pricing; oil as the marginal fuel does not earn any rents in this calculation since it assumes the absence of market power.

(b) *Infra-marginal rent with* CO_2 *(free allocation)*: the total rents generated by the electricity system with carbon-pricing under the assumption of free allocation of allowances.

[25] In some instances, a peak-load technology can be used to produce base-load power. Depending on relative prices, it may even be profitable to do so. In the United Kingdom, for instance, gas-fired power generation is now widely used for base-load power production as well, which supports the finding for fuel-switching in this particular country (see above).

Table A.2 Rents in the European power sector due to carbon-pricing, period 1 (million euros, average period 1 price of €12/tCO$_2$)

Technology	TWh	(a) Infra-marginal rent without CO$_2$	(b) Infra-marginal rent with CO$_2$	(c) Additional type I rent due to EU ETS	(d) Infra-marginal rent with CO$_2$	(e) Difference free allocation versus auctioning	(f) Type II rent (one-off)	(g) Sum of period 1 type I and type II rents
Allocation		Free	Free	Free	Auctioning		Free	Free
Geothermal	6	153	186	33	186	–	–	33
Hydro	304	5 638	7 303	1 665	7 303	–	–	1 665
Nuclear	998	16 325	21 790	5 465	21 790	–	–	5 465
Wind	78	1 209	1 636	427	1 636	–	–	427
Coal	1 001	11 137	17 657	6 520	8 562	(9 095)	7 360	13 881
Biomass	84	935	1 211	276	1 211	–	–	276
Gas	664	3 572	7 141	3 569	4 273	(2 868)	2 203	5 772
Solar	2	2	4	2	4	–	–	2
Oil	139	–	1 301	1 301	–	(1 301)	999	2 300
Total	3 276	38 971	58 230	19 259	44 966	(13 265)	10 562	29 821

(c) *Type I rent due to CO_2*: this is the additional rent due to the increase in the price of electricity; it is equal to the difference between (a) and (b); see the text for the explanations concerning the different types of rent; this the most important result of the table.

(d) *Infra-marginal rent with CO_2 (auctioning)*: the total rents generated by the electricity system with carbon-pricing under the assumption that allowances were auctioned; this is an information item only, since in period 1 virtually all allowances were allocated for free.

(e) *Difference free versus auctioning*: conceptually self-explanatory but politically relevant; note that the difference is zero for carbon-free technologies but substantial for coal-based production.

(f) *Type II rent (one-off)*: power producers received allowances for free in an oversupplied system in which allowances commanded an average price of €12; in practice much less; it is also a one-off limited to period 1.

(g) *Sum of type I and type II rents*: the theoretical maximum that power producers might have gained during period 1; due to the overestimation of type II rents, the total amounts might be substantially less.[26]

From table A.2 it emerges that the sums in play were substantial even with a relatively modest carbon price of €12. Total type I rents are more than €19 billion without including scarcity rents from temporary pricing power. Carbon-intensive power producers in particular gained because of the free allocation of allowances. The sum total of type I and type II rents of €30 billion should not be quoted without the necessary caveats surrounding the uncertainty of the precise amount of type II rents. During period 1, with free allocation, all technologies – whether carbon-free or carbon-intensive – gained.

With a full auctioning of allocation, as envisaged by the Commission for 2013 and beyond in its Climate and Energy Package of 23 January 2008, carbon-intensive producers are instead bound to lose heavily. Coal will even be significantly worse off than before the introduction of the EU ETS, while gas and oil will be roughly as well off as they were beforehand. Carbon-free producers based on nuclear

---

[26] It should also be noted, however, that the average price for electricity on the German EEX power exchange during period 1 was €42 per MWh, whereas with marginal cost pricing on the basis of our load-curve an average price of €33 per MWh would have resulted. Both higher fuel costs during 2006 and 2007 and scarcity pricing are responsible for this difference.

and renewables, however, will not be affected and will continue to enjoy the full amount of infra-marginal rents generated by the EU ETS.

Conclusions

There is no doubt that the EU ETS has had an impact on the European power sector, though not necessarily in the way most people had expected. Price formation in carbon markets and electricity markets remained complex when identifiable influences such as the gas price, information about the true severity of the carbon constraint and the psychology of traders interacted. One may safely conclude, however, that gas prices and the prices of long-term electricity futures had (and continue to have) an important influence. There is also evidence that carbon prices themselves drove electricity prices, most notably in the spot market. So far European electricity demand has not decreased perceptibly in response to carbon-pricing, even though electricity demand has stopped rising, and 2007 even began to see a levelling off of electricity demand. The verdict as to the extent to which carbon-pricing contributed to this levelling off is still uncertain, however. These facts need to be looked at in perspective, though: (1) electricity demand is very inelastic; (2) retail price regulations shielded consumers from development in the wholesale market; and (3) the short timeframe of only three years prevented major changes in the structure of European power generation. Carbon-pricing probably contributed to some fuel-switching in the United Kingdom, but there is no evidence for this from the publicly available statistical evidence for the rest of Europe.

The EU ETS had its largest impact on the profitability of Europe's power companies, which gained additional annual rents in excess of €15 billion. The result was – in combination with market-opening and regulatory uncertainty – a historic spending spree that saw the forma-tion of a European oligopoly of five (EDF, E.ON, GDF Suez, Enel-Endesa and RWE) or six (if one includes Vattenfall) transnational electricity majors. Auctioning will change this state of affairs signifi-cantly, with coal producers taking the brunt of the new arrangements. On the investment side, the three-year period 1 was too short to make a significant difference. The most important long-term impact of the EU ETS on the European power sector is that carbon-pricing is now part and parcel of the business of producing and selling electricity. The complete potential for structural reform will be realized only by a combination of full auctioning and longer allocation periods.

Appendix A: Sequence of events in the development of the EU ETS and Linking Directives

Date	Action	Implications
1986	Single European Act.	A single market for the economy makes a single market for the environment both feasible and necessary.
1990	European Communities' publication of '1992', *The Environmental Dimension: Task Force Report on the Environment and the Internal Market*.	This study both reinforced the significance of the single market for environmental policy and advocated the use of market based instruments.
1992	(1) Rio 'Earth Summit': EU argues for quantitative restrictions. (2) Commission proposes Community-wide carbon energy tax.	Once quantitative restrictions are accepted, then the logic of trading quantities flows therefrom. The Commission proposes a tax, however.
1997	Carbon energy tax proposal is withdrawn.	This eliminates one alternative for climate policy.
July	Byrd–Hagel resolution passed in US Senate.	This established conditions for ratification of the Kyoto Protocol by the US Senate, as would be required by the US constitution.
December	Kyoto Protocol is agreed.	Commission disappointed; it had aimed for greater reductions and opposed emissions trading. Did not meet Byrd–Hagel conditions, thereby greatly complicating US ratification.

Date	Action	Implications
1998		
May	(1) Council welcomes measures with emphasis on market-based instruments. (2) Burden-sharing agreement signed.	Burden-sharing agreement sets quantitative targets for each member state. Council endorses a market-based approach. The logic of trading begins to crystallize.
June	(1) Commissioner Ritt Bjerregaard (Environment) gives support. (2) Commission communication *Towards an EU Post-Kyoto Strategy* published.	Commissioner argues for Europe to lead on trading. Commission argues for Community-wide approach, with 'demonstrable progress' to be achieved by 2005.
1999		
May	Commission communication *Preparing for Implementation of the Kyoto Protocol* published.	'Best preparation might be to develop our own trading experience.'
May	First GHG and energy-trading simulations (GETS) launched.	Utilities get experience, and (probably) realize that rent capture is a prospect for some if there is free allocation.
June	Council urges Commission to submit further proposals for common measures and Green Paper.	Trading is the most obvious 'common measure'. Commission has green light to develop and promote its trading agenda.
October	COP Buenos Aires fails to define trading rules.	This provides further impetus for EU to 'do its own thing' as regards trading.
2000		
March	Green Paper on the EU ETS is launched.	This sets out all the issues and the Commission's preferences, most of which ultimately prevail.
	Support from Green MEP Hiltrud Breyers, but only if stringent conditions, monitoring and penalties for non-compliance.	This support was helpful in muting the antagonism in some NGO quarters and encouraging the (reluctant) German government.

Date	Action	Implications
June	European Climate Change Programme (ECCP) is launched.[1]	This was the main vehicle – via WG1 – for progressing discussions and identifying key blockages and opportunities.
July	First meeting of ECCP WG1 is held.	All key stakeholders engage for the first time.
October	German working group on emissions trading is started.	Germany was late in establishing its own domestic group – a reflection of reluctance and divided interests.
December	Collapse and adjournment of COP6 in The Hague.	Differences between US-led Umbrella Group and the EU15 do not allow international trading rules to be agreed.
2001		
January	The Commission starts to draft the EU ETS proposal.	
March	The Bush administration rejects the Kyoto Protocol.	This triggers a major effort to secure sufficient votes to bring Kyoto into effect, and also adds impetus to develop the EU ETS.
May	Draft proposal completed.	
June	European Council is determined to meet member state commitments under the Kyoto Protocol.	See above.
September	(1) Consultation meetings are held. (2) Germany submits a separate paper.	German commitment to voluntary agreements with industry inhibits support for trading, especially the obligation to participate in the pilot period.
October	EU ETS proposal is adopted by the Commission – based on article 175 (1), which provides for qualified majority voting.	Qualified majority voting means that no small group of countries can exercise a veto.
October	COP Marrakech agrees rules for international trading.	This provides further validation for the EU ETS and ensures the potential for the use of CDM and JI credits.

Date	Action	Implications
December	First debate held by the Council. Free allocation, but 'large majority preferred that costs be borne by electricity producers'.	The inconsistency between the enthusiasm for free allocation and the view that costs be borne by electricity producers is notable.
2002		
February	The Netherlands announces plans for a domestic scheme.	This provides a further impetus for a Europe-wide scheme.
March	(1) First reading in the Legal Affairs Committee. (2) Ministers adopt a legal instrument obliging members to ratify the Kyoto Protocol using qualified majority voting.	Parliament action begins, and the use of qualified majority voting is re-emphasized.
April	(1) The Environment Committee of the European Parliament meets. (2) The EEA publishes a report showing that more progress is needed. (3) UK domestic trading begins.	The evidence on emissions indicates that further action is needed to meet the Kyoto target, and the EU ETS is perceived as a key response. The UK move creates an incentive for the UK to support the opt-out and voluntary participation in the pilot period of the EU scheme, and provides more pressure to implement the European scheme before inconsistent national schemes become the norm.
May	Burden-sharing becomes law. The EU ratifies the Kyoto Protocol.	These developments further intensify the logic for the EU ETS.
July	Denmark assumes the EU presidency.	Denmark provides skilful leadership in overcoming pressure from Germany, the UK and Finland for voluntary participation in the pilot period.

Date	Action	Implications
August	Disastrous flooding in Germany along the Elbe and Danube.	This both convinced the German public that climate change was 'real' and potentially catastrophic and generated support for the Greens in the forthcoming general election.
September	(1) The German government is re-elected with stronger Green representation. (2) Parliament adopts its plenary position – 80 amendments.	The new German government is more sympathetic to trading. The European Parliament is supportive but wants more auctioning, and more centralization of allocation.
October	The German government agrees emissions trading, but with free allocation and pooling.	This is the key to progress and finalization of the Council position.
2003		
March	(1) The Council adopts a common position. (2) Communication from Commission to Parliament.	A final effort is made by the Commission to convince Parliament that it has secured some of its key priorities.
June	(1) Second reading by Parliament. (2) The Environment Committee adopts the main position. (3) Compromise proposals are tabled and agreed.	This clears the stage for enactment.
July	(1) Formal adoption by Council of the EU ETS Directive. (2) The Linking Directive is proposed. (3) The Environment Working Group meets.	The Linking Directive had been 'parked' pending agreement on the EU ETS. Now it moves centre stage.
October	The EU ETS Directive is published in the *Official Journal*.	The EU ETS Directive becomes law.

Date	Action	Implications
December	Rapporteur Alexander de Roo MEP wants agreement on a linkage directive before the 2004 Parliament elections.	The fact that the sands of time are running out for MEPs adds urgency to the task of agreeing the Linking Directive.
2004		
April	The European Parliament is dissolved.	
October	(1) The Russian Duma approves the Kyoto Protocol. (2) The Irish presidency, rapporteur and Commission reach an informal agreement on the Linking Directive. (3) The Linking Directive is formally adopted by the European Parliament and Council.	The quid pro quo for Russian support is EU support for its membership of the WTO. Russian ratification provides the necessary condition for entry into force of the Kyoto Protocol. Rapid progress on the Linking Directive is a product of the Parliament not being too ambitious in pressing its amendments; from proposal to final agreement takes only fifteen months.
2005	The Kyoto Protocol enters into force.	

Note: [1]The European Climate Change Programme consisted of six working groups (WGs) focused on (1) flexible mechanisms (including trading); (2) energy supply; (3) energy consumption; (4) transport; (5) industry; and (6) research. Most of the work relative to the EU ETS took place in WG1.

Appendix B: Data tables

Item a – Allowance allocations, verified emissions and net positions by member states

Item b – Allowance allocations, verified emissions and net positions by sector

Item c – Carbon and energy prices, 2005–8

Item d – EUA trading: transaction volumes by platform, 2005–8

Item e – Origin and destinations of surrendered allowances over the first phase

Item a *Allowance allocations, verified emissions and net positions by member*

	Allocation[1,2]				Installations[3]		
	Three–yr total allocated to installations	CITL reserves (NER, auctions, etc.)	Reserves remaining at the end of the period	Issued reserves[5]	2005	2006	2007
Austria	97,711	990	878	112	199	199	199
Belgium	178,691	7,653	8,371	−718	307	307	308
Denmark[6]	93,114	7,384	2,216	5,168	372	372	371
Finland	133,904	2,596	164	2,432	484	483	480
France	450,155	14,573	11,362	3,211	1,074	1,078	1,079
Germany	1,486,273	6,767	0	−55,233	1,850	1,850	1,845
Greece	213,487	9,713	3,898	5,815	140	149	149
Ireland	57,715	9,245	225	9,020	106	106	106
Italy	624,456	44,756	39	44,717	950	990	1,029
Luxembourg	9,688	387	355	32	15	15	15
Netherlands	259,317	7,510	3,005	4,505	207	210	211
Portugal	110,726	3,758	945	2,813	240	250	254
Spain	498,064	41,056	858	40,198	793	1,028	1,005
Sweden	67,619	2,010	1,834	176	644	660	665
United Kingdom	627,834	46,542	5,928	40,614	693	708	756
EU15 subtotal	**4,908,754**	**204,940**	**40,078**	**102,862**	**8,074**	**8,405**	**8,472**
Cyprus	16,983	120	60	60	13	13	13
Czech Republic	290,760	1,044	186	858	396	404	390
Estonia	56,290	569	204	365	42	48	48
Hungary	90,708	4,274	330	3,944	235	237	244
Latvia	12,163	1,517	950	567	91	95	100
Lithuania	34,394	2,392	0	2,392	92	97	99
Malta	6,538	2,288	2,288	0	2	2	2
Poland	712,503	2,472	2,450	22	853	862	860
Slovakia	91,444	25	0	25	175	174	176
Slovenia	26,076	200	4	196	97	98	99
Romania[7]	74,343						244
Bulgaria[7]	42,270						128
New member states	**1,454,474**	**14,901**	**6,472**	**8,429**	**1,996**	**2,030**	**2,403**
Total EU ETS	**6,363,228**	**219,841**	**46,550**	**111,291**	**10,070**	**10,435**	**10,875**

Notes:

[1]CITL totals may differ from totals authorized in NAP decisions due to opt-outs, opt-ins and other changes in the list of included installations.

[2]Unless otherwise noted, and excepting reserves, allowances were allocated to installations equally in each year.

[3]Installations are those reporting non-zero entries for either emissions or allocations.

[4]Annual data reflect differences from initial allocations to installations as recorded in the CITL and verified emissions.

[5]Remaining reserves may be higher than initial reserves due to the later inclusion of forfeited or unclaimed allowances. An unspecified portion of the remaining reserves in Austria, Belgium, Ireland and the United Kingdom were either sold or auctioned. The entry for Germany is a net withdrawal as a result of *ex post* corrections.

states (thousand EUAs)

Verified emissions				Net position[4]				Period (taking reserves into account)
2005	2006	2007	Period	2005	2006	2007	Period	
33,373	32,383	31,746	97,502	−960	267	903	209	321
55,363	54,775	52,795	162,934	2,947	5,177	7,633	15,757	15,039
26,469	34,191	29,374	90,034	10,835	−6,284	−1,471	3,080	8,248
33,082	44,508	42,358	119,947	11,584	110	2,263	13,957	16,389
131,264	126,979	126,583	384,826	19,148	22,988	23,193	65,329	68,540
474,991	478,017	487,004	1,440,011	18,492	17,472	10,298	46,262	−8,971
71,268	69,965	72,712	213,945	−105	1,197	−1,550	−458	5,357
22,379	21,642	20,756	64,778	−3,143	−2,404	−1,516	−7,063	1,957
225,989	227,439	226,362	679,791	−9,839	−22,389	−23,107	−55,336	−10,619
2,603	2,713	2,567	7,884	626	516	662	1,804	1,836
80,351	76,701	79,829	236,882	6,101	9,687	6,647	22,435	26,940
36,426	33,084	31,183	100,693	483	3,825	5,726	10,034	12,847
182,930	179,697	184,456	547,083	−10,769	−13,511	−24,740	−49,019	−8,821
19,382	19,884	15,348	54,614	2,907	2,599	7,498	13,005	13,181
242,470	251,116	250,700	744,286	−36,437	−45,151	−34,864	−116,452	−75,838
1,638,339	1,653,095	1,653,775	4,945,210	11,870	−25,902	−22,424	−36,456	66,406
5,079	5,259	5,396	15,734	392	353	503	1,249	1,309
82,455	83,625	87,575	253,654	14,465	13,295	9,345	37,106	37,964
12,622	12,109	15,327	40,058	4,125	6,091	6,017	16,232	16,597
26,162	25,846	26,835	78,843	4,075	4,390	3,401	11,865	15,809
2,854	2,941	2,849	8,644	1,216	1,118	1,186	3,519	4,086
6,604	6,517	5,999	19,120	6,896	4,060	4,320	15,275	17,667
1,971	1,986	2,027	5,984	114	182	258	554	554
202,871	209,343	209,576	621,790	34,635	28,163	27,915	90,713	90,735
25,232	25,543	24,517	75,292	5,239	4,944	5,970	16,153	16,178
8,721	8,842	9,049	26,611	418	−150	−803	−535	−339
		69,616	69,616			4,727	4,727	4,727
		39,182	39,182			3,088	3,088	3,088
374,570	382,011	497,948	1,254,529	71,574	62,444	65,926	199,945	208,374
2,012,909	2,035,106	2,151,723	6,199,739	83,444	36,543	43,502	163,489	274,780

[6]Denmark distributed 40 per cent of the allocation to installations in 2005 and 30 per cent in each of the subsequent years.

[7]Romania and Bulgaria entered the EU ETS in 2007 when these countries acceded to the European Union. The Bulgarian allocation is not yet available from the CITL; the figure here is the maximum allocation amount allowed by the European Commission in the decision on 2007 NAP (http://ec.europa.eu/environment/climat/pdf/nap2006/bulnap1finalen.pdf).

Sources: CITL as of 4 May 2008 (www.ec.europa.eu/environment/ets) and EEA (2008: 62).

Item b *Allowance allocations, verified emissions and net positions by*

	Allocation	Installations		
	Three-yr total	2005	2006	2007
1 Combustion	4,370,738	6,585	6,903	6,996
1a Electricity production[1]	3,086,972	776	786	782
1b Rest of combustion[1]	1,283,766	5,809	6,117	6,214
2 Refineries	472,572	147	147	139
3 Coke ovens	68,367	20	20	20
4 Metal ore	26,285	12	12	12
5 Iron and steel	504,311	227	228	229
6 Cement	570,772	508	514	520
7 Glass	66,853	402	407	404
8 Ceramics	54,312	1,114	1,124	1,115
9 Paper and board	111,714	783	797	786
99 Other activities	692	272	283	282
Total EU ETS	**6,246,615**	**10,070**	**10,435**	**10,503**

Note:
[1]The CITL does not separate electricity production from the combustion category.
The division presented here was made by the Mission Climat based on a detailed analysis
of the six largest member states and a listing of electric utility facilities in the other member
states. Because of uncertainties concerning the treatment of combined heat and power
plants, this estimate for electricity production should be regarded as a minimum.
See McGuinness and Trotignon (2007) and Trotignon and Delbosc (2008).
Source: CITL as of 4 May 2008.

*sector (**without Romania and Bulgaria**) (thousand EUAs)*

Verified emissions				Net position			
2005	2006	2007	Period	2005	2006	2007	Period
1,460,133	1,471,650	1,478,524	4,410,308	10,653	−23,776	−26,446	−39,569
1,094,218	1,102,413	1,108,037	3,304,669	−47,556	−80,208	−89,933	−217,696
365,915	369,237	370,487	1,105,639	58,209	56,432	63,486	178,127
150,019	148,543	148,439	447,002	8,092	8,909	8,568	25,570
19,193	21,301	22,074	62,568	3,596	1,488	715	5,798
7,756	8,015	8,404	24,174	995	736	380	2,111
134,109	138,874	134,558	407,542	34,325	29,057	33,388	96,769
176,722	181,556	188,271	546,548	13,043	7,243	3,937	24,223
19,906	19,829	19,652	59,386	2,398	2,456	2,613	7,467
14,794	14,988	14,204	43,986	3,286	3,265	3,775	10,326
30,126	30,212	28,660	88,999	6,973	7,075	8,667	22,715
152	138	138	428	82	91	91	264
2,012,909	2,035,106	2,042,925	6,090,940	83,444	36,543	35,688	155,675

Item c *Carbon and energy prices, 2005–8*

2005

		Unit	Jan.	Feb.	Mar.	Apr.	May	Jun.	Jul.	Aug.	Sep.	Oct.	Nov.	Dec.
Carbon prices	Phase I EUA spot price[1]	€/tCO2	7.13	7.82	11.47	16.14	17.44	24.13	24.65	22.02	22.82	22.68	21.59	21.11
	Phase I EUA futures price[2] – Dec. 05	€/tCO2	7.05	7.86	10.66	16.69	17.6	21.28	24.60	22.05	22.80	22.65	21.54	21.27
	Phase I EUA futures price[2] – Dec. 06	€/tCO2	7.15	7.93	10.7	16.73	17.69	21.43	24.86	22.25	22.88	22.56	21.57	21.66
	Phase I EUA futures price[2] – Dec. 07	€/tCO2	7.2	8.01	10.78	16.78	17.77	21.56	25.10	22.44	22.99	22.63	21.65	22.08
	Phase II EUA futures price[2] – Dec. 08	€/tCO2				16.83	17.88	21.73	25.32	22.63	22.11	21.75	19.61	19.25
Energy prices	Electricity price – base[3]	€/MWh	33.64	33.23	34.12	38.78	40.54	45.42	51.63	46.82	48.88	51.89	56.40	72.00
	Electricity price – peak[3]	€/MWh	43.91	42.68	43.63	49.07	52.84	65.42	72.51	62.67	67.06	69.25	79.50	103.72
	Natural gas price[4]	€/MMBTU							4.71	4.62	5.49	6.51	11.26	13.50
	Coal price[5]	€/t	52.22	49.87	50.5	51.95	51.77	50.76	51.78	47.77	47.14	45.16	43.86	44.42
	Brent crude oil[6]	$/bbl	44.46	45.86	53.27	53.35	49.62	55.42	57.91	63.62	63.80	59.50	56.23	57.63

2006

		Unit	Jan.	Feb.	Mar.	Apr.	May	Jun.	Jul.	Aug.	Sep.	Oct.	Nov.	Dec.
Carbon prices	Phase I EUA spot price[1]	€/tCO2	23.92	26.19	26.37	26.71	14.81	14.99	16.24	15.88	14.83	12.13	9.04	6.78
	Phase I EUA futures price[2] – Dec. 06	€/tCO2	24.70	26.88	27.07	27.18	15.09	15.31	16.53	16.13	15.05	12.26	9.14	6.89
	Phase I EUA futures price[2] – Dec. 07	€/tCO2	25.34	27.80	28.03	28.14	15.73	15.95	17.15	16.71	15.50	12.51	9.38	6.90
	Phase II EUA futures price[2] – Dec. 08	€/tCO2	21.58	26.60	24.33	28.09	21.26	19.98	19.42	17.90	17.20	15.73	16.71	17.98
Energy prices	Electricity price – base[3]	€/MWh	74.94	68.76	54.83	46.11	39.29	44.87	54.21	52.26	51.62	63.42	63.11	62.65
	Electricity price – peak[3]	€/MWh	109.56	93.48	72.73	59.64	58.74	67.62	82.83	76.26	72.39	91.18	95.79	96.41
	Natural gas price[4]	€/MMBTU	10.41	8.32	7.25	6.09	5.80	5.63	5.90	6.37	5.81	7.59	7.05	5.74
	Coal price[5]	€/t	45.29	50.79	53.54	51.25	46.67	49.61	48.87	54.59	51.55	51.96	52.66	51.69
	Brent crude oil[6]	$/bbl	63.86	61.14	63.03	70.54	70.98	69.78	74.26	73.90	63.64	59.84	59.86	62.69

2007

	Unit	Jan.	Feb.	Mar.	Apr.	May	Jun.	Jul.	Aug.	Sep.	Oct.	Nov.	Dec.
Carbon prices													
Phase I EUA spot price[1]	€/tCO$_2$	3.80	1.23	1.10	0.69	0.35	0.18	0.12	0.09	0.08	0.07	0.07	0.03
Phase I EUA futures price[2] – Dec. 07	€/tCO$_2$	3.85	1.28	1.14	0.72	0.36	0.19	0.13	0.10	0.08	0.07	0.08	0.03
Phase II EUA futures price[2] – Dec. 08	€/tCO$_2$	15.67	14.09	15.69	17.38	21.25	22.54	20.30	19.48	20.96	22.25	22.59	22.53
Energy prices													
Electricity price – base[3]	€/MWh	49.47	34.58	28.54	28.31	37.51	37.67	30.01	32.20	38.07	60.05	75.70	88.35
Electricity price – peak[3]	€/MWh	74.87	45.54	36.03	36.80	59.38	63.23	46.09	48.19	52.55	87.25	115.24	123.48
Natural gas price[4]	€/MMBTU	4.56	2.96	3.12	2.88	3.40	2.88	4.25	4.21	4.85	6.65	7.32	7.35
Coal price[5]	€/t	51.98	52.57	53.38	53.38	53.42	57.23	56.65	62.57	66.58	76.99	85.42	87.06
Brent crude oil[6]	$/bbl	54.66	58.81	62.46	67.63	67.93	70.44	75.63	71.38	76.67	82.48	92.20	91.44

2008

	Unit	Jan.	Feb.	Mar.	Apr.	May	Jun.	Jul.	Aug.	Sep.	Oct.	Nov.	Dec.
Carbon prices													
Phase II EUA spot price[1]	€/tCO$_2$		20.82	21.33	24.11	25.24	27.03	25.30	23.29	23.73	20.91	17.02	14.96
Phase II EUA futures price[2] – Dec. 08	€/tCO$_2$	22.47	20.65	21.77	24.28	25.39	27.39	25.72	23.52	23.95	21.07	17.07	14.86
Energy prices													
Electricity price – base[3]	€/MWh	75.84	60.41	62.18	57.82	67.00	79.32	69.22	78.04	94.41	109.40	79.06	70.04
Electricity price – peak[3]	€/MWh	98.92	72.89	75.89	72.86	94.54	114.54	96.02	102.84	123.09	150.17	102.66	91.00
Natural gas price[4]	€/MMBTU	7.25	6.68	6.97	7.67	7.70	8.59	8.38	7.58	9.45	9.39	7.67	6.36
Coal price[5]	€/t	88.51	95.62	91.94	84.77	98.18	114.39	135.56	126.26	122.99	97.00	74.10	59.10
Brent crude oil[6]	$/bbl	91.91	94.09	102.87	110.43	124.68	133.74	134.56	114.96	100.84	73.68	54.75	43.51

Notes and sources:
[1] Average closing price, Powernext Carbon (now BlueNext); the source for the first half of 2005 is Point Carbon.
[2] Average closing price for considered contracts, ECX; the source for the first half of 2005 is Point Carbon.
[3] Month ahead contracts, Powernext Futures.
[4] Monthly average, Zeebrugge, first maturity.
[5] Monthly average CIF ARA, first maturity.
[6] Monthly average, Brent, first maturity.

Item d EUA trading: transaction volumes by platform, 2005–8 (million tonnes)

2005

	Jan.	Feb.	Mar.	Apr.	May	Jun.	Jul.	Aug.	Sep.	Oct.	Nov.	Dec.
ECX	0.00	0.00	0.00	0.33	1.00	4.19	8.05	4.33	6.39	6.15	6.34	7.60
BlueNext	0.00	0.00	0.00	0.00	0.00	0.00	0.00	0.00	0.00	0.00	0.00	0.00
Nord Pool		0.73	0.87	1.21	0.76	1.16	1.31	1.55	0.46	0.28	0.33	0.38
EEX		0.00	0.11	0.03	0.03	0.21	0.21	0.28	0.08	0.14	0.18	0.52
EXAA		0.00	0.00	0.00	0.00	0.00	0.07	0.08	0.03	0.03	0.04	0.05
OTC		7.85	15.00	10.55	9.62	15.65	20.44	14.92	28.94	28.42	30.20	19.34
Total	**0.00**	**8.58**	**15.98**	**12.12**	**11.41**	**21.22**	**30.08**	**21.16**	**35.90**	**35.02**	**37.09**	**27.90**

2006

	Jan.	Feb.	Mar.	Apr.	May	Jun.	Jul.	Aug.	Sep.	Oct.	Nov.	Dec.
ECX	21.89	15.56	11.47	24.06	23.65	10.29	12.79	10.27	14.45	16.27	28.77	21.57
BlueNext	0.00	0.00	0.00	0.00	0.00	0.00	0.00	0.00	0.45	1.08	1.90	2.95
Nord Pool	1.15	0.37	0.33	1.20	0.81	0.40	0.38	0.37	0.42	0.18	0.53	2.27
EEX	0.65	0.61	0.61	0.74	0.54	0.32	0.35	0.28	0.23	0.36	0.53	0.57
EXAA	0.09	0.03	0.00	0.00	0.01	0.01	0.01	0.01	0.01	0.01	0.01	0.01
OTC	44.07	35.03	37.76	55.89	58.24	37.14	44.28	38.60	58.37	64.93	67.09	35.81
Total	**67.85**	**51.60**	**50.17**	**81.88**	**83.25**	**48.16**	**57.81**	**49.54**	**73.93**	**82.83**	**98.83**	**63.18**

2007

	Jan.	Feb.	Mar.	Apr.	May	Jun.	Jul.	Aug.	Sep.	Oct.	Nov.	Dec.
ECX	25.66	27.69	25.40	23.83	32.97	35.30	43.67	39.37	34.20	34.97	33.28	24.13
BlueNext	2.12	2.71	1.29	0.87	0.93	0.40	0.18	0.30	0.21	0.22	0.61	0.36
Nord Pool	2.19	2.28	2.06	1.53	2.53	3.39	1.72	2.11	3.12	3.57	5.95	3.42
EEX	0.77	0.42	0.29	1.11	0.60	0.87	1.00	1.26	1.09	0.45	0.60	0.49
EXAA	0.02	0.01	0.01	0.01	0.01	0.01	0.01	0.01	0.01	0.01	0.01	0.00
OTC	77.91	71.04	82.26	66.60	84.58	95.36	111.14	80.39	89.34	100.59	87.65	62.55
Total	108.68	104.16	111.31	93.96	121.63	135.33	157.71	123.43	127.97	139.80	128.11	90.95

2008

	Jan.	Feb.	Mar.	Apr.	May	Jun.	Jul.	Aug.	Sep.	Oct.	Nov.	Dec.
ECX	56.75	48.61	41.51	58.21	42.64	77.12	108.89	73.36	103.68	154.23	121.35	83.40
BlueNext	0.28	0.90	0.70	0.61	0.68	1.71	4.37	9.14	16.11	13.10	39.50	57.75
Nord Pool	5.83	6.54	5.42	3.70	3.80	2.51	3.28	0.85	0.00	0.00	0.00	0.00
EEX	2.06	2.43	1.89	2.42	1.05	1.68	2.72	4.69	3.97	7.91	6.46	0.94
EXAA	0.01	0.00	0.00	0.00	0.00	0.00	0.00	0.00	0.00	0.00	0.00	0.00
OTC	115.73	109.52	99.52	138.24	101.89	156.13	178.02	93.77	152.77	179.76	136.60	33.96
Total	180.66	168.01	149.03	203.19	150.06	239.14	297.27	181.81	276.52	355.01	303.90	176.05

Sources: ECX, BlueNext, Nord Pool, EEX, EXAA and Point Carbon.

Item e *Origin and destinations of surrendered allowances over the first phase*

2005–7 combined	AT	BE	DK	FI	FR	DE	GR	IE	IT	LU	NL	PT	ES
AT	91.63	0.20	0.11	0.20	0.52	1.03		0.00	0.05		0.83	0.01	0.03
BE	0.21	148.38	0.17	0.12	0.96	0.80	0.01	0.04	0.95	0.38	0.23	0.08	0.75
DK	0.00	0.15	72.62	0.15	0.10	0.65			0.01		0.85	0.11	0.15
FI	0.20	0.11	0.06	114.34	0.87	0.22	0.25		0.07		0.15	0.14	0.03
FR	0.01	0.07	0.04	0.29	379.71	0.15	0.12		0.07		0.13	0.07	0.43
DE	0.48	4.02	0.87	2.83	6.72	1391.19	0.08	0.86	1.26	0.27	7.34	0.96	0.96
GR	0.02	0.01			0.06	0.00	212.91				0.01	0.02	
IE	0.08	0.02	0.06	0.29	0.12	0.06		64.04	0.19	0.01	0.09	0.18	0.02
IT	0.46	1.18	0.66	1.07	6.45	5.42	0.26	0.09	629.12	0.01	1.16	1.19	1.54
LU										7.88			
NL	0.12	2.98	0.27	0.79	2.30	2.84	0.08	0.02	0.15	0.02	216.80	0.08	0.38
PT	0.01	0.15	0.01	0.01	0.05	0.06			0.06		0.04	99.44	0.28
ES	0.27	1.68	2.47	3.77	5.92	3.47	0.13	0.13	1.05	0.10	3.74	3.32	499.67
SE	0.01	0.03	0.07	0.36	0.09	0.19	0.01			0.01	0.01	0.01	0.00
GB	0.41	10.09	4.69	5.11	20.59	11.29	1.17	0.16	3.45	0.26	18.52	1.78	2.60
CY													
CZ	0.00	0.08	0.07	0.04	0.07	0.12			0.12		0.26	0.23	0.03
EE		0.02	0.00			0.03							
HU		0.01			0.14	0.03					0.02	0.00	0.02
LV													
LT		0.03	0.05	0.00	0.39	0.18	0.00		0.03			0.01	
MT													
PL	0.04	0.18	0.10	0.00	0.26	0.20	0.02	0.00	0.05		0.02	0.02	0.09
RO		0.01		0.03	0.05	0.04	0.18	0.13			0.23		0.01
SK	0.00	0.03		0.00	0.22	0.02			0.08		0.01		
SI	0.04		0.02	0.00	0.02	0.40	0.00		0.02		0.09	0.02	0.06
Total	93.99	169.42	82.36	129.40	425.61	1418.40	215.23	65.47	636.74	8.94	250.53	107.66	507.06
Exports	2.36	21.03	9.74	15.07	45.90	27.21	2.32	1.42	7.62	1.06	33.73	8.21	7.39
%	1%	6%	3%	4%	13%	8%	1%	0%	2%	0%	10%	2%	2%

The left margin is labelled "Surrendered in ..." and the top right "Originating from ...".

Notes:

AT = Austria, BE = Belgium, DK = Denmark, FI = Finland, FR = France, DE = Germany, GR = Greece, IE = Ireland, IT = Italy, LU = Luxembourg, NL = the Netherlands, PT = Portugal, ES = Spain, SE = Sweden and GB = the United Kingdom.
CY = Cyprus, CZ = the Czech Republic, EE = Estonia, HU = Hungary, LV = Latvia, LT = Lithuania, MT = Malta, PL = Poland, RO = Romania, SK = Slovakia and SI = Slovenia.
Bulgarian data were not available at the time of analysis and are not included here.
Source: Trotignon and Ellerman (2008).

(MtCO$_2$)

SE	GB	CY	CZ	EE	HU	LV	LT	MT	PL	RO	SK	SI	Total	Imports	%
0.05	0.26		0.30	0.00	0.03	0.14	0.13		0.42		0.31	0.02	96.27	4.64	1%
0.03	0.08		0.46	0.17	1.49	0.01	0.66		6.89		0.07		162.92	14.54	4%
0.21	0.37		0.43	0.02	0.06		0.02		0.08		0.11		76.09	3.47	1%
0.34	0.78		0.93	0.26	0.02	0.06	0.21		1.09		0.10		120.24	5.90	2%
0.02	0.26	0.04	0.25		0.02		0.12		1.73		0.13		383.67	3.96	1%
1.21	8.40	0.01	7.06	1.35	2.53	0.28	2.39		5.31		1.67		1448.08	56.89	16%
	0.03				0.01		0.01		0.84		0.02		213.93	1.03	0%
0.00	0.43	0.02	0.06	0.56		0.04	0.03		0.06		0.03		66.38	2.33	1%
0.57	4.13	0.23	3.68	2.05	1.08	0.85	1.14		6.83		2.84	0.05	672.06	42.94	12%
													7.88	0.00	0%
0.23	2.72	0.05	1.79	0.58	0.38	0.23	0.75		2.44		0.93	0.00	236.94	20.14	6%
0.00	0.46		0.22	0.00	0.00	0.01	0.00		0.01		0.02		100.84	1.40	0%
0.91	4.69	0.01	3.54	1.06	1.13	0.56	0.74		8.21		1.64		548.22	48.55	14%
57.05	0.18		0.08	0.15	0.00	0.01	0.08		0.12		0.01		58.46	1.41	0%
1.20	619.10	0.14	13.83	5.29	2.81	0.75	5.40		17.76		4.33		750.72	131.62	37%
		15.73											15.73	0.00	0%
0.07	0.96	0.01	247.03	0.11	0.48	0.01	0.10		2.02		0.61		252.42	5.39	2%
0.02				39.94					0.04				40.05	0.11	0%
	0.01		0.15	0.04	78.63				0.24		0.02	0.00	79.30	0.67	0%
			0.03	0.00		8.55	0.06				0.00		8.64	0.09	0%
	0.01		0.00	0.00	0.03	0.02	17.98		0.39		0.01		19.13	1.15	0%
								3.96					3.96	0.00	0%
0.01	0.62	0.01	0.17	0.00	0.08	0.04	0.02		620.34		0.25		622.53	2.19	1%
0.18	0.01		0.74	0.04	0.25		0.07		1.37	55.24	0.03	0.03	58.65	3.41	1%
0.01	0.05		0.07	0.10	0.01	0.11	0.20		0.17		74.30		75.37	1.07	0%
0.04	0.19		0.02	0.07	0.01	0.04	0.02		0.19		0.00	25.37	26.61	1.24	0%
62.14	643.75	16.25	280.83	51.78	89.05	11.73	30.13	3.96	676.55	55.24	87.44	25.49	6145.13	354.16	100%
5.09	24.65	0.52	33.79	11.84	10.42	3.18	12.15	0.00	56.22	0.00	13.14	0.11	354.16		
1%	7%	0%	10%	3%	3%	1%	3%	0%	16%	0%	4%	0%	100%		

Bibliography

Alberola, E. 2008. 'Essay on the European Union Emissions Trading Scheme: organization, market efficiency and carbon price drivers'. PhD thesis, economics, University Paris I Panthéon-Sorbonne.

Alberola, E., and J. Chevallier. 2009. 'European carbon prices and banking restrictions: evidence from phase I (2005–2007)'. *Energy Journal* **30** (3): 107–36.

Alberola, E., J. Chevallier and B. Chèze. 2007. *European Carbon Price Fundamentals in 2005–2007: The Effects of Energy Markets, Temperature and Sectoral Production. EconomiX Working Paper no. 2007–33.* Université Paris X Nanterre, Paris.

2008. 'Price drivers and structural breaks in European carbon prices 2005–2007'. *Energy Policy* **36** (2): 787–97.

Alexeeva-Talebi, V., C. Böhringer and U. Moslener. 2007. *'Climate and competitiveness: an economic impact assessment of EU leadership in emission control policies'.* Paper presented at 15th European Association of Environmental and Resource Economists annual conference. Thessaloniki, Greece, 30 June.

André, Y., A. Bodiguel and B. Leguet. 2008. *Domestic Offset Projects: Implementing the Kyoto Protocol.* Paris, Mission Climat, Caisse des Dépôts.

Baron, R., J. Reinaud, M. Genasci and C. Philibert. 2007. *Sectoral Approaches to Greenhouse Gas Mitigation: Exploring Issues for Heavy Industry.* Information paper. Paris, IEA.

Bart, I. 2007. 'Hungary'. In A. D. Ellerman, B. K. Buchner and C. Carraro (eds.). *Allocation in the European Emissions Trading Scheme: Rights, Rents and Fairness.* Cambridge, Cambridge University Press: 246–68.

Betz, R. 2005. *'Emissions trading to combat climate change: the impact of scheme design on transaction costs'.* Paper presented at seminar at British Institute of Energy Economics academic conference in association with UK Energy Research Centre. Oxford, 22 September.

Böhringer, C., T. Hoffman, A. Lange, A. Loschel and U. Moslener. 2005. 'Assessing emission regulation in Europe: an interactive simulation approach'. *Energy Journal* **26** (1): 1–21.

Böhringer, C., T. Hoffmann and C. Manrique-de-Lara-Penate. 2006. 'The efficiency costs of separating carbon markets under the EU emissions trading scheme: a quantitative assessment for Germany'. *Energy Economics* **28** (1): 44–61.

Brennan, M. 1958. 'The supply of storage'. *American Economic Review* **48** (1): 50–72.

Bunn, D., and C. Fezzi. 2007. *Interaction of European Carbon Trading and Energy Prices*. Working Paper no. 63. Milan, Fondazioni Eni Enrico Mattei.

Capoor, K., and P. Ambrosi. 2008. *State and Trends of the Carbon Market 2008*. Washington, DC, World Bank.

Capros, P., and L. Mantzos. 2000. '*The economic effects of industry-level trading to reduce greenhouse gases: results of the PRIMES model*'. Unpublished manuscript. Institute of Communication and Computer Systems, National Technical University of Athens.

Carbon Trust. 2004. *The European Emissions Trading Scheme: Implications for Industrial Competitiveness*. Report no. CT-2004-04. London, Carbon Trust.

Cembureau. 1997. *World Cement Market in Figures 1913–1995*. Brussels, Cembureau.

2008. *World Statistical Review 1996–2006*. Brussels, Cembureau.

CEMEX UK. 2007. 'CEMEX UK gets approval for new grinding and blending facility at Tilbury'. CEMEX UK press release, 6 February.

Center for Clean Air Policy. 1999. *Design of a Practical Approach to Greenhouse Gas Emissions Trading Combined with Policies and Measures in the EC*. Washington, DC, Center for Clean Air Policy.

ČEZ. Undated. 'ČEZ action plan for CO_2 reduction and annex: calculation of profits from the sale of saved allowances by ČEZ in the CR'. www.cez.cz/en/power-plants-and-environment/environment/cez-action-plan-for-co2-reduction.html (accessed 26 January 2009).

Chmelik, T. 2007. 'Czech Republic'. In A. D. Ellerman, B. K. Buchner and C. Carraro (eds.). *Allocation in the European Emissions Trading Scheme: Rights, Rents and Fairness*. Cambridge, Cambridge University Press: 269–300.

Coase, R. 1960. 'The problem of social cost'. *Journal of Law and Economics* **3** (1): 1–44.

Convery, F. 2009. 'Origins and Development of the EU ETS'. *Environmental and Resource Economics* **43** (3):391–412.

Convery, F., and L. Redmond. 2007. 'Market and price development in the European Emissions Trading Scheme'. *Review of Environmental Economics and Policy* **1** (1):88–111.

COWI. 2004. *Competitiveness and EU Climate Change Policy*. Kongens Lyngby, Denmark, COWI.

Crocker, T. D. 1966. 'The structuring of atmospheric pollution control systems'. In H. Wolozin (ed.). *The Economics of Air Pollution.* New York, W. W. Norton: 61–86.

Dales, J. H. 1968. *Pollution, Property and Prices.* Toronto, University of Toronto Press.

DEHst. 2009. *Emissionshandel: Auswertung der ersten Handelsperiode 2005–2007.* Berlin, Federal Ministry for the Environment.

Del Rio, P. 2007. 'Spain'. In A. D. Ellerman, B. K. Buchner and C. Carraro (eds.). *Allocation in the European Emissions Trading Scheme: Rights, Rents and Fairness.* Cambridge, Cambridge University Press: 182–212.

Delarue, E., A. D. Ellerman and W. D'haeseleer. 2008. *Short-term CO_2 Abatement in the European Power Sector. Working Paper no. 2008–008.* Boston, Center for Energy and Environmental Policy Research, MIT.

Delarue, E., K. Voorspools and W. D'haeseleer. 2008. 'Fuel switching in the electricity sector under the EU ETS: review and prospective'. *Journal of Energy Engineering* **134** (2): 40–6.

Delbeke, J. (ed.). 2006. *EU Energy Law*, vol. IV, *EU Environmental Law: The EU Greenhouse Gas Emissions Trading Scheme.* Leuven, Belgium, Claeys & Casteels.

Delbosc, A., and C. de Perthuis. 2009. *Carbon markets: the simple facts.* Caring for Climate Series, UN Global Compact.

Demailly, D., and P. Quirion. 2006. 'CO_2 abatement, competitiveness and leakage in the European cement industry under the EU ETS: grandfathering vs. output-based allocation'. *Climate Policy* **6** (1): 93–113.

2008. 'European Emission Trading Scheme and competitiveness: a case study on the iron and steel industry'. *Energy Economics* **30** (4): 2009–27.

2009. 'Leakage from climate policies and border-tax adjustment: lessons from a geographic model of the cement industry'. In R. Guesnerie and H. Tulkens (eds.). *The Design of Climate Policy.* Boston, MIT Press: 333–58.

Deutsche Bank. 2008. *Summarizing the EU Summit: A Qualified Success.* Frankfurt, Deutsche Bank.

Drax Group. 2008. 'Half year report 2008'. www.draxgroup.plc.uk (accessed 22 January 2009).

Dufour, C., and A. Leseur. 2006. *Overview of National Allocation Plans.* Research Report no. 8. Paris, Mission Climat, Caisse des Dépôts (available at www.caissedesdepots.fr/missionclimat).

EEA. 2002. *Annual European Community Greenhouse Gas Inventory 1990–2000 and Inventory Report 2002.* Technical Report no. 75. EEA, Copenhagen.

2004. *Greenhouse Gas Emission Trends and Projections in Europe 2004: Progress by the EU and Its Member States towards Achieving Their Kyoto Protocol Targets.* Technical Report no. 5/2004. EEA, Copenhagen.

2005. *Market-based Instruments for Environmental Policy in Europe.* Technical Report no. 8/2005. EEA, Copenhagen.

2007. *Greenhouse Gas Emission Trends and Projections in Europe 2007: Tracking Progress towards Kyoto Targets.* Technical Report no. 5/2007. EEA, Copenhagen.

2008. *Application of the Emissions Trading Directive by EU Member States: Reporting Year 2008.* Technical Report no. 13/2008. EEA, Copenhagen.

Egenhofer, C., N. Fujiwara, M. Åhman and L. Zetterberg. 2006. *The EU Emissions Trading Scheme: Taking Stock and Looking Forward.* European Climate Platform Report no. 2. Centre for European Policy Studies and Mistra, Brussels.

Ellerman, A. D. 2000. *Tradable Permits for Greenhouse Gas Emissions: A Primer with Particular Reference to Europe.* Report no. 69. Boston, MIT Joint Program on the Science and Policy of Global Change.

2007. 'New entrant and closure provisions: how do they distort?' *Energy Journal* **28** (Special Issue): 63–78.

Ellerman, A. D., and B. K. Buchner. 2008. 'Over-allocation or abatement? A preliminary analysis of the EU ETS based on the 2005–06 emissions data'. *Environmental and Resource Economics* **41** (2): 267–87.

Ellerman, A. D., B. K. Buchner and C. Carraro (eds.). 2007. *Allocation in the European Emissions Trading Scheme: Rights, Rents and Fairness.* Cambridge, Cambridge University Press.

Ellerman, A. D., P. L. Joskow, R. Schmalensee, J.-P. Montero and E. M. Bailey. 2000. *Markets for Clean Air: The US Acid Rain Program.* Cambridge, Cambridge University Press.

Ellerman, A. D., and J. Parsons. 2006. 'Shortage, inter-period pricing, and banking'. *Tendances Carbone* **5**: 1.

Ellerman, A. D., and S. Feilhauer. 2008. 'A Top-down and Bottom-up look at Emissions Abatement in Germany in response to the EU ETS. Working Paper no. 2008–017.' Boston, Center for Energy and Environmental Policy Research, MIT.

ENAM Research. 2007. 'Aluminium sector – China visit – all set for a big upswing'. ENAM Research, Mumbai, 13 December.

Environment News Service. 2003. 'Europe adopts climate emissions trading law'. Environment News Service, Washington, DC, 22 July (available at www.ens-newswire.com).

Estonia. 2007. 'Action brought on 16 July 2007 – Estonia v Commission (Case T-263/07)'. In *Official Journal of the European Union*, Brussels, European Commission, 22 September (available in material for hearing on 11 February 2009 at http://curia.europa.eu/en/actu/activities/index.htm).

European Commission. 1992. *Proposal for a Council Directive Introducing a Tax on Carbon Dioxide Emissions and Energy*, COM(92) 226 final. Brussels, European Commission.

1998.*Climate Change: Towards an EU Post-Kyoto Strategy.* COM(98) 353 final. Brussels, European Commission.

1999. *Preparing for Implementation of the Kyoto Protocol.* COM(99) 230. Brussels, European Commission.

2000. *Green Paper on Greenhouse Gas Emissions Trading within the European Union.* COM(2000) 87 final. Brussels, European Commission.

2005a. *Further Guidance on Allocation Plans for the 2008 to 2012 Trading Period of the EU Emissions Trading Scheme.* COM(2005) 703 final. Brussels, European Commission.

2005b. *Communication from the Commission to the Council, the European Parliament, the European Economic and Social Committee and the Committee of the Regions: Reducing the Climate Change Impact of Aviation.* COM(2005) 459 final. Brussels, European Commission.

2005c. 'EU action against climate change: EU emissions trading – an open scheme promoting global innovation'. Brussels, European Commission.

2006a. *Building a Global Carbon Market: Report Pursuant to Article 30 of Directive 87/2003/EC.* COM(2006) 676 final. Brussels, European Commission.

2006b. *On the Assessment of National Allocation Plans for the Allocation of Greenhouse Gas Emission Allowances for the Second Period of the EU Emissions Trading Scheme accompanying Commission Decisions of 29 November 2006 on the National Allocation Plans of Germany, Greece, Ireland, Latvia, Lithuania, Luxembourg, Malta, Slovakia, Sweden and the United Kingdom in accordance with Directive 2003/ 87/EC.* COM(2006) 725 final. Brussels, European Commission.

2007. 'Emissions trading: Commission adopts amendment decision on the Slovak National Allocation Plan for 2008 to 2012'. Press release no. IP/ 07/1869. Brussels, European Commission.

2008a. 'Accompanying document to the proposal for a directive of the European Parliament and the Council amending Directive 2003/87/EC so as to improve and extend the EU greenhouse gas emission allowance trading system: impact assessment'. Working document. Brussels, European Commission.

2008b. *Commission Decision concerning the Unilateral Inclusion of Additional Greenhouse Gases and Activities by the Netherlands in the Community Emissions Trading Scheme pursuant to Article 24 of Directive 2003/87/EC of the European Parliament and of the Council.* COM(2008) 7867. Brussels, European Commission.

2008c. *Proposal for a Directive of the European Parliament and of the Council Amending Directive 2003/87/EC so as to Improve and Extend the Greenhouse Gas Emission Allowance Trading System of the Community.* COM(2008) 16 final. Brussels, European Commission.

European Commission, McKinsey & Company and Ecofys. 2006. *EU ETS Review: Report on International Competitiveness*. Brussels, European Commission.

European Council. 1998. 'Annex I'. In 'Document no. 9702/98 of 19 June 1998 of the Council of the European Union reflecting the outcome of proceedings of the Environment Council of 16–17 June 1998'. Brussels, European Council.

  2003. 'Council's common position on the adoption of a Directive establishing a scheme for greenhouse gas emissions allowance trading within the Community and amending Council Directive 96/61/EC of 18 March 2003'. Brussels, European Council.

  2007. 'EU objectives for the development of the international climate regime beyond 2012: Council conclusions.' Information Note no. 6621/07. Brussels, European Council.

  2008. 'Energy and climate change: elements of the final compromise'. Information Note no. 17215/08. Brussels, European Council.

European Court of First Instance. 2007. 'Judgment of the Court of First Instance in Case T-374/04, Federal Republic of Germany v Commission of the European Communities'. Press Release no. 80/07. Luxembourg, European Court of First Instance.

European Economic Area Joint Committee. 2007. 'Decision of the EEA Joint Committee no. 146/2007 of 26 October 2007 amending Annex XX (Environment) to the EEA Agreement'. Brussels, European Economic Area Joint Committee.

European Parliament. 2003. 'Draft recommendation for second reading on the Council common position for adopting a European Parliament and Council directive establishing a scheme for greenhouse gas emission allowance trading within the Community and amending Council Directive 96/61/EC'. Strasbourg, Committee on the Environment, Public Health and Consumer Policy, European Parliament.

  2008a. 'Draft report on the proposal for a directive of the European Parliament and of the Council amending directive 2003/87/EC so as to improve and extend the greenhouse gas emission allowance trading system of the Community'. 2008/0013 (COD). Strasbourg, Committee on the Environment, Public Health and Food Safety, European Parliament.

  2008b. 'Legislative resolution of 17 December 2008 on the proposal for a directive of the European Parliament and of the Council amending directive 2003/87/EC so as to improve and extend the greenhouse gas emission allowance trading system of the Community,' provisional edition. Strasbourg, European Parliament (available at www.europarl.europa.eu/sides/getDoc.do?pubRef=-//EP//TEXT+TA+P6-TA-2008–0610+0+DOC+XML+V0//EN).

European Parliament and Council. 2003. 'Directive 2003/87/EC of the European Parliament and of the Council of 13 October 2003 establishing a scheme for greenhouse gas emissions trading within the Community and amending Council Directive 96/61/EC'. Brussels, European Parliament and Council.

2004 'Directive 2004/101/EC of the European Parliament and of the Council of 27 October amending Directive 2003/87/EC establishing a scheme for greenhouse gas emission allowance trading within the Community, in respect of the Kyoto Protocol's project mechanisms'. Brussels, European Parliament and Council.

Eurostat. 2008a. 'Regional GDP per inhabitant in the EU27: GDP per inhabitant in 2005 ranged from 24% of the EU27 average in Nord-Est Romania to 303% in Inner London'. News Release no. 19/2008. Brussels, Eurostat.

2008b. *Energy: Monthly Statistics, January*. Brussels, Eurostat.

Favennec, J.-P. 2001. *Petroleum Refining*, vol. V, *Refinery Operation and Management*. Paris, Technip Editions.

Fazekas, D. 2008a. 'Auction design, implementation and results of the European Union Emissions Trading Scheme'. Unpublished working paper, available at www.aprec.net/documents/08–04–28_eu_ets_auctions_fazekas.pdf.

2008b. 'Hungarian experiences with the EU ETS: carbon market implications for the new EU member states'. Unpublished working paper, available at www.aprec.net/documents/08–08-hungarian_experience_with_the_eu-ts.pdf.

France. 2008. 'Loi n° 2008–1443 du 30 décembre 2008 de finances rectificative pour 2008' *In Journal officiel de la République française*, Paris.

Gale, J., and P. Freund. 2001. 'Greenhouse gas abatement in energy intensive industries'. In R. A. Durie, P. McMullan, C. A. J. Paulson, A. Y. Smith and D. J. Williams (eds.). *Proceedings of the 5th International Conference on Greenhouse Gas Control Technologies*. Collingwood, Australia, CISRO: 1211–16.

Gielen, D., and Y. Moriguchi. 2002. 'CO_2 in the iron and steel industry: an analysis of Japanese emission reduction potentials'. *Energy Policy* **30** (10): 849–63.

Godard, O. 2005. 'Politique de l'effet de serre: une évaluation du plan français de quotas de CO_2'. *Revue française d'économie* **19** (4): 147–86.

Herold, A. 2007. *Comparison of Verified CO_2 Emissions under the EU Emission Trading Scheme with National Greenhouse Gas Inventories for the Year 2005*. Technical Paper no. 2007/3. Bilthoven, the Netherlands, European Topic Centre on Air and Climate Change.

Hidalgo, I., L. Szabó, I. Calleja, J. C. Ciscar, P. Russ and A. Soria. 2003. *Energy Consumption and CO_2 Emissions from the World Iron and*

Steel Industry. Report no. EUR 20686. Seville, Institute for Prospective Technological Studies, European Commission Joint Research Centre.

Houpert, K., and A. de Dominicis. 2006. *Trading in the Rain: Rainfall and European Power Sector Emissions.* Climate Report no. 9. Paris, Mission Climat, Caisse des Dépôts.

Hourcade, J.-C., D. Demailly, K. Neuhoff, M. Sato, M. Grubb, F. Matthes and V. Graichen. 2008. *Differentiation and Dynamics of EU-ETS Industrial Competitiveness Impacts: Final Report.* London, Climate Strategies.

IAI. 2007. *Energy Efficiency and Greenhouse Gas Reduction Potentials in the Aluminium Industry.* London, IAI (available at www.iea.org/ textbase/work/2007/aluminium/proceedings.pdf).

IEA. 2007a. *Mind the Gap: Quantifying Principal–Agent Problems in Energy Efficiency.* Paris, IEA.

2007b. *Tracking Industrial Energy Efficiency and CO_2 Emissions.* Paris, IEA.

2007c. *World Energy Outlook 2007.* Paris, IEA.

2007d. *Climate Policy Uncertainty and Investment Risk.* Paris, IEA.

2008. *Oil Market Report.* Paris, IEA (available at http://omrpublic.iea. org).

IEA and NEA. 2005. *Projected Costs of Generating Electricity: 2005 Update.* Paris, IEA/OECD.

IISI. 2005. *Steel Statistical Yearbook 2005.* Brussels, World Steel Association.

2007. *Steel Statistical Yearbook 2007.* Brussels, World Steel Association.

Institute for Prospective Technological Studies. 2000. 'Preliminary analysis of the implementation of an EU-wide permit trading scheme on CO_2 emissions abatement costs: results from the POLES model'. Institute for Prospective Technological Studies, Seville.

Jankowski, B. 2007. 'Poland'. In A. D. Ellerman, B. K. Buchner and C. Carraro (eds.). *Allocation in the European Emissions Trading Scheme: Rights, Rents and Fairness.* Cambridge, Cambridge University Press: 301–36.

Jaraite, J., F. Convery and C. Di Maria. 2009. *Transaction Costs of Firms in the EU ETS.* Working paper, UCD (available at www.aprec.net/ documents/09-02-17_transaction_costs_of_firms_in_theu_ets.pdf).

Joskow, P. 2006. *Competitive Electricity Markets and Investment in New Generating Capacity.* Working Paper no. 06–009. Boston, Center for Energy and Environmental Policy Research, MIT.

Jourdan de Muizon, G. 2006. *'Articuler les marchés de permis d'émission avec des autres instruments dans les politiques de lutte contre le changement climatique'.* PhD thesis, economics, University of Paris X Nanterre.

Kemfert, C., M. Kohlhaas, P. T. Truong and A. Protsenko. 2006. 'The environmental and economic effects of European emissions trading'. *Climate Policy* 6 (4): 441–55.

Keppler, J. H. 2005. 'The future of nuclear power in Europe: a lesson in risk management from Finland'. *Revue de l'énergie* **556** (5): 305–10.

    2007a. 'Causality and cointegration between energy consumption and economic growth in developing countries'. In J. H. Keppler, R. Bourbonnais and J. Girod (eds.). *The Econometrics of Energy Systems*. London, Palgrave: 75–97.

    2007b. 'We do not yet have the answers, but we know the right questions: lessons learned from the 2005–2007 trial phase of the EU Emission Trading System'. In J. Lesourne and J. H. Keppler (eds.). *Abatement of CO$_2$ Emissions in the European Union*. Paris, Institut français des relations internationals: 137–56

Klaassen, G. 1997. 'Practical experience, international agreements and the prospects for emission trading in the CEE'. In P. Kaderjak and J. Powell (eds.). *Economics for Environmental Policy in Transition Economies: An Analysis of the Hungarian Experience*. Cheltenham, Edward Elgar: 90–109.

Klepper, G., and S. Peterson. 2005. *Emissions Trading, CDM, JI and More: The Climate Strategy of the EU*. Working Paper no. 1238. Kiel, Germany, Kiel Institute for the World Economy.

Krugman, P. 1994. 'Competitiveness: a dangerous obsession'. *Foreign Affairs* **73** (2): 28–44.

Lacombe, R. 2008. 'Economic impact of EU ETS: evidence from the refining sector'. *Master's thesis, technology and policy program*, MIT, Boston.

Lefton, S. A., and P. Besuner. 2006. 'The cost of cycling coal fired power plants'. *Coal Power Winter*: 16–20.

Leguet, B., and G. Elabed. 2008. 'A reformed CDM to increase supply'. In K. Holm and J. Fenhann (eds.). *A Reformed CDM: Including New Mechanisms for Sustainable Development*. Frederiksborgvej, Denmark, UNEP Risoe Centre on Energy, Environment and Sustainable Development: 73–83.

Lekander, P. 2006. 'CO$_2$ price still too low'. *Carbon Market Europe*, 21 April.

Mansanet-Bataller, M., A. Pardo and E. Valor. 2007. 'CO$_2$ prices, energy and weather'. *Energy Journal* **28** (3): 72–92.

Marks, J. 2007. '*Present progress and scope for further GHG emissions reduction during production*'. Paper presented at IEA Energy Efficiency and GHG Emission Reduction workshop, Paris, 24 May.

Marshall, C. 1998. *Pre-Budget 1998: Economic Instruments and the Business Use of Energy*. London, HM Treasury.

Matthes, F. C., V. Graichen and J. Repenning. 2005. *The Environmental Effectiveness and Economic Efficiency of the European Union Emissions Trading Scheme: Structural Aspects of Allocation*. Berlin, Öko-Institut.

Matthes, F. C., and F. Schafhausen. 2007. 'Germany'. In A. D. Ellerman, B. K. Buchner and C. Carraro (eds.). *Allocation in the European Emissions Trading Scheme: Rights, Rents and Fairness*. Cambridge, Cambridge University Press: 72–105.

McCann, L., B. Colby, K. W. Easter, A. Kasterine and K. V. Kuperan. 'Transaction cost measurement for evaluating environmental policies'. *Ecological Economics* 52 (4): 527–42.

McGuinness, M., and A. D. Ellerman. 2008. CO_2 *Abatement in the UK Power Sector: Evidence from the EU ETS Trial Period*. Working Paper no. 2008–010. Boston, Center for Energy and Environmental Policy Research, MIT.

McGuinness, M., and R. Trotignon. 2007. *Technical Memorandum on Analysis of the EU ETS using the Community Independent Transaction Log*. Working Paper no. 2007–012. Boston, Center for Energy and Environmental Policy Research, MIT.

Millock, K., and T. Sterner. 2004. 'NO_x emissions in France and Sweden: advanced fee schemes versus regulation'. In W. Harrington, R. D. Morgenstern and T. Sterner (eds.). *Choosing Environmental Policy: Comparing Instruments and Outcomes in the United States and Europe*. Washington, DC, Resources for the Future: 117–32.

Ministry of Finance. 2006. 'CO_2 taxes 2006'. Oslo, Ministry of Finance.

Ministry of the Environment. 2008. *Norwegian National Allocation Plan for the Emissions Trading System in 2008–2012*. Oslo, Ministry of the Environment.

Mission Climat. 2008. 'Tableau de bord de Tendances carbone, September 2008'. Unpublished document. Mission Climat, Caisse des Dépôts, Paris.

Montgomery, W. D. 1972. 'Markets in licenses and efficient pollution control programs'. *Journal of Economic Theory* 5 (3): 395–418.

Muehlegger, E. 2002. *The Role of Content Regulation on Pricing and Market Power in Regional Retail and Wholesale Gasoline Markets*. Working Paper no. 02–008. Boston, Center for Energy and Environmental Policy Research, MIT.

Neuhoff, K., K. Keats and M. Sato. 2006. 'Allocation, incentives and distortions: the impact of EU ETS emissions allowance allocations to the electricity sector'. *Climate Policy* 6 (1): 73–91.

OECD. 1996a. *Industrial Structure Statistics 1994*. Paris, OECD.

1996b. *Industrial Competitiveness*. Paris, OECD.

2003. *Environmental Policy in the Steel Industry: Using Economic Instruments*. Paris, OECD.

2008a. 'Crude steelmaking capacity developments'. Paris, Steel Committee, OECD.

Oil & Gas Journal. 2005. '2005 worldwide refining survey'. *Oil & Gas Journal*, 19 December.

  2006. '2006 worldwide refining survey'. *Oil & Gas Journal*, 18 December.

  2007. '2007 worldwide refining survey'. *Oil & Gas Journal*, 24 December.

Peterson, S. 2006. *Efficient Abatement in Separated Carbon Markets: A Theoretical and Quantitative Analysis of the EU Emissions Trading Scheme.* Working Paper no. 1271. Kiel, Germany, Kiel Institute for the World Economy.

Pigou, A. C. 1920. *The Economics of Welfare.* London, Macmillan.

Point Carbon. 2007a. 'SAB Miller cuts carbon intensity 12% in 2006'. Carbon Market Daily, 4 July.

  2007b. *Carbon 2007: A New Climate for Carbon Trading.* Oslo, Point Carbon.

  2008a. 'RWE to build new coal plant in Poland'. Point Carbon News, 12 June.

  2008b. 'Union Fenosa switches from coal to gas'. Point Carbon News, 16 July.

  2008c. 'Spanish utility Iberdrola cuts carbon emissions'. Point Carbon News, 23 October.

  2008d. 'EUAs cost RWE €1 billion in Jan–Sep 08'. *Carbon Market Daily*, 11 November.

  2008e. *Carbon 2008: Post-2012 Is Now.* Oslo, Point Carbon.

  2009. 'Iberian power sector emissions fall in 2008'. Point Carbon News, 15 January.

Poland. 2007. 'Action brought on 28 May 2007 – Poland v Commission (Case T-183/07)'. In *Official Journal of the European Union*, Brussels, European Commission, 7 July (available in material for hearing on 10 February 2009 at http://curia.europa.eu/en/actu/activities/index.htm).

Ponssard, J.-P., and N. Walker. 2008. 'EU emission trading and the cement sector: a spatial competition analysis'. *Climate Policy* 8 (5): 467–93.

Porteous, H. 2007. 'Alcan's view on a global sectoral approach for the aluminium sector'. Paper presented at the European High Level Group on International Action on Climate Change, Brussels, 11 September.

Purvin & Gertz. 2008. *Global Petroleum Market Outlook.* Houston, Purvin & Gertz.

Reguant, M., and A. D. Ellerman. 2008. *Grandfathering and the Endowment Effect: An Assessment in the Context of the Spanish National Allocation Plan.* Working Paper no. 2008–018. Boston, Center for Energy and Environmental Policy Research, MIT.

Reilly, J., and S. Paltsev. 2006. 'European greenhouse gas emissions trading: a system in transition'. In C. de Miguel, X. Labandeira and B. Manzano (eds.). *Economic Modelling of Climate Change and*

Energy Policies. Cheltenham, Edward Elgar: 45–64 (also available as Reprint 2006–11 of the MIT Joint Programme on the Science and Policy of Global Change).

Reinaud, J. 2003. *Emissions Trading and Its Possible Impacts on Investment Decisions in the Power Sector.* Information paper. Paris, IEA.

2005a. *Industrial Competitiveness under the European Union Emissions Trading Scheme.* Information paper. Paris, IEA.

2005b. *The European Refinery Industry under the EU Emissions Trading Scheme.* Information paper. Paris, IEA.

2007. *CO_2 Allowance and Electricity Price Interaction: Impact on Industry's Electricity Purchasing Strategies in Europe.* Information paper. Paris, IEA.

2008a. *Issues behind Competitiveness and Carbon Leakage: Focus on Heavy Industry.* Information paper. Paris, IEA.

2008b. *Climate Policy and Carbon Leakage: Impacts of the European Emissions Trading Scheme on Aluminium.* Information paper. Paris, IEA.

Roques, F. A., W. J. Nuttal and D. M. Newberry. 2006. *Using Probabilistic Analysis to Evaluate Investments in Power Generation Investments under Uncertainty.* Working Paper no. CWPE 650. Cambridge, University of Cambridge.

RTE. 2007. 'Courbe de charge de la journée du 5 decembre 2007'. www. rte-france.com/htm/fr/accueil/courbe.jsp.

Schleich, J., and R. Betz. 2004. 'EU emissions trading and transaction costs for small and medium sized companies'. *Intereconomics* **39** (3): 121–3.

Sijm, J., K. Neuhoff and Y. Chen. 2006. 'CO_2 cost pass-through and windfall profits in the power sector'. *Climate Policy* **6** (1): 49–72.

Sijm, J., K. E. L. Smekens, T. Kram and M. G. Boots. 2002. *Economic Effects of Grandfathering CO_2 Emission Allowances.* Petten, Energy Research Centre of the Netherlands.

Skidelsky, R. 2003. *John Maynard Keynes, 1883–1946.* London, Macmillan.

Skjaerseth, J. B., and J. Wettestad. 2008. *EU Emissions Trading: Initiation, Decision-making and Implementation.* Aldershot, Ashgate.

Smale, R., M. Hartley, C. Hepburn, J. Ward and M. Grubb. 2006. 'The impact of CO_2 emissions trading on firm profits and market prices'. *Climate Policy* **6** (1): 29–47.

Sorrell, S., and J. Skea (eds.). 1999. *Pollution for Sale: Emissions Trading and Joint Implementation.* Northampton, Edward Elgar.

Stavins, R. N. 1995. 'Transaction costs and tradeable permits'. *Journal of Environmental Economics and Management* **29** (2): 133–48.

Szabó, L., I. Hidalgo, J. C. Ciscar and A. Soria. 2006. 'CO_2 emission trading within the European Union and Annex B countries: the cement industry case'. *Energy Policy* **34** (1): 72–87

Szabó, L., I. Hidalgo, J. C. Ciscar, A. Soria and P. Russ. 2003. *Energy Consumption and CO_2 Emissions from the World Cement Industry.* Report no. EUR 20769. Seville, Institute for Prospective Technological Studies, European Commission Joint Research Centre.

Szabo, M. 2008. 'Carbon's correlation to energy prices strengthens'. *Reuters News* 22 May (available at www.reutersinteractive.com/Carbon).

Tanaka, K. 2008. *Assessing Measures of Energy Efficiency Performance and Their Application in Industry.* Information paper. Paris, IEA.

Tietenberg, T. H. 2006. *Emissions Trading: Principles and Practice* (2nd edn.). Washington, DC, Resources for the Future.

Trotignon, R., and A. Delbosc. 2008. *Allowance Trading Patterns in the European CO_2 Market's Trial Period: What Does the CITL Reveal?* Climate Report no. 13. Paris, Mission Climat, Caisse des Dépôts.

Trotignon, R., and A. D. Ellerman. 2008. *Compliance Behavior in the EU ETS: Cross-border Trading, Banking and Borrowing.* Working Paper no. 2008–012. Boston, Center for Energy and Environmental Policy Research, MIT.

UNFCCC. 2008. *National Inventory Submissions 2008.* Bonn, UNFCCC.

Voorspools, K. 2004. 'The modelling of the power generation of large interconnected power systems in the framework of emission reduction strategies and the liberalization of the market'. PhD thesis, Catholic University of Leuven, Belgium.

Voorspools, K., and W. D'haeseleer. 2006. 'The modelling of electric generation of large interconnected systems: how can a CO_2 tax influence the European generation mix?'. *Energy Conversion and Management* **47** (11–12): 1338–58.

Walker, N. 2006. *Concrete Evidence? An Empirical Approach to Quantify the Impact of EU Emissions Trading on Cement Industry Competitiveness.* Working Paper no. 06/10. Department of Planning and Environmental Policy, UCD.

2007. 'The impact of CO_2 emissions trading on the European cement industry'. PhD thesis. School of geography, planning and environmental policy, UCD.

Working, H. 1949. 'The theory of the price of storage'. *American Economic Review* **39** (5): 1254–62.

Worrell, E., and C. Galitsky. 2005. *Energy Efficiency Improvement and Cost Saving Opportunities for Petroleum Refineries.* Technical report. Energy Analysis Department, Environmental Energy Technologies Division, Ernest Orlando Lawrence Berkeley National Laboratory, University of California, Berkeley.

Zapfel, P. 2007. 'A brief but lively chapter in EU climate policy: the Commission's perspective'. In A. D. Ellerman, B. K. Buchner and

C. Carraro (eds.). *Allocation in the European Emissions Trading Scheme: Rights, Rents and Fairness*. Cambridge, Cambridge University Press: 13–38.

Zetterberg, L. 2007. 'Sweden'. In A. D. Ellerman, B. K. Buchner and C. Carraro (eds.). *Allocation in the European Emissions Trading Scheme: Rights, Rents and Fairness*. Cambridge, Cambridge University Press: 132–56.

Index